The Future in Greek

*"Something there is in beauty
which grows in the soul of the beholder
like a flower:
fragile—and imperishable."*

Stephen Donaldson,
"The Chronicles of Thomas Covenant, The Unbeliever"

The Future in Greek

From Ancient to Medieval

THEODORE MARKOPOULOS

OXFORD
UNIVERSITY PRESS

Great Clarendon Street, Oxford OX2 6DP

Oxford University Press is a department of the University of Oxford.
It furthers the University's objective of excellence in research, scholarship,
and education by publishing worldwide in

Oxford New York

Auckland Cape Town Dar es Salaam Hong Kong Karachi
Kuala Lumpur Madrid Melbourne Mexico City Nairobi
New Delhi Shanghai Taipei Toronto

With offices in

Argentina Austria Brazil Chile Czech Republic France Greece
Guatemala Hungary Italy Japan Poland Portugal Singapore
South Korea Switzerland Thailand Turkey Ukraine Vietnam

Oxford is a registered trade mark of Oxford University Press
in the UK and in certain other countries

Published in the United States
by Oxford University Press Inc., New York

© Theodore Markopoulos 2009

The moral rights of the author have been asserted
Database right Oxford University Press (maker)

First published 2009

All rights reserved. No part of this publication may be reproduced,
stored in a retrieval system, or transmitted, in any form or by any means,
without the prior permission in writing of Oxford University Press,
or as expressly permitted by law, or under terms agreed with the appropriate
reprographics rights organization. Enquiries concerning reproduction
outside the scope of the above should be sent to the Rights Department,
Oxford University Press, at the address above

You must not circulate this book in any other binding or cover
and you must impose the same condition on any acquirer

British Library Cataloguing in Publication Data

Data available

Library of Congress Cataloging in Publication Data

Data available

Typeset by SPI Publisher Services, Pondicherry, India
Printed in Great Britain
on acid-free paper by
Biddles Ltd., King's Lynn, Norfolk

ISBN 978–0–19–953985–7

1 3 5 7 9 10 8 6 4 2

Contents

Abbreviations	vii
List of Tables	ix
List of Figures	xi
Preface	xiii

1	Introduction: aims, theory, and method	1
	1.1 Theoretical preliminaries	2
	1.1.1 *Grammaticalization from different perspectives*	2
	1.1.2 *The notion of futurity*	8
	1.1.3 *Auxiliary verbs and "periphrasis"*	11
	1.2 Main aims of the study	13
	1.3 Corpus: problems and methodology	14
	1.4 The structure of the book	18
2	Classical Greek (5th–3rd c. BC): the origins	19
	Introduction	19
	2.1 Μέλλω / Ἔμελλον + Infinitive: future-referring AVC (?)	20
	2.2 Ἔχω / Εἶχον + Infinitive: possession and ability	33
	2.3 (Ἐ)θέλω + Infinitive: future-referring alternative?	38
	2.4 Classical Greek: a summary	45
3	Hellenistic–Roman Greek (3rd c. BC–4th c. AD): proliferation of AVCs	46
	Introduction	46
	3.1 Μέλλω / Ἔμελλον + Infinitive: relative stability	47
	3.2 Ἔχω / Εἶχον + Infinitive: from ability to futurity	60
	3.3 (Ἐ)θέλω + Infinitive: volition, futurity, and new developments	73
	3.4 Conclusions: the interaction of three AVCs	84
4	Early Medieval Greek (5th–10th c. AD): the misty transition	87
	Introduction	87
	4.1 Μέλλω + Infinitive: apparent stability	88
	4.2 Ἔχω + Infinitive: the dominant AVC	94

vi   Contents

   4.3 Θέλω + Infinitive: remaining under shadow   104
   4.4 Conclusions: FCs and registers   113

5 Late Medieval Greek (11th–15th c. AD): the dominance
   of a single AVC   115
   Introduction: texts and methodology   115
   5.1 High registers and specialization: the case of μέλλω/ἔμελλον   121
      5.1.1 *The early stages*   121
      5.1.2 *The later stages*   124
      5.1.3 *Conclusions: the status of μέλλω*   136
   5.2 Ἔχω + Infinitive / subordinate clause: future-reference
      and modality   140
      5.2.1 *The early stages*   140
      5.2.2 *The later stages*   145
      5.2.3 *"Νά ἔχω + Infinitive": new evidence and
           a new interpretation*   149
      5.2.4 *Conclusions: ἔχω AVC and futurity*   155
   5.3 Εἶχα + Infinitive: modality and pluperfect   156
   5.4 The case of θέλω: untangling the evidence of dominance   164
      5.4.1 *The early stages*   165
      5.4.2 *The later stages*   173
      5.4.3 The emergence of "θέ νά": phonological
           reduction and language contact   186
      5.4.4 *Summary: the story of θέλω*   208
   5.5 Ἤθελα + Infinitive / clause: conditionals and volition   209
   5.6 Conclusions: future reference in LMG   223

6 Conclusions   225
   6.1 Methodology of historical linguistic investigations   225
   6.2 Theoretical implications: typological predictions
      and frameworks   229
   6.3 Three answers—and some further questions   232

Appendix: Abbreviations of texts   234
Bibliography   243
   Primary sources   243
   Secondary sources   271
Name Index   283
Subject Index   286

Abbreviations

(see Appendix for text abbreviations)

ACC	Accusative
adv	adverb
AG	Ancient Greek
AOR	Aorist (Perfective Past)
AVC	Auxiliary Verb construction
cl	clitic
co-ref	co-reference
disj	disjoint reference
EMG	Early Medieval Greek
FC	Future-referring construction
FUT	Future
GEN	Genitive
H–RG	Hellenistic–Roman Greek
IMP	Imperative
IMPER	Imperfective
IND	Indicative
INF	Infinitive
LMG	Late Medieval Greek
NOM	Nominative
OCS	Old Church Slavonic
OPT	Optative
OV	Object-Verb
PASS	Passive
PCIPLE	Participle
PER	Perfective

PERF	Perfect
PERS	Person
PL	Plural
PLUPERF	Pluperfect
prep	preposition
PRES	Present
PRET	Preterite (Imperfective Past)
prt	particle
rel	relative
SING	Singular
SUBJ	Subjunctive
TAM	Tense-Aspect-Modality
V	Verb
VO	Verb-Object

List of Tables

2.1	The paradigm of 3rd person singular of λύω (=undo, dissolve) in AG	20
2.2	Token frequency of the forms of future-referring μέλλω	23
2.3	Linear order of μέλλω + Infinitive	27
2.4	Linear order of volitional (ἐ)θέλω + Infinitive	28
2.5	Type of infinitival complement of μέλλω	28
2.6	Aspectual readings of μέλλω AVC	30
2.7	('E)θέλω + Infinitive in AG	41
3.1	Forms of μέλλω in H–R times (non-papyri)	48
3.2	Forms of μέλλω in H–R times (papyri)	49
3.3	Linear order of μέλλω + Inf. in H–R times (non-papyri)	52
3.4	Linear order of μέλλω + Inf. in H–R times (papyri)	52
3.5	Type of infinitival complement of μέλλω (non-papyri)	53
3.6	Type of infinitival complement of μέλλω (papyri)	53
3.7	Pattern of complementation for ἐλπίζω (non-papyri)	56
3.8	Pattern of complementation for ἐλπίζω (papyri)	56
3.9	Ἔχω AVC in the H–R period (non-papyri)	63
3.10	Ἔχω AVC in the H–R period (papyri)	67
3.11	Volitional (ἐ)θέλω in the H–R period (non-papyri)	74
3.12	Volitional (ἐ)θέλω in the H–R period (papyri)	76
3.13	The (ἐ)θέλω AVC in the H–R period	83
3.14	Properties of AVCs in H–R Greek	85
4.1	Infinitival complementation of μέλλω (non-papyri)	90
4.2	Infinitival complementation of μέλλω (papyri)	90
4.3	Complementation of ἐλπίζω (papyri)	93
4.4	Complementation of ἐλπίζω (non-papyri)	93
4.5	Ἔχω + Infinitive in EMG	101
4.6	Εἶχον + Infinitive in EMG	103
4.7	Complementation of volitional θέλω in EMG	104
4.8	Θέλω AVC in EMG	111

5.1 *Μέλλω* in 14th-c. literary texts	126
5.2 *Μέλλω* in 15th-c. literary texts	132
5.3 The *ἔχω* AVC in 14th-c. literary texts	146
5.4 "*Νά ἔχω* + Infinitive" construction in 14th-c. literary texts	150
5.5 The *εἶχα* AVC in 14th-c. literary texts	159
5.6 *Θέλω* + Infinitive in 14th-c. literary texts	175
5.7 *Θέλω* + Finite complementation in 14th-c. literary texts	175
5.8 The *ἤθελα* AVC in 14th-c. literary texts	213

List of Figures

2.1	Aspect and Infinitive in the $\mu\acute{\epsilon}\lambda\lambda\omega$ AVC	31
3.1	Token frequency of the forms of $\mu\acute{\epsilon}\lambda\lambda\omega$	49
3.2	Adjacency in $\mu\acute{\epsilon}\lambda\lambda\omega$ AVC	52
3.3	Development of Inf. complementation of $\mu\acute{\epsilon}\lambda\lambda\omega$ AVC	54
3.4	Ability / possibility and futurity	69
4.1	Token frequency of future reference in the $\check{\epsilon}\chi\omega$ AVC	101
4.2	$\Theta\acute{\epsilon}\lambda\omega$ complementation	105
5.1	The complementation of $\mu\acute{\epsilon}\lambda\lambda\omega$ AVC	134
5.2	Token frequency of FCs in LMG (14th c.)	174
5.3	The sequence of developments of the $\theta\acute{\epsilon}\lambda\omega$ AVC	209

Preface

This book is a revised and extended version of my Ph.D. dissertation, submitted to and approved by the University of Cambridge (July 2006). A lot of people have contributed to the final shaping of my ideas in one way or another. First of all, I am profoundly grateful to my Ph.D. supervisor, Geoffrey Horrocks, who, with his great knowledge and enquiring mind, has been a great source of inspiration, help, and encouragement. I would also like to thank Peter Mackridge, Torsten Meissner, and two anonymous reviewers, for providing me with detailed comments on the contents of the thesis, which have proven to be particularly helpful. Although they may not wholly agree with what is written here, they have greatly contributed to a better understanding and treatment of the issues discussed in the book.

A very warm "thank you" goes to David Holton, for all his support during my stay in Cambridge, Dimitra Theophanopoulou-Kontou, for showing great confidence in me, Tina Lentari, for all her help and especially for showing me why manuscripts are better than editions, Amalia Moser, for encouraging me to study in Cambridge, and Amfilochios Papathomas, for getting me acquainted with the various electronic sources of the papyri.

For various comments and discussions, I would like to thank Dora Alexopoulou, Napoleon Katsos, Ian Roberts, Anna Roussou, and Christina Sevdali. I would also like to thank Theocharis Detorakis, Giannis Mavromatis, Stavros Skopeteas, and Marina Terkourafi for helping me assemble a greater amount of material. I have also greatly benefited from comments I received from the audiences of the 6th, 7th, and 8th International Conferences in Greek Linguistics, the Linguistics seminar of the Faculty of Classics (University of Cambridge), and the Modern Greek seminar of the Faculty of Modern and Medieval Languages (University of Cambridge), whom I would like to thank here. Finally, a warm "thanks" should go to the staff of the Research Centre of the History of Greek Law (Academy of Athens), as well as to the staff of the Benaki Museum Library (Athens), for letting me consult their archives.

I would also like to thank all the academic staff (including Ph.D. students) at the Greek section of the Department of Linguistics and Philology, University of Uppsala, where the book took its final shape, for their warm support and encouragement from the first moment of my arrival in Sweden. Particularly, I would like to express my gratitude to Ingela Nilsson, for all her help, Jan Olof Rosenqvist, for his excellent co-operation, and Eva Nyström, for her warm welcome to Uppsala. Finally, many thanks are also due to Johan Heldt, for his crucial technical support when needed.

A special thanks should go to John Davey and Chloe Plummer from Oxford University Press, for their constant encouragement and support through all the stages of publication of the book.

This research has been financially supported by the Greek State Scholarships Foundation, the Onassis Foundation, the Cambridge European Trust, Trinity College, the Faculty of Classics (University of Cambridge), and a STINT scholarship.

I would like to thank my friend, Michalis Kalamaras, who, throughout the years, has helped me shape my ideas about language and society. I would also like to thank all my friends in Cambridge, and especially Napoleon Katsos, Marios Mavrogiorgos, and Christina Sevdali for bearing with me on an everyday basis, and for some beautiful memories. Finally, Vangelis Tolis has always been there when I needed him, and has strengthened my belief in friendship.

My parents have always shown me what parental love means. This book is dedicated to them and to my dear brother, Philippos, his wife Maria, and my wonderful niece Nefeli.

And to Maria, for being a rose in a winter garden, always.

Theodore Markopoulos

Uppsala, January 2008

1

Introduction: aims, theory, and method

This is an investigation on the development of the notional category "Future" in Greek as manifested in three future-referring "periphrases", mainly from the post-classical (3rd c. BC) to the Late Medieval period (15th c. AD). The diachronic investigation of a grammatical category of Greek, supposedly one of the most studied languages in the world, might seem superfluous at first glance. But this impression is not well grounded, for two reasons: first, because the great majority of the extant investigations belong to the paradigm of "traditional grammar", predating modern linguistic theories, and may thus be found inadequate in various respects; and secondly, because all these studies are not equally distributed along the time axis of Greek: specifically, while Classical and Modern Greek (and Hellenistic–Roman Greek to a lesser extent) have attracted the interest of many scholars, Medieval Greek has remained hitherto largely unexplored. The focus of this investigation, the category of Future, constitutes one of the best exemplifications of these problems.

With regard to the extant literature, the only specialized treatment of this grammatical category in the post-classical period (Bănescu, 1915) was written in a strictly philological context, without the help of modern linguistic tools, and at a time when many texts of the Medieval (and also of the Hellenistic) period remained unpublished, thus rendering the corpus quite limited from today's perspective. Apart from this monograph, there exist two types of relevant studies. On the one hand we have historical grammars of Greek (e.g. Jannaris, 1897, Schwyzer, 1950–71, Horrocks, 1997, among others), which contain various comments on the development of future-referring constructions, but their necessarily broad character does not allow them to go into much detail: to these we may add investigations of specific periods of Greek (e.g. Browning, 1983 for Medieval Greek and Christidis, 2007 for Classical and Hellenistic Greek), which again are of a similar character to the grammars of broader scope. On the other hand, there are also investigations of specific future-referring constructions (e.g. Magnien, 1912 for the ancient synthetic Future Tense and Joseph & Pappas, 2002 for the θέλω "periphrasis"), though these are still quite scarce and usually do not attempt to incorporate their analysis in the wider picture of the "system" of future reference for any particular period.

As can be seen, the research undertaken hitherto regarding the category "Future" in Greek leaves a lot to be desired. This book aims first and foremost to eliminate these gaps in our understanding of the development of this grammatical category in Greek, investigating specifically those periods that are least known and well studied, i.e. the Hellenistic–Roman and the Medieval period. In order to understand the origin of the state of affairs obtaining in the Hellenistic–Roman period, the classical period (5th–4th c. BC) will also be briefly investigated. The current examination focuses on the three major future-referring "periphrastic constructions" that emerged and / or were established in these periods, namely 'μέλλω / ἔχω / (ἐ)θέλω + Infinitive / complement clause'. Before presenting the main issues addressed in the book, however, the theoretical framework of this investigation will be first discussed, followed by some considerations related to the notion of futurity and to the status of the term "periphrasis".

1.1 Theoretical preliminaries

1.1.1 *Grammaticalization from different perspectives*

The emergence of new future-referring constructions (FCs) out of lexical verbs, typically conveying notions such as volition, movement or obligation (e.g. Bybee & Pagliuca, 1987: 109), is commonly regarded as a prototypical case of grammaticalization, i.e. of a process through which formerly lexical elements acquire a grammatical meaning or elements of an already partly grammatical character become even more grammatical. Even though the first definition of grammaticalization as a distinct process can be traced back not only to Meillet (1912), as is commonly assumed to be the case, but also to the leading Neogrammarian Paul (cf. Itkonen, 2005: 109–10), it is in the last two decades that it has attracted most interest, especially from scholars working in a functional–typological perspective (cf. for example, Lehmann, 1995, Hopper & Traugott, 1993, 2003, Haspelmath, 1999b, and Heine, 2003), though not exclusively, as we shall see below. Recently, there has been criticism of the assumption that grammaticalization constitutes a theory of language change in its own right (cf. for example, the collection of papers in Campbell, 2001), even though Traugott (1999) and Heine (2003) correctly point out that the term "theory" has seldom been used by those actually working on grammaticalization. This investigation of the developments of the Greek FCs is phrased in terms of the functional–typological perspective of grammaticalization, which is considered to be a type of process rather than a theory *sensu stricto*. This process does not affect lexical elements but rather constructions: for instance, it would be meaningless to say that the English verb "have" is grammaticalized, without specifying the context of grammaticalization, since "have" can convey different meanings *depending on its complement and the construction it is found in* (e.g. "I have to go" = obligation, "I have gone" = perfect). In other words, it has been correctly stressed that grammaticalization can only occur in a specific context involving a string of lexical elements, a construction, and not isolated lexical elements (cf., for example, Fischer, 2007: 59). In this investigation, any mention of grammaticalized elements should be taken to mean elements participating in a grammaticalized construction.

Even the assumption of grammaticalization as a distinct process rather than a theory has not remained impervious to criticism, since it has been argued (cf., for example, Joseph, 2001a, 2004) that all phenomena usually considered as instances of such a process can be analyzed and well understood without it. But there are two reasons why this criticism is probably exaggerated. First, the great majority of cases of grammaticalization involve the co-occurrence of different phenomena across grammatical levels (semantic "bleaching", phonological erosion, syntactic irregularities), a fact that was emphasized by Lehmann (1995) and has hitherto remained largely undisputed, although there exist obviously instances where the correlation between the different types of change is not fully observed. Since this combination of phenomena is, to my knowledge, peculiar to grammaticalization, it is only reasonable to assume that grammaticalization constitutes a distinct process rather than an epiphenomenon, crucially combining together convergent developments at different levels of grammar. Secondly, grammaticalization studies (e.g. Heine, 1993, Bybee, Perkins, & Pagliuca, 1994, Kuteva, 2001, Heine & Kuteva, 2002) have shown that the constructions that are finally grammaticalized belong to specific cognitive domains and follow distinct cognitive paths: for instance, verbs denoting movement to a place can come to denote movement towards a more abstract goal, and subsequently become future-referring forms. Importantly, this type of investigation accounts for the repetitive patterns of change observed in the languages of the world, manifested by the grammaticalization of similar elements (semantically speaking) time and again. Without this notion of cognitive paths and cognitive sources of change, we would be at a loss to explain the repetition of specific patterns of language change. Arguably, such a systematic account is preferable to the one appealing to randomness.

This investigation follows largely the "(conceptual) transfer – context" (Heine, 2003: 586–8) or "metonymic-metaphorical" model of grammaticalization (Heine, Claudi & Hünnemeyer, 1991: 13), according to which both the cognitive sources and the specific linguistic context constitute integral parts of one and the same overall process. In other words, without ignoring the importance of specific cognitive sources for subsequent developments (notably, the "metaphorical transfer" to a different cognitive domain), the equally important role of specific contexts in order for certain changes to take place in the diachrony of the FCs will also be highlighted (cf., for example, Traugott & Dasher, 2002 for a recent application of this model). However, this will be coupled with careful attention to the particulars of the "grammatical systems" associated with the FCs, that is to the formal (but not necessarily formalized) properties of the FCs in question. This is in accordance with Fischer's (2007: 82) plea for historical linguists to "give equal weight to form and function". So, the current investigation intends to underline all different factors (semantic, pragmatic / contextual, functional, formal and sociolinguistic, cf. further below) that might be at play at the diachronic development of the FCs.

It has been widely documented that, despite all possible facilitating factors, grammaticalization might not occur or, to be more precise, there is no predictability concerning the occurrence and the final outcome of any grammaticalization process; what can be more or less predicted is the development of the construction being grammaticalized and its passing through various, largely predictable, stages (cf. Bybee, Perkins, & Pagliuca, 1994). The lack of predictability might seem a drawback for a framework seeking to account for language change; but I would argue that this is not so, basically because *speakers* change their language, and the outcome of the actions of rational agents cannot be predicted in any absolute way. This has been already argued for language change (cf. mainly Itkonen, 1983, 2005). One cannot predict what will happen but only explain what happened *a posteriori*. Therefore, no theory should aim to predict language change but simply provide an understanding of the mechanisms used by speakers to shape their language and point out the main *tendencies* observed in language change.

There are two main assumptions associated with the study of grammaticalization: the unidirectionality and the gradualness of grammatical change. The former implies that a lexical element that is being grammaticalized cannot become again an independent element; this alleged property has sparked great controversy (cf., for example, Janda, 2001 for criticism and counter-examples) and, even though it seems that it cannot be taken as an absolute, it nevertheless represents a very strong tendency, as even the strongest critics of grammaticalization admit (cf., for example, Newmeyer, 2001: 213). Unidirectionality partly refutes the "no-prediction" principle mentioned above, but only regarding the stages of development, not its occurrence or its outcome, as clarified. Actually, functionalists should feel more at ease knowing that unidirectionality represents a tendency instead of an absolute principle, since this complies well with the overall preference of tendencies instead of absolutes (cf., for example, Dryer, 1998). As to what constrains the availability of 'de-grammaticalization', no consensus exists. A possible suggestion would be to look into the often neglected factor of phonological erosion. It looks only plausible that elements participating in a grammaticalized construction can be put to uses "less grammatical" only if they are not so phonologically eroded as to have lost their paradigmatic association with fully articulated elements. Obviously, further research is required before we have any concrete results on the issue.

Regarding the gradualness of change, this has been denied mainly by scholars working in the generative framework (cf., for example, Lightfoot, 1999), who favor a theory of catastrophic change. According to the generative view, change in a speaker's grammar can only take place instantaneously, while the diffusion of the change in the whole population of the language is gradual. This follows from the view of language as an internal "organ" of the individual, and not as a means of communication or anything similar of a collective nature. This continuing debate cannot be evaluated here: suffice it to say that I do not subscribe to the catastrophic view of language change and to the generative diachronic investigation in general, for reasons stated further below. For this investigation, gradualness is a property of language change evident in the diachrony of all FCs.

Both properties (unidirectionality and gradualness) are implemented in the notion of a "cline", i.e. the pathway of change that the various lexical elements follow. In the case of the verbal domain, the "Verb-to-affix" cline is of the following form (Hopper & Traugott, 1993: 108): Full verb > Auxiliary Verb > Clitic > Affix. According to what has been said above, it follows that a cline does not imply that all verbs starting to follow this pathway will necessarily reach the end and become affixes but simply how the process will continue to develop, if it develops. The passing from one stage to another is manifested in a variety of parameters related to the semantic, pragmatic, morphosyntactic as well as phonological properties of the elements involved. Not all practitioners of grammaticalization framework are in agreement over the exact nature of these parameters, but according to a recent formulation (Heine & Kuteva, 2005: 15) they should look like the following:

(a) extension, i.e. the rise of novel grammatical meanings when linguistic expressions are extended to new contexts (context-induced reinterpretation)
(b) desemanticization (or "semantic bleaching"), i.e. less (or generalization) in meaning content
(c) decategorialization, i.e. loss in the morphosyntactic properties characteristic of lexical or other less grammaticalized forms
(d) erosion (or "phonetic reduction"), i.e. less in phonetic substance.

An important observation should be made here: the development along these four parameters is not isomorphic, i.e. a construction may be fully grammaticalized from a semantic point of view without any obvious phonological consequences, a point that will be relevant for the analysis of the Greek FCs. However, these four factors tend to correlate, a feature characteristic of grammaticalization, which encompasses all linguistic levels.

The gradualness assumed for grammaticalization clines predicts that there are no clear-cut boundaries between the various stages of development, indeed between the assumed grammatical categories of the linguistic elements. This is one of the hallmarks of the functional framework, as it distinguishes it rather sharply with the generative grammar, which is based on the distinctiveness of grammatical categories. The non-concreteness of categories stems from typological findings (cf. below for the extreme difficulty in defining Auxiliaries), but also from neurological studies: Pulvermüller (2002: 116) observes that there is no brain localization for lexical as opposed to "grammatical" words, a fact that implies that there is a gradience, a continuum between all linguistic elements, and not any sharp dichotomy. As Fischer points out (2007: 68), the same findings had already been reported by Slobin (1997: 282) and she concludes, therefore, that the "categories continuum" seems rather more plausible from a psycholinguistic point of view. On the basis of these observations, the current analysis will be phrased in terms of a cline of grammaticality, with elements or constructions being more or less grammatical (according to various criteria, cf. 1.1.3), and with no clear-cut boundaries between categories.

As can be seen from the discussion so far, the assumptions made in this analysis follow the functional–typological perspective on grammaticalization, and are in contrast with the generative paradigm, since the former is much more convincing and can arguably account better for this type of phenomena. Any generative analysis of diachronic change starts at the point when the frequency of a specific construction rises or a new construction emerges, and "it has nothing to say about why the distribution of the cues [i.e. primary data] should change" (Lightfoot, 2003: 503). But since it is the change in the frequency of cues that triggers reanalysis and subsequent parametric change, as Lightfoot (ibid.) admits, such a view excludes the original cause of the subsequent changes in the grammar, since it is the primary data that undeniably trigger such a grammatical change: in other words, people change their language, a fact ignored (and often refuted) by practitioners of generative grammar, which, therefore, cannot account for change in a global way, being much more restricted in scope. The admittedly difficult task of revealing the reasons for the change in distribution of the primary data should arguably be part of any explanation of diachronic linguistic phenomena, and the functional perspective of grammaticalization is clearly oriented towards that goal, paying attention to factors such as contexts of use, which belong to the domain of language use and not to the intrinsic knowledge of language (or to the domain of performance and not competence, in generative terms).

Recently, however, there have been attempts to tackle grammaticalization from a generative perspective (e.g. Roberts & Roussou, 2003, van Gelderen, 2004), despite denials of the existence of the phenomenon from some practitioners (e.g. Lightfoot, 2002). Although these attempts are clearly helpful for the formalization of the syntactic aspects of grammaticalization, they are intrinsically linked to syntax, thus largely excluding semantico-pragmatic and phonological aspects of the phenomenon, and so have little to say about the reasons, possibly non-syntactic, for the changes in the use of specific constructions. As a consequence, they only partly illuminate the phenomenon of grammaticalization (cf. Fischer, 1997). Fischer (2004: 730) summarizes rather neatly what the historical linguist should and should not do:

For me, this means that he [i.e. the historical linguist] must concentrate on physical data, on their context, and on the variations that occur on the performance level, and not on how grammar changes. Grammar, at this stage, is a theoretical construct, not something that has been established empirically.

Nevertheless, Fischer (2007) attempts to pursue an "equal distance" attitude towards the two frameworks (functional–typological / generative), stating that "each approach practises a different kind of 'cleaning' of the facts" (2007: 57) and arguing for a new framework incorporating elements from both paradigms or, in her own words (2007: 82), "a theory that looks at performance facts, takes account of variation, and gives equal weight to form and function". However, regarding these three criteria, the functional–typological approach can in principle satisfy all three, while the generative approach would have severe conceptual problems dealing with performance facts and giving equal weight to form and function; as to variation, it has only recently started to constitute an explanandum for generativists. Therefore, Fischer's "equal distance" approach seems rather unmotivated, not least because she herself points out conceptual problems with the most basic assumptions of the generative paradigm, e.g. the innateness of grammar (Fischer, 2007: 67–74).

These are the main reasons why the functional perspective will be followed in this study (for extensive criticism on various other aspects of diachronic generative investigations, cf. Itkonen, 1983, 2005, Keller, 1994, Croft, 2000, among others). Following Fischer's (2004) quote, particular attention is paid to the data itself, so as no cleaning (either conscious or unconscious) occurs. This is of the outmost importance, since, as Haiman (1998: 172) most fittingly observed:

Every theory may begin its career as an attempt to preserve the phenomena, but once the theory gets a good hold on life and becomes entrenched in the minds of its adherents, there ensues a drive to sacrifice the phenomena to preserve the theory.

Therefore, priority is given to the in-depth investigation of the data, and what it reveals concerning the predictions of the functional–typological framework, which will be taken into account, but only as mere guidelines, as will be seen in the conclusions of the investigation, where examples of refuting of some of these predictions will be provided.

The attention to textual evidence itself leads most naturally to the sociolinguistic perspective of grammaticalization, often overlooked by functionalists and generativists alike. Following Nevalainen (2004), among others, a careful analysis of the social embedding of each construction under investigation will be pursued, on the basis of a sociolinguistically sensitive corpus (for more details, cf. 1.3). It is thus highlighted that only such a combination of perspectives can shed more light on diachronical developments in general, and on grammaticalization phenomena affecting FCs in particular.

1.1.2 *The notion of futurity*

Futurity as a notional / grammatical category is surrounded by controversy, which has its roots both in theoretical issues and in specific cross-linguistic observations. With regard to the former, the fact that reference to future time is inherently related to events as yet unrealized and therefore unknown obviously separates the Future tense (and in general all FCs) from all other tenses. Consequently, future-referring assertions are always associated with probabilities of realization, hence the well-known debate whether the Future tense can ever be a true 'tense', in the sense of having a 'purely' temporal value, or if it should be best placed within the realm of modality which covers the domains of probability / possibility. However, it has been observed that speakers can refer to the future with strong conviction and without any trace of uncertainty, irrespective of whether this is epistemologically or logically correct or not (Lyons, 1977: 815, Fleischman, 1982: 20). It follows that the status of Future as a tense cannot be refuted solely on the basis of epistemological assumptions, according to which the future, being unknown to the human mind, is not strictly liable to confident predictions or assertions: the way that speakers refer to the external world and, as a result, the way that languages grammaticalize specific notions such as futurity, do not necessarily coincide with what would logically be expected. In other words, the fact that it is not possible for humans to actually know the future does not entail that speakers cannot make assertions referring to the future as if they knew it (cf. also Tsangalidis, 1999 and McCawley, 1981: 343).

Having said that, the inter-relation between Future tense and modality is not restricted to the domain of semantics but is robustly manifested cross-linguistically in various ways. Firstly, many of the forms that develop into FCs (either "periphrastic" or synthetic) are of modal origin (Fleischman, 1982: 24–7, Bybee, Perkins, & Pagliuca, 1991, 1994: 252–3). Secondly and most importantly, FCs are almost without exception used to convey epistemic and deontic modal meanings, such as possibility, necessity etc. (cf., for example, Bybee, Perkins, & Pagliuca, 1994: 243–4). Despite this close relationship, however, it is not always the case that future reference is tied to an obviously modal meaning: Dahl (1985: 106) reports that, cross-linguistically, "future time reference" is more often a part of the meaning of an FC than the various modalities, even though Comrie (1989: 52) argues that only rarely do FCs convey exclusively a temporal meaning.

These observations allow us to conclude that treating the Future solely as a modal or a temporal category is arguably an over-simplification, probably due to the extension of purely logical assumptions to the actual use of linguistic elements, which does not always follow what is scientifically or logically dictated. In most—if not all—future forms, there exists a balance between their modality and their temporality, determined mostly by their correlations with other future-referring forms of the particular language they belong to (Fleischman, 1982: 153) and the retention of smaller or bigger parts of their former lexical meaning (Bybee, Perkins, & Pagliuca, 1994: 15–17). This assumption seems to fit rather neatly with Dahl's (1985: 3) property of "Impreciseness", according to which all Tense–Aspect–Modality (TAM) categories cannot be defined in any systematic way that could guarantee that a specific linguistic form belongs to just one of them to the exclusion of the others. Arguably, the Future tense is the ideal category to demonstrate the validity of this property, and this will become evident from the investigation of the Greek FCs.

The tight linking between futurity and various kinds of modality might be regarded as one of the major factors behind the formal instability of the FCs. The propensity of these constructions towards semantic change is a well-known fact manifested in a great variety of unrelated languages (Fleischman, 1982: 23) and is thus considered to be one of the universal characteristics of futurity. It is further taken as evidence for the "marked" nature of Future tense and futurity in general in comparison with other grammatical categories in the domain of Tense. Apart from the common modal uses of the FCs already mentioned, the "markedness" of Future is arguably supported by typological findings that indicate that the Future is the member of the category Tense that is least likely to occur cross-linguistically (Croft, 1990: 93), as well as by the observation that it is acquired rather late by children during the process of first language acquisition (Fleischman, 1982: 22–3). Since the notion of "markedness" is not sufficiently strictly defined to be helpful in a grammatical description or analysis, it could be argued that, if true, all these observations constitute simply the result of the idiosyncratic semantics of the category of Future, which rests on the very border of temporality and modality. From this perspective, these "markedness" properties of the FCs are to be expected.

In the analysis of the Greek FCs, it is therefore assumed that Future is a category spreading through both the domains of Tense and Modality (and Aspect to some extent); accordingly, the whole range of uses of each FC needs to be investigated in order to fully comprehend its properties. On the other hand, only those FCs will be treated whose uses clearly—insofar as the evidence permits one to tell—include a "pure" prediction value, given that: (a) a future-referring assertion can be considered as "equivalent to a prediction on the part of the speaker that the situation in the proposition, which refers to an event taking place after the moment of speech, will hold" (Bybee, Perkins, & Pagliuca, 1994: 244), and (b) prediction constitutes the core semantic element common to all future-referring constructions cross-linguistically, independently of the lexical source of the future formation (cf. Bybee, Perkins, & Pagliuca, 1994: 243–80 for cross-linguistic data, and Coates, 1983 for a similar analysis of English "will"). Therefore, instances of modal meaning, e.g. permission, which are inherently future-referring, will be investigated, but will not be considered as instances of a future meaning, since they do not make any prediction concerning a future state of affairs. Arguably, in this way the dual character of futurity is best reflected.

Before proceeding to the notions of Auxiliary Verbs and "periphrastic constructions", a note on the use of the terms of modality is in order here. Numerous definitions and categorizations of the various modality types have been proposed, but no consensus has emerged: for instance, Bybee, Perkins, & Pagliuca (1994: 177) distinguish four types of modality, namely "agent-oriented, speaker-oriented, epistemic and subordinating", while Palmer (2001) prefers a tripartite distinction between deontic / dynamic / epistemic modality, while things become even more confusing if sub-categorizations are taken into consideration. However, most accounts coincide to a great degree on the overall distinction between epistemic and non-epistemic modality (Van der Auwera & Plungian, 1998: 84). As it is not the aim of the book to propose a new categorization of modality, it follows this broad distinction, with more specific terms given when specific meanings of constructions need to be defined (ability, obligation, etc.). On the other hand, attention will be paid to the verification or falsification of typological predictions regarding modal pathways of FCs, on the basis of the Greek data.

1.1.3 *Auxiliary verbs and "periphrasis"*

The linguistic constructions undergoing grammaticalization are often labeled "periphrastic". Despite its widespread use, the term "periphrasis" has not been strictly defined and is mostly used in an intuitive sense, as shown in the following definition: "When a form in a paradigm consists of two or more words, it is periphrastic" (Matthews, 1981: 55). In all discussions of the term (cf., for example, Aerts, 1965 and especially Haspelmath, 2000 and references therein), the notion of the paradigm is most important: a "periphrasis" can only be described in relation to an inflectional paradigm that consists of at least some synthetic forms. When this paradigm is extant in the language exhibiting the "periphrasis" under investigation, then this "periphrasis" can be called a "suppletive periphrasis". In some cases, though, a construction is considered "periphrastic" although no synonymous synthetic form exists in the language; consequently, it can be regarded as "periphrastic" only in relation to a paradigm of a different language, which would presumably contain analogous synthetic forms; for instance, the English "will" future is called "periphrastic", although English has no corresponding monolectic form. This type of "periphrasis", called "categorial periphrasis" by Haspelmath (2000: 660), is especially problematic, since it is not evident why for instance the "have perfect" in English, although it has no corresponding monolectic form, should be considered a "periphrasis", simply because this meaning traditionally belongs to the paradigm of Tense, while the obligation construction "have to + Infinitive" is not usually referred to as a "periphrasis", although it forms a semantic pattern / paradigm with other modal expressions. Nevertheless, it is common practice for many linguists to use the term "periphrasis" in this manner.

The overall basic problem associated with this notion is deciding when a construction involving two or more words (typically a verb and a type of complement) should be considered a "periphrasis". Various criteria have been proposed (cf., for example, Bertinetto, 1990 and Vincent, 1991), but no agreed answer has emerged. Nevertheless, there do exist some typical properties of "periphrases", the most prominent being: (a) semantic non-compositionality of the integral parts ("constructional meaning", cf., for example, Kuteva, 2001: 100), (b) syntactic unity (rigid order and linear adjacency of the verb and its complement in the case of verbal "periphrases"), and (c) morphological poverty of the verbal form, i.e. restrictions on the possible forms of the verb in a "periphrastic" construction. Unfortunately, these properties do not always co-occur, hence the difficulty of isolating any necessary and sufficient properties of such constructions.

This state of affairs should probably be attributed to the fact that "periphrases" typically contain Auxiliaries. The category of Auxiliary has been much discussed under a variety of frameworks (cf., for example, Steele, 1978, Harris & Ramat, 1987, Heine 1993, Warner, 1993, Kuteva, 2001, Anderson, 2006), and many criteria have been proposed for identifying an element as an Auxiliary. Ramat (1987), for example, proposes four, while the result of a survey of most of the existing analyses concerning Auxiliaries at the time (Heine, 1993: 22–4) has raised the number of their plausible properties to twenty-two! While some are undoubtedly robust, and have been widely accepted as such (e.g. an auxiliary must have the same Subject as the uninflected dependent verb; the order of the two elements must be fixed; no—or very few—elements can be interposed between these), no fully satisfactory definition has emerged. This is clearly reflected in the definition proposed by Heine (1993: 70): "An auxiliary is a linguistic item covering some range of uses along the Verb-to-TAM chain."

The difficulty in defining precisely a distinct category of Auxiliaries has led many scholars to employ the more general notion of a prototypical Auxiliary (Heine, 1993, Warner, 1993, Anderson, 2000), reflecting their most typical characteristics: most importantly, lack of argument structure, loss of morphological distinctions, and non-finite complementation. This notion is related to the overall issue of 'prototypical' and 'non-prototypical' members of all linguistic categories, which cannot be further discussed here (cf. Borsley, 2000).

What emerges from this discussion is the non-availability of necessary and sufficient criteria for the definition of Auxiliaries, as already stressed by Kuteva (2001: 10) and followed by Anderson (2006) in his typological survey of Auxiliaries. As expected, given the gradualness of grammaticalization and the non-distinctiveness of categories, Auxiliaries can be described only in terms of relevant properties, and cannot be strictly defined using categorial criteria. Their properties vary from language to language to such an extent that only a definition such as the following can capture the whole range of variation manifested cross-linguistically:

"Auxiliary verb" is here considered to be an item on the lexical verb-functional affix continuum, which tends to be at least somewhat semantically bleached, and grammaticalized to express one or more of a range of salient verbal categories, most typically aspectual and modal categories, but also not infrequently temporal, negative polarity, or voice categories. (Anderson, 2006: 4)

Given that Auxiliaries (and, as had been argued, grammaticalization in general) can only occur in a construction, one can only speak of Auxiliary Verb Constructions (AVCs), a term that covers the vague notion of "periphrasis" (at least in the verbal domain, which is of interest here) and will be used in the analysis below. It is noteworthy that Anderson (2006: 24) can only distinguish one variable in his typological examination of AVCs, namely the head of inflection, isolating four types of AVCs (AUX-headed, LEX-headed, double inflection and mixed systems).

On the basis of the above discussion, no clear-cut boundaries regarding the extent of grammaticalization of various AVCs will be postulated, and AVCs will only be analyzed as "more / less" grammaticalized, based on properties found to be relevant for the language in which they occur (i.e. Greek in its various stages).

1.2 Main aims of the study

A thorough investigation of *all* FCs in the period covered in the book, i.e. from the 5th and mainly from the 3rd c. BC to the 15th c. AD, would constitute a huge endeavor, since there was massive variation in the means of expressing futurity throughout these centuries. Consequently, as already mentioned, the examination will focus on the future-referring AVCs and, to be more precise, on the three main representatives: μέλλω / ἔχω / (ἐ)θέλω + Infinitive / complement clause. All three constitute future-referring forms in the sense discussed above, that is they can convey the temporal meaning of prediction, apart from the various modal meanings most commonly associated with FCs (cf. 1.1.2). The motivation for their selection as the focus of this investigation is twofold. First, as AVCs, they are typically linked to grammaticalization, and therefore they provide a good opportunity to assess the validity of the assumptions usually made with regard to their development. They also constitute the most frequently used AVCs, albeit each one in a different period. But even though the focus of the current investigation will be on the three specified FCs, occasional comments with regard to various other future-referring forms will be made (e.g. the ancient morphological Future Tense and the νά-Subjunctive), since it is clearly necessary to determine the place of these main AVCs in the overall domain of future reference in the various periods.

More generally, the study of the three FCs seeks to answer the following basic research questions:

(a) What was the exact process of development for each of the constructions? Is there any interconnection between them? And if so, what exactly?
(b) Which are the possible causes of the attested developments?
(c) What can this investigation tell us about the theory(ies) of language change? More specifically: (i) the phenomenon of grammaticalization and how this is best captured (formal / functional approaches), and (ii) the predictions of the typological literature concerning FCs.

Obviously, these general aims can be further subdivided into more specialized goals regarding each particular AVC (for example, What is the role of language contact in the development of the AVCs, and especially of ἔχω and θέλω? How is the "θέ νά" construction related to the future-referring θέλω + Infinitive? and so forth). These more specific questions will be formulated and addressed in the relevant chapters.

1.3 Corpus: problems and methodology

As is well known, any diachronic linguistic investigation faces severe problems regarding the available linguistic material. The necessarily complete absence of spontaneous spoken data for periods before the advent of sound recording constitutes an important obstacle for any linguistic analysis, since it is generally accepted that texts always deviate to a greater or lesser extent from the everyday language of their time, as this is mainly manifested in the spoken language. The only method at our disposal to circumvent this problem is to identify texts of genres that usually employ a form of language closely related to the spoken language of their time, e.g. comedies etc. But even in the case of such texts, a comparison with more elaborate styles is needed to determine whether they are really linguistically different. And, even if they are, it is often tricky for the historical linguist to decide whether the differences correspond to any diachronic developments or are simply the result of the genre factor (cf. Herring, van Reenen & Schøsler, 2001: 3, Gregersen & Pedersen, 2001).

The second major issue relates to the scarcity of the available material. Historical records are usually far from complete, containing numerous gaps in documentation for a variety of reasons, such as extended periods of warfare and social instability or the use of writing material with limited resistance to time. These gaps may seriously undermine any attempt to trace instances of linguistic change along a continuous line. Yet a third problem is associated with the nature of the surviving texts: in many cases, they are of a literary or official character and as such do not necessarily constitute a reliable source of information about the 'normal' use of the contemporary language, since they may contain archaisms or other unusual forms, which could be mistakenly taken as belonging to the "norm" in the absence of any other textual source. Moreover, most of the texts are copies of older originals, lost to us now. Historical linguists are usually aware of these problems of the available material; however, they sometimes examine the surviving texts stripped of their social embedding, undermining in this way the validity of their results. The salience of the social embedding is immediately relevant in the case of Greek.

On the face of it, Greek seems an almost ideal language for a diachronic investigation: it contains surviving linguistic material from the 2nd millennium BC to the present day, with no complete gap in the record after the classical period (5th–3rd c. BC). This ideal picture quickly vanishes, though, when one looks into this material in more detail. The most prominent and widely discussed problem is that of Atticism, an intellectual movement originating in the Hellenistic period, which considered the classical Attic language of higher value than the contemporary Koine and its spoken dialects. This attitude resulted in the production of numerous texts in an "Atticizing" language that had rather loose ties with the spoken language of that period (cf., for example, Horrocks, 1997: 50–1). Thus, a situation of diglossia was initiated, which would actually last till the 20th century (!) and according to which "learned" authors wrote in this artificial, archaizing language, while all other writers employed a more vernacular variety of Greek. Unfortunately, the great bulk of the surviving material from the Hellenistic to the Late Medieval period belongs to the learned tradition, is written in a language quite different from the spoken language of their time, and consequently is of little—if any—help for a historical linguistic investigation, which is necessarily focused on change in the spoken language as reflected in vernacular texts. Diglossia therefore forces us to include in our corpus of investigation only low-register texts that avoid Atticism.

As the register of each text plays a crucial role in determining whether it can be of any help for this investigation, a note on the use of this term is due here: it has been observed that there is a strong correlation between informal registers of discourse and lower-ranked social groups in terms of the linguistic features they exhibit (cf. Finegan & Biber, 1994). Consequently, in this investigation, the term "low-register" is used for texts of a more or less informal register of use (e.g. private letters) or texts written by an individual assumed to belong to the lower social / educational ranks or both.

The surviving low-register texts constitute only a small proportion of the surviving texts in Greek and, in addition, there are gaps in their tradition, especially in the Early Medieval period (5th–10th c. AD) (cf. ch. 4). The only period, however, for which we possess numerous low-register texts in the vernacular is the Late Medieval period (11th–15th c.). But even these texts are not devoid of problems, as we shall see in more detail below (cf. ch. 5). Perhaps the most important among them is their quite problematic manuscript tradition: apparently, the scribes felt more at ease when copying texts that did not belong to the archaizing tradition and, as a result, there is extensive variation in the different versions of numerous texts that have come down to us (for relevant discussion, cf., for example, Beaton, 1996: 164–88). Moreover, the great majority of these manuscripts are of a considerably later date than the assumed date of original production of the texts, and this gap may seriously undermine any conclusions about the language of the date of production, given the propensity of scribes to adapt and modify. This is not the case for the non-literary texts of the same period, which are usually autographs of notaries and are therefore very useful for the investigation of Late Medieval Greek (cf. ch. 5). The issue of manuscript tradition has long been the traditional domain of philologists, while linguists were either unaware of its complexities or tended to ignore it. Lately, this tendency has started to reverse, as more and more historical linguists stress the importance of the individual manuscripts instead of published (usually critical) editions of older texts for the diachronic study of language (cf. mainly Lass, 2004 and Grund, 2006). Obviously, the study of manuscripts is not always easy, as manuscripts are sometimes difficult to get hold of, and the separate study of each manuscript of all works in a specific corpus is very time-consuming. Hopefully, more diplomatic editions of individual manuscripts will see the light of day, so that diachronic investigations can count on more solid evidence.

On the basis of these observations, it can be argued that Greek, despite its rich and continuous documentation, presents serious obstacles to a diachronic examination of any particular phenomenon. Bearing this in mind, the corpus for this study has been compiled in an attempt to address these problems as effectively as possible, and thereby to maximize the validity of the conclusions. The near totality of the available textual sources normally considered to be written in a low register was examined, taking into account the genre and character of each text, its social embedding, and any available information concerning its author. In some cases (especially for the Early Medieval period), texts of a middle register have also been included, owing to the scarcity, or even absence, of low-register sources. The inclusion of almost every available text that belongs to a lower register, and the systematic exclusion of texts written in higher, i.e. archaizing, registers, minimizes the dangers of any serious distortion. It is acknowledged, nonetheless, that even the investigation of all appropriate texts cannot guarantee that we acquire a complete picture of the contemporary vernacular, though it is hoped that the results are the best that can be achieved with the evidence that is currently available.

More specifically, the corpus for the brief investigation of the classical period (5th–3rd c. BC) consists of texts representative of different genres (historiography, philosophical writings, tragedy, and comedy), which correspond to both low and high registers of use, since in this period formal diglossia had not yet become an issue. As far as the Hellenistic–Roman period (3rd c. BC–4th c. AD) is concerned, the texts selected comprise the surviving non-literary papyri and works of early Christian literature, when "pagan" Atticism was consistently avoided (indeed many writers would have been incapable of such a style, even in principle). The following period (Early Medieval, 5th–10th c.) is the most problematic in terms of the existing material; apart from the last surviving papyri, dating from the 8th century, the corpus includes mostly middle-register texts, which can shed at least some light on the developments that occurred in that period, especially in combination with the papyrological evidence. Finally, with regard to the Late Medieval period (11th–15th c.), the corpus consists of all literary texts written in the vernacular, while, in compliance with the discussion above on manuscript tradition, an attempt has been made check and account for manuscript variation whenever possible. In addition, various official documents (agreements, treaties, notary books, etc.) have also been consulted, which, despite various difficulties related to their official character (cf. ch. 5), are most important, since their non-literary character allows them to constitute the controlling factor for the conclusions drawn on the basis of the literary texts. More information on the textual sources of each period will be provided in the relevant chapters, and a complete list of all texts included in the corpus is given in the bibliography.

The analysis of the textual evidence will be both quantitative and qualitative. Concerning the former, it is crucial to ascertain the frequency of use of the AVCs in each text, each genre, and each period, since frequency has been proved to be a crucial factor not only for diachronic developments (cf. Fischer, 2007: 128–9, Haiman 1994) but also for the very organization of human language ability (cf. Bybee, 2006a and Haiman, 1999). We will be mostly dealing with "token frequency", which "counts the number of times a unit appears in running text" (Bybee, 2006b: 9). On the other hand, given the problems of the surviving material, a quantitative investigation must be accompanied by a qualitative examination in order to critically evaluate the quantitative results and to filter out factors that might cloud our judgments (e.g. the rarity of use of an FC in specific text(s) might be due to its mainly oral character or to a dialect differentiation or to author preferences etc.).

1.4 The structure of the book

The investigation of the FCs will proceed in chronological order, following the different periods of the history of the Greek language, so that each chapter provides an overall picture of the interaction of the FCs in a specific period. Thus, chapter 2 presents the properties of the AVCs in the classical period, which can be considered as the starting point for subsequent developments. The next chapter discusses their properties in the Hellenistic–Roman period, when AVCs were more frequently used. Chapter 4 deals with the Early Medieval period, and chapter 5 investigates the Late Medieval period. The considerable bulk of this last chapter is due to the fact that in this period the AVCs (and especially θέλω + Infinitive) have at last come to constitute the main and most frequently used FCs, while Late Medieval Greek in general is perhaps the least studied stage of the language. The investigation concludes with the overall picture of development that has emerged from the analysis, and some theoretical remarks based on the evidence presented.

2

Classical Greek (5th–3rd c. BC): the origins

Introduction

This chapter can be seen as a preface to the actual point of interest, i.e. the developments from the Hellenistic–Roman period onwards. Its inclusion is based on the fact that all three AVCs can be seen to have their origins in Ancient Greek (AG),[1] and even though this has been sporadically observed in the literature, mostly concerning μέλλω (e.g. Goodwin, 1875, Basset, 1979 among many others for μέλλω, Aerts, 1965 for ἔχω, and Chila-Markopoulou, 2000 for θέλω), it has not been paid its due attention, perhaps because speakers of AG mainly used a synthetic Future Tense that constituted the main means of future reference during that period. Overall, the extensive TAM paradigm of AG is traditionally assumed to include three Voices (Active, Passive, and Medio-Passive, although the last two were distinguished morphologically only in the Future and Aorist Tense), seven Tenses (Present, Preterite / Imperfective Past,[2] Future, Aorist, Perfect, Pluperfect, and Future Perfect, although the last is more sporadically attested) and four Moods (Indicative, Subjunctive, Optative, and Imperative, although, with the exception of the Indicative, there are no forms for all moods in all tenses). In all these finite forms, all grammatical persons have distinct endings. Moreover, AG had two non-finite forms, the Participle and the Infinitive, with distinct forms in the Present, the Future, the Aorist, and the Perfect tense. The Participle in particular exhibited grammatical gender distinction in all its occurrences, as gender agreement with the noun it modified was obligatory. Leaving aside

---

[1] A term used here to refer to classical Attic, excluding other Ancient Greek dialects.
[2] The term "Preterite" is used throughout the book to refer to the Imperfective Past form of the Greek verbs, while the term "Aorist" is used to refer to the Perfective Past form. Notice that, as far as the AVCs are concerned, the only past form they are found in is the "Preterite" (with a partial exception for μέλλω in AG), which for their case is synonymous to the more general term "Past form".

TABLE 2.1 *The paradigm of 3rd person singular of* λύω (=undo, dissolve) *in AG*

	INDIC	SUBJ	OPT	IMP	PCPLE	INF
PRES	λύει	λύῃ	λύοι	λυέτω	λύων–ουσα –ον	λύειν
PRET	ἔλυε	–	–	–	–	–
FUT	λύσει	–	λύσοι	–	λύσων –ουσα –ον	λύσειν
AOR	ἔλυσε	λύσῃ	λύσαι/ειε	λυσάτω	λύσας-ασα -αν	λῦσαι
PERF	λέλυκε	λελυκώς ᾖ	λελυκώς εἴη	λελυκώς ἔστω	λελυκώς –υῖα–ός	λελυκέναι
PLUPERF	ἐλελύκει	–	–	–	–	–

numerous complications concerning the formation of different verbal paradigms (on the basis of the verbal stem), an illustration of a typical paradigm of a verb in the active voice would be as shown in Table 2.1.

AG verbal morphology will only be referred to in relation to the investigation of the AVCs, to which we now turn our attention.

2.1 Μέλλω / Ἔμελλον + Infinitive: future-referring AVC (?)

The AG Future Tense could be "replaced" by an AVC comprising 'μέλλω + Infinitive (INF)', a construction existing as early as Homer and surviving in various forms in Modern Greek and its dialects. Even though this has been repeatedly observed in the relevant literature (cf. Goodwin 1875, Jannaris 1897, Schwyzer, 1950–71, among many others), the actual properties of the particular construction and the exact manner of its association with the synthetic Tense are still hard to determine. Moreover, little has been said concerning the thorny issue of the formal status of μέλλω itself: the fact that the original meaning of μέλλω remains controversial (contrary to the situation concerning the constructions involving ἔχω and (ἐ)θέλω, cf. 2.2–2.3) hinders any firm assumptions with regard to the exact status and meaning of the verb and the construction. Despite these difficulties, it will be demonstrated in this section that μέλλω was a verb with a modal core meaning which, together with its Infinitival complement, formed a construction that can be called an AVC mostly on semantic grounds. An attempt will also be made to clarify various related issues regarding the semantic and syntactic properties of this construction, e.g. the type of the INF and what determines it. The fact that μέλλω + Infinitive constitutes the only future-referring AVC which proliferated in AG requires us to draw particular attention to its properties at that time.

Semantically, as is well known, μέλλω + Infinitive constituted an FC with, where appropriate, a strong nuance of intention (cf. Magnien, 1912: 99–106), perhaps the most crucial future-referring notion, since it is hypothesized that all future-referring AVCs pass through this semantic stage (Bybee, Perkins, & Pagliuca, 1994: 254). Bearing this in mind, we can assume that the meaning of μέλλω itself would be "I intend to do something (for wilful animate subjects)—something is about to / will happen" (in the case of inanimate subjects). The "critical" / "bridging" (in the sense of Diewald, 2002 and Heine, 2002, respectively) context for the passing from intention to prediction is assuredly the 3rd person (with inanimate subject), where intention is excluded and gives rise to a predictive utterance, as can be seen from the examples below, illustrating intention (1) and prediction (2):

(1) Ἀκούω   τινὰ   διαβάλλειν, ὦ ἄνδρες, ἐμὲ ὡς ἐγὼ ἄρα ἐξαπατήσας
    Hear   someone slander,   men,   me that I prt deceived-PCIPLE
    ὑμᾶς   μέλλω   ἄγειν   εἰς Φᾶσιν.[3]
    you   intend-1st PERS. SING. lead-INF. to Phasin.
    "Men, I hear somebody slandering me, saying that, having deceived you, I intend to / I will lead you to Phasin"

(Anabasis, 5.7.5)

(2) Ἡμεῖς πορευόμεθα ὅπου   μέλλει   ἕξειν τὸ στράτευμα τροφήν
    We   march   wherever   intends-3rd PERS. SING. have-INF. the army food
    "We march wherever the army will have / find food"

(Anabasis, 7.3.8)

According to Aristotle, μέλλω was not exactly equivalent to the Future Tense, as it implied less commitment on the part of the speaker concerning the realization of the action described, in other words it was more modal than temporal.[4] Consequently, the μέλλω construction and the synthetic Future were not semantically and functionally equivalent, and this fact is also depicted in the differences concerning their use in participial contexts for instance, as we shall see below.

---

[3] Throughout the book, the examples are given in exactly the form they occur in the edition used, unless stated otherwise.

[4] "ὅλως γὰρ οὐ πᾶν γίνεται τὸ μελλῆσαν, οὐδὲ τὸ αὐτὸ τὸ ἐσόμενον καὶ τὸ μέλλον". "It is not the case that all that was intended-about to happen will actually happen, and what will happen is not the same with what is intended-about to happen" (De div. somn., 463b 28).

Unfortunately, the situation regarding the semantics of μέλλω is not so simple, as there is still a complication to be investigated, namely the fact that this verb can also bear the meaning "be late at, delay, stay idle" (henceforth μέλλω₂), usually in intransitive contexts, but not always. At first glance, one could argue that this use of μέλλω illustrates its proper lexical meaning: There is an obvious semantic relation between the two uses of μέλλω, as the postponement of an action inevitably implies that the action will or may take place in the future; and there are cases which seemingly exemplify how this semantic shift could take place (Basset, 1979: 14).[5] There remains, though, the question of the directionality of this semantic change, in other words, is the future-referring meaning the origin of μέλλω₂ or *vice versa*? This is not a trivial point, as it might shed light on the formal status of μέλλω in AG and its path of development. Even though it is not an easy task to decide on such subtle issues on the basis of the available material, there are two types of evidence, one intra-linguistic and the other cross-linguistic, which suggest that, in all probability, μέλλω₂ should be regarded as the subsequent development. With regard to the former evidence, the Homeric texts contain no instance of μέλλω₂, while they do contain 91 occurrences of future-referring μέλλω and, in addition, μέλλω₂ is only present in the Attic writers (cf. the relevant entry in LSJ: 1996), hinting at a specific dialectal development. From a cross-linguistic perspective, in their recent survey of all documented grammaticalization instances, Heine & Kuteva (2002) do not report any instance of a verb with the meaning "delay, be idle" becoming the source of a future-referring construction.

On the basis of this evidence, it seems reasonable to assume that μέλλω₂ constitutes a development particular to Attic writers, and that intention should possibly be seen as the primary meaning of μέλλω.[6] If this assumption is correct, then we are faced with an interesting case of a rather modal verb (μέλλω) acquiring another lexical meaning. This does not constitute a reversal of a grammaticalization process, in other words a case of de-grammaticalization, but simply an extension of the original meaning of the verb.

More interesting for our purpose is the examination of the morphosyntactic properties of the μέλλω FC, to determine its formal status as an AVC. Regarding morphology, little attention has been given to the form in which μέλλω is mostly used. This could shed some light on the frequent syntactic

---

[5] These cases usually involve μέλλω with an infinitival complement, with the meaning of "delay to do something" (e.g. *Agamemnon*, 908–9). It is easy to discern the association between "always delaying to do something" and "always going to do something (but never actually doing)".

[6] Obviously, one cannot exclude the possibility that Attic simply retained an old meaning that did not survive in other dialects (i.e. μέλλω₂), but there is no evidence to support such a claim, as mentioned.

TABLE 2.2 Token frequency of the forms of future-referring μέλλω

	5th c.	5th–4th c.	4th c.	4th–3rd c.	Total
PRES	78 (16.1)	267 (27.5)	124 (19.2)	31 (33.0)	500 (22.8)
PRET	154 (31.7)	143 (14.7)	111 (17.2)	6 (6.4)	414 (18.9)
AOR	4 (0.8)	2 (0.2)	2 (0.3)	1 (1.1)	9 (0.4)
PCPLE (V)	110 (22.7)	324 (33.4)	214 (33.2)	32 (34.0)	680 (31)
PCPLE (N)	84 (17.3)	101 (10.4)	122 (18.9)	13 (13.8)	320 (14.6)
INF	15 (3.1)	15 (1.5)	23 (3.6)	4 (4.3)	57 (2.6)
SUBJ	14 (2.9)	45 (4.6)	39 (6.1)	7 (7.4)	105 (4.8)
OPT	26 (5.4)	72 (7.4)	9 (1.4)	–	107 (4.9)
TOTAL	485	969	644	94	2192

contexts of the AVC, as can be seen in Table 2.2, which summarizes the results of a quantitative investigation of this kind (numbers represent occurrences, while percentages are given in parentheses).[7]

The striking fact emerging from this table is the very high token frequency of μέλλω in the participial form: as illustrated in the table, μέλλω can occur either as a verbal participle (PCPLE V in the table), i.e. with an Infinitival complement, or as an adjectival / nominal participle, i.e. "τοῦ μέλλοντος καιροῦ" "of the year to come" or "εἰς τό μέλλον" "in the future", respectively. If we count together the instances of both types of participial forms, the total reaches 45.6% of the total number of attestations. And even the verbal participle alone is the most frequent token form of μέλλω in absolute numbers (31%). This observation had completely eluded the previous research on μέλλω, and may be the key to understanding at least some of the developments of this AVC. It is also particularly interesting that participial μέλλω is completely absent from the Homeric texts, while there is a total of 91 instances of μέλλω in the Indicative and the Optative. So, there seems to be a clear development, namely the increase in the frequency of use of the participial form of μέλλω from Homeric to classical times. This appears to be a case of the well-known phenomenon of "specialization" (Hopper & Traugott, 1993: 113–6), whereby one construction perceived by speakers as functionally similar to another is used in a specific, specialized context / sense: in this particular case, the μέλλω construction came to be utilized quite regularly in its participial form, since the participle of the Future Tense of any verb had arguably a strong, goal-oriented (purposive) connotation and was regularly used to denote the goal of movement / action (e.g. Παρελήλυθα συμβουλεύσων, "I have risen to give my advice": Goodwin, 1875: 335). This might constitute the reason why μέλλω was used quite often in its participial

---

[7] As mentioned, the corpus, consisting of authors of various genres, is given in the bibliography.

form, usually with the meaning of "the one who is about to / will do something". In other words, the participial μέλλω construction was used to convey posteriority in a participial syntactic configuration, while the Future participle was used to render explicit the goal of the action described by the verb of the clause (typically, a movement verb). Consequently, one would predict that, from the moment the μέλλω AVC became almost indispensable for a particular context in the overall domain of FCs, it started gaining ground and competing with the Future in other contexts as well.

The fact that participial μέλλω could have both verbal and nominal / adjectival uses comes as no surprise, considering the peculiar nature of the category of Participle, which is cross-linguistically associated both with nominal and verbal constructions (cf., for example, Haspelmath, 1995). In the case of μέλλω, the "non-verbal" participial use seems to have its origin in an elliptical construction involving the verbal one, as exemplified in (3a–b):

(3a) εἰ   μὲν   γὰρ ἦν   σοὶ   πρόδηλα   τὰ   μέλλοντ᾽,
      If   though   prt were to-you   obvious   the-PL will-PCPLE.PL
      "If the future were obvious to you..."

(De corona, 196.4)

(3b) εἰ γὰρ ἦν   ἅπασι   πρόδηλα   τὰ   μέλλοντα   γενήσεσθαι
      If prt were to-everyone obvious   the-PL will-PCPLE.PL be-INF.FUT.
      "If what will come to pass were obvious to everybody..."

(De corona, 199.4)

The similarity between (3a) and (3b) is quite striking, the only difference being the inclusion of a FUT.INF. as a complement of μέλλοντα in (3b), which apparently is redundant, as the meaning is the same as (3a). It seems reasonable to conclude that variation of the kind exemplified gave rise to the proliferation of the nominalized use of participial μέλλω, already attested in Aeschylus and all the authors of the 5th c. BC.[8]

The development of the nominalized participle of μέλλω may be neatly accounted for by examples such as (3), but, on the other hand, raises serious doubt with regard to the grammatical status of μέλλω AVC. First of all, the very abundance of participial occurrences argues against an auxiliary status for μέλλω, since such elements usually tend to lose large parts of their conjugation paradigm, at least when used as auxiliaries (cf., for example,

---

[8] The only exception being Herodotus, who uses only once an adjectival participle of μέλλω, but, on the other hand, frequently utilizes the verbal participle (39 instances in total). Perhaps this is an archaizing element of his language (recall that Homer contains no participle of μέλλω) or reflects an Ionic dialectal peculiarity. The matter needs further investigation.

Heine, 1993: 23). Accordingly, neither ἔχω nor (ἐ)θέλω in their future-referring meaning ever occur in a participial form (cf. 2.2–2.3 and 3.2–3.3). Instead, μέλλω apparently developed its participial forms while already having a future-referring meaning! This contrast is most important, as properties of a construction should be judged in relation to similar constructions of the same language, since there are no cross-linguistic regularities that cannot be refuted in any particular language concerning AVCs (cf. 1.1.3). Furthermore, the fact that the participle by itself could have future reference, without any infinitival complement, argues strongly in favor of the idea that the future-reference of the AVC was due to the lexical meaning of μέλλω itself, which could be retained—as expected—even in the absence of a complement.

Elliptical constructions such as in (3a), which gave rise to the adjectival / nominal participial use of μέλλω, also occur in contexts where the "missing" Infinitive is not the verb "to be", which can quite easily and widely be dropped. In the following example, the 'missing' Infinitive must be inferred from the linguistic context:

(4) καὶ ἐπειδὴ καλῶς αὐτοῖς   εἶχεν, ὑπερεφάνησαν τοῦ λόφου καὶ ἔθεντο τὰ
and when good   to-them had, appeared-over the hill   and placed the
ὅπλα τεταγμένοι ὥσπερ ἔμελλον
arms arranged   as   intended-PRET.3rd PL.
"and when everything was arranged to their satisfaction, they appeared over the hill, and halted in the order which they had determined on"

(*Thuc.*, 4.93.3)

In (4), the complement of ἔμελλον should probably be inferred from the participle τεταγμένοι. Importantly, this elliptical construction, attested not only in Thuc. (e.g. 4.69.1, 7.20.2) but in other writers as well (e.g. *Lysias Fragm.* 335.5), corroborates the assumption of an inherent, intentional / future-referring meaning for μέλλω. Ellipsis can be attested after modal verbs in other languages (e.g. in German: "Ich muss zum Arzt"="I have to go to the doctor"), but AG (similarly to Hellenistic–Roman and Medieval Greek) seems not to have allowed such constructions unless the verb involved had a clear lexical meaning, hence the absence of any similar attestations with the other future-referring AVCs involving ἔχω and (ἐ)θέλω.[9]

---

[9] However, there exist two similar attestations of the future-referring (ἐ)θέλω AVC (*Parm.*, 146d8, 149a2). They are found in dialogue, and more specifically, in very short answers ("Οὐκ ἐθελήσει") to immediately preceding questions containing a full AVC, where ellipsis is highly facilitated. Therefore, they differ from the narrative of Thucydides, for instance, who uses μέλλω in elliptical constructions with more indirect clues regarding the 'missing' complement.

Another piece of evidence of a syntactic nature arguing for an initial grammaticalization stage for the μέλλω AVC relates to the relevant order of μέλλω and its infinitival complement, as well as their linear adjacency. It has been suggested (Lehmann, 1995), and is generally accepted, that the "syntagmatic bondedness" of two linguistic elements increases as the auxiliary becomes more and more of a grammatical element. This is related to the rise in frequency of use that more grammatical constructions exhibit: more frequent juxtapositions become closely associated as a unit both in production and in processing, hence the linear adjacency. As always, this grammaticalization criterion should be considered in association with word-order requirements of the various languages, since there is clearly an interaction between the position of the auxiliary and its complement with respect to each other and with the overall clause structure; for example, in German, due to the well-known V2 constraint, the auxiliary occupies the second position in the clause, while its complement is in the final position. In the case of μέλλω, what can be observed is that strict adjacency of its infinitival complement does not seem to have been a requirement or at least a pattern predominantly followed, as shown in Table 2.3 below.

The data is illuminating in many respects. First of all, it is clearly indicative of the relatively low degree of syntactic cohesion between μέλλω and its complement, since the token frequency of the V + INF/INF + V (i.e. adjacent) pattern is only slightly higher than that of the non-adjacent (V + ... + INF/ INF + ... + V) one (55%–45%, respectively); what is more, in the case of the non-adjacent pattern, the actual linear distance of the two elements can vary, as the intervening unit could be a particle, a phrase of any kind or a whole sentence (ex. 5)!

(5) κατὰ νώτου τε αἰεὶ ἔμελλον αὐτοῖς, ᾗ χωρήσειαν,
    prep back prt always will-3rd PL.PRET for-them, wherever would-advance,
    οἱ πολέμιοι ἔσεσθαι ψιλοὶ
    the enemies be-INF.FUT. light-armed
    "Wherever they went, they would always have the light-armed enemies behind them"

(*Thuc.*, 4.32.4)

According to my knowledge, there is no 'overriding' principle of any kind in the word-order requirements of Ancient Greek which could dictate the linear separation of μέλλω from the infinitival complement. Even so, the interaction with word-order characteristics is—at least—twofold. On the one hand, as can be seen in the table, there is an overwhelming tendency for V + INF order

TABLE 2.3 Linear order of μέλλω + Infinitive

Pattern	5th c.	5th–4th c.	4th c.	4th–3rd c.	Total
V + INF	164 (43.4)	346 (39.7)	260 (51.0)	40 (52.6)	810 (44.2)
INF + V	42 (11.1)	84 (9.6)	53 (10.4)	17 (22.4)	196 (10.7)
V + ... + INF	155 (41.0)	420 (48.2)	184 (36.1)	13 (17.1)	772 (42.1)
INF + ... + V	17 (4.5)	21 (2.4)	13 (2.5)	6 (7.9)	57 (3.1)
TOTAL	378	871	510	76	1835

(86.3%), which could be seen in the light of the overall change from OV to VO order, arguably completed between the Homeric and the classical period (Taylor, 1994). On the other hand, the frequent intervention of an argument of the Infinitive between the verb and its complement is presumably an instance of the well-known phenomenon of hyperbaton, a schema possibly triggered by stylistic and pragmatic factors (Devine & Stephens, 2000). However, even these considerations argue for a low degree of grammaticalization for the μέλλω AVC; the fact that, despite the dominance of V + INF order, the reverse order is still possible is, according to Heine (1993:87), an indication that the development has not reached its final stages; and the licensing of hyperbaton is characteristic, apart from μέλλω, for a verbal class assumed to have modal nuances of meaning but not to construct AVCs with their complements, e.g. οἶμαι (believe) (cf. Devine & Stephens, 2000: 138).

The fact that μέλλω behaves morphosyntactically as a common lexical verb is further strengthened if this data is compared with the equivalent data involving the lexical (volitional) (ἐ)θέλω, illustrated in Table 2.4.

Evidently, there is a close similarity in the distribution of the data in the two tables, clearly suggesting that μέλλω + Infinitive had a parallel morphosyntactic status to (ἐ)θέλω + Infinitive. Notice that in the case of (ἐ)θέλω, the token frequency of adjacency is even slightly higher than that involving μέλλω (57%–55%, respectively), although the difference is marginal.

There is further evidence, of a morphosyntactic nature, in favor of the intentional / future-referring meaning being inherent in μέλλω as a lexical element. Apparently, μέλλω could participate in compounding bearing this meaning: relevant examples are attested mainly in poetry (e.g. μελλόνυμφος "one who is about to marry", *Antigone* 633) but not exclusively (μελλόνυμφος in *Epigr.Gr.*, 364.3). This use, which remained productive in the Hellenistic–Roman period (cf. 3.1), and even beyond (cf. 5.1), is particular to μέλλω among the verbs forming FCs (i.e. ἔχω / (ἐ)θέλω) and constitutes a crucial argument in favor of the future-referring meaning of μέλλω.

TABLE 2.4 Linear order of volitional (ἐ)θέλω + Infinitive

Pattern	5th c.	5th–4th c.	4th c.	4th–3rd c.	Total
V + INF	178 (29.0)	337 (40.8)	165 (45.6)	14 (38.9)	694 (37.8)
INF + V	185 (30.2)	91 (11.0)	66 (18.2)	10 (27.8)	352 (19.2)
V + … + INF	170 (27.7)	306 (37.1)	104 (28.7)	4 (11.1)	584 (31.8)
INF + … + V	80 (13.1)	91 (11.0)	27 (7.5)	8 (22.2)	206 (11.2)
TOTAL	613	825	362	36	1836

Different types of evidence (morphological, semantic, and syntactic) converge on the conclusion that the μέλλω construction can be regarded as an AVC inclusively on the basis of its semantics, that is of the passing from intention to prediction in specific contexts. The fact that no morphosyntactic developments accompany this semantic extension indicates that the future reference of the μέλλω construction is still very much context-dependent, as no evidence for a tighter association, invariably common in AVCs, between μέλλω and its complement is to be found. In other words, of the four grammaticalization parameters proposed by Heine & Kuteva (cf. 1.1.1), only 'semantic extension' is evident in μέλλω, leading us to conclude that this AVC is basically still in its infancy from a grammaticalization perspective.

All these observations relate mostly to the grammaticalization status of the μέλλω AVC. However, one basic syntactic problem of this AVC that has attracted scholarly attention and needs to be addressed here concerns the type of the Infinitival complement. Μέλλω could take both a Present and a Future Infinitive (and in some cases, even the Aorist, cf. below).

Table 2.5 shows that the FUT. and the PRES. INF. were of the same token frequency, while the AOR. INF. constituted only a marginal choice. The FUT. INF. seems to have been more popular in the early writers, while the PRES. INF. apparently became increasingly popular from the 4th c. onwards. The figures are only telling as we approach the end of this period, but the tendency becomes clear in the Hellenistic–Roman times (cf. 3.1).

TABLE 2.5 Type of infinitival complement of μέλλω

Infinitive	5th c.	5th–4th c.	4th c.	4th–3rd c.	Total
PRES	145 (38.7)	378 (43.3)	277 (54.2)	63 (82.9)	863 (47.0)
FUT	196 (52.4)	471 (54.0)	222 (43.4)	12 (15.8)	901 (49.0)
AOR	33 (8.8)	24 (2.7)	12 (2.3)	1 (1.3)	70 (4.0)
TOTAL	374	873	511	76	1834

The variation in the complementation of μέλλω led many scholars to seek a specific semantic difference in the selection of the INF. Magnien (1912: 99–106) argued that if μέλλω was followed by a PRES. or AOR.INF., then it meant logical necessity or imminence, while if followed by a FUT.INF., it would be desire- or goal-oriented. This is apparently a distinction too neat to hold, as demonstrated by (6):

(6) ἠριθμοῦντο δὲ πολλοὶ ἅμα τὰς ἐπιβολάς, καὶ ἔμελλον   οἱ μέν
    counted   prt many together the lines, and will-3rd PL.PRET. the prt
    τινες ἁμαρτήσεσθαι   οἱ δὲ πλείους τεύξεσθαι   τοῦ ἀληθοῦς
    some be wrong-FUT.INF. the prt more   achieve-FUT.INF. the correct
    λογισμοῦ,
    calculation.
    "Many counted simultaneously the stone lines, and it was natural that some would make a mistake on the calculation, but most of them would get the right number"

(Thuc., 3.20.3)

Contrary to Magnien's claim, the use of the FUT.INF. in (6) almost undoubtedly entails high probability (logical necessity in his terms), as the meaning of the complement of the verb lies beyond the power of the subject to 'control'. It seems more likely that his semantic differentiation is heavily influenced by his overall argument that Future in AG has a strong volitional meaning, and therefore the use of the FUT.INF. should also have a similar semantic nuance, which is not the case, as shown.

Furthermore, the task of determining a specific meaning on the basis of the accompanying Infinitive becomes even more difficult, when one considers cases as the following:

(7) ἆρ' οὖ πᾶν   τὸ   μέλλον   ἅψεσθαί   τινος   ἐφεξῆς
    prt not everything the will-PCIPLE.PRES. touch-FUT.INF. something adv
    δεῖ κεῖσθαι   ἐκείνῳ   οὗ   μέλλει   ἅπτεσθαι;
    must lie- INF. to-that which-GEN. will-3rd SING.PRES. touch-PRES.INF.
    "Must not everything which is to touch anything be next to that which it is to touch?"

(Parm., 148e5–6)

In this example, which is by no means the only one of its kind,[10] the infinitival complement of μέλλω is different in two consecutive instances of the construction (Future and Present, respectively) in the very same context,

[10] Cf. also, for example, Respublica 347a4 / 347c1, Olynth III, 36.8.

without any apparent reason for this varied choice, since there is nothing to suggest that the two instances of the μέλλω construction should have a different interpretation.

Examples such as (7) also undermine an alleged aspectual choice in the selection of the Infinitival complement, argued repeatedly in the past (e.g. Jannaris, 1897: 443–4). According to this view, the Present Infinitive has an imperfective value, while both Future and Aorist Infinitives have a perfective value, mainly because of the sound -σ- /s/ incorporated in the verbal stem in these tenses and considered to be a perfective marker (cf. Table 2.1). However, there are both conceptual and empirical problems with that particular claim. Firstly, the aspectual character of the FUT.INF. is taken for granted, apparently ignoring the fact that the FUT. could convey both perfective and imperfective readings, being aspectually neutral in AG (Goodwin, 1875: 19); therefore, it is not evident why the FUT.INF. should be of a particular aspectual value. Moreover, the AOR.INF. as complement of μέλλω is hardly attested in the AG texts, during which the main opposition—if any—was undoubtedly between the Present and the Future Infinitive. Bearing in mind the aspectual underspecification of the Future Infinitive, and the relative rarity of the Aorist, there seems to be no clear path by which the alleged aspectual differentiation in the complementation of μέλλω could have arisen.

A survey of all instances of the μέλλω AVC in two prose writers of the 5th–4th c. BC, namely Thucydides and Lysias, confirms these assumptions. Obviously, the aspectual interpretation of each occurrence of the AVC is not an easy task, but, in the closest possible approximation, the picture emerging of this survey is illustrated in Table 2.6 and Figure 2.1.[11]

Contrary to what would be traditionally expected, the vast majority of the Present Infinitive occurrences apparently convey a perfective reading (33 / 36–91.6%, cf. Figure and ex. 8), while the domain of imperfective is clearly dominated (26 / 29–89.7%) by the Future Infinitive (ex. 9 and *Thuc.*, 2.24.1, *Areop.*, 16.3, *In Alcib. I*, 5.1):

TABLE 2.6 Aspectual readings of μέλλω AVC

	Perfective			Imperfective		
Author	FUT.INF	PRES.INF	AOR.INF	FUT.INF	PRES.INF	AOR.INF
Thuc.	72	25	8	11	3	–
Lys.	25	8	1	15	–	–
Total	97(69.8%)	33(23.7%)	9 (6.5%)	26(89.7%)	3(10.3%)	–

[11] Ambiguous examples that could have as easily both aspectual readings (six in Thucydides, four in Lysias) have been excluded from the table.

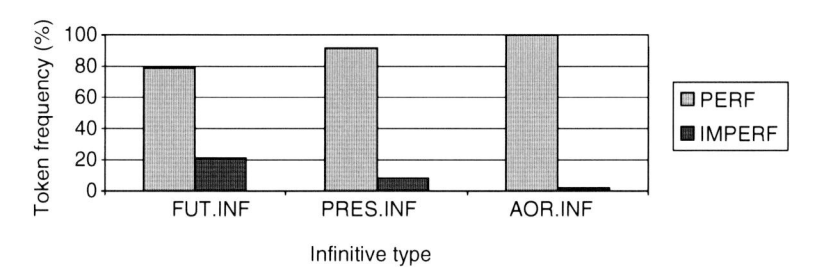

FIGURE 2.1 Aspect and Infinitive in the μέλλω AVC

(8) καὶ   μελλόντων   αὐτῶν,   ἐπειδὴ ἑτοῖμα ἦν,   ἀποπλεῖν
and will-PCIPLE.PRES.GEN.PL. they-GEN.PL.,since ready were,sail-PRES.INF.
ἡ   σελήνη ἐκλείπει
the moon   disappears
"and when they were about to sail, as they were ready, the moon disappeared"

(Thuc., 7.50.4)

(9) αὐτὰ τὰ προσγενόμενα ἐκεῖθεν χωρία   ἔμελλε   διαρκῆ
these the added   from-there villages will-3RD SING. PRET.
continuous
ἄνευ   τῆς ἐνθένδε προσόδου παρέξειν.
without   the local   income   provide-FUT.INF.
"These villages that were conquered from that area would continuously provide (us) [with the necessary income] without the need of the local income"

(Thuc., 6.90.4)

As a result, the notion of aspect being the basis for the choice of the infinitival complement is very difficult to maintain.

Perhaps then, instead of Aspect, we should look at Tense. To be more precise, the Future Infinitive is exclusively used as a complement of verbs with inherent future-referring meaning, for instance μέλλω and ἐλπίζω "hope", or to convey posteriority in reported speech (Goodwin, 1875: 45–6). In the former case, which is of more interest to us, it basically renders explicit the future reference contained and demanded by the verb. On the other hand, the Present Infinitive is probably, as we have observed, neutralized with respect to aspect, and presumably could also refer to the future, following the indicative of the Present. These two facts are not randomly but causally associated. Even though it is generally assumed that, except for specific cases, the Present Tense in most languages has only an imperfective reading, one of the very well-known cases whereby this generalization does not hold is the future-referring use of the Present, widely attested cross-linguistically (Comrie, 1985), and, more crucially, attested also in the Classical and all subsequent periods of Greek (cf., for example, Jannaris, 1897: 553). Therefore, it is only to be expected that, when used as a complement of μέλλω, the Present Infinitive was aspectually neutralized, i.e. it did not have a specific aspectual value, and could also convey a future-referring meaning. It could be argued, consequently, that the infinitival complement of μέλλω should in principle be "compatible" with the inherent future reference of the verb itself.

Recently, De Melo (2007) discussed a similar situation in Latin, whereby the Present Infinitive could convey future reference in contexts where the Future Infinitive was more readily expected. According to his arguments, the main factor controlling the choice of the Infinitive is the telicity of the construction: the Future Infinitive is used both in telic and atelic events, while the Present Infinitive is restricted to telic events, with very few exceptions, possibly accounted for as instances of a change in progress. A similar situation seems to have obtained in the case of the μέλλω AVC: a survey on the basis of the two authors examined in the case of aspect (i.e. Thucydides and Lysias) revealed that, indeed, the Future Infinitive could be used in both telic and atelic situations (97 vs. 31 cases, respectively), while the Present Infinitive is effectively restricted to telic cases (40 vs. 5 cases, respectively). Suggestive as this data may seem, there remains to be ascertained whether similar findings can be reported for other verbs as well, and how all the infinitival complementation system ties together. Clearly, more research is needed before we reach any firm conclusions regarding this matter.

A relative issue remains to be addressed, namely where the Aorist Infinitive fits in this context. According to the figures in Table 2.5, the token frequency of this infinitival form is the lowest among the different options of the AVC. The reason for this limited use of the Aorist Infinitive is elusive. Interestingly, a great percentage of the cases attested (55 / 70, approximately 80%), involve the Strong Aorist[12] Infinitive. Even though the verbs exhibiting Strong Aorists are quite frequently used (e.g. ἦλθον "I came"), still their limited number does not readily justify such a high percentage. One possible explanation might be to assume that this is related to intonational and metrical factors, as 25 instances of the Strong Aorist Infinitive are found in poets (22 in Euripides alone). James Diggle (personal communication) suggests that, firstly, Strong Aorist Infinitives are metrically convenient (usually x–), and, secondly, metre can often guarantee a Strong Aorist instead of a Future

---

[12] The Aorist of some AG verbs was formed in a different, peculiar way, with different endings, called "Strong Aorist".

Infinitive, as the latter is usually a syllable longer (e.g. λαβεῖν vs. λήψεσθαι), but this does not usually happen when a weak Aorist is involved (e.g. χωρῆσαι vs. χωρήσειν); as a result, copyists would be likely to change a weak Aorist Infinitive into a Future of a similar metrical shape. These observations might partially explain the proliferation of the Strong Aorist Infinitive in drama (especially compared to the weak Aorist Infinitive), but one would also have to assume an analogical extension of this use in prose or a rather elaborated intonational structure for non-poetical texts. Independently of its exact origin, the use of the Aorist Infinitive in this particular context instantiates an increasingly popular tendency to utilize the Aorist or the Present Infinitive in contexts where the Future Infinitive would normally surface; this tendency, which does not affect only μέλλω, acquired great impetus presumably in the later stages of the classical period and in the subsequent period, as we shall see (cf. 3.1). The fact that such use represents a tendency allows us also to assume safely that the instances of the Aorist Infinitive as complement of μέλλω are not due to scribal errors: in fact, according to the critical editions consulted, in only 18 of the 70 cases are there varied readings in the manuscripts (e.g. *Thuc.*, 1.114.1: ἐσβαλεῖν E / ἐσβάλλειν CG, 4.116.2: προσβαλεῖν E / προσβάλλειν CG). Therefore, the issue of the authenticity of this pattern of the AVC even in AG does not really arise (on the comment of the Alexandrian grammarian Phrynichus concerning μέλλω and its complements, cf. 3.1).

To recapitulate, in this section it has been argued that the μέλλω AVC lies in the initial stages of grammaticalization, not manifesting any morphosyntactic properties usually associated with AVCs. Μέλλω itself should be seen as a modal verb with an "intention" meaning which, in the appropriate context (i.e. 3rd person inanimate subject) acquires a predictive sense through an implicature. The issue of the complementation of μέλλω in this AVC has also been addressed, and it has been shown that the choice of the Infinitive in AG was not determined on aspectual grounds, as traditionally assumed, but probably on a combination of factors, including the telicity of the event described. Finally, the use of the Aorist Infinitive in this AVC could perhaps be attributed to metrical reasons, at least for the drama cases, and it represents the beginning of a systematic pattern, as we shall see further below.

2.2 Ἔχω / Εἶχον + Infinitive: possession and ability

It is well known that ἔχω ("have") in AG could be followed by an Infinitive to form an AVC with the meaning "having the ability / the means to", as illustrated in (10):

(10) ὧν   ἐγὼ οὔτε γένος ἔχω   εἰπεῖν   οὔτε ὁπόθεν ἐσῆλθον
which-GEN I nor race have-1st PRES. tell-AOR.INF. nor whence entered
"...whose race I am not able to say or whence they came..."

(*Thuc.*, 6.2.1)

This construction is not an innovation of AG, as five examples of the εἶχον + Infinitive AVC can be found as early as Homer (*Il.* 7, 217—cf. ex. 13 / 20,242 / 21, 474 / *Od.* 11, 584 / 12, 433–4). It is rather safe to assume, therefore, that the development which led to the emergence of this construction must be dated before the 8th c. BC.

Even though the presence and the meaning of this construction are well documented in all grammars of AG, there has been no attempt to account for its emergence in the first place. How did "ἔχω + Infinitive" come to mean "I have the means / the ability to do something"? It is proposed here that this AVC constitutes an instantiation of the cognitive schema proposed by Heine (1993, 1997) for Possession – Purpose, which also accounts for similar developments observed in Latin (e.g. *dicere habeo*) and in English (e.g. *I have to go to the doctor*). According to this schema, the lexical verb of possession is first associated with an object (stage I); subsequently, the whole Verb Phrase (Verb + Object) is followed by a goal-denoting Infinitive (stage II) and after the original meaning of possession is lost (stage III), ἔχω is exclusively linked with the Infinitive (stage IV). The stages of this development are schematically represented in (11) (Heine 1993: 42):

(11) Stage I: ἔχω τι (possessive)="I have something"
 Stage II: ἔχω τι εἰπεῖν (goal-denoting Infinitive)="I have something to say"
 Stage III:[13] ἔχω τι εἰπεῖν (the possessive meaning is neutralized—"bleached")
  = "I have something to say"
 Stage IV: ἔχω εἰπεῖν τι (ἔχω now has a different meaning)

As is always the case in grammaticalization processes, constructions belonging to different developmental stages can co-exist for long periods of time. AG seems to conform to this tendency and to this schema in general, with one important exception: while Heine (1993) claims that at stage IV ἔχω should

---

[13] Even though stage III might seem necessary from a theoretical point of view, in order to illustrate the semantic transition from the lexical to the grammatical meaning, it is extremely difficult to find a suitably corresponding example which could not be associated with stage II. This is expected, as the difference between stage II and III is the reanalysis of "τι" becoming associated with the Infinitive instead of the verb, and reanalysis by definition causes no alteration in the actual utterances.

have an obligation meaning, it instead has a different modal meaning, namely that of "ability", defined here as "having the (mental or material) resources to do something"; in other words, the enabling conditions stem from the agent (cf. Bybee, Perkins, & Pagliuca, 1994: 177–8). Thus, the Possession / Purpose schema sketched in (11) predicts to a great extent accurately all morphosyntactic stages of the particular development, but fails to allow the possibility of variation in the final semantic outcome in the transition from stage III to stage IV. But the ability meaning is easily derivable for this AVC: "I have something with the intention / goal of saying it" naturally implies "I can say something", since the possession (mental or physical) of an object allows you to make use of it. Therefore, an elaboration of Heine's schema is proposed: the transition from stage III to stage IV should have multiple branching in order to capture different, albeit closely connected, semantic developments (cf. also below, 3.2). The tight association between various modal values involved in this construction can even be illustrated in an AG example:

(12) Λακεδαιμόνιοι περὶ τοὺς καιροὺς τούτους πολλῶν ἀγαθῶν αἴτιοι τοῖς
Spartans   prep the times   those   many goods responsible to-the
Ἕλλησιν κατέστησαν· ἀλλὰ διὰ τοῦτο καὶ μᾶλλον   ἐπαινεῖν
Greeks became;   but for this and more   praise-PRES.INF.
ἔχω   τὴν πόλιν...
have-1st SING.PERS. the city
"The Spartans at that time had done many good deeds for the Greeks; but because of this I am able to / I may / I should praise our city more..."

(*Panegyricus*, 73.1–4)

In this example, it is almost equally possible to argue for three different modal meanings: the ability meaning of the AVC can be interpreted in this context as permission or obligation. Nevertheless, the case presented in (12) is the only one of such ambiguity in the whole corpus. However, the AVC gave rise to various modal meanings, manifested in subsequent periods (cf. discussion in 3.2).

AG contains numerous attestations of stages II / III and IV, illustrating the continuous development of this construction: there are 159 attestations of stage IV type and 92 attestations of stage II / III type in the corpus. These numbers do not include the instances involving the verb λέγω (=say) (306 in total), as in most of these cases it is quite difficult to tell whether the object of the verb construction is associated with ἔχω or with the following Infinitive (as in ex. 10). The high token frequency of the ἔχω AVC with verbs of saying might simply reflect an accident brought about by the *genre* of the texts handed down to us, but, interestingly enough, an identical phenomenon can be observed for the earliest attestations of this construction in Latin (Pinkster, 1987). The relationship between the Greek and the Latin equivalent construction will be discussed further below (cf. 3.2).

From the numbers given above it could be implied that the stage IV AVC constitutes an innovation of AG and is gradually taking over from the older stages, whose instances are fewer in number. Convenient as this might be, it is nevertheless an illusion: an examination of the Homeric epic poems reveals that all five instances found in these texts belong to stage IV, as can be seen in the example (13):

(13) ἀλλ' οὔ πως ἔτι εἶχεν   ὑποτρέσαι   οὐδ' ἀναδῦναι
    but not adv adv have-3rd SING.PRET. flee-INF.AOR. nor shrink-INF.AOR.
    "but he could not anymore flee or shrink [into the crowd] ..."

(*Il.* 7, 217)

In this example εἶχεν is complemented only by an intransitive Infinitive, since there is no concrete object that could be linked to the verb, and therefore (13) represents a prototypical instance of stage IV. Consequently, as already mentioned, AG constitutes another typical example of the well-known phenomenon of "layering", i.e. the situation whereby a certain AVC can be simultaneously utilized in more than one form corresponding to different stages of its development (cf., for example, Hopper & Traugott, 2003: 49). As the stage IV construction is already present in Homer, no innovative use can be argued to have originated in AG.[14]

In the numbers given so far the relevant attestations of the past equivalent of the AVC, i.e. εἶχον + Infinitive, have not been included, since they are significantly fewer in number (97 in total comparing to 557 for ἔχω) and they do not diverge in any way from the pattern already observed for the non-past counterpart. There is, though, one quite interesting example involving εἶχον:

(14) ἀλλ' ἢ   σάφ' ἤνει τόνδ' ἀποπτύσαι   πλόκον,
    but prt clear said this   disregard-INF.   tress
    εἴπερ γ' ἀπ' ἐχθροῦ κρατὸς ἦν   τετμημένος,
    if   prt from enemy   head   were cut-PCIPLE
    ἢ   ξυγγενὴς ὢν   εἶχε   συμπενθεῖν   ἐμοί
    or kinsman is-PCPLE have-3rd SING.PRET. mourn-with-INF.PRES. with-me

---

[14] Perhaps one could assume that stage II / III instances in AG are an innovation compared to the situation in Homer. In that case, the AG instances might simply constitute a repetition of the process that led to the examples found in Homer. It is difficult to imagine a plausible syntactic context that would favor a reanalysis in the opposite direction, i.e. from stage IV to stage II / III.

"but [I wish] it clearly said to disregard this tress / if it were cut from the head of an enemy / or if it were a kinsman's that it could / would mourn with me..."

(*Choephoroe*, 197–9)

In this passage from Aeschylus, the AVC εἶχε συμπενθεῖν is the apodosis of the conditional participle ὤν. The ability / potential reading for the AVC in this context is still possible, while that of an irrealis, counterfactual apodosis is equally plausible (in the sense of "would mourn"), even though the distinction in the scope of a conditional is too subtle to tell with certainty. In any case, this example illustrates the close connection of the "ability-in-the-past" AVC with irrealis modal interpretations (especially if the AVC lies in the scope of a conditional), an observation that will become vital for the explanation of subsequent developments, as we shall see in following sections.

A note regarding the complementation of ἔχω should also be made: in some cases, ἔχω is followed by a clause in the Subjunctive introduced by an interrogative / relative pronoun or an adverb, as exemplified in (15):

(15) ἐπειδὴ οὐκ   ἔχει   ὅ τι   εἴπῃ...
    because not have-3rd SING.PRES.   what-rel   say-3rd SING.SUBJ.
    "because he has nothing to say..."

(*De Halonneso*, 36.2)

The appearance of this construction is conditioned by the presence of a negative element, such as the clausal negation οὐκ in (15), not only in AG but throughout the history of Greek and effectively till the equivalent contemporary construction in Modern Greek ("δεν ἔχω τι να πω" "I cannot say anything / I do not know what to say"). This negative polarity construction instantiates an abstract possession meaning (according to Heine's, 1997: 33–41 categorization of possessive notions, i.e. a possession whereby "the possessee is a concept that is not visible or tangible"), as the object of possession is the abstract complement clause of ἔχω. This meaning, which has little to reveal regarding the development from ability to futurity for this AVC, will not be further examined.

As to the choice of the Infinitival complement of ἔχω, since this AVC did not belong yet to the domain of future reference, the choice of the Infinitive is part of the otherwise established system of infinitival complementation, which cannot be discussed here. Suffice it to say that the ability ἔχω was followed either by a Present or an Aorist Infinitive, although the latter was more productive in this context.

On the whole, the ἔχω AVC in AG is grammaticalized as a construction expressing ability, without any obvious traces of the later prediction meaning (cf. 3.2). The only context where ability becomes noticeably more tightly associated with futurity is the past conditionals (ex. 14), where both ability ("could") and futurity ("would") are plausible interpretations of the AVC.

2.3 (Ἐ)θέλω + Infinitive: future-referring alternative?

The verb (ἐ)θέλω "want" is very frequently attested in classical texts. In Plato alone (ἐ)θέλω is found 407 times. It is almost without exception complemented by an Infinitive, whether the subject of the Infinitive is the same as that of the main verb or not. The fact that the following Infinitive is usually the Present or the Aorist, and rarely the Future (cf. LSJ), differentiates (ἐ)θέλω rather radically from μέλλω, which, as noted, was usually followed by a Future or a Present Infinitive (cf. 2.1). Apparently, even though both verbs had an inherent future-referring meaning, the choice of the infinitival complement might not have been solely dependent on the semantics of the verb, as already argued for μέλλω.

There are five instances of a different pattern of complementation for volitional (ἐ)θέλω, which needs particular attention, as it can arguably still be traced in Late Medieval Greek (cf. ch. 5), and has been a puzzle for many scholars. In this pattern, in the case of disjunctive reference, i.e. when the subject of the Infinitive is different from that of the verb, the complement of (ἐ)θέλω is not an Infinitive but a finite Subjunctive, as in (16):

(16) θέλεις   μείνωμεν   αὐτοῦ
     want-2ndSING.PRES. stay-1st PL.PRES.SUBJ. there
     κἀνακούσωμεν   γόων;
     and listen-1st PL.PRES.SUBJ. sobs
     "do you want us to stay there and listen to sobs?"

(*Electra*, 80–1)

The "Verb + Verb$_{Subj.}$"(V + V$_S$) pattern, as far as (ἐ)θέλω is concerned, is solely attested in tragedy.[15] Goodwin (1875: 98–9) cites further examples of this construction for the near synonym βούλομαι "want", but also one example for κελεύω "urge" (*Philip.* 3, 46.5). A thorough investigation of the corpus has revealed that there are two more attestations involving κελεύω (*Helena*, 1590 and *Phaedrus*, 235d5), both occurring in questions, as all other examples of this construction. Obviously, this pattern is not peculiar to (ἐ)θέλω and verbs of similar meaning, but has spread to other verb types, such as jussive (e.g. κελεύω). We cannot exclude the possibility that even more verbs were involved in this syntactic pattern, probably in colloquial speech,

---

[15] *O.T.* 651, *Bacchae* 719, and *Frag Eur.* 1036, 1.

since all instances of the "V + V$_S$" construction in Attic appear in dialogue. This observation should be considered as indirect evidence in favor of the assumption that the pattern was mainly a feature of the spoken language.

With regard to its origin, Goodwin (1875) remarks that the pattern is reminiscent of the Interrogative Subjunctive (e.g. Τί πράξωμεν; "What should we do?") and that the main verb must have been originally felt as a distinct clause, followed by an Interrogative Subjunctive (e.g. Θέλεις; Μείνωμεν; = Do you want...? We stay?). He admits, though, that, by the time of the AG authors, some kind of subordinate relation between the two verbal forms must have existed. The fact that there is a specific syntactic licensing of the pattern, i.e. disjunctive reference, arguably renders the existence of a subordination relation very plausible.

The origin of the "V + V$_S$" construction is not readily accessible, more so because Homer provides no relevant examples.[16] It is important to note here that Early Latin makes extensive use of such a pattern with a wide variety of (semantic) verbal categories, including even impersonal forms, such as *oportet* ("must"), *decet* ("it is fitting") etc. (Bennett, 1910: 208–45). The Latin data strongly suggest that, at least by the time of the written evidence, the "V + V$_S$" construction is clearly a pattern of complementation / subordination. Bennett (1910), aware of the Greek parallel, rejects the possibility of borrowing from Greek into Latin. Indeed, even though syntactic borrowing *is* attested (e.g. Harris & Campbell, 1995: 149–50), the type and the extent of language contact it presupposes could not presumably hold between Greek-speaking and Latin-speaking populations that early (with the possible exception of specific areas, e.g. S. Italy). On the face of it, it is more feasible to assume that this pattern is an inherited Indo-European feature or simply an independent innovation; one would be inclined to go one step further and assume that this pattern might have predated the appearance of particular complementizers with the appropriate semantic features, and survived considerably later, mainly in the spoken language. The Subjunctive morphology of the linearly second verb would be then regarded as marking the subordination.[17] Promising as it may be, this assumption clearly needs further investigation in order to be verified or rejected.

---

[16] Curiously enough, in *Il.* 1,133 we find an example of ἐθέλω complemented by a subjunctive subordinate clause introduced by ὄφρα (an archaic equivalent of ἵνα, the goal complementizer). This is clearly a different case from the one discussed so far, as the Homeric example involves controlled and not disjunctive reference. The fact that no such example is found in AG (but it represents a subsequent chain in the development, cf. 3.3) renders this issue even more puzzling, although no general assumptions can be made on the basis of one example.

[17] Cf. Cristofaro (2003: 51–82) for SUBJ marking subordination in a typological perspective; according to her framework, this is a type of "deranking", a situation whereby different types of TAM distinctions apply to main and dependent clauses, with various possible combinations.

More importantly, the (ἐ)θέλω + Infinitive construction was also used as an AVC to express future-reference as well as generic truths.[18] This fact, even though already known (cf. LSJ: 1996 in (ἐ)θέλω) has not been given much attention (for a recent exception, cf. Chila-Markopoulou, 2000). These two meanings are exemplified in (17) and (18), respectively:

(17) εἴπερ—ὃ   μὴ γένοιτο—
     if—which not happen–3rd SING.OPT.AOR.–
     νῦν   ἐθέλει   κρατῆσαι.
     now   want-3rd SING.PRES.   win-INF.AOR.
     "if—God forbid— / he is going to win now"

(Vespae, 536–7)

(18) Θέλει   γὰρ   εἶναι
     Want-3rd SING.PRES.   prt   be-INF.PRES.
     διμερὴς ὁ πλεύμων   ἐν   ἅπασι
     two-sided the lung   in   everybody
     τοῖς   ἔχουσιν   αὐτόν.
     the have-PCIPLE.PRES.   it.
     "for the lung has two parts in all those [animals] which have it"

(Hist. Anim., 495a32)

Even though these meanings of the construction (ἐ)θέλω + Infinitive are obviously much less widely attested than its lexical one, they are nevertheless sufficiently common to enable us to claim with relative certainty that these attestations represent a "real" situation in AG. Table 2.7 provides the relative figures according to the *genre* of the various texts.

With the exception of the orators, the non-volitional meanings of the construction are attested in all other *genres*, and especially in philosophical texts, an observation that should probably be attributed to their particular character. Evidently, the volitional meaning is by far the dominant one of the three. This has a twofold explanation: on the one hand, the TAM meanings of (ἐ)θέλω + Infinitive must have been a relatively recent development with the volitional meaning as their source (no such meanings are attested in the Homeric epics); and on the other hand, both future reference and genericness could be conveyed by various other constructions in AG: future-reference

---

[18] This meaning should not be confused with habitual aspect, as it is not about the repetition of an action in a specific time interval but conveys instead the timeless character of generic truth, usually expressed through Present Tense (e.g. English: Dogs have four legs). For a brief account of the uses of Present Tense and their association with Future Tense, cf. Binnick, 1991: 247–52.

TABLE 2.7 (’E)θέλω + Infinitive in AG

(’E)θέλω + Inf.*	Volitional	Future-referring	Generic[19]
Orators	464	–	–
Dramatists	413	2	–
Historians	471	1	4
Philosophers	488	7	17
Total	1,836	10	21

* The figures given include all attestations of the construction in all morphological forms of the verb.

was mainly conveyed by the Future Tense and the μέλλω AVC, while generic statements were most commonly made in the Present Tense and also in the so-called "Gnomic Aorist" (Goodwin, 1875: 53–4). The strong competition from already established morphosyntactic constructions is at least partially responsible for the scarce attestations of these two meanings of (ἐ)θέλω + Infinitive. On the other hand, this competition does not prevent new constructions from emerging, in other words the emergence of new AVCs is not strictly conditioned on functional grounds.

But how did these meanings emerge in the first place? With regard to future reference, it could be safely argued that it constitutes an instantiation of the well-known and widely documented development "volition → intention → futurity". Volitional verbs are one of the most frequent sources for the emergence of future-referring constructions, not only in various Indo-European languages (e.g. Old English "willan = to want" → Modern English "will = future"), but in other unrelated language families (e.g. in Nimboran and Swahili, both African languages, and in Tok Pisin, a Melanesian English pidgin language, among many others: cf. Bybee, Perkins, & Pagliuca, 1991, 1994: 254). As volition is inherently associated with intention and intention with futurity, the step from the one meaning to the other is necessarily a small one. It has been repeatedly argued (cf. Fleischman, 1982, among others) that the most crucial stage for this development is reached when the condition requiring a human (or at least animate) agent of the volitional verb is weakened, in other words, when the verb takes an inanimate subject. In this case, the desire component of the meaning of the verb is suppressed, whereas the future reference is the dominant meaning, since inanimate subjects have no desire by necessity.[20] AG offers further evidence to support this observation and to

---

[19] This category includes both "omnitemporal" and "timeless" meanings, in the sense of Lyons (1977: 680).
[20] The condition on the animacy of the subject is first weakened to include metaphorical uses of inanimate subjects used as animate ("personification"), either from the world of nature (e.g. rivers etc.) or from the spiritual world (e.g. love, revenge, etc.). For a possible example of the former, cf. *Herodotus*, 2.99.14.

strengthen the claim with regard to the importance of this intermediate stage of development. Consider the following example:

(19) ἴδω   τί   λέξαι   δέλτος ἥδε μοι θέλει.
see-1st SING.AOR.SUBJ. what say-INF.AOR.   letter this to-me want-3rd PRES.
"let me see what this letter wishes to tell me (?) / will tell me"

(*Hippolytus*, 865)

As can be seen, the verb θέλει has as its subject the inanimate δέλτος and, consequently, the meaning of the construction θέλει λέξαι becomes blurred, since the desire / intention meaning can only be maintained if δέλτος stands for the sender of the letter through a metaphorical extension. Even so, (19) illustrates how close the relevant notions (volition, intention, and futurity) can be, and provides a good example of a stage of ambiguity and fluctuation between them. This is not the case for (17), where the future-referring meaning is quite clear, as the conditional protasis is accompanied by a future-referring wish (ὃ μὴ γένοιτο). Therefore, AG provides us also with unambiguous evidence in favor of an (ἐ)θέλω FC.[21]

On the basis of the existing evidence, it is quite difficult to try and find the actual frequency of use and contextual distribution of this future-referring form. Obviously, compared to μέλλω (cf. 2.1), the (ἐ)θέλω AVC has a much lower token frequency, leading us to assume fairly easily that, at least in the written language, the μέλλω AVC was more productive than the (ἐ)θέλω one. This said, the fact that almost all occurrences of the (ἐ)θέλω AVC are attested in drama (one in tragedy and one in comedy) and in Plato (seven attestations), i.e. in dialogues, seems to indicate that this AVC may have been used mainly in the oral language, and only rarely did it find its way into written texts, in specific contexts demanding features of colloquial speech. Given that our knowledge of the non-written varieties of AG is meagre at best, we can only hypothesize that this construction might have been more frequent in the everyday language.

Regarding the type of Infinitive used in this AVC, it follows the pattern observed concerning the volitional uses of (ἐ)θέλω: in 70% of the cases (7/10), it is the Present Infinitive that appears, and in the remaining 30% the Aorist. Obviously, the fact that this FC is derived from the volitional verb is also reflected in the same choice of the Infinitive in both meanings. This contrasts with future-referring μέλλω, which does not have a different prior lexical source and usually takes a Future Infinitive as a complement (cf. 2.1).

---

[21] Cf. also *Parm.* 146d8, where this AVC is used as an equivalent of the Future Tense ἔσται (= will be).

The existence of the generic meaning (ex. 18) of this AVC is also worth discussing.[22] The generic interpretation of FCs, manifested also for the morphological Future Tense (Goodwin, 1875: 19), is not a phenomenon particular to AG, as has been observed in other languages as well (cf., for example, English: "boys will be boys"). It is generally assumed that the ability of a construction to express generic meaning presupposes the emergence of future reference (Dahl, 1985, Bybee, 1988: 373). However, it has been argued (Ziegeler, 2006) that, in a similar development concerning Old and Middle English "willan" ("will"), this verb was first employed in generic predicates before being used for prediction. Ziegeler comes up with data to support her claims, and builds a possible semantic scenario to show how this development might come about. She argues firstly, that there are no clear examples of predictive "willan" before the occurrence of generic "willan", and, secondly, that there are no examples ambiguous between volition / intention and prediction, which could be seen as manifesting the common pathway assumed for similar verbs cross-linguistically; on this basis, she goes on to argue for an alternative semantic path of development. Nevertheless, the situation in AG is different: there *are* clear instances of future-referring (ἐ)θέλω occurring simultaneously with cases of genericness (cf. ex. 18 and fn. 20), while there *are* also examples exhibiting the passing from volition / intention to prediction (cf. ex. 19). Therefore, it is proposed here that AG (ἐ)θέλω followed the commonly assumed development, a possibility that Ziegeler (2006: 110) herself admits is possible for every language, in parallel with her "genericness → prediction" route.

If we then assume, *contra* Ziegeler, that the generic meaning is a development conditioned by the previous existence of a future-referring meaning, then we can make two interesting observations: firstly, that the (ἐ)θέλω FC may have been rather more productive than we are led to assume by the textual evidence, in order to generalize in various contexts and constitute the source of a subsequent development; and, secondly, the semantic development from volition to futurity must have taken place at a pre-classical period, as the earliest attestations not only of the future-referring but also of the generic meaning of the AVC date from the 5th century BC (*Electra* 330 and *Thuc.*, 2.89.11, respectively). Should we take the evidence of Homer at face value, according to which there is no instance of either of the two TAM

---

[22] It is maintained here that it is the same AVC expressing two different, but clearly related meanings, as will be shown in the following discussion. The same principle is followed throughout the analysis, relation defined mainly as semantic and historical association, although the decision on the number of AVCs has no significant bearing on the findings of the current investigation.

meanings, we could assume that the development occurred at some point between the 8th and the 5th c. BC. It goes without saying that this is only a rough approximation, due to the notorious problems of the Homeric texts and the possibly oral / colloquial character of this AVC, as argued above.

The generic meaning of the AVC is significant in another respect: it differentiates the two FCs based on μέλλω and (ἐ)θέλω, since the former apparently could not convey this meaning, despite its wide distribution. As a consequence, on a semantic level, (ἐ)θέλω + Infinitive could "replace" the morphological Future Tense in more varied contexts than μέλλω + Infinitive could. On the other hand, while μέλλω could also form an AVC when used in non-finite forms (participial or infinitival), (ἐ)θέλω always has a lexical, volitional meaning when attested in such a form. It seems that, syntactically speaking, the μέλλω AVC had a wider applicability.

This is typical in the so-called "functional layering" situation (cf. Hopper, 1991: 22–3), which means that various constructions of a language are used for the same functional domain (e.g. future reference). Semantic or morphosyntactic specializations usually result from the lexical, original meaning of the verbal element participating in the AVC, for instance motion or volitional verbs for the case of future reference (the phenomenon of retention, cf. Bybee, Perkins, & Pagliuca, 1994: 15–19). Regarding the situation in AG, the differences could arguably be ascribed to the fact that the μέλλω AVC was on an initial stage of grammaticalization, intention constituting the core lexical meaning of μέλλω itself (cf. 2.1). This allowed the μέλλω AVC to surface in a broad variety of non-finite forms, a fact rarely observed for AVCs in subsequent stages of development, where the Auxiliary loses large parts of its morphological paradigm (consider, for instance, the non-availability of infinitival forms for the English modal verbs). In this initial stage, the μέλλω AVC could not generalize in varied related contexts, hence its unavailability for the expression of generic truths.

Two conclusions can be drawn from the brief comparison between the two FCs: first, as expected, they were not freely interchangeable, as there existed specific semantic (timeless generic statements) and morphosyntactic (non-finite forms) contexts where only one of them could be used. And, second, the (ἐ)θέλω AVC can arguably be considered as more grammaticalized than the μέλλω one because of its broader semantics and restricted morphology. However, the (ἐ)θέλω AVC had not yet achieved strict syntactic cohesion, as, similarly to the μέλλω AVC, it did not manifest any preference for adjacency of the verb and its infinitival complement; in fact, in only three out of a total of ten instances are the two elements adjacent. Obviously, despite the more grammatical status in comparison to μέλλω, the degree of bondedness between (ἐ)θέλω and the following Infinitive is not yet significantly different than the one μέλλω exhibits.

2.4 Classical Greek: a summary

All of the three future-referring AVCs studied in this book are found in AG. Ἔχω + Infinitive does not belong yet to the domain of future reference, but conveys a modal meaning (ability), which nonetheless becomes more tightly linked with futurity in past conditionals. Of the remaining two AVCs, μέλλω + Infinitive is evidently the more common (at least in written language), while (ἐ)θέλω + Infinitive is seen to emerge as a competing form (at least in the spoken language), bearing partially overlapping properties with the μέλλω construction. Concerning their morphosyntactic status, while the ἔχω and (ἐ)θέλω AVCs provide evidence of a continuous development and of a rather grammatical status at the synchronic level, μέλλω + Infinitive remains in its initial stage of grammaticalization.

3

Hellenistic–Roman Greek (3rd c. BC–4th c. AD): proliferation of AVCs

Introduction

The Hellenistic–Roman (H–R) period is of great importance for the study of the Greek language. During this period Greek became a *lingua franca* in the Eastern Mediterranean world (and even beyond), and the populations acquiring Greek as their native language or learning Greek as a foreign language for various practical needs (administrative, commercial, etc.) far outnumber those of AG. Nonetheless, the importance of the H–R period has not been fully reflected in the amount of attention it has drawn from scholars, as it was traditionally overshadowed by the highly valued AG, in terms not only of linguistic analysis but of most aspects of social and political life as well. This is not to say, obviously, that the linguistic developments of H–R times have been completely neglected but rather that, with the exception of various grammars (e.g. Mayser, 1934, Mandilaras, 1973, Gignac, 1976–81, among others) and histories of the language (e.g. Jannaris, 1897, Horrocks, 1997, Christidis, 2007, among others), there have been relatively few systematic and thorough accounts of specific linguistic phenomena (cf., for example, Humbert, 1930, Janse, 1993, Manolessou, 2000). Apparently, the serious difficulties associated with the study of the low-register texts of these centuries (mostly papyri and religious texts), including the problematic tradition of many, has prevented scholars from attempting to tackle particular aspects of their language.

The H–R period sees considerable linguistic changes in all respects, phonological, morphological, semantic, and syntactic. A survey of these developments would necessarily be too long and lies beyond the scope of the book (for more details, cf. Horrocks, 1997 and Christidis, 2007, among others). Suffice it to say that there occurred considerable changes in the overall tense system, such as the merger of Aorist and Perfect (cf. Horrocks, 1997: 118–9) and the phonological overlap between the Subjunctive and Indicative (cf. Horrocks, 1997: 75–6, 102–3). Regarding the domain of futurity, the AG Future Tense is declining in use (especially its non-finite forms), mainly to the benefit of the Present Indicative and the Subjunctive which is widely used as a future-referring form, while the AVCs, especially μέλλω + Infinitive, gain in popularity and seem to become more productive. No comprehensive account has hitherto been put forward concerning the various paths of development for these AVCs and their semantic and syntactic properties. This investigation aims to clarify the necessarily blurred picture, based on two kinds of evidence: various middle- / low-register, religious (in their majority) texts on the one hand, and the papyri on the other.

More specifically, the corpus of this investigation consists of all the collections of the papyri available, as well as various other texts, chiefly—but not solely—religious in character (e.g. the Septuaginta and the New Testament, Acts and Lives of Saints, etc.). Arguably, most of these texts—the majority of the papyri included—represent either low registers of language use (private correspondence, notes, etc.) or at least low written varieties, devoid of any evident Atticizing influence. They offer glimpses of the spoken language of that time, thus providing us with indirect evidence of the actual spoken varieties and the linguistic developments occurring therein during this period. On the other hand, the papyri occasionally contain texts of official character, but given that most of the times the genre and register of the text is readily established, these texts can prove to be helpful in determining register differences between the AVCs, hence their inclusion in the corpus. Moreover, they constitute a material that has hardly been systematically exposed to linguistic scrutiny, and this examination seeks to start redressing the balance. As to the dating of the available material, it is highly dubious in some cases, and this might confuse matters when an historical development needs to be established with relative precision. The investigation follows the—more or less—elaborated guess of the editors concerning dating of the texts, but the indeterminacy will be taken into account when necessary.

3.1 Μέλλω / Ἔμελλον + Infinitive: relative stability

It has been argued that, in AG (cf. 2.1), μέλλω + Infinitive should be considered an 'initial stage' AVC; a similar situation obtains in the H–R period. Firstly, regarding semantics, it continued to convey future reference, based on the notion of intention when the agent is animate. The only significant development attested in this period is illustrated in the following example:

(1) καὶ περὶ   τοῦ βορρᾶ εἰ μέλλει   ποτισσεσθαι
                                                        (leg. ποτίζεσθαι)
    and for   the north if will-3rd SING.PRES.   water-INF.
                                                        PRES.PASS.
    μελησάτω   σοι   περὶ αὐτοῦ
    arrange-3rd IMP.AOR.   you-DAT.   for it
    "and regarding the northern [field], if it needs to be watered, take care of it"

(POslo, 155 / 2nd c. AD)

In (1), as in two other cases (PMichael, 17 / 2nd–3rd c. AD, POxy, 113 / 2nd c. AD), μέλλω seems to have developed a deontic or at least a "deontic-future" meaning, thus becoming akin to Bybee, Perkins, & Pagliuca's (1994: 248) 'future certainty marker'. Since all three attestations of this development are of similar date, we can safely conclude that the μέλλω AVC probably acquired this deontic meaning in the first century AD. The association between deontic modality and future reference is very well known and widely attested cross-linguistically (cf. for example, Bybee, Perkins, & Pagliuca, 1994) and, therefore, this development is rather expected (cf. Lyons, 1977: 846 and Aijmer, 1985: 16 for a similar development regarding English "will"). The deontic undertone in the meaning of this AVC features prominently in its subsequent developments (cf. especially 5.1).

On the morphological level, similarly to AG, μέλλω continues to occur in various forms including non-finite (mainly participial) ones, showing no evidence of a morphological reduction usually associated with auxiliaries.

TABLE 3.1 Forms of μέλλω in H–R times (non-papyri)

FORM	3rd c. BC	1st c. BC–1st c. AD*	1st c. AD	2nd c. AD	3rd c. AD	4th c. AD	Total
PRES	15 (35.7)	5 (83.3)	64 (36.2)	50 (55.6)	15 (34.9)	15 (19.5)	164 (37.7)
PRET	3 (7.1)	–	26 (14.7)	11 (12.2)	5 (11.6)	5 (6.5)	50 (11.5)
PCPLE (V)	18 (42.8)	–	51 (28.8)	20 (22.2)	10 (23.3)	30 (38.9)	129 (29.7)
PCPLE (N)	3 (7.1)	1 (16.7)	20 (11.3)	4 (4.4)	13 (30.2)	26 (33.8)	67 (15.4)
INF	1 (2.4)	–	6 (3.4)	3 (3.3)	–	1 (1.3)	11 (2.5)
SUBJ	2 (4.8)	–	10 (5.6)	2 (2.2)	–	–	14 (3.2)
TOTAL	42	6	177	90	43	77	435

* In this period, apart from the Vita Adam et Evae, I have also included Apocalypsis Esdrae, which is of uncertain date (possibly between 2nd c. BC and 2nd c. AD).

TABLE 3.2 Forms of μέλλω in H–R times (papyri)

FORM	3rd c. BC	2nd–1st c. BC	1st c. AD	2nd c. AD	3rd c. AD	4th c. AD	Total
PRES	15 (55.6)	4 (57.1)	24 (68.6)	35 (45.5)	40 (50.0)	15 (25.0)	133 (46.5)
PRET	4 (14.8)	–	4 (11.4)	12 (15.6)	8 (10.0)	4 (6.7)	32 (11.2)
PCPLE (V)	6 (22.2)	2 (28.6)	4 (11.4)	19 (24.7)	26 (32.5)	21 (35.0)	78 (27.3)
PCPLE (N)	–	1 (14.3)	2 (5.7)	10 (12.9)	6 (7.5)	18 (30.0)	37 (12.9)
INF	2 (7.4)	–	1 (2.9)	1 (1.3)	–	2 (3.3)	6 (1.3)
SUBJ	–	–	–	–	–	–	–
TOTAL	27	7	35	77	80	60	286

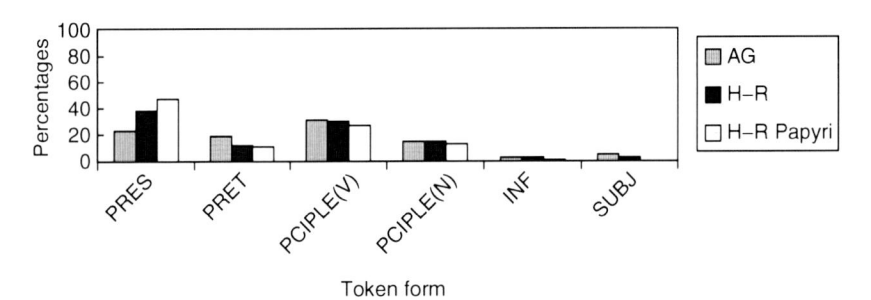

FIGURE 3.1 Token frequency of the forms of μέλλω

The token frequency of the forms of μέλλω both in the religious texts and in the papyri are illustrated in Tables 3.1 and 3.2, respectively.[1]

In both types of textual evidence, μέλλω occurs regularly in its participial forms (Verbal and Nominal), while its paradigm remains unchanged.[2] It has been argued (Blass & Debrunner, 1961: 181) that the disappearance of the non-finite forms of the ancient Future Tense during the Hellenistic period is the reason why μέλλω is more often found in non-finite contexts. This assumption is most probably erroneous in two respects: firstly, participial μέλλω AVC is at least as frequent in AG as in subsequent periods; and, secondly, the fast disappearing Future Infinitive is not being replaced by the μέλλω AVC, which is hardly ever used in an infinitival form, as can be seen from the tables above. The proliferation of the participial forms of μέλλω is simply a continuation of its use in AG, and evidence in favor of a still early stage of grammaticalization for this AVC.

---

[1] Μέλλω₂ is still attested, even though rarely (e.g. SB, 11648 / 222 AD).
[2] The only exception being the disappearance of the perfective Past (Aorist), a form that was quite rare even in AG (cf. Table 2.2).

One might raise some objections as to the actual productivity of the participial use of μέλλω in the H–R period on the basis of cases such as the following:

(2) γεινωσκιν   σε   θέλω,   ὅτι τὸν μέλλων
    know-INF.PRES. you want-1st SING.PRES., that the will-PCPLE.NOM.
    ηνιαυτον[leg. ἐνιαυτὸν]
    year-ACC.
    "I'd like you to know that in the following year…"

(*SB*, 9636 r 4 / 135–6 AD)

In this example, μέλλω is found in its participial form, in an adjectival function. As a consequence, it should morphosyntactically agree in Number, Case, and Gender with the following Noun. However, this is not the case, as there is no Case agreement: the participle is in the Nominative (μέλλων), while it should be in the Accusative (μέλλοντα), as is the Noun. Examples like (2) constitute an indication of the unstable status of participles (exactly like the Infinitives), at least as far as their morphological properties are concerned. This lack of stability, most probably associated with the devastating changes in the Noun declension during the same period,[3] could be attributed solely to lack of knowledge, as it is well known that many of the scribes were not native speakers of Greek, and they did not always have a good command of the language (cf. relevant discussion in Fewster, 2002). Having said that, there are good counter-arguments to this claim: the extent of the phenomenon, which correlates with the simultaneous weakening of the whole system of the non-finite forms of the verbs (Horrocks, 1997: 45–6), hints at an explanation along the lines of an actual tendency and not of random grammatical mistakes caused by ignorance. Moreover, since lack of full agreement can be found in other texts of this period as well (e.g. *Acta Joannis*, 86.5 / 2nd c. AD, *PHeid.*, 297.33 / 171–6 AD) (cf. Manolessou, 2005 for discussion and numerous examples), it would be relatively safe to conclude that this phenomenon is a real, authentic feature of H–R Greek. It is important to note that this lack of morphosyntactic agreement does not concern only μέλλω but all types of verbs and, therefore, it cannot be taken as evidence of a reduction in the morphological paradigm of μέλλω specifically but as an indication of a restructuring of the verbal and, more specifically, the non-finite verbal system of Greek.

---

[3] Consider, for instance, the partial merger of the 1st and 3rd declension or the decline of the dative case (cf. Horrocks, 1997: 69–70 / 124–5).

Another pattern of use of μέλλω that remained productive in H–R times was its ability to form compounds, which, as already argued, manifests quite explicitly its inherent 'intention / future-referring' meaning. There are a total of 11 instances of such words in the papyri, the most characteristic being the one below:

(3a) ὑπό τε   τοῦ πρυτάνεως οὐδ' ὑπὸ τοῦ μελλοπρυτάνεως
     by and   the prytanis   nor by   the prytanis-to-be
     "by neither the prytanis nor the future prytanis..."

(P.Oxy, 2110.1.13 / 370 AD)

(3b) οὔτε   ὑπὸ τοῦ νῦν πρυτάνεως οὔτε ὑπὸ [μελλόντ]ων   πρυτάνεων,
     neither by the now prytanis nor by   will-PCPLE.PRES. prytanis
     "by neither the present prytanis nor the future prytanis..."

(P.Oxy, 2110.1.20 / 370 AD)

(3c) οὔτε   ὑπὸ <τοῦ νῦν πρυτάνεως οὔτε ὑπὸ?> τῶν μελλόντων
     neither by   the now prytanis nor by   the will-PCPLE.PRES.
     πρυτανεύειν.
     be-prytanis-INF.PRES.
     "by neither the present prytanis nor those that will be prytanis..."

(P.Oxy, 2110.2.30 / 370 AD)

In these examples, attested in the same papyrus, we can easily observe the contemporary use of three stages of development: in (3c), μέλλω is found in its verbal participle form, in (3b) in an adjectival participle form, while (3a) exemplifies a compound based on μέλλω. Apparently, speakers retained the knowledge that all these constructions are intrinsically related and did not treat μελλοπρύτανις as a fully independent lexical element but as a word associated with μέλλω. It should be noted that most probably there is no semantic difference whatsoever between the above sentences, as the context of use is identical for all three of them. This example indicates that as late as H–R Greek, the μέλλω AVC was most probably treated by speakers as a construction involving two parts and not as an indistinguishable unit, since μέλλω retained its future-reference outside the construction (e.g. in compounding).

This assumption is corroborated by the fact that, similarly to AG, the past form ἔμελλον exhibits the same properties with the present form μέλλω. Importantly, in the case of the other two AVCs, the developments attested in the present and the past forms are clearly divergent (cf. 3.2, 3.3, and ch. 4).

No significant change can be observed with regard to the syntax of the AVC either. First, three instances of ellipsis are attested (*PAmh*, 38 / 2nd c. BC, *POxy*, 1293 / 2nd c. AD [dubious] and *Vita Antonii*, 26, 928.20 / 4th c. AD); the scarcity of this construction might be due to the low register of the texts, or it can reflect increasing difficulty on the part of speakers in the use of such a construction. Since there is no evidence as to whether this difficulty extended to other verbs apart from μέλλω, this evidence can only be of limited value.

Regarding the bondedness of μέλλω and its complement, the picture in the H–R period is similar to the one shown for AG, as is illustrated in Tables 3.3 and 3.4:

TABLE 3.3 Linear order of μέλλω+Inf. in H–R times (non-papyri)

PATTERN	3rd c. BC	1st c. BC–1st c. AD	1st c. AD	2nd c. AD	3rd c. AD	4th c. AD	Total
V + INF	19	4	93	60	20	28	224 (62.2)
INF + V	4	–	12	3	–	2	21 (5.8)
V + ... + INF	14	1	50	22	10	8	105 (29.2)
INF + ... + V	2	–	5	1	1	1	10 (2.7)
TOTAL	39	5	160	86	31	39	360

TABLE 3.4 Linear order of μέλλω+Inf in H–R times (papyri)

PATTERN	3rd c. BC	2nd–1st c. BC	1st c. AD	2nd c. AD	3rd c. AD	4th c. AD	Total
V + INF	13	2	22	35	34	20	126 (49.6)
INF + V	6	1	3	7	13	8	38 (15.0)
V + ... + INF	9	3	8	27	27	14	88 (34.6)
INF + ... + V	–	–	–	–	1	1	2 (0.8)
TOTAL	28	6	33	69	75	43	254

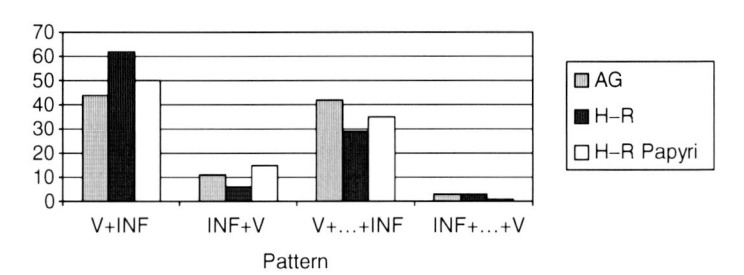

FIGURE 3.2 Adjacency in μέλλω AVC

The stability depicted in these tables is remarkable: in each century, the adjacency of the elements is more frequent than non-adjacency; the V + INF configuration is clearly much more popular than the INF + V. No clear indication of any significant development can be observed, not only inside the H–R period but also in relation to the AG (cf. Figure 3.2). This fact verifies the observation already made that, apart from acquiring a new modal (deontic) undertone in its meaning, this AVC does not exhibit any major changes between the classical and post-classical period regarding its grammatical status.

The only important development affecting the μέλλω AVC is related to the choice of the infinitival complement. A rather different pattern than the one found in AG is now attested, as illustrated in Tables 3.5 and 3.6.

As already mentioned (cf. 2.1), in AG μέλλω could normally have either a Present or a Future Infinitive as a complement, while the Aorist Infinitive was used only rarely. The Tables and Figure below show an altered picture for the H–R period: the Present Infinitive is undoubtedly the main means of complementation for μέλλω, while the Aorist is now also rather more frequently employed, and the formerly dominant Future Infinitive is fast retreating. This fact had been already observed in general for the Hellenistic–Roman texts (cf. Jannaris, 1897, Blass & Debrunner, 1961, among others), but not in relation specifically to μέλλω. The data apparently suggest that the process had begun

TABLE 3.5 Type of infinitival complement of μέλλω (non-papyri)

Infinitive	3rd c. BC	1st c. BC–1st c. AD	1st c. AD	2nd c. AD	3rd c. AD	4th c. AD	Total
Present	33	2	138	65	20	50	308 (81.5)
Future	1	–	18	4	–	–	23 (6.1)
Aorist	5	3	13	16	8	2	47 (12.4)
TOTAL	39	5	169	85	28	52	378

TABLE 3.6 Type of infinitival complement of μέλλω (papyri)

Infinitive	3rd c. BC	2nd–1st c. BC	1st c. AD	2nd c. AD	3rd c. AD	4th c. AD	Total
Present	16	4	23	48	50	19	160 (63.2)
Future	2	–	–	1	2	4	9 (3.6)
Aorist	10	2	10	20	22	20	84 (33.2)
TOTAL	28	6	33	69	74	43	253

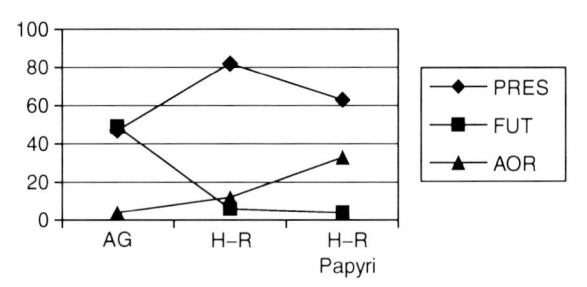

FIGURE 3.3 Development of Inf. complementation of μέλλω AVC

earlier, in the late classical period (4th–3rd c. BC), given the scarce number of instances of Future Infinitive both in the papyri and in the other textual sources of the 3rd c. BC. This issue is to an extent related to the overall retreat of the Infinitive as a category in Greek, with the Future Infinitive being the first to be lost (cf. Joseph, 1983).

More importantly for our purposes, a striking observation to be drawn from Figure 3.3 is the abundance of the Aorist Infinitive in the papyri, especially in relation to the other non-papyri texts of the period. In the papyri, the Aorist Infinitive is used in the 33% of the total instances, compared to the 12% in the non-papyri texts. It is worth noting that, of the occurrences of the Aorist Infinitive in the papyri, exactly 50% involve the weak Aorist, attesting to a rather expected generalization of the pattern of AG: the Aorist Infinitives following μέλλω do not belong any more in their majority to the class of verbs exhibiting a strong Aorist, as was apparently the case in the previous centuries.

An immediate response to this data would be to assume that the numerous instances of the Aorist Infinitive in the papyri are simply mistakes. It is well established that these texts contain many grammatical mistakes (cf. the issue of the morphosyntactic agreement of the participle above), reflecting the low level of knowledge of the Greek language that even many scribes possessed, let alone the majority of the population, which learned Greek as a foreign language and only as a means of oral communication. However, it is argued that this type of complementation should be seen as authentic for the following reasons.

First of all, the sheer number of token instances found in the papyri constitutes an argument by itself for the popularity of this pattern. But even if one assumes that the papyri are texts of dubious validity (at least in some cases) as far as linguistic developments are concerned, there still exist numerous instances of μέλλω + Aorist Infinitive in the other textual sources, as seen in Table 3.5. Moreover, the occurrence of the Aorist Infinitive in this context in AG as well argues in favor of a pattern rather than illiteracy mistakes. Apart from the textual findings, there is also one metalinguistic source in favor of the authenticity of this particular pattern. The contemporary grammarian Phrynichus (2nd c. AD), in his work *Eclogae*, dedicates two entries (313 / 347) to this particular construction, in order to advise all the users of Greek to avoid at all costs accompanying μέλλω (or, to be more precise, ἔμελλον) with an Aorist Infinitive, and to prefer the Present and the Future one instead. As is the case in every work of a prescriptive linguistic nature, the mention of a particular linguistic construction which, according to the author, is characteristic of "vulgar" speech is evidence by default of the popularity of its use. Consequently, it is evident that μέλλω + Aorist Infinitive constituted an authentic linguistic feature of the Greek-speaking world, at least in the Roman period.

Thus far, the authenticity of this gradual change in the pattern of complementation has been established. Still, the exceptionally high frequency of use of this type of Infinitive in the papyri requires an explanation. The generalized use of the Aorist Infinitive in the μέλλω AVC does not constitute an isolated development but a manifestation of a wider tendency to replace the ancient Future Infinitive with the Aorist one or with a subordinate clause. Recall that, in AG, the Future Infinitive was almost exclusively used with a limited class of inherently future-referring verbs, such as ἐλπίζω "hope", ὄμνυμι "swear", ὑπισχνοῦμαι "promise" and, obviously, μέλλω. So, we should expect that these verbs would parallel the developments regarding the complementation of μέλλω. Indeed, this is what is actually found. Tables 3.7 and 3.8 illustrate the pattern of complementation for ἐλπίζω in both AG and H–R Greek (H–RG), which is the verb with the most attestations in the corpus, as far as this particular verbal class is concerned.[4]

The tables are undoubtedly revealing; they show that, as the Future Infinitive was becoming more and more obsolete, the Aorist Infinitive came to be used in its place as a complement of verbs like ἐλπίζω. This fact, which is exactly similar to the development of the complementation of μέλλω (cf. Figure 3.3), suggests that there exists a clear parallelism between the two verbs, and, presumably, between all the verbs belonging to the class which selected a

---

[4] In Table 3.7, the data from Thucydides and Demosthenes include "periphrastic" constructions such as ἐλπίς ἐστί "there is hope that…". In addition, the tables do not contain types of complementation that are rather rarely attested and of relatively little importance for our purposes, such as an articular Infinitive (τοῦ + Inf.). Finally, the non-papyri texts of the 2nd–4th c. AD contain very few attestations of ἐλπίζω, hence their exclusion from the table.

TABLE 3.7 Pattern of complementation for ἐλπίζω (non-papyri)

Complement (᾽Ελπίζω)	Thucydides (5th c. BC)	Demosthenes (4th c. BC)	Septuaginta (3rd c. BC)	NT (1st c. AD)	Total
INF.PRES	4 (8.7)	2 (5.6)	1 (11.1)	–	7 (6.7)
INF.FUT	39 (84.8)	27 (75.0)	2 (22.2)	–	68 (64.8)
INF.AOR	3 (6.5)	7 (19.4)	2 (22.2)	10 (71.4)	22 (21.0)
ὅτι + INDIC.	–	–	4 (44.4)	4 (28.6)	8 (7.6)
TOTAL	46	36	9	14	105

TABLE 3.8 Pattern of complementation for ἐλπίζω (papyri)

Complement (᾽Ελπίζω)	3rd c. BC	1st c. BC	1st c. AD	2nd–2nd c. AD	3rd c. AD	4th c. AD	Total
INF.PRES	–	–	1	–	–	–	1 (3.7)
INF.FUT	1	1	1	3	–	1	7 (25.9)
INF.AOR	1	–	1	7	3	1	13 (48.2)
ὅτι+INDIC.	–	–	2	1	2	1	6 (22.2)
TOTAL	2	1	5	11	5	3	27

Future Infinitive in AG. Therefore, the Aorist Infinitive in the μέλλω AVC does not constitute a peculiarity of this specific lexical element, since there seems to be a clear tendency in the post-classical period to use the Aorist Infinitive in contexts where the Future Infinitive was formerly much more productive. Moreover, this fact lends crucial support to the authenticity of the μέλλω + Aorist Infinitive construction, which can now be seen as an instance of diffusion of a syntactic pattern affecting a particular class of verbs.

On the other hand, Tables 3.7 and 3.8 also show that, apart from the ever-growing use of the Aorist Infinitive in this particular context, there began in the Hellenistic–Roman period the change which ultimately led to the disappearance of the Infinitive in Greek, as implied by the many cases of subordinate clauses after ἐλπίζω, introduced by ὅτι "that". Μέλλω, though, does not seem to follow this development, as it is solely accompanied by an Infinitive. This gives us indirect evidence of a more grammatical status of the μέλλω AVC than previously assumed. It has been convincingly demonstrated (cf. Bybee, 2006a: 715, Bybee & Thompson, 1997) that new morphosyntactic patterns are more likely to occur in low-frequency units, since high-frequency elements "become entrenched and resist restructuring". Since, by definition, grammatical constructions are very frequent, they are likely to retain a more conservative structure. Consequently, the differentiation in the complementation pattern constitutes evidence of the high frequency of use for the μέλλω AVC, and, in addition, the first morphosyntactic evidence distinguishing this AVC from all other lexical verb + Infinitive constructions.

So, the pattern μέλλω + Aorist Infinitive *was* authentic and gained widespread popularity in the Roman period. It is part of a more general pattern, presumably involving all the verbs which used to take a Future Infinitive as a complement in AG. The important question about μέλλω that remains to be investigated is if there is any motivation—functional or not—for the choice of the following Infinitive from Hellenistic times onwards, since the speakers made use of two main options, the Present and the Aorist Infinitive.

One possible—functional—candidate would be the notion of aspectual differentiation. We could perhaps assume that when the Future Infinitive, which had an unclear aspectual value, ceased to be used (i.e. in the Hellenistic–Roman period), then speakers could re-organize the Infinitival system on a more transparent basis, with Present expressing the Imperfective and Aorist the Perfective value. As with what has been observed concerning AG, this again does not standup to scrutiny, because of the peculiar semantics of the Present Infinitive, which could be used to convey both perfective and imperfective meanings, as can be seen in the following examples from the papyri:

(4) καλῶς οὖν ποιήσῃς ἐξαυτῆς ἐλεύσῃ πρὸς ἐμέ. ἐὰν δὲ μὴ
good prt do-2ndSUBJ. from-her come-2nd SUBJ. to me. If prt not
μέλλῃς ἔρχεσθαι, πάλιν μοι ἐξαυτῆς φάσιν πέμψον,
will-2nd SING.SUBJ. come-INF.PRES., again to-me from-her notice send-IMP.,
ἵνα ὧδε αὐτὰ ἀναβαλῶ.
so here these postpone-1st FUT.
"I'd rather you leave there and come to me. But if you are not going to come, send me notice, so that I postpone these"

(*PBerl Zill*, 9r11 / 68 AD)

(5) μέλλω σοι ἀεὶ γράφειν καὶ πειν [leg. ποιεῖν]
will-1st PRES. to- you always write-INF.PRES. and make-INF.PRES.
σοι δαπάνην
to-you costs
"I will be continuously writing to you and buying what you need"

(*PMeyer*, 20 / 3rd c. AD)

In (4), ἔρχεσθαι clearly conveys a perfective meaning. It goes without saying that this is not the only instance where we find a discrepancy between the traditionally expected aspectual value of the Present Infinitive and its actual value in the particular context (cf., for example, *PCair Zen*, 59496 r9 / 248 BC, *PEnteux*, 86 r9 / 221 BC, *PFlor*, 278 r2.12 / 203 AD, *PCollYoutie* 2, 67 34 / 260–1 AD, *PFlor*, 127r, A9 / 266 AD among many others). Example (5), on the other hand, is one of the few cases where the Present Infinitive most likely conveys an imperfective meaning (other cases being *PIand*, 97 / 3rd c. AD, *POxy*, 1665 / 3rd c. AD, among others).

There is a crucial difference with the pattern in AG, however. Unlike the aspectually neutral Future Infinitive, the Aorist Infinitive in H–R times apparently had an inherent perfective value: there is no instance in the corpus of an Aorist Infinitive in the μέλλω AVC used with an imperfective aspectual value. Consequently, it could be argued that, contrary to AG, in the H–R period the choice of the Infinitive was at least partially based on Aspect: for an imperfective meaning, speakers used exclusively the Present Infinitive, while for the perfective meaning they could use both Present and Aorist Infinitive. In the latter case, the choice might also be determined by other factors, such as the paradigm of specific verbs, patterns of use, phonological considerations, etc. Apparently, the system of complementation of μέλλω underwent a development which rendered it more transparent in terms of aspect, a grammatical category presumably present in the finite forms of the AG / H–RG verbal system. Viewed from a speaker's perspective, this might give us an insight in to the reasons behind the decrease in popularity of the Future Infinitive: this form was used only in very specific contexts, it did not convey a clear aspectual meaning, and it also seemed superfluous in terms of tense, as the verbs it complemented were inherently future-referring. In a process of restructuring of the non-finite system on the basis mainly of Aspect, the Future Infinitive would be a prime candidate for elimination. As we have seen, speakers may have refrained from using the Future Infinitive possibly because of its peculiar properties already from the late classical period (4th c. BC), thus setting in motion a wholesale restructuring of the infinitival system in the complement of μέλλω and, presumably, of all future-referring verbs that followed—to some extent—the syntactic pattern of μέλλω. Obviously, the functional explanation has nothing to say by itself about why the restructuring took place in that specific period, and not earlier or later. Perhaps this issue is also linked to the language contact situation of the H–R period, and the numerous speakers of other languages who learned Greek as a second language, but more research is needed before any conclusions can be reached.

Even though Aspect could be the driving force behind the developments concerning the complements of μέλλω, it does not readily explain why the Aorist Infinitive is much more frequent in the papyri than in the non-papyri texts of this period. There is, however, a hitherto unknown fact which could prove illuminating in this respect: of the 84 instances of the Aorist Infinitive in the papyri, 78 (93%) are attested in private letters (e.g. *PCair Zen*, 59043 / 257 BC, *PHamb*, 90 / 3rd c. AD)! Apparently, this type of Infinitive was quite common in low-register contexts (such as private correspondence), and, since the papyri contain documents belonging to this register, they are most likely to contain more instances of the Aorist Infinitive. Therefore, apart from Aspect, there was probably a sociolinguistic parameter that partially determined the choice of the Infinitive following μέλλω as well; recall also the comment of Phrynichus, who considered the use of this Infinitive as βάρβαρον ("pertaining to barbarians"); such normative comments are a safe indication of the pattern described being used in the lower registers.

But why would the Aorist Infinitive be more popular in low registers? We could tentatively assume that its semantic—and mainly aspectual—properties were more transparent to most of the speakers of Greek who were not very familiar with AG: in other words, the speakers were fairly sure that the Aorist Infinitive would convey a perfective meaning and used it with ease, while the Present Infinitive might seem semantically more opaque to them.[5] In any case, the use of the Aorist Infinitive as a complement of μέλλω signalled a rather low-register text, and this can be an important new tool in determining the register of certain texts, especially in subsequent periods (cf. 4.1).

To conclude, the μέλλω AVC in H–R times only made small steps towards a more grammatical status, retaining most of its properties already present in the previous period. Apart from the emergence of a new, deontic undertone in the meaning of this construction, the most notable development affected the complementation of μέλλω. On the one hand, the almost obsolete Future Infinitive gave way mainly to the Aorist Infinitive, thus allowing for a more symmetrical system of complementation in terms of Aspect. The frequent use of the Aorist Infinitive also came to be associated with low-register contexts, as revealed by its high-token frequency in the private correspondence contained in the papyri. On the other hand, the retention of infinitival complementation instead of the new clausal one is a fairly safe indication that the μέλλω AVC was morphosyntactically differentiated by speakers of Greek and was not associated any longer with the patterns of other, lexical classes of verbs.

---

[5] This implies that the restructuring was initialized by—or quickly diffused in—speakers with little grasp of Greek. This remains to be seen by further research.

3.2 Ἔχω / Εἶχον + Infinitive: from ability to futurity

There is a general consensus in the literature that the ἔχω AVC is first used as an FC beginning in this period. Apart from this observation, though, no uncontroversial facts are yet to be acknowledged, with the possible exception of the (semantic) stages through which the development of the AVC proceeded: it has been widely suggested (e.g. Bănescu, 1915, Aerts, 1965) that ἔχω + Infinitive first came to convey an obligation meaning before becoming a future-referring construction. The chronology of this development remains unclear, as neither Bănescu (1915) nor Aerts (1965) provide any specific examples of the obligation meaning. There is even controversy associated with the dating of the emergence of future reference: while Bănescu (1915) and Aerts (1965) place it in the late Roman period (approximately 5th c. AD), Jannaris (1897) tacitly and Horrocks (1997) argue for a slightly earlier chronology, possibly in the 3rd–4th centuries AD.

However, a careful examination of the data reveals that the acquiring of the future-referring meaning took place probably earlier, in the first Christian centuries (in the 1st–2nd c. AD, if not earlier), and does not presuppose any prior obligation meaning, as it is directly linked to the AG meaning of ability and the closely associated notion of possibility. The evidence from the mostly Christian literature will first be presented before proceeding to the papyri to examine whether they validate the conclusions already drawn. The main point of interest will be the present form ἔχω, as its past equivalent is seldom attested in the corpus; however, εἶχον will be referred to when its attestations, despite their scant number, shed some light on developments affecting both the present and the past forms of the verb.

The well-known ability meaning is frequently attested throughout all these centuries, but this is not surprising, as old meanings of AVCs tend to continue in use well after the same construction has undergone a generalization in its use in various contexts and meanings. It is worth mentioning that the ability ἔχω AVC was often used in negative contexts, which is probably related to the emergence of the future-referring meaning, as will be proposed below.

The first attestations of this new meaning are arguably found in *Apoc. Esdrae*, a rather obscure text of uncertain chronology (2nd c. BC–2nd c. AD), a fact that to some extent undermines the usefulness of these attestations. Nevertheless, this text offers a relatively straightforward instance of future-referring ἔχω AVC, as it makes use alternatively of the morphological Subjunctive as a future-referring form in the same context:

(6) καὶ ἐξαλείψω   τὸ γένος τῶν ἀνθρώπων, καὶ οὐκέτι   ᾖ
    and annihilate-1st FUT. the race of   men,   and no-more   is-3rd
                                                                     PRES.SUBJ.
    κόσμος.   καὶ εἶπεν ὁ   προφήτης· καὶ πῶς ἔχει
    world.   and said   the prophet;   and how have-3rd PRES.
    δοξάζεσθαι   ἡ   δεξιά σου;
    glory-INF.PRES.PASS.   the right yours?

    "... and I will annihilate the race of man, and there will be world
    no more. And the prophet said: and how will your right side be glorified?"

(Apoc. Esdrae, 27.15)

The future reference of this example is indisputable, as God is talking to one of his prophets, revealing what will happen on the day of the Apocalypse. Moreover, the use of the ἔχω AVC is preceded by a morphological Future Tense (ἐξαλείψω) and a future-referring Subjunctive (ᾖ). The use of the Subjunctive as a future-referring form is well known even for Homeric and AG (cf. Goodwin, 1875), and it spreads in the H R period (cf. Jannaris 1897, Schwyzer, 1950–71, and Horrocks, 1997 for an overview).[6]

The example in (6) is not the only attestation of the future-referring meaning of the ἔχω construction in this text (cf. also *Apoc. Esdrae*, 31.11–14), and there is another possible instance of this development in a different text of roughly the same period:

(7) λέγει τῷ   'Αδὰμ   ἡ Εὔα· διὰ τί σὺ ἀποθνῄσκεις κἀγὼ   ζῶ;
    say   to-the   Adam   the Eve; for what you die   and-me live?
    ἢ πόσον χρόνον ἔχω   ποιῆσαι   μετὰ τὸ ἀποθανεῖν σε; ...
    prt how time have-1st PRES.   make-INF.AOR. after the die-INF.AOR. you?
    οὐ γὰρ βραδύνεις   ἀπ' ἐμοῦ, ἀλλ' ἴσα ἀποθνῄσκομεν ἀμφότεροι·
    not prt delay-2nd PRES.   after me, but adv die-1st PL.   both
    "Eve says to Adam: why are you dying while I'm still alive? And how long will I live after you die? ... You will not be long after me, but we'll both die together"

(Vita Ad. et Ev., 31.2–7)

In this case the future reference of the construction is highly preferred in comparison to the ability meaning, as Eve does not question her 'ability' to

---

[6] This partial functional equivalence led to "mixed" forms such as ἐνεγκῶ "I will bring", built from the Aorist Subjunctive stem ἐνεγκ- and the endings of the Future Tense (while the AG equivalent of this form would be οἴσω). These forms are occasionally attested in the papyri (Gignac, 1981: 287).

survive after Adam's death but rather wants to know how long she will live alone. This is evident in the response given to this question in the following lines of the text. Another possibility would be to postulate an obligation meaning, which is not excluded by the context, even though (7) has a strong future reference (we will return to the issue of an obligation meaning for this construction below).

The dating of this text is not certain, but it is assumed to lie between 1st c. BC and 1st c. AD. This is approximately the period of the composition of the other text previously mentioned, namely *Apoc. Esdrae*. On this basis, we could argue that the emergence of the future-referring meaning for the ἔχω AVC should be dated close to the 1st c. AD, much earlier than is traditionally recognized.

The chronology of that development is crucial with regard to its origin, as it rather uncontroversially refutes the claim (put forward originally in Jannaris, 1897: 553), that the future-referring ἔχω AVC constitutes simply a Latinism, a construction borrowed from Latin due to the extensive contact between Greek-speaking and Latin-speaking populations in the Eastern Mediterranean. The full development of the roughly equivalent Latin "habeo" + Infinitive cannot be articulated here; suffice it to say that it has been convincingly argued (Fleischman, 1982, Pinkster, 1987, among many others) that the Latin construction can only be said to have acquired a future-referring meaning in the 2nd–3rd c. AD, as its first attestations are found in the texts of the writers of this period (mostly Tertullian). It has already been shown that the ἔχω AVC could have a future-referring meaning at least as early as the 1st c. AD (cf. ex. 6). Therefore, it seems quite unlikely that it had been borrowed from Latin, since the earliest Latin attestations of the equivalent construction are later. One might suggest that the future-referring meaning of the Latin AVC might have developed earlier, without this development being reflected in the texts. However, exactly the same could hold for the Greek construction, as the lack of oral evidence is obviously total for any ancient language. Consequently, the relative chronology of the parallel development of the two equivalent constructions in Latin and Greek rather strongly suggests that the future-referring meaning of the Greek AVC does not constitute a case of syntactic / semantic borrowing (or "grammatical replication", in Heine & Kuteva's 2005 terms), but a language-internal phenomenon in each case. On the other hand, this conclusion does not exclude the possibility, suggested by Horrocks (1997), of the mutual reinforcement of the two developments because of the extensive communication and bilingualism (Adams, 2003) manifested at that time between the two communities (Greek- and Latin-speaking). It is actually

TABLE 3.9 *Ἔχω* AVC in the H–R period (non-papyri)

Meaning	3rd c. BC	1st c. BC–1st c. AD	1st c. AD	2nd c. AD	3rd c. AD	4th c. AD	Total
Ability	1	1	24	23	6 (60.0)	13 (56.5)	68 (75.6)
Futurity	–	7	–	1	4 (40.0)	10 (43.5)	22 (24.4)
TOTAL	1	8	24	24	10	23	90

very likely that such reinforcement must have taken place after the future reference of the specific construction emerged *independently* in the two languages, even though exact evidence to support the claim is almost impossible to find.[7]

Indirect evidence in favor of the reinforcement argument can be found in the rise in the frequency of use of the future-referring ἔχω AVC in comparison to the old ability meaning in the late Roman period. Table 3.9 illustrates the relevant figures. As can be seen, the future-referring meaning must have emerged by the end of the 1st c. AD, while its spread should be chronologically placed in the 3rd and 4th c. AD: it is noteworthy that, in the two last centuries of this period, the number of future-referring attestations of the AVC almost equals that of the ability ones. The near complete absence of the future-referring meaning in the 1st and 2nd c. AD (the exception being *Acta Joannis*, 63.8 / 2nd c. AD), on the other hand, at a time when it has presumably emerged, as has been argued, calls for an explanation, possibly on a sociolinguistic level. There is always the possibility of historical accident, but, if taken at face value, it suggests that at this early stage of its development as a future-referring construction ἔχω + Infinitive was not yet considered as a feature of the written norm, and was possibly used predominantly in oral communication, with sporadic attestations in texts bearing evidence of its existence. On the whole, these texts offer a typical picture of a linguistic change in progress: early attestations of a new meaning / construction are sporadically attested, while the diffusion of this innovation is much more systematically attested in the texts of subsequent centuries.

Recall here that the traditional account for the development of the ἔχω AVC presupposes an obligation meaning as an intermediate stage between

---

[7] Biville (2002) actually talks about a "well-entrenched bilingualism" between speakers of the two languages on the basis mostly of epigraphic material from Delos and elsewhere. If this is indeed the case, then one could assume that the main mechanism through which mutual reinforcement came about is "code alternation", to use Thomason's (2001: 136) term, i.e. alternation between different languages in different linguistic and sociolinguistic situations.

ability and futurity (cf., for example, Jannaris, 1897 and Bănescu, 1915), and Heine (1993, 1997) has incorporated this intuition into his cognitive schema of Possession / Purpose. Despite its semantic feasibility, this assumption is hard to maintain on the basis of the data available. Excluding the ambiguous example in (7), the one and only possible example of such a use in the corpus is found in the New Testament:

(8) βάπτισμα δὲ   ἔχω   βαπτισθῆναι,   καὶ   πῶς
    baptism   prt have-1st PRES.   baptize-INF.AOR.PASS.,   and   how
    συνέχομαι   ἕως ὅτου τελεσθῇ.
    distress-1st PRES.PASS.   till when done
    "I have a baptism to be baptized / I will be baptized a baptism, and how distressed I am until it is accomplished"

(Luc. 12.50)

Even though an obligation meaning seems possible in this context, the future-referring one is not excluded, since it is Jesus who is talking to his disciples, and therefore we may assume that he was simply making a statement concerning his future. To be more precise, the meaning of the AVC in this case seems to belong either to the notion of "predestination", commonly involving the verbs "be" or "have" (cf. Bybee, Perkins, & Pagliuca, 1994: 262–3) or to "planned / scheduled" future, which refers to events that are pre-arranged to occur (cf. Bybee, Perkins, & Pagliuca, 1994: 249).[8] In any case, it constitutes a sole and debatable example, and cannot effectively support the claim for an *intermediate* obligation stage, being rather more future-referring.[9] If we consider the early attestation of the future meaning, established above to be around the 1st c. AD, and its simultaneous use with the ability meaning throughout the period, then the absence of the hypothetical obligation stage seems bizarre. It could be argued that the gap presented in the development of the Greek AVC is due to a poor textual tradition, but even this assumption

---

[8] In this respect, it is interesting to note that the Modern Greek AVC "ἔχω να + subj.", e.g. "ἔχω να δουλέψω απόψε = I have work to do tonight" seems to belong to the 'scheduled future' domain also.

[9] LSJ provides another alleged obligation example from a fragmentary text of the 3rd c. AD (*Contra Christianos*, 63: ὁ δέ γε Χριστὸς εἰ καὶ παθεῖν εἶχε κατ' ἐντολὰς τοῦ θεοῦ, ἐχρῆν μὲν ὑπομεῖναι τὴν τιμωρίαν = Christ, although he would / had to suffer following God's order, he had to tolerate this punishment). The context seems to favor, though, the future-in-the-past interpretation, since the obligation meaning of the AVC gives the awkward reading "Christ, although he had to suffer, he had to tolerate this", instead of the much better "Christ, although he would suffer, he had to tolerate this". In any case, the example comes from a time that the future-referring meaning of the AVC seems well established, so it does not provide any evidence for an *intermediate* obligation stage between ability and futurity.

is arguably oversimplifying, since the inherent problem of the existing data did not affect the attestation of both ability and futurity meanings. On the basis of the data given, it seems reasonable to argue that the obligation meaning, if it emerged at all in the H–R period, could not have predated the development of the future-referring meaning, and, therefore, should not be considered its immediate source. It will also be demonstrated further below that the obligation stage is not essential from a conceptual point of view either.

Before moving to the thorny issue of the source and the pathway of development of the future-referring meaning, though, let us examine the evidence from the papyri, in order to determine whether they verify the picture emerging from the other textual sources. Despite the fact that, as mentioned, the character of these texts varies immensely, the overall picture remains to a great extent unaltered. The ability meaning is attested throughout the period, and is also found in formulaic expressions, such as "εἰδέναι ἔχω: I am able to learn / know". The future-referring meaning is possibly attested as early as the 1st c. BC, as shown in the following example:

(9) Εἰς αὔριον   ἔχομεν   πρὸς Σωτήριχον ἐλθεῖν,
    prep tomorrow have-1st PL.PRES. to   Soterichos   come-INF.AOR.
    ἐπεὶ ἐπιβάλλεταί τις   ἐπ'αὐτόν. Ὡς ἂν γενώμεθα   ἐκεῖ, ...
    for be-hostile someone against him. When prt be-1st PL.SUBJ. there
    "Tomorrow we have to / will go to Soterichus, as someone is being hostile against him; when we get there,..."

(*BGU*, 2629 / 4 BC)

This example constitutes an excerpt from a private letter, where the sender tells the recipient his plans for the near future. This context apparently favors the future-referring interpretation, and, more specifically, the 'scheduled future' interpretation of the AVC, since the sender is plainly describing the actions to be undertaken in the immediate future. On the other hand, ability is excluded, but there is nothing to exclude an obligation meaning; it is simply impossible to retrieve the exact meaning of the AVC on the basis of the available context. Still, the high likelihood of a future-referring meaning for the ἔχω AVC in this example, at such an early date, fits well with the evidence presented of the non-papyri texts.

Even though there is not much room for certainty, the future-referring use may also occur in the texts of the following centuries. However, most future-looking occurrences are actually ambiguous between a 'possibility' and a 'future reference' reading, as exemplified in (10):

(10) δὸς οὖν τὴν ἀρτάβην τοῦ σίτου Ζακαῶνι, ἣν κακῶς
give prt the artaba the grain-GEN. Zakaon-DAT., which bad-adv
[ἔ]λαβας παρ' α[ὐ]τοῦ εἰ δὲ μή, μεταμεληθῆναι
receive-2nd AOR. from him; otherwise, regret-INF.AOR.PASS.
ἔχεις.
have-2nd PRES.
"give the artaba of grain to Zakaon, which you should not have taken from him; otherwise, you may / will regret it"

(*PSakaon*, 55rp16 / 3rd–4th c. AD)

In this example, as in other cases (*PRyl*, 242r12 / 3rd c. AD, *PGrenf*, 82r17 / 4th–5th c. AD), the context is strongly future-referring, since it constitutes a threat, a speech act inherently associated with futurity. The modal notion of possibility is also very likely, though, as it is also quite productive in similar contexts and is tightly linked with the notion of ability, both semantically and cross-linguistically (Bybee, Perkins, & Pagliuca, 1994: 192). The transition from ability to possibility is easy, and can be seen as the loss of the requirement that the enabling conditions of the action lie within the agent. Therefore, it is also easy to assume that the ἔχω AVC could express the meaning of possibility as well. Obviously, (10) aptly demonstrates how readily ability gives rise to possibility, and how the latter is ambiguous with future reference in specific contexts. It is a well-known fact that ambiguity is typical in constructions expressing various modal meanings, and it is hardly possible to determine the exact meaning in every case.

Moreover, such examples could be seen as the linking context between an already extant possibility meaning and a new, future-referring meaning for the ἔχω AVC. In this case, the latter meaning would have emerged through the mediation of a possibility stage. Even though the association between the two types of meaning is well known, and is particularly favored in contexts such as the one exemplified in (10), the scarcity of the possibility meaning as well as the relative chronology of attestations do not seem to favor such an account at a first glance. Moreover, it seems that, cross-linguistically speaking, the emergence of FCs from a possibility meaning is rather rarely manifested (cf. Bybee, Perkins, & Pagliuca, 1994: 266). However, the association between possibility and futurity must have played a role in the transition from ability to future reference, as will be argued further below.

Concerning the issue of the assumed obligation stage, the papyri are even more telling than the other H–R texts, since there is no attestation whatsoever of this modal meaning. This observation corroborates the conclusion drawn on the basis of the non-papyri texts, namely that, even if such a meaning had developed,

TABLE 3.10 *Ἔχω* AVC in the H–R period (papyri)

Meaning	3rd c. BC	2nd–1st c. BC	1st c. AD	2nd c. AD	3rd c. AD	4th c. AD	Total
Ability*	18	3	3	9	8	2	43
Futurity	–	1	–	1	–	1	3
Futurity / Possibility	–	–	–	–	2	1	3
TOTAL	18	4	3	10	10	4	49

*Excluding the formulaic construction "Εἰδέναι ἔχω"

the scarcity of its attestations, especially in relation to the—admittedly few, but relatively more numerous—instances of the future-referring construction, renders the assumption of an obligation stage highly improbable. Schematically, the attestations of the various meanings of the ἔχω AVC are shown in Table 3.10.

The low total of token instances prevents us from drawing any conclusions with certainty, but, as already stated, the basic tendencies found in the non-papyri texts are also attested in the papyri: the continuous usage of the ability meaning, the emergence of the future-referring meaning, as well as the absence of any obligation meaning (with the exception of one or two ambiguous cases); consequently, the papyri confirm the authenticity of the picture emerging from the other textual sources. To these we should add the interplay between possibility and futurity, manifested more clearly in the papyri.

We have yet to provide a convincing answer to the basic question, however: how exactly did the future-referring meaning emerge? We have already established that it does not constitute a case of 'grammatical replication' from Latin but mostly a language-internal development. Moreover, we have observed that the data do not readily comply with the scenario of an intermediate obligation stage between ability and futurity. It is therefore realistic to assume that, somehow, the future-referring ἔχω AVC constitutes a direct descendant of the ancient ability use of this particular construction and its closely related notion of possibility.

Clearly, the transition from ability / possibility to futurity in the case of this AVC is not an instance of "exaptation", a term adopted by Lass (1990) to denote the use of an old form to express a novel function, after having lost its original function. If we followed such an account, we would have to accept a developmental discontinuity between the former and the later function of the particular form, a logical "leap" from one morphosyntactic area to another; in other words, we would have to maintain that ability / possibility cannot be a direct semantic source for future reference, contrary to the evidence presented above. There is, however, cross-linguistic evidence that ability can in fact be the source of an FC (Bybee, Perkins, & Pagliuca, 1994: 264–6), and that such linguistic developments as the one regarding ἔχω + Infinitive do not fall under the scope of exaptation. Consequently, we need to illustrate explicitly the semantic / syntactic route of the development "ability → futurity" without making reference to the notion of exaptation.

Apparently, there exists a logical / semantic relationship between ability and futurity, even though the former has not been widely recognized as a future-referring modality, contrary to other modal meanings (such as obligation). Consider example (11):

(11) ἀλλ' εἰμὶ Χριστιανὸς καὶ   πλέον τούτου παρ'ἐμοῦ ἀκοῦσαι
     but   am   Christian   and   more   this   from-me   hear-INF.AOR'.
     οὐκ ἔχεις·
     not have-2nd PRES.
     "but I am a Christian and you cannot / will not hear anything more than that from me"

(*Mart. Carpi*, 34.3 / 2nd c. AD)

Even though this example has been included in the instances of ability meaning in Table 3.9, it is actually ambiguous between ability, possibility ("it is not possible that you hear") and a future-referring meaning. The reason for the ambiguity is partly the *pragmatic* context, since in (11) the speaker asserts the inability of the hearer (the agent of the AVC) to perform an action (i.e. to hear anything more). But such assertions necessarily imply a possibility meaning, as the ability conditions lie outside the agent. Moreover, the negation further ambiguates the interpretation of the AVC, as a negated ability necessarily implies a negated possibility (cf. Iakovou, 2003 for other cases from Greek), which, in its turn, implies the negation of a future action, i.e. "I cannot (I am not able) → I cannot (it is not possible that I) → I will not". This implication arises each and every time that an ability / possibility construction is negated, and, consequently, ability and future reference are semantically tightly linked through the mediation of possibility. Their association can be schematically represented by the well-known "logical square", where all constructions occupying a corner of the square are linked with another construction occupying a different corner through the logical relation of contradiction or entailment. The square was originally used by the Medieval philosophers, but was recently re-introduced by Horn (1989) and adopted by Levinson

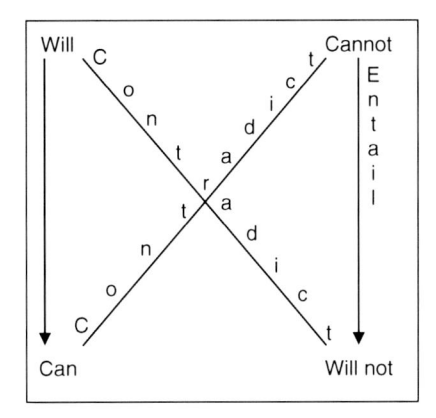

FIGURE 3.4 Ability / possibility and futurity

(2000) to account for scalar implicatures (i.e. the relation between "all", "some", etc.) and by Van der Auwera (2001) and Traugott & Dasher (2002) to explain instances of semantic change in the domain of modality.

As can be seen, the same square also describes successfully the association between ability / possibility and future reference. Figure 3.4 illustrates that, while "can" does not entail "will", the negative "cannot" entails "will not". Therefore, the hitherto unexplained association between ability / possibility and futurity is adequately captured through the logical square. This is arguably one of the main mechanisms of transition from ability to futurity, since in every negative utterance of the ἔχω AVC, possibility and future reference were logically implied. Obviously, negative contexts are quite common for almost every linguistic expression, while negative expressions give rise to other semantic phenomena as well (such is the case for the scalar implicatures mentioned above). Therefore, the semantic change from ability to futurity is now—at least partially—captured from a contextual point of view.

With regard to ἔχω, this argument does not explain why the ἔχω AVC developed the new meaning at this particular period but rather illustrates the possible mechanism of transition and how this change was facilitated by the intrinsic semantic properties of the construction. Furthermore, it demonstrates the reason why an obligation stage in the development of the ἔχω AVC is not essential conceptually, an observation complying with the evidence provided by the data that supported this view. On the other hand, the mediation of possibility in negated contexts, as well as in other contexts such as threats (cf. ex. 10), cannot be denied, and, consequently, a possibility stage must be assumed between ability and future reference. This stage is mostly of a semantic nature and is hard to manifest as a distinct stage in the data, which, as mentioned above, do not contain one unambiguous instance of a possibility meaning, a fact partly expected, given the close association of possibility with ability.

The path "ability → possibility → futurity" has been noted by Bybee, Perkins, & Pagliuca (1994: 266), although they remark that it is not very common, as possibility does not readily give rise to intention, which they consider as a prerequisite for futurity to arise. True as this may be, it has been illustrated above how an AVC can pass from possibility to futurity, especially in the case of negative contexts; consequently, the Greek data complements the above semantic pathway by showing how exactly the bridging between these meanings might come to pass. Furthermore, the development of this AVC is not a simple manifestation of this semantic route: instead, the ἔχω AVC underwent a *series* of developments, giving rise to related but distinct meanings, such as possibility and future reference, but also 'scheduled future' or even 'predestination'. As illustrated above, all these meanings are probably attested in the H–R texts. Therefore, the development of ἔχω AVC can best be captured if a multiple modal branching is assumed, similarly to its Latin equivalent "habeo + INF", which, according to Coleman (1971), could also express possibility, while, on the other hand, must have come to express future reference through an obligation stage (Adams, 1991). In a multiple branching scenario, the occurrence of sporadic obligation instances is rather to be expected and, consequently, even if some of the ambiguous examples mentioned favor an obligation reading, they do not constitute counter-examples to the overall scenario of the ἔχω AVC development.

But perhaps one more facilitating factor for the transition from ability to futurity can be isolated. The past equivalent of the ἔχω AVC, namely εἶχον + Infinitive, was inherently associated with futurity (in the past) as well. As it conveyed the meaning of ability-in-the-past, it would approximate to the meaning of futurity-in-the-past, especially in the cases of an unrealized action. Unfortunately, the attestations of the past form of the ἔχω AVC are extremely scarce: ten in the literary texts and only three in the papyri. Despite the scarcity, two examples are found that show this ambiguous ability / futurity-in-the-past meaning in two different contexts:

(12) καὶ γὰρ εἰ μὴ ἦν   ἡ   δεξιὰ χεὶρ τοῦ θεοῦ μετά σου ἐν   τῇ ὥρᾳ ἐκείνῃ,
     and prt if not were the right hand the God with you prep the time that

καὶ σὺ   τοῦ βίου   τούτου ἀπαλλάξαι   εἶχες.
and you the life-GEN. this   release-INF.AOR. have-2nd SING.PRET.
"if the right hand of God had not been with you at that time, you
could / would also have left this world"

(*Test. Abr (A)*, 18.17 / 1st c. AD)

(13) ἀλλὰ λειαν ἐλυπήθην ὅτι οὐ παρεγένου ις τὰ γενέσια τοῦ παιδίου μου
but much saddened that not you-came to the birthday the child mine
καὶ σὺ καὶ ὁ ἀνήρ σ[ο]υ, εἶχες   γὰρ ἐπὶ πολλὰς ἡμέρας
and you and the man your, have-2nd PRET. prt prep   many   days
ευφ[ρ]ανθης [leg. εὐφ[ρ]ανθῆναι (?)] σὺν αὐτῷ.
delight- 2nd AOR.SUBJ?   with him
"but I was really saddened that you and your husband were not here
at my child's birthday, because you could / would have enjoyed yourself
for many days with him"

(*POxy*, 1676r13 / 4th c. AD)

In (12), the εἶχον construction is found in the apodosis of a counterfactual conditional, and it is crucially not accompanied by the potential / irrealis marker ἄν;[10] therefore the irrealis interpretation can solely be attributed to the meaning of the AVC. This example illustrates nicely how ability-in-the-past, in such contexts, would be indistinguishable from futurity-in-the-past. The relatively early chronology of this text fits neatly with the date of emergence of the future-referring meaning suggested above (*ca.* 1st c. BC–1st c. AD), while similar examples are attested in texts of the subsequent centuries (*Acta X. et P.,* 16.5 / 3rd c. AD), indicating a continuous line of existence. Counterfactuals, then, must have been another specific context whereby the semantic change from ability to futurity was facilitated. It is worth mentioning that a similar use has been reported (Denison, 1993: 355) for the Old and Middle English "have + Infinitive" construction, verifying the suggested semantic link.

The irrealis interpretation was not restricted to conditional apodoses, as shown in example (13). In this case, the εἶχον AVC simply refers to an unrealized action in the past. This attestation demonstrates that the past equivalent of the AVC could convey this meaning in simple declarative clauses, at least by the end of the H–R period, if not earlier. After all, an apodosis is a main clause, so we could expect speakers would generalize the use of εἶχον + Infinitive in contexts outside the scope of a conditional.

---

[10] This marker was mainly used in AG to mark "irrealis", depending on the verbal form it accompanied (cf. Goodwin, 1875: sec. VI).

Note incidentally that the papyrus in (13) reads εἶχες ευφ[ρ]ανθης, which constitutes a manifestation of the construction "V+V_S" (cf. 2.3); the editor had corrected it, though, by replacing the finite form with the "correct" Infinitive εὐφ[ρ]ανθῆναι. However, seen in the light of the wider pattern attested already in AG, this correction is superfluous; apparently, this pattern was generalized to include other verbs (apart from (ἐ)θέλω and κελεύω), but its exact distribution needs further investigation, which lies beyond the scope of the book. This example also constitutes the earliest attestation of this pattern involving ἔχω, and should probably be regarded as the syntactic source for similar attestations found in subsequent periods (Early and Late Medieval, cf. ch. 4–5).

The future-referring ἔχω AVC bears again the characteristics of a more grammaticalized AVC in comparison to the μέλλω AVC. Firstly, it manifests a constructional meaning, while the meaning of the AVC is still largely dependent on the lexical meaning of μέλλω. Secondly, although no radical morphological reduction in the paradigm of ἔχω is observed, it is important that in all attestations of the future-referring meaning ἔχω occurs in a finite form, or, in other words, ἔχω cannot appear in a participial form when forming the AVC, contrary to μέλλω (cf. 3.1). As to the syntagmatic bondedness between ἔχω and its complement, there is a very clear and strong tendency for the two elements to appear linearly adjacent (22 / 27 occurrences, 81%), while again no such tendency could be observed for the μέλλω AVC (cf. 3.1). Therefore, the combined evidence seems to be quite conclusive on that matter.

On the whole, the examination of the texts of H–R times reveals that the ἔχω AVC acquired a future-referring meaning, probably around the 1st c. BC– 1st c. AD, which gained in use in the subsequent centuries. At the same time, the old ability meaning was continuously used throughout this period. Future-reference came about as a possible meaning for this AVC through multiple pathways, the most important being (negated) possibility. The reason why the new meaning appeared in that specific period is elusive, as always. Mutual influence from the equivalent Latin construction could constitute a partial answer, but mainly for the generalization of use of the AVC in the future-referring meaning, not its original emergence. Another possible relevant factor might be the tendency of speakers of Demotic (Egyptian), the common variety of Egyptian mainly employed at that period, to use "periphrastic" constructions, although of a different character (Loprieno, 1995: 91). The vast majority of the surviving papyri come from Egypt, and there is no doubt that the language contact situation in that area must have influenced the Greek as we see it today in the papyri; still no thorough understanding of the sociolinguistic situation and, especially, its outcome in Hellenistic–Roman Egypt is yet available.

As expected, not all FCs were used in the same contexts. The μέλλω AVC could not apparently be used in irrealis contexts of the type exemplified in (12–13), as no similar example has been found containing the μέλλω AVC, despite its relative abundance in the very same texts. This observation indicates a specialization in meaning for the two AVCs, which could provide a communicative reason for the co-existence of (at least) two AVCs expressing future reference. Moreover, a different kind of specialization was also manifested: sociolinguistic specialization to certain registers, since the ἔχω AVC was undoubtedly restricted to lower registers of use, contrary to μέλλω, which enjoyed a sociolinguistically unrestricted use. Such a specialization is commonly not taken into account by grammaticalization studies: for instance Bybee, Perkins, & Pagliuca (1994: 243) only mention the different range of uses that AVCs belonging to the same functional domain might have, depending largely on the retention of previous lexical meanings. However, the sociolinguistic specialization can more readily account for the co-occurrence of multiple AVCs with similar meanings, since it illustrates that, irrespective of retained properties, speakers choose which AVC to use on a sociolinguistic basis.

3.3 (Ἐ)θέλω + Infinitive: volition, futurity, and new developments

Already in AG (cf. 2.3), the construction (ἐ)θέλω + Infinitive manifested a semantic 'split': on the one hand, it was normally used to convey the lexical meaning of volition and, on the other hand, it had acquired a grammatical status and was used as an AVC to convey the meaning of future reference as well as to express generic, timeless statements. This semantic divergence also became gradually syntactically marked starting in the H–R period, as the infinitival complementation of the lexical (ἐ)θέλω gave way slowly but surely to a clausal complementation introduced by ἵνα or to a bare finite (Subjunctive) form. In contrast, the TAM meanings were always conveyed by the (ἐ)θέλω + Infinitive construction, solidifying little by little into a syntactic / semantic divergence between the lexical and the grammatical verb which would prove crucial in the development of the AVC, as we shall see below (cf. 5.4). Following this line of development, the findings of the investigation on the lexical and the grammatical meaning(s) of the construction will be presented separately.

Regarding the volitional (ἐ)θέλω, what is of particular interest is the issue of complementation. The replacement of the Infinitive by a clausal complement constitutes part of a wider pattern of change, which ultimately resulted in the almost total loss of the Infinitive by the end of the Late Medieval period (15th c.) (for more details, cf. Joseph, 1983). Concerning the stages of this development, the traditional account has been oversimplified, according to the evidence provided by the investigation of (ἐ)θέλω. To be more precise, it has ignored the pattern V + V$_S$, already mentioned here on previous occasions (cf. 2.3–3.2). The texts of the H–R period suggest that this pattern was actually more productive than the alternative involving clausal complementation, as far as (ἐ)θέλω is concerned. It should be noted that the replacement of the Infinitive took place almost exclusively in cases of disjoint reference, that is to say in cases where the subject of the Infinitive was different from the subject of the verb, similar to the instances of the V + V$_S$ pattern in AG. The development of the complementation of volitional (ἐ)θέλω, as this is depicted in the non-papyri texts, is illustrated in Table 3.11.

As can be seen, the infinitival complementation is still the norm by far, while the instances of the V+V$_S$ pattern clearly outnumber those of clausal complementation. This fact has remained hitherto unnoticed, even though it should be expected given that this alternative existed even in AG. The abundance of attestations of non-infinitival complementation when disjoint reference is involved immediately suggests that this specific syntactic configuration was originally the target of change. This is expected, since it has been found that, cross-linguistically, the complement of "want" verbs has predominantly the same subject with the verb (Haspelmath, 1999a) and, therefore, the *less* frequent pattern, i.e. disjoint reference, would be the first to be replaced in case of syntactic change, according to the frequency effects

TABLE 3.11 Volitional (ἐ)θέλω in the H–R period (non-papyri)

Complement	3rd c. BC	1st c.BC–1st c.AD	1st c. AD	2nd c. AD	3rd c. AD	4th c. AD	Total
INF.	35	6	318	75	35	89	558 (92.7)
ἵνα+SUBJ (disj.)	–	–	9	–	–	2	11 (1.8)
ἵνα+SUBJ (co-ref.)	–	–	1	–	–	–	1 (0.2)
V$_S$(co-ref.)	1	1	24	3	–	3	32 (5.3)
TOTAL	36	7	352	78	35	94	602

already discussed. Surprisingly enough, there is one instance of a clausal complement involving a co-referent subject:

(14) 'Μᾶλλον θέλω',   φησίν, 'ἵν' ἐκεῖνος αὐτὰ ἀφέληται   ἢ ἵν' ἐγὼ
     More   want-1st PRES, says, that he these lose-3rd SUBJ. or that I
     μὴ πέμψω'.
     not send-1st SUBJ.
     "I prefer, [she] said, that he lose these rather than that I do not send [them]"

(*Diss.*, 2.7.8 / 1st c. AD)

This example is even more interesting since it is found in a text by Epictetus, which arguably belongs to a higher register of use than the other texts of the corpus[11] (Horrocks, 1997: 91). Furthermore, as it is taken from a dialogue, it leads us to assume that in spoken language the clausal complementation could have been more widespread than what the texts make us believe. The above example manifests one of the contexts that might have facilitated the generalization of the clausal complement in the case of co-referent subject: as a disjoint subject complement immediately follows the verb, the complement with co-referent subject that comes after could not presumably appear in an infinitival form (with the subject itself left unexpressed), as this would most probably invite a co-referential interpretation with the intervening disjoint subject, and not with the subject of the verb θέλω! Moreover, as the two complement clauses in (14) are contrasted in terms of their subject, this contrast is made more explicit by using the same complementation pattern.

The papyri comply with the picture emerging from the other texts of the H–R period. Generally, the Infinitive constitutes the dominant means of complementation for the volitional (ἐ)θέλω, while the two other alternatives already mentioned are also attested, with the same relevant token frequency of use, i.e. the V + V$_S$ pattern[12] being slightly more common than the ἵνα-clause. Moreover, (ἐ)θέλω, like ἔχω, constitutes the basis for a formula

---

[11] Therefore, it is excluded from the quantitative study of the period, but it is examined as representative of a different register, to control for the register factor in the development of the AVCs. The list of all texts consulted, but not included in the quantitative analysis, is given in the bibliography.

[12] Mandilaras (1973: 257) mentions this pattern, although he refers to it using the term "deliberative subjunctive", not being aware that it constituted a general pattern of complementation, as illustrated here.

76   *The future in Greek*

TABLE 3.12   Volitional (ἐ)θέλω in the H–R period (papyri)

Complement	3rd c. BC	2nd c. BC– 1st c. BC	1st c. AD	2nd c. AD	3rd c. AD	4th c. AD	Total
INF.	9	19	30	74	44	46	222 (93.4)
ἵνα+SUBJ (disj.)	–	–	1	1	–	–	2 (0.8)
V$_S$ (disj.)	1 (?)	–	–	5	5	1	12 (5.0)
V$_S$ (co-ref.)	–	–	–	1	–	1	2 (0.8)
TOTAL	10	19	31	81	49	48	238

("γι(γ)νώσκειν σὲ θέλω" "I'd like you to know"), very frequently attested in the papyri containing private and official correspondence (its attestations are excluded from the table). These observations are illustrated in Table 3.12.

The sole new development, not attested in the other textual sources and hitherto unknown, is the generalization of the V + V$_S$ pattern to include cases of co-referentiality, as in (15):

(15) εἰ μὲν σὺ θέλεις   ἀποσπάσῃς   τὴν φιλ[ί]αν,
      If prt you want-2nd PRES. end-2nd AOR.SUBJ. the friendhsip,
      ἔστω.
      be-3rd PRES.IMP.
      "if you want to end the friendship, so be it"

(*SB*, 10841rp r11 / 4th c. AD)

As with clausal complementation, the alternative V + V$_S$ pattern came gradually to be used in co-referential contexts, 'creeping' into the last context where the Infinitive was exclusively used in previous periods. The papyri fill in the picture drawn from the other textual sources regarding the complementation of the lexical verb, by showing that the two syntactic alternatives could be used in all contexts. However, the Infinitive appears—not only in the papyri but in all texts of this period—to constitute undoubtedly the norm in written language, despite the traces of its gradual weakening.

Of more interest to this investigation are the various TAM meanings that the (ἐ)θέλω AVC could convey in this period. Recall that in AG, this AVC was occasionally used as an FC and could also express genericness, i.e. timeless truths (cf. Table 2.7). However, in the corpus of the H–R period (papyri excluded), the (ἐ)θέλω AVC is hardly ever attested. The only possible example of a future-referring meaning for the (ἐ)θέλω construction comes from the very late stages of the period:

(16) καὶ διὰ τὴν πονηρίαν αὐτῶν, ἀσεβεῖς ὄντες, οὐ
and for the wickedness their, impious are-PCIPLE.PRES., not
θέλουσιν ἐκ νεκρῶν ἀναστῆναι, διὸ καὶ τὴν ἀνάστασιν
want-3rd PL.PRES. from dead rise-INF.AOR.PASS., hence and the resurrection
διαβάλλουσιν
mock-3rd PL.PRES.
"and because of their wickedness, as they are impious, they will not (?) / do not want to (?) rise from the dead, hence they mock the resurrection"

(*Constit. Apost.*, 6.26.16 / 4th c. AD)

This example comes from a text with advice against heretics, who, in this case, mock the resurrection; hence, although future reference would seem a plausible interpretation in this instance, the volitional meaning also looks at least equally possible: "they do not want to rise from the dead, and that's why they mock the resurrection". There is another example where a future-referring meaning might also be possible, this time from the New Testament:

(17) Τί θέλετέ μοι δοῦναι κἀγὼ ὑμῖν
What want-2nd PL.PRES. to-me give-INF.AOR. and-I to-you
παραδώσω αὐτόν;
deliver-1st SING.FUT. him
"what will you / are you willing to give me so that I give him to you?"

(*Matth.*, 26.15 / 1st c. AD)

Arguably, however, in this example the favored notion is intention, so (17) does not constitute a clear example of future reference but only of the path leading from volition, through intention, to futurity. This near-total absence of the future-referring meaning of the construction calls for an explanation, bearing in mind two facts: its limited, but still more frequent use in AG, and the relevant (more than 20 in number) attestations of the future-referring ἔχω AVC (cf. 3.2) in the very same texts. We will comment on these observations after the investigation of the contemporary papyri.

With regard to the generic meaning, it is attested in the texts of Epictetus (*Diss.* 1.2.17 / 3.13.3), a writer who, as already mentioned, could be placed in the middle register of use. A further investigation of three more contemporary authors whose language is comparable (if belonging to a higher register overall) to that of Epictetus, namely Strabo, Plutarch, and Pausanias, revealed that they all contained attestations of the (ἐ)θέλω AVC conveying either generic or habitual meaning, the latter being very close semantically to both volition and genericness (Bybee, Perkins, & Pagliuca, 1994: 157) (*Strabo*: 11.2.17[13] / *Quaest. Conv.* 678,D,5 / *Pausanias*: 3.26.3, 8.29.2, 8.54.2, 9.39.6). Apparently, the AVC was used in these meanings only in middle and higher registers of the written language requiring a specific sort of context (such as 'popular philosophy'), hence its absence in the other texts of the corpus.

Apart from these meanings already attested in AG (with the possible exception of habitual), the construction (ἐ)θέλω + Infinitive developed new modal meanings, frequently expressed cross-linguistically by FCs. The first of them is exemplified in (18):

(18) καὶ διηπόρουν, ἄλλος πρὸς ἄλλον λέγοντες, Τί   θέλει
and wondered one   prep other saying,   what want-3rd PRES.
τοῦτο εἶναι;
this be-INF.PRES?
"and they wondered, saying one to the other: What can / must this be?"

(*Acta*, 2.12 / 1st c. AD)

In this example, (ἐ)θέλω + Infinitive conveys rather unambiguously the modal meaning of epistemic possibility. The development of this meaning, which is once more attested in the same text (*Acta*, 17.20), illustrates the multi-functionality of the (ἐ)θέλω construction that will become even more evident below. Interestingly, although epistemic possibility is commonly expressed by FCs, it supposedly arises in the last stages of the development of an FC (Bybee, Perkins, & Pagliuca, 1994: 279). This prediction cannot easily account for the Greek data. There is no doubt that the (ἐ)θέλω AVC could convey future reference already in AG (cf. 2.3), and, strictly chronologically speaking, there had been a considerable lapse of time from that period to the texts of the New Testament (*ca.* 4–5 centuries). On the other hand, there is no indication whatsoever of an 'advanced' development of this FC: apparently, it was seldom used, and, more importantly, it is never found in the very same text that contains this instance of epistemic possibility meaning. Therefore, it seems unlikely that this meaning argues for an advanced stage of development of the (ἐ)θέλω FC. Rather, one should look for a different path of development.

Related to this issue is, perhaps, a further novelty, attested, unexpectedly enough, in the writings of a well-known grammarian of the 2nd c. AD, namely Apollonius Dyscolus. Apollonius is using the (ἐ)θέλω construction to convey a different, deontic meaning:

---

[13] Even though Strabo mentions that, in this line (probably a proverb), he cites Euripides.

(19) καὶ γὰρ τὰ πρωτότυπα θέλει   ὁπωσδήποτε περισπᾶσθαι...
     and prt the simple   want-3rd SING.PRES. absolutely   stress- INF.PRES.PASS.
     "and the simple (non-compounds) [adverbs] must absolutely be marked with a circumflex"

(*De adv.*, Part 2, 1.1, p. 158/2nd c. AD)

There are in total 15 attestations of this deontic meaning for the (ἐ)θέλω construction in similar contexts in Apollonius (e.g. *De pronom.*, Part 2, 1.1, p. 31 / p. 92, among others). In all these examples, the subject of θέλει is inanimate, suggesting that θέλει has a grammatical status, since the lexical verb would require an animate agent (and the possibility of metaphor is too far-fetched to consider in these cases). The deontic meaning in (19) is revealed and emphasized at the same time by the adverb ὁπωσδήποτε ("absolutely"). The development of such a modal meaning for this construction should not be regarded as unexpected, because the transition from "want" to "need" is very common and predictable, especially in case of a weakening of the semantic requirement for an animate subject: a "want" verb, when accompanying an inanimate subject, can readily be interpreted as "need", since inanimate subjects cannot have volition of their own by definition. In this case, this modal meaning does not presuppose the emergence of the future-referring meaning of the construction. It is rather unexpected, though, that the deontic modality is first attested in the writings of a grammarian who, particularly in this period of the rise of Atticism (cf. 1.3), must have been very cautious and rather prescriptive in his use of language. It is, consequently, fairly safe to assume that the use of (ἐ)θέλω to convey a deontic meaning was quite common and well established, at least in certain registers or dialects.

The emergence of the deontic meaning is interesting from a theoretical point of view as well. Despite the well-known and widely-documented association between deontic modality and futurity, especially in the 2nd person (cf., for example, Aijmar, 1985, among many others), it has been argued that FCs originating from volition verbs should not, in principle, exhibit uses belonging to a different semantic source of FCs, such as obligation (Bybee, Perkins, & Pagliuca, 1994: 257). However, the Greek data leaves no room for doubt that this restriction is too strong, and that FCs stemming from verbs of volition can also convey deontic meanings; in any case, Bybee, Perkins, & Pagliuca (1994: 257) admit that, in the case of this restriction, they have some "unresolved anomalies". It is proposed here that these "anomalies" need not arise at all if we consider that AVCs may also express meanings from various semantic paths, possibly (at least originally) unrelated; in the case of the (ἐ)θέλω construction, it could convey both deontic modality and futurity, probably through different paths: "want → intend" for the future, "want → need" for deontic modality. There is no reason to postulate an incompatibility of these two meanings being expressed by the same AVC, as the semantics of the Auxiliary can give rise to multiple modal developments (as with the ἔχω AVC, cf. 3.2). Moreover, this assumption also resolves the inconsistency between the presumed (but not justified by the data) 'advanced' stage of the (ἐ)θέλω FC in accordance with its conveying epistemic possibility. This meaning is easily derived from the deontic meaning of the (ἐ)θέλω construction, independently developed, as argued above: it is commonly accepted that deontic modalities give rise to epistemic modalities (already suggested by Horn, 1972). If we assume, accordingly, that the possibility meaning exemplified in (18) originates in the deontic meaning attested in contemporary works, then the apparent inconsistency of the early stage of development of the FC and availability of epistemic meaning never arises.

In the light of these facts, the examination of the papyri becomes even more crucial in order to arrive at a relatively clear picture for the (ἐ)θέλω AVC. As we have mentioned, the low-level (non-papyri) texts of the H–R period contain only two possible instances of the (ἐ)θέλω AVC, one perhaps conveying a future-referring meaning and the other epistemic possibility. Moreover, texts of the middle register contained attestations of two further meanings, the generic / habitual and the deontic. With regard to the future-referring meaning, the papyri provide five more instances where this interpretation is the preferred one, the clearest being the following:

(20) οὔπω   μέχρι σήμερον τὰ   πλοῖα τῆς ἀννώνας ἐξῆλθεν ἵνα
     not-yet till   today   the   ships of annona sailed so-that
     δυνηθῶμεν   ἐξελθεῖν. . . . λέγουσι δὲ ὅτι   μέχρι
     can-1stPL.AOR.SUBJ.   sail-INF.AOR. . . . say   prt that by
     15 θέλομεν
     15 want-1st PL.PRES.
     ἐξελθεῖν   σὺν θεῷ.
     sail-INF.AOR. with God
     "The ships of annona have not yet sailed, so that we be able to sail . . .
     But they say that by the 15th we will sail, God willing"

(*POxy*, 1763r10 / 3rd c. AD)

This example is the most unambiguously future-referring attestation of the (ἐ)θέλω AVC. Similarly unambiguous are two more attestations (*PBingen*, 74 / 2nd c. AD, *PRyl*, 691r9 / 3rd c. AD), while in another two cases the context provides no certain clue, even though future reference is possible (*PBad*, 35v8 / 1st c. AD – *SB*, 9026 / 2nd c. AD). These examples prove to a great extent that the (ἐ)θέλω AVC continued to be used as an FC in the H–R period.

If we compare these attestations with the relevant attestations of the equivalent ἔχω AVC in the papyri, which are six in number (if we include the three instances of ambiguity between future reference and possibility in the overall total), we can draw the conclusion that the two AVCs might have been equally (un)common in use, at least in the papyri. In the other texts of the period, though, the picture is completely different, with ἔχω being much more common than (ἐ)θέλω (the relevant numbers are 22 and 1(?), respectively). This inconsistency between the two types of texts is the only major one manifested with regard to the FCs. Are these facts reconcilable, then?

In the papyri, as with ἔχω, the future-referring (ἐ)θέλω AVC is found in low-register texts: the example (20) constitutes an excerpt from a note of a sailor, being therefore quite representative of the actual speech of that time. The other four possible examples of this meaning are all attested in private letters, supporting the assumption that the future-referring (ἐ)θέλω AVC must have been productive in the low registers of use, just like ἔχω. Apparently, though, the latter had already 'infiltrated' higher registers to some extent, i.e. the texts of those authors not aiming to imitate or achieve the 'eloquence' of the language of the Attic writers. It is very likely that there was a difference in register of use between the two constructions: the ἔχω AVC had wider application than the (ἐ)θέλω AVC which was presumably still restricted to the lower registers. The reason for this sociolinguistic specialization is now almost impossible to ascertain, but the equivalence of the ἔχω AVC with the Latin "habeo" AVC must have greatly facilitated the spread of ἔχω in contrast to (ἐ)θέλω (cf. 3.2).

A new development of the (ἐ)θέλω construction is attested solely in the papyri, from the 3rd c. AD onwards: the construction is now used in requests (cf. also Mandilaras, 1973: 251–2), in which case (ἐ)θέλω appears either in the Subjunctive (21) or in the Imperative (22):

(21) κύριε ἡμῶν αδελφαι. μὴ θέλῃς αμαιλησαι [leg. ἀμελῆσαι]
 lord our brother. not want-2nd SING.SUBJ. disregard-INF.AOR.
 "our dear brother: please, do not disregard [this case]"

 (*PWisc*, 74r20 / 4th c. AD)

(22) θέλησον ὅσον χρήζουσι ἔν τε σίτῳ ἢ οξους [leg. ὄξει]
 want-2nd IMP.AOR. as-much they-need in prt grain or vinegar
 παρασχοῦ αὐτοῖς
 provide-2nd IMP.AOR. to-them
 "please, provide them with grain and vinegar, as much as they need"

 (*POxy*, 1776r6 / late 4th c. AD)

The example in (22) constitutes a further stage in this development in comparison to (21), since, in this case, (ἐ)θέλω, attested in the Imperative, is followed by a verb again in the Imperative (παρασχοῦ), and it consequently functions as an uninflected form not adding much to the propositional meaning of the utterance, similarly to particles such as "please". This particle-like usage is straightforwardly reminiscent of the classical Latin (negative) Imperative particle "noli / nolite", an observation that, combined with an exact parallel in French (e.g. "Veuillez aller"="Please, go"), illustrates that such a usage is typical for volitional verbs, at least in the Indo-European language family.

Finally, another previously unknown development (with regard to this period) is also manifested in the papyri, namely the disjunctive θέλεις ... θέλεις ... :

(23) πρὸς τὸ αιξουσιαν [leg. ἐξουσίαν] αὐτ[ὸ]ν αιχιν [leg. ἔχειν] δεια ταύτης μου
prep the authority   him have-INF.PRES.   through this mine
τῆς ἐντολῆς θέλης   πωλει   θέλης   χαρίζεσθαι
the act want-2nd SING.PRES. sell-INF? want-2nd SING. PRES. offer-INF.
[τὴ]ν δούλην μου [θ]εοδωρα ...
the slave mine Theodora
"in order that he has the authority, through this act of mine, to either sell or give away my slave Theodora ..."

(*POxy*, 2771r6 / 4th c. AD)

Even though this new non-lexical use of (ἐ)θέλω is not surprising by itself, since there is a close cross-linguistic parallel again from Latin ("vel ... vel") and there is also another example in the papyri which illustrates the semantic path leading to this construction,[14] its attestation in the papyri of this period is remarkable and of interest to us for a different reason: as this construction is still in use today in Modern Greek, and the next (in chronological order) example is found in a text of the 10th century (!) (cf. 4.3), this attestation of the disjunctive θέλεις reveals quite emphatically our limited knowledge of the actual linguistic developments in the spontaneous, spoken language of this period.

It has been mentioned that in the non-papyri texts there are—limited—instances of other TAM uses of the (ἐ)θέλω construction: one conveying epistemic possibility is attested in the religious texts of the corpus, while the

---

[14] *PTebt*, 421 / 3rd c. AD: ἀλλὰ θέλις αὐτὸ πωλῆσα[ι] πώλησον, θέλις αὐτὸ ἀφεῖναι τῇ θυγατρί σ[ου] ἄφες. "but if you want to sell it, sell it, if you want to leave it to your daughter, leave it".

generic and the deontic meanings are attested in works of middle register. In the papyri, the generic meaning is not found, which is to be expected given the register of these texts, which mostly deal with everyday matters. The modal meaning of possibility is also not attested, a fact probably indicative of its infrequent use. There exists, however, one example where the deontic interpretation for the construction is preferable:

(24) οἶδας ὅθι [leg. ὅτι] καὶ τὰ ἐνέχυρα ἡ[μ]ῶν ἔξω εἰσὶν καὶ ὁ πατὴρ ἡμῶν
    know that   and the loans ours out are and the father ours
Διόσκορος ἔχρησεν ἡμῖν καὶ αὐτὸν θέλομεν πληρῶσαι·
Dioskorus lent us and him want-1st PL.PRES. pay-INF.AOR.
διὸ σπουδή σοι γενέσθω συνβαλέσθαι αὐτῷ
for-this haste to-you become pay-INF.AOR. him
"You know that our loans are out (?) and that our father Dioskorus has lent us [money] and that we need to pay him. So, hasten to give him money…"

(POxy, 3419 / 4th c. AD)

Although a volitional reading is not excluded, the context arguably favors a deontic interpretation. This example, though unique, lends some justification to the abundance of attestations of such a modal meaning in the writings of Appollonius Dyscolus, which should arguably presuppose a rather extensive use of the deontic (ἐ)θέλω AVC.

The discussion above reveals an important difference between the future-referring AVCs: the (ἐ)θέλω construction acquired a great variety of TAM meanings in a range of different registers following different paths of grammaticalization, while ἔχω and especially μέλλω had more specialized uses. On the other hand, the (ἐ)θέλω AVC is in general quite rare, despite this semantic and sociolinguistic variation. This is depicted in Table 3.13, which illustrates

TABLE 3.13 The (ἐ)θέλω AVC in the H–R period

Meaning	3rd c. BC–1st c. BC	1st c. AD	2nd c. AD	3rd c. AD	4th c. AD	Total
Future-ref.	–	1	2	2	1(?)	6
Possibility (epistemic)	–	2	–	–	–	2
Deontic	–	–	–	–	1	1
Requests	–	–	–	3	13	16
TOTAL	–	3	2	5	15	25

the token frequency of TAM meanings of (ἐ)θέλω + Infinitive both in the papyri and the other textual sources (excluding the texts belonging to middle registers).

Regarding the past form ἤθελον, contrary to the development of εἶχον + Infinitive which must have been associated with the development of the equivalent present form, no attestation of any non-lexical meaning has been found. Apparently, no such meaning of the (ἐ)θέλω construction was analogically extended to the past form, probably because of their limited use. It will be seen that the two forms of the (ἐ)θέλω AVC had mostly divergent developments (cf. mainly ch. 5).

Concerning the grammatical status of the (ἐ)θέλω AVC, all the observations with regard to ἔχω apply also to (ἐ)θέλω: morphologically, even though (ἐ)θέλω is still frequently used in the participial form, none of the future-referring attestations occurs in this non-finite form; and, syntactically, (ἐ)θέλω + Infinitive were apparently very tightly linked when they conveyed future reference (Adjacent: 5/6, 83%). Recall that, in AG (cf. 2.3), in only 30% of the future-referring examples of this construction were the two elements adjacent. Although the actual number of attestations is too small to draw firm conclusions, there seems to be a development in terms of bondedness, which would be expected as the construction became more and more grammatical.

On the whole, the (ἐ)θέλω AVC continued to be used as an FC in the H–R period, probably in the lower registers. Simultaneously, it developed into a multi-functional form, as it could convey a wide variety of TAM meanings, either related to the FC (generic) or as possible independent developments (deontic, possibility, requests). In all such instances, the verb was complemented by an Infinitive. However, the volitional (ἐ)θέλω was occasionally complemented by a bare finite form (Subjunctive) or a subordinate ἵνα– clause. Contrary to what is traditionally assumed, the former was more common than the latter, at least in this period. Finally, the present and the past forms of the construction apparently followed completely different paths, as ἤθελον was still solely used in its lexical meaning.

3.4 Conclusions: the interaction of three AVCs

In the H-R period, all three AVCs were used in the domain of future reference. The two AVCs built on μέλλω and (ἐ)θέλω could convey the future-referring meaning already in AG (with μέλλω having obviously a much wider use), while ἔχω + Infinitive became an FC during this period. These three constructions were not equivalent in all respects. Sociolinguistically speaking, μέλλω was most readily accepted in all registers of use, as it had a wide applicability and was presumably associated with the language of the classical period, whereas the other two AVCs originated from the lower registers, but ἔχω came to be more easily accepted in middle registers, while (ἐ)θέλω remained restricted and was not used outside low-register texts. Apart from this sociolinguistic difference, there were specific semantic / pragmatic contexts particular to only one of the AVCs: only εἶχον, for instance, could be used in counterfactuals. Furthermore, the different lexical meanings of the three constructions played, as expected, an important role in their distribution: this is easy to tell in the case of (ἐ)θέλω, which could express a variety of TAM meanings related to its volitional meaning.

Moreover, new accounts have been put forward concerning the semantic route of emergence of various meanings of the AVCs, and typological predictions were found to be too restrictive, since multiple modal branching has apparently been quite common in the diachronic development of the Greek AVCs. Finally, regarding the grammaticalization stage, we have argued extensively that μέλλω + Infinitive constituted an AVC in early stages of grammaticalization, although it started to show evidence of further grammaticalization beginning this period. Schematically, the various properties of the FCs in the H–R period are shown in Table 3.14.

TABLE 3.14 Properties of AVCs in H–R Greek

Properties	Μέλλω	Ἔχω	(Ἐ)θέλω
1. Futurity	✓	✓	✓
2. Other TAM meanings			
a. Obligation	✓ (?)	✓ (?)	✓
b. Possibility	–	✓	–
c. Epist. possibility	–	–	✓
d. Generic	–	–	✓
e. Ability	–	✓	–
f. Requests	–	–	✓
3. Past form			
a. Futurity	✓	–	–
b. Counterfact.	–	✓	–
4. Reduction of morph. paradigm (non-availability of non-finite forms)	–	✓	✓
5. Register			
a. Low	✓	✓	✓
b. Middle	✓	✓ (?)	–
c. High	✓	–	–

On the whole, despite the seeming similarity at first glance, the three constructions diverged in important respects, in relation to their semantic, syntactic, and sociolinguistic properties. Consequently, their parallel existence should not come as a surprise but should be seen as a manifestation of the fluctuation of the domain of future reference, especially in a period when the whole verbal system was being restructured.

4

Early Medieval Greek (5th–10th c. AD): the misty transition

Introduction

The end of the 4th century sees the end of antiquity, since in the subsequent centuries the political, social, and cultural environment alters dramatically not only in the Eastern Mediterranean but in Western Europe as well. In the Greek-speaking world, from the beginning of the 5th c., the new Byzantine empire was being gradually built. This process was not smooth but rather full of both external and internal problems and crises: invasions by the Arabs, the Avars, the Slavs, and other tribes / "nations" on the one hand, which, despite the heavy territorial losses, did not destroy the Byzantine power, but also, and perhaps more importantly, a religious crisis of extreme magnitude, spanning over a century (8th–9th c.), concerning the sacredness of icons, the so-called "Iconoclasm". This crisis took a heavy toll on every aspect of the social life of the empire, and, therefore, on the study and even the production of texts (for more details, cf. ODB, 1991: 975–7, Bryer & Herrin, 1977 and Schreiner, 1988). It is widely assumed that this "war of the icons" constitutes one of the main reasons for the scarcity of texts surviving from this period, in particular from the mid-8th till the mid-9th c. This scarcity led many scholars to label this period, especially from the 7th till the 9th c., the "Dark Ages" of Byzantium.

Even though recent studies have shown that the so-called "Dark Ages" were not so dark as originally presumed (cf., for example, Kazhdan, 1999 and Kountoura-Galaki, 2001, for a collection of papers regarding this period), still an important fact remains: the textual sources for Early Medieval Greek (EMG) are scarce not only in absolute terms but in comparison with the previous and the subsequent periods. And, more importantly, the low-register texts surviving from Early Medieval times are very limited, for a number of reasons: the religious texts, which proved to be quite helpful for the Roman period, are now written in their vast majority in a more elaborated style, mainly due to the establishment of the Christian Church as the official religion of the empire and an altered, more favorable attitude towards the language of the classical period by high-profile figures of the Church, such as John Chrysostom, already from the early 5th c. On the other hand, papyri are still available for the beginning of this period, but they become exceedingly rare and are no longer to be found after the 8th c., since papyrus is replaced by other writing materials, less costly and easier to obtain. In any event, Egypt and North Africa, i.e. the area where most of the Greek papyri are found, fell into Arab hands in the 7th c., and, even though some documents were still written in Greek under Arab rule, Arabic quickly asserted itself as the dominant language in these areas (cf. Haldon, 1997). As a result, the Early Medieval period is probably the least documented period in the history of the Greek language, at least with regard to low-register texts.

Consequently, the close tracking of the linguistic developments attested in EMG becomes an almost impossible task, especially after the 8th c. Before that time, there still exist ample papyri (some of which belong to rather low registers), various religious texts, and the first Byzantine chronicles written in a style relatively devoid of archaizing features. After the 8th c. though, there are only occasional chronicles and very few other texts to help us follow the developments under investigation. This lack of evidence is in sharp contrast with the evidence of the Late Medieval period, which is relatively richly documented, particularly from the 12th c. onwards. Despite all these problems, an attempt will be made to trace as accurately as possible the developments of the AVCs in EMG.

4.1 Μέλλω + Infinitive: apparent stability

At first glance, no significant development can be observed in EMG with regard to the μέλλω AVC. The semantic range of meanings conveyed remains stable, the variety of morphological forms of μέλλω used is not diminished, and the syntactic properties of this AVC seem unchanged. I would like to suggest, though, that this apparent stability is mostly due to the problematic textual sources of this period, and hides possible developments in the lower registers of use. This observation rests mainly on the basis of the pattern of complementation of μέλλω, which, as already mentioned (cf. 3.1), becomes a useful guide in order to determine the actual register of the relevant texts.

It has been shown (cf. 2.1 and 3.1) that the type of Infinitive complementing μέλλω changed from the Future and the Present (and rarely the Aorist) in AG, to the Present and the Aorist (and only rarely the Future) in the H–R period. It has also been argued that, even though the Present Infinitive could convey both perfective and imperfective aspect, the Aorist Infinitive could be seen as the prototypical form expressing the perfective aspect, and its use can be associated with the need for explicitness in the aspectual domain, especially from speakers who either did not know the classical pattern or were uncertain of the semantic properties of the Present Infinitive, hence the proliferation of the Aorist Infinitive in the lower registers.

The Aorist Infinitive as a complement of μέλλω remains in use throughout the EMG period: for instance, it is attested four times (Caput LXXVI / LXXVIII / CLXXVI / CLXXX)[1] in the *Spiritual Meadow* by John Moschos, a text traditionally assumed to represent, at times quite faithfully, the actual speech of the educated of the 6th c. (cf. Browning, 1983: 35 and Horrocks, 1997: 185–8), since it is written in a straightforward and plain style, containing extensive dialogue. From the very end of the period comes an interesting and previously unknown example of this complementation, in the death poem for Constantine VII:

(1) ἔμελλεν   ἡ γλυκύτης   σου, δέσποτα Κωνσταντίνε,
    will-3rd PRET. the sweetness yours, lord   Constantine,
    δριμύξαι   τῶν   ποθούντων   σε τὰ σπλάγχνα μετὰ τέλος.
    hurt-INF.AOR. the-GEN. mourn-PCIPLE.PRES. you the inside prep end
    "Your sweetness, lord Constantine, would deeply hurt the hearts of those who miss you after your passing"

(*Death Poems*, 14–15 / 959–60 AD)

This is the only instance of the μέλλω AVC in these four songs on the death of emperors (the first three on Leo VI and the fourth on Constantine VII). Apart from the complementation pattern, it also illustrates the uninterrupted use of the past form equivalent of the AVC to convey the futurity-in-the-past meaning. On the complementation issue, it is noteworthy that Constantine himself also used the μέλλω + INF.AOR. pattern quite frequently in his writings, as illustrated in (2):

---

[1] It should be noted that Moschos does not often use the Aorist Infinitive after μέλλω. The Present Infinitive is found 17 times in this construction, while there are also four cases of the Future Infinitive, certainly obsolete at that time. The frequency of the attestations of the Aorist Infinitive will be extensively discussed below.

(2) ἰδόντες τὸν ῥῆγα Πιπῖνον μετὰ τῆς ἑαυτοῦ δυνάμεως κατ' αὐτῶν
seeing the king Pipinos with the his-own force against them
ἐπερχόμενον καὶ μέλλοντα   μετὰ τῶν ἵππων ἀποπλεῦσαι
coming   and will-PCIPLE.PRES. with the horses sail-INF.AOR.
πρὸς τὴν νῆσον τοῦ   Μαδαμαύκου
to   the island the-GEN. Madamaukos
"When they saw that the King Pipinos with his force was coming against them and that he would sail to the island of Madamaukos together with his horses..."

(*De adm. imp.* 28, 24 / 10th c.)[2]

Consequently, it is safe to conclude that the construction μέλλω + Aorist Infinitive does not constitute a peculiarity of the papyri or even of the H–R period but a widely existing pattern which clearly survived into Byzantine times, at least up to the 10th c. Nevertheless, there is a sharp contrast between the complementation pattern attested in the textual sources and that found in the papyri of EMG, which unfortunately only go up to the 8th c. These two patterns are shown in Tables 4.1[3] and 4.2:

TABLE 4.1. Infinitival complementation of μέλλω (non-papyri)

Complement	5th c.	6th c.	7th c.	8th–9th c.	10th c.	Total
PRES	122 (80.8)	38 (64.4)	61 (85.9)	39 (81.3)	42 (51.9)	302 (73.6)
FUT	21 (13.9)	13 (22.0)	2 (2.8)	4 (8.3)	12 (14.8)	52 (12.7)
AOR	8 (5.3)	8 (13.6)	8 (11.3)	5 (10.4)	27 (33.3)	56 (13.7)
TOTAL	151	59	71	48	81	410

TABLE 4.2 Infinitival complementation of μέλλω (papyri)

Complement	5th c.	6th c.	7th c.	8th c.	Total
PRES	1	6	–	–	7 (10.8)
FUT	2	3	–	–	5 (7.7)
AOR	2	19	3	29	53 (81.5)
TOTAL	5	28	3	29	65

---

[2] Cf. also ibid. 29.165 / 29.203 / 42.35 et al.
[3] The appearance of a relatively high number of the Future Infinitive should be attributed to the middle register of the writings of Constantine VII Porphyrogenitus, and not to any real revival of this pattern.

It is evident that, while in the papyri the Aorist Infinitive is definitely the norm in the complementation of μέλλω, this is not the case for the other textual sources, where, first, the Future Infinitive is still in use, and, second, the Aorist Infinitive is relatively rarely represented, the Present Infinitive being the dominant complement. Compared to the picture of the H–R period (cf. 3.1), there is one major difference: in the previous period, both the papyri and the other texts converged in the domination of the Present Infinitive as the most frequent means of complementation for μέλλω; in EMG, the papyri (especially of the last two centuries) provide almost exclusively instances of the Aorist Infinitive, while the non-papyri texts contain only occasional attestations of this type of Infinitive.

Arguably, this important difference can be attributed to the different register which the papyri and the other textual sources belong to. In other words, the latter were written by people who had—to a greater or lesser extent—a good grasp of the Greek language and, more precisely, of AG syntax and morphology, and thus could be seen as representatives of a middle register of use. On the other hand, the personal papyri, as is well known, were often written by people with a limited competence in Greek, and especially in AG; for instance, all the occurrences of the Aorist Infinitive in the 8th c. are attested in a corpus of correspondence of an Arabian ruler of Egypt (Korrah ben Scharik), who, apparently, was competent enough to use the μέλλω construction often, but only with the post-classical Aorist Infinitive. The sociolinguistic distribution of the complement of μέλλω is further illustrated by examples such as found in a text of the 5th century, namely *Historia monachorum,* where there are only two instances of μέλλω + Aorist Infinitive (9.6 / 9.58), both in the context of reported speech, which must have been considered as appropriate for the use of such a low-register pattern.

The clearest indication, though, in support of this sociolinguistic analysis comes from a later period, from the texts of the emperor Constantine VII. In the prologues of two of his works, namely *De adm. imp.* and *De cerimoniis,* he explicitly states (in Attic) that he (thereafter) writes in an everyday language, avoiding features of a "high", "learned" style. As far as we can tell, this is mostly true, since the language of these texts is considerably different from his other writings.[4] With regard to μέλλω, there are 78 instances of the AVC to be found, 26 of which involve the use of the Aorist Infinitive (33%) (cf. ex. 2). Similar research into another historical text of his, namely *De insidiis,* written in a more elaborated style, illuminates a striking difference: in a total of 49

---

[4] For a more detailed analysis of the language of these texts and, in general, of all the writings of the emperor, cf. Moravcsik (1938).

attestations of the particular construction, only three involve an Aorist Infinitive (6% approximately). This contrast provides reliable evidence in favor of a socially determined choice of the Infinitive in the construction of μέλλω, as the texts come from the very same writer, who consciously chooses, in the case of the first two "popular" works, to use the Aorist Infinitive much more often, and then, in the case of his historical work, to hardly use it at all. On the other hand, this fact does not imply that the μέλλω AVC as such was characterized as being rather low-register, since this would be refuted by the vast number of attestations of this construction in works of learned writers, which should be contrasted with the relatively limited number of instances of the other future-referring AVCs (ἔχω / θέλω[5] + Infinitive) in such contexts. This point will be discussed after the investigation of the other AVCs.

The sociolinguistic distribution of the complement of μέλλω, hitherto unknown, can shed light on a "mystery" associated with μέλλω. To be more precise, the observation that in Medieval Cypriot μέλλω + Infinitive was replaced by μέλλω + νά + Aorist Subjunctive is not surprising, according to my findings and *contra* Aerts (1983), who obviously was not aware either of the papyrological or of the Byzantine data and expected the Present Subjunctive instead, according to the pattern shown in Table 4.1.

It is more important to note that the divergence of the evidence between the papyri and the non-papyri textual sources reveals that the evidence in the latter cannot be taken at face value, since these texts only occasionally contain patterns of everyday language. Therefore, they are bound to obscure the linguistic developments occurring in this period, not only as far as μέλλω is concerned but in general. This is clearly exemplified in the case of ἐλπίζω, a verb whose complementation, even though originally similar to that of μέλλω, started diverging in the H–R period, a fact possibly related to the inclusion of μέλλω in the core of more frequent, grammatical verbs that retained their infinitival complements after the advent of clausal complements (cf. 5.1). Again, the papyri dating from EMG reveal a completely different pattern from the one found in the non-papyri texts, as shown in Tables 4.3 and 4.4, respectively.

The striking contrast between the papyri and the other textual sources is entirely clear: while the papyri contain only instances of a clausal complementation for ἐλπίζω (with just one exception), the other texts categorically favor an infinitival complement. Given that we know that the overall development

---

[5] From this point onwards, the form θέλω instead of (ἐ)θέλω will be exclusively used, since the latter becomes rare in EMG and is mainly restricted to the archaizing texts of the higher registers.

TABLE 4.3 Complementation of ἐλπίζω (papyri)

Complement	5th c.	6th c.	7th c.	8th c.	Total
ἵνα-clause	2	–	–	–	2 (11.8)
ὅτι-clause	1	10	2	1	14 (82.4)
INF.AOR	–	1	–	–	1 (5.8)
TOTAL	3	11	2	1	17

TABLE 4.4 Complementation of ἐλπίζω (non-papyri)

Complement	5th c.	6th c.	7th c.	8th–9th c.	10th c.	Total
ὅτι-clause	–	–	3	–	1	4 (11.1)
INF.PRES	3	2	1	1	2	9 (25.0)
INF.AOR	4	1	5	9	2	21 (58.3)
INF.FUT	1	–	–	1	–	2 (5.6)
TOTAL	8	3	9	11	5	36

proceeded along the lines indicated by the papyri, resulting in the replacement of the Infinitive by a subordinate clause, the evidence presented above argues quite clearly for a lack of trustworthiness in the non-papyri textual sources of EMG, at least with respect to lower registers.

Therefore, regarding the μέλλω AVC, its apparent stability in all linguistic levels (with the possible exception of the proliferation of the Aorist Infinitive in its complementation pattern) is most probably a result of the problems in the textual evidence and does not represent an actual stage of stability in its use in the lower registers. This will become convincingly clear when the evidence from the following period is presented (cf. 5.1). Moreover, the evidence of the papyri suggests that μέλλω became increasingly differentiated from the other future-referring lexical verbs, since it could not be complemented by a subordinate clause (cf. Table 4.2), contrary to ἐλπίζω (and, presumably, most of the other verbs of this class by that time), which were almost exclusively complemented by a subordinate clause (cf. Table 4.3). The contrast between μέλλω and the complementation pattern of other, lexical future-referring verbs, originating in the H–R period (cf. 3.1), is now beyond doubt established. Even though corroborating semantic or morphosyntactic evidence is lacking, indirect evidence (the difference with ἐλπίζω in terms of complementation) argues that the μέλλω AVC has progressed a stage in the grammaticalization chain.

4.2 Ἔχω + Infinitive: the dominant AVC

The construction ἔχω + Infinitive proliferates in the texts of EMG, the papyri included. Bănescu (1915) cites numerous examples of this FC from this period, and all subsequent investigations (cf., for example, Aerts, 1965, Joseph, 1983, Horrocks, 1997) seem to agree that it constituted, if not the dominant means overall, at least the dominant AVC to express future reference. This well-known fact is further supported by this investigation: ἔχω + Infinitive is richly attested throughout the period, both in the papyri and the non-papyri texts. No attention has been paid, though, to the sociolinguistic parameters of its distribution, i.e. the genre and the register of the texts wherein it is found.

In the H–R period this FC could be regarded as a feature mostly of low-register texts and, presumably, of low-register oral communicative contexts (cf. 3.2). This situation gradually changes, so that by the end of the Early Medieval period, ἔχω + Infinitive could be used in texts of a rather higher register, as is the case for some works of the emperor Constantine Porphyrogenitus, as we shall see below.

Interesting in this respect is the *Spiritual Meadow*; Browning (1983: 35) has attempted a survey of all FCs attested in this work, which, according to his count, amount to 55 attestations in total. It is rather unfortunate that he does not provide us with the exact number of attestations for each form, even though he argues that the most frequent FC is the Present Tense. In any case, the actual number given above is proven to be inaccurate: the ἔχω AVC is attested 31 times conveying a future-referring meaning and the equivalent μέλλω AVC is attested 25 times. Obviously, the total number of all FCs is much higher than the one given by Browning, since two of the forms alone amount to 56 attestations. More interesting, though, is the relative number of attestations of these two constructions: despite the high frequency of μέλλω, the ἔχω AVC is even more frequent, according to the figures given above. In most other texts, when μέλλω is frequently used, the other AVCs are less common, a fact that can be attributed to the higher register of use for μέλλω: when writers are competent enough in Greek to regularly use the μέλλω AVC, they avoid employing the other semantically similar AVCs. In the case of the *Spiritual Meadow*, the altered picture can be attributed to a great extent to the particular character of the text, which contains prose and dialogue intermixed. Ἔχω + Infinitive as an FC is almost exclusively found in the dialogue parts, as in (3):

(3) «Κύρι ἀββά, ἄρτι ἔχω   ἀποθανεῖν». Καὶ μετὰ τρεῖς ἡμέρας

Father abbot, soon have-1st PRES. die-INF.AOR. And after three days
ἀνεπάη
died
"'Father abbot, I will die soon'. And after three days he died."

(*Spiritual Meadow*, Caput v)

On that basis, it can be argued that, regarding ἔχω + Infinitive, the text by Moschos reflects a transitional period in terms of register, whereby ἔχω is found alongside μέλλω in the domain of future reference, even though it is only attested in dialogue. Importantly, Moschos sees no reason to replace ἔχω by μέλλω in these instances, a fact that reveals both the plain style of this particular text but, more interestingly, the easy acceptance of the ἔχω AVC by a writer who uses μέλλω almost as often as ἔχω. Moreover, the same situation regarding the ἔχω AVC is observed in the texts of Leontius (7th c.), which contain eight instances of this AVC with a future-referring meaning, all of them in dialogue. Recall that, on the basis of the evidence concerning μέλλω (cf. 4.1), we have argued that these texts of EMG belong most probably to a middle register of use. The pattern they exhibit regarding ἔχω should therefore be expected: on the one hand, as this AVC becomes more popular and acceptable in higher registers, it is often included in texts of middle register; on the other hand, as it has yet to reach the—higher—status of μέλλω in terms of sociolinguistic prestige, it is mostly restricted in parts reflecting the everyday language, i.e. dialogues.

It is interesting to note this correlation between the rise in the frequency of use of an AVC and its rise in the sociolinguistic scale: as the ἔχω AVC became more frequent in lower registers, it became more acceptable in middle registers. The same observation will be made in relation to the θέλω FC (cf. ch. 5). This sociolinguistic parameter has not been properly explored in grammaticalization studies, and it will be discussed further below (cf. ch. 6).

Corroborating evidence for the ascent of this construction into higher registers comes from a papyrus:

(4) οὐκ ἔχει   ἡσυχάσαι,   ἀλλὰ καὶ   γονιορτον[leg. κονιορτὸν]
    not have-3rd PRES. calm-INF.AOR., but and trouble
    ἐγερεῖ   πάντως κατὰ   τῶν μοναστηρίων καὶ καθ' ἑνὸς 1
    raise-3rd FUT. adv   against the abbeys   and against one
    ἑκάστου   ἡμῶν.
    each   of-us
    "...he will not calm down, but he will create trouble to all abbeys and to every one of us"

(*PFuad*, 86r10 / 6th c.)

In this example, the future-referring ἔχει ἡσυχάσαι is attested in the apodosis of a future-referring conditional, alongside the ancient morphological Future Tense (ἐγερεῖ), a fact that constitutes by itself an indication of the ἔχω AVC 'infiltrating' higher registers than it was originally associated with, since the Future Tense, and especially in the contracted form (ἐγερεῖ) used for this type of verb, should be considered if not obsolete for EMG, at least indicative of an official text (Bănescu, 1915: 21–3). This example, combined with the evidence from Moschos and Leontius, leads us fairly naturally to assume that ἔχω + Infinitive as an FC is no longer restricted to low registers.

It has been established that the ἔχω AVC gained middle and higher registers in this period. As to its frequency of use, it was fairly common in texts of all these centuries. It is continuously attested in the papyri (e.g. *PSI*, 301 / 5th c., *PFuad*, 86r10 / 6th c., *SB*, 4635 / 7th c.), and it outnumbers the instances of the ability meaning in the texts of every century of EMG, irrespective of the fact that these texts are very limited in number. It is already suggested that these two factors, frequency of use and sociolinguistic registers of use, correlate. By the 10th c., ἔχω + Infinitive found its way into two of the works of the emperor Constantine VII Porphyrogenitus, specifically those that he himself states have been written in an everyday language (cf. 4.1), as in (5):

(5) ἐπειδὴ   ἔχειν   ἔχομεν   μετὰ τῶν   Ῥωμαίων μάχας
     because   have-INF.PRES.   have-1st PL. PRES.   with the Romans   war
     καὶ πολέμια
     and fighting
     "because we shall have war and fighting with the Romans…"

(*De adm. imp.*, 46.133 / 10th c.)

The very fact that the ἔχω AVC is attested in the writings of an emperor, even though less often than the μέλλω construction (cf. 4.1), argues quite convincingly in favour of the generalization of use for ἔχω in middle registers. The same conclusion can be drawn on the basis of another text, a letter from the well-known and highly educated scholar Arethas (9th–10th c.) to the ruler of Damascus, on the alleged 'superiority' of the Christian religion. In this letter, written obviously in a style aiming to facilitate understanding from a non-native speaker of Greek, Arethas utilizes the future-referring ἔχω six times (e.g. *opus 26*, p.234 / 27–8, p.243 / 17–18). Given the high level of education of Arethas, which would not allow him to use any "vulgar" construction in any official context, and the fact that the very same text also contains synthetic future tenses and instances of the μέλλω AVC (three occurrences for each form), both undoubtedly related to a rather elaborated style, we can quite safely assume that the ἔχω FC must have found its place in the middle registers of use by that time, if not earlier.

Despite the apparent generalization of use for ἔχω + Infinitive, there is one example in *Spiritual Meadow* of a construction that slightly undermines this conclusion, although from a different aspect. This example is shown in (6):

(6) Βλέπεις, ἀδελφὴ Μαρία, ποίας ἁμαρτίας ἔχω, καὶ δι' ἐμὲ ὑμεῖς ὅλοι
    See,   sister   Maria, what sins   I-have, and for-me you   all
ἕξετε   ἀπολέσθαι.
have-1st PL.FUT. lose-INF.AOR.PASS.
"You see, sister Mary, what sins I have, and because of me you will be all lost"

(*Spiritual Meadow*, Caput LXXVI)

In this case, the verb ἔχω is found in its old Future form ἕξω, which was still independently in use in the early centuries of this period, both in the papyri and the various other textual sources (cf. Mandilaras, 1973: 175 and Bǎnescu, 1915: 23, respectively). In (6), the construction 'ἕξετε ἀπολέσθαι' conveys most probably a future-referring meaning (although a possibility meaning is not excluded), not only because of the favorable context but also because the synonymous μέλλετε ἀπολέσθαι is attested a few lines below this example, in the very same context. Even though Browning (1983: 35) mentions this construction, he makes no comment with regard to its possible significance: it is very plausible that it constituted an attempt to strengthen the future reference of the ἔχω AVC by using the old Future form of the verb. If this assumption is correct, then a likely conclusion would be that the future-referring meaning of ἔχω + Infinitive was not yet totally evident or acceptable in EMG, at least for some speakers, and as a result it could / should be strengthened. This example might then be seen as an attempt, perhaps by a relatively educated person such as Moschos, to construct a less opaque FC by using the ancient Future Tense of ἔχω to highlight the future reference of the AVC. However, the construction ἕξω + Infinitive is not attested even once in the whole corpus of the papyri, and is to be found nowhere else in the other textual sources. Moreover, the rather problematic edition of the *Spiritual Meadow*, dating from the 19th c., provides no safe ground for conclusions. For these reasons, the evidence of this example cannot be considered as conclusive concerning the development of the ἔχω AVC in EMG.[6]

Apart from the future-referring meaning and its development, the ἔχω construction continued to convey the old ability meaning, although less

---

[6] Nevertheless, Bǎnescu (1915: 59–60) mentions two instances of an FC ἕξω + Participle, the first in *Syntipas* (11th c.) and the second in Chalkokondyles (15th c.). The fact that both texts are written in a non-vernacular, quite elaborated style fits well with the scenario sketched above for the attestation of a similar construction (involving an infinitival complementation, though) in the *Spiritual Meadow*. Notice also that an exactly equivalent construction is attested in Old Italian (Rohlfs, 1949: 384), manifesting perhaps a common pathway. In any case, the evidence is too meagre to allow for any firm conclusions.

frequently than before. More interestingly, further morphosyntactic developments of the ἔχω AVC are first attested in EMG. In one example found in the papyri, the AVC is used in a context where the Subjunctive would be normally expected:

(7) καὶ τὴν δὲ ἐπιστολήν... γράφω καὶ ἀποδίδωμι μετὰ καὶ προσκυνήσεως
and the prt letter...   write and deliver   with and reverence
μήπως καὶ μετὰ ταῦτα ζητῆσαι   ἔχει   σου   ἡ δεσποτεία
in-case and after these ask-INF.AOR. have-3rd PRES. you-GEN. the ladyship
καὶ αὐτὰ τὰ   χειροψέλλια
and these the armbands
"and this letter... I send and deliver faithfully in case / in the event that, after these, your ladyship asks [i.e. will ask] for these armbands as well"

(PKöln, 166 / 6th–7th c.)

In this example, the construction ζητῆσαι ἔχει is preceded by the complementizer μήπως, which would normally be followed by a Subjunctive, similarly to its ancient predecessor μή. Obviously, the clause introduced by μήπως in (7) conveys future reference, and that is the reason why not only in this case but in various other contexts the Subjunctive and the morphological Future Tense could be interchanged already in the classical period (Goodwin, 1875), although not wholly freely. As already mentioned (cf. ch. 3), this partial overlap between the two grammatical categories became even more extensive in the H–R period, and the texts manifest quite abundantly the interchangeability of these two categories, most plainly so by the extensive use of the Subjunctive as a future-referring form in main clauses throughout the H–R and the Medieval period. Given this situation, it is not surprising that the ἔχω FC is found in the context of the example above: firstly, it constituted a semantic equivalent of the morphological Future Tense and, secondly, it could also convey a future-referring possibility meaning (cf. 3.2), a modal interpretation that is highly likely in the context above.

Arguably, this example constitutes the oldest attestation of a pattern according to which a future-referring AVC is used in a subjunctive context. Similar examples are also attested in the works of Constantine VII Porphyrogenitus (*De admin. imp.* 13.76, 43.94), providing evidence for the continuous existence of such a construction, especially because this pattern is further manifested in Later Medieval Greek not only in the case of ἔχω (in the controversial "νά ἔχω + Infinitive" form, cf. 5.2.3) but also of θέλω ("νά θέ νά", cf. 5.4.3). The hitherto unexamined example in (7) places similar developments of the subsequent period in a different light, since it illustrates: (a) that they form a systematic pattern originating from Early Medieval times, and (b) that this pattern did not include only ἵνα–clauses but various other subordinate clauses introduced by other complementizers. In this last case we should also include instances of this pattern whereby the subordinate clause is introduced by ὅτι, a complementizer with no Subjunctive requirement: two such examples are found in the papyri (*PSI*, 301 / 5th c., *SB*, 4635 / 7th c.). Moreover, this pattern manifests a well-known development which sees old FCs being employed in subordinate clauses where a subordinate mood is commonly expected (Bybee, Perkins, & Pagliuca, 1994: 274). The whole pattern in its various manifestations will be discussed in detail in the following chapter (cf. 5.2.3).

Another example of the ἔχω AVC used in a Subjunctive context, albeit a different one, is found in *Malalas*:

(8) Τί   ἔχω   ποιῆσαι   τῷ   κυνὶ τούτῳ,   ὅτι οὕτως
    What have-1st PRES. do-INF.AOR. to-the dog this,   that adv
    ταράσσει με   καὶ τὴν πολιτείαν, φιλόσοφε;
    pester   me   and the city,   philosopher?
    "What shall I do [am I to do] to this dog, which is pestering me and the city, philosopher?"

(*Malalas*, 330.34–6 / 6th c.)

In this kind of clause, where what is questioned is the solution to a particular problem or the best way to act under specific circumstances, the Subjunctive constituted the norm already in AG, even though the Future Tense could occasionally appear (Goodwin, 1875: 19). Apparently, this situation remained unchanged in EMG, with the ἔχω AVC in the place of the ancient morphological tense. Furthermore, the ἔχω AVC in (8) can be arguably considered as expressing a deontic meaning, since the speaker wonders what he "should do", given the circumstances.

Recall that, contrary to traditional beliefs, the future-referring meaning of the AVC did not pass through an obligation stage, as there were no clear instances of the deontic meaning in H–R times. The first clear instances of an obligation meaning are manifested in the EMG period: apart from the similar-looking meaning in (8), there are more clear-cut cases, as in (9):

(9) καὶ ἀναγκαῖον ἐνόμισα τα[ῦ]τα μαθὼν
    and necessary believed these learn-PCIPLE
    εὐθέως   γράψαι   ὥστε
    immediately   write-INF.AOR. that

μὴ συγ[χ]ωρῆσαι τοὺς ζυγοστάτας
not allow-INF. the weighers
παρὰ τὸ ἔ[θο]ς διαστρέψαι τινά, ... τ[ὰ] γὰρ
prep the custom   twist-INF. someone ... the prt
χρήματα κατὰ τὸ ἔθος   πάλιν ἐν Ἀλεξανδρείᾳ   ἔχει
money prep the custom again in Alexandria have-3rd PRES.
καταβληθῆ[ν]αι καὶ   οὐκ ἐνταῦθα.
pay-INF.AOR.PASS.   and not here
"And when I learned this, I thought it necessary to write immediately [to you] so that we do not allow the public weighers to twist someone, thus ignoring the tradition ... for the money shall [must] be paid in Alexandria and not here, according to custom."

(*SB*, 9285 / 6th c.)

In this example, the ἔχω construction conveys a deontic (obligation) meaning, in which it became productive probably in the late H–R period or at least by the end of the 5th c., as it is attested more than once in the texts of EMG: there is another example in the papyri (*PLond*, 77rp75 / 7th c.), one in the *Spiritual Meadow* (CL / 6th c.) and two more in *Miracula* (43.15, 44.1 / 7th c.). As argued previously (3.2), the acquisition of this modal meaning might have occurred in the H–R period even though no unambiguous example can be found. The fact that the first clear instances of obligation are attested in EMG, in a period when the future-referring meaning is well established even at middle registers of use, suggests that a conspiracy of factors / meanings leading to future reference, instead of an account based solely on the schema "obligation → futurity", constitutes the most plausible scenario for the development of the ἔχω AVC, as already established (cf. 3.2).

On the whole, the ἔχω AVC could convey a variety of modal meanings in EMG, similar to H–R times, the important difference being that the dominant meaning of the AVC is now future reference instead of ability. The various TAM meanings / contexts of use of the AVC and their token frequency in the texts are illustrated in Table 4.5.

It should be noted that in the table are included the attestations of the various meanings of the constructions in both the papyri and the non-papyri texts, as both types of documents create the same picture for ἔχω. Only the "should" meaning in questions, attested in *Malalas* (ex. 8), is nowhere to be found in the papyri, but since it is only attested once, its absence from the papyri is not particularly surprising.[7] Figure 4.1 illustrates quite strikingly the

---

[7] Despite its possible significance, the controversial "ἔξω + Infinitive" construction has not been included in the table, as its authenticity is debatable.

Early medieval Greek 101

TABLE 4.5 Ἔχω + Infinitive in EMG

MEANING	5th c.	6th c.	7th c.	8th–9th c.	10th c.	Total
Future	17 (60.7)	37 (58.7)	16 (64.0)	13 (86.7)	14 (70.0)	97 (64.2)
Ability	11 (39.3)	22 (34.9)	6 (24.0)	2 (13.3)	4 (20.0)	45 (29.8)
Subordinate	–	1 (1.6)	–	–	2 (10.0)	3 (2.0)
"Should"(Q.)	–	1 (1.6)	–	–	–	1 (0.7)
Obligation	–	2 (3.2)	3 (12.0)	–	–	5 (3.3)
TOTAL	28	63	25	15	20	151

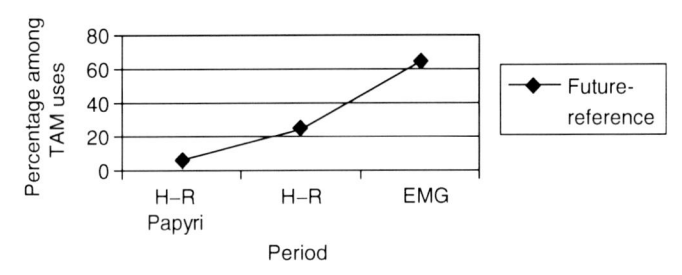

FIGURE 4.1 Token frequency of future reference in the ἔχω AVC

major development of the ἔχω AVC in EMG, namely the dramatic increase in the frequency of use of the construction as an FC. This fact, together with the employment of this AVC in subordinate contexts, argues convincingly for the continuation of the grammaticalization process of this AVC, which is now frequently and widely used (both from a morphosyntactic and a socio-linguistic perspective).

Similarly to ἔχω + Infinitive, the dominant use of the equivalent past formation, εἶχον + Infinitive, is not the modal sense of ability any more, as was the case in the H–R period, but the irrealis interpretation. The latter is contained numerous times in the texts of the EMG, not only in the apodosis of a counterfactual but outside the scope of a conditional, too. These two cases are exemplified in (10) and (11), respectively:

(10) κ(αὶ) εἰ μὴ ἡ θεία πρόνοια ἐβοήθησεν..., ειχαν ἀλλήλ[ους]
and if not the godly providence helped, have-3rd PL.PRET. each-other
αναιλιν [leg.ἀνελεῖν] καὶ ερημωθη πᾶσα ἡ κώμη ἡ [ἡμετέρα].
kill-INF.AOR. and devastated all the village the ours
"And if God had not helped... they would have killed each other and the whole village of ours would have been devastated"

(*PSI*, 71 / 6th c.)

(11) Τὸ δὲ πλοῖον οὕτως ἔπλευσεν, ὅτι διὰ τριῶν ἡμίσεως ἡμερῶν
The prt ship thus sailed, that prep three a-half days
ἠνύσαμεν πλοῦν, ὃν εἴχομεν ποιῆσαι
covered distance, which have-1st PL.PRET. make-INF.AOR.
διὰ δεκαπέντε ἡμερῶν
prep fifteen days
"The ship sailed in such a way that in three and a half days we covered such a distance that we would have covered in fifteen days"

(*Spiritual Meadow*, Caput LXXVI / 6th c.)

Example (10) represents a straightforward case of a counterfactual, while in (11) the irrealis interpretation emerges without the co-occurrence of any overt conditional. The two attestations in (10, 11) simply prove the continuing existence of this meaning of the construction, as similar examples for both contexts have already been found in the H–R period. Recall that it has been argued that this irrealis interpretation of the past construction must have been one of the facilitating factors for the emergence of the future-referring meaning of the ἔχω AVC (cf. 3.2). In the texts of EMG, there are examples that manifest the opposite direction of influence, i.e. from the future-referring present construction to its past equivalent. In other words, we come across the first clear instance of the εἶχον AVC with the future-in-the-past meaning, as in (12):

(12) καὶ ἐξῆλθεν ἀπὸ Δαμασκοῦ ἐπὶ τὴν Μελιτηνὴν διὰ τὸ τὸν τύραννον
and left from Damascus prep the Melitini for the the tyrant
εἶναι ἐν τοῖς μέρεσιν ἐκείνοις, ἐν οἷς καὶ Σέργιος εἶχε
is-INF. prep the parts those, prep which and Sergios have-3rd
πορεύεσθαι
PRET. go-INF.PRES.
"And he left Damascus for Melitini, since the tyrant was in that place, where Sergios would also go"

(*Theophanes*, 350.3 / 8th–9th c.)

Apart from (12), there is another possible attestation of the future-in-the-past in EMG (*L.Asc.*, 22.11 / 6th c.). The fact that the first instances (with the possible exception of a dubious attestation in the Roman period, cf. fn. 9, ch. 3) of this meaning of the εἶχον AVC are attested late in comparison with the present ἔχω AVC should not come as a surprise, if we take into account that, firstly, the future-referring meaning originally emerged in the present form and, secondly, that in the semantic domain of the future-in-the-past ἔμελλον was still quite common (cf. ex.1). In any case, such a meaning is probably not very common from a textual point of view, historical texts (as the one from which the above example is taken) being the most obvious candidates to contain it.

Finally, the obligation meaning, attested for the ἔχω AVC, is probably attested in its past equivalent as well, as can be seen in the following example:

(13) ἀνθ' ὧν   σὺ πρὸς ἐμὲ εἶχες   ἐλθεῖν,
    prep which you prep me   have-3rd PRET. come-INF.AOR.,
    ἐγὼ πρὸς σὲ ἦλθον,   καὶ διώκεις   με τοῦ   οἴκου   σου
    I prep you came   and send-away me the-GEN. house yours
    "For all [the things] that you should have come to me, I came to you, and you send me away from your home"

(Miracula, 33.3 / 7th c.)

In example (13), a doctor is talking to a potential patient, stating his displeasure at being sent away without giving his advice. In this context, obligation is apparently the preferred interpretation. Moreover, the example comes from the very same text that contains two more attestations of this meaning for the ἔχω AVC (cf. above), a fact that strengthens the possibility of the same interpretation here. In any event, a rather obscure excerpt in the *Spiritual Meadow* (Cap. XC) might constitute another instance of the same meaning for the εἶχον AVC. The various meanings of the εἶχον AVC and their token frequency are represented in Table 4.6.

Thus, contrary to the situation regarding the μέλλω construction, the past equivalent of the ἔχω AVC apparently followed a different path of development from its present counterpart. While ἔμελλον + Infinitive mainly conveyed the past future meaning, the εἶχον + Infinitive construction had predominantly an irrealis interpretation, which, as already mentioned, is due to the originally different lexical meaning of the two verbs. Nevertheless, it seems that the ἔχω and the εἶχον AVCs were still related in the speaker's perspective, since the developments of the former had apparently exercised an influence on the latter (cf. the emergence of the future-referring and the obligation meaning). Moreover, they were both still associated with the overall morphological paradigm of the verb, since, for instance, the ἔχω

TABLE 4.6 *Εἶχον* + Infinitive in EMG

Meaning	5th c.	6th c.	7th c.	8th–9th c.	10th c.	Total
Irrealis	2	9	4	1	–	16 (53.3)
Ability	1	4	4	1	–	10 (33.3)
Past Future	–	1	–	1	–	2 (6.7)
Obligation	–	1	1	–	–	2 (6.7)
TOTAL	3	15	9	3	–	30

AVC always refers to the future, while the εἶχον AVC to the future-in-the-past, according to the morphological specification of the verb forms (present and preterite, respectively). This will change in the subsequent period, as we shall see (cf. 5.2–5.3).

On the whole, the ἔχω FC seems to have been much more common in EMG than in the previous period. The attestations of this meaning are abundant in comparison to the old ability meaning, which has lost considerable ground in both the present and the past forms of the construction. The rise in frequency for ἔχω is further manifested in its use in additional contexts with the appropriate meaning (e.g. the Subjunctive contexts for ἔχω, the future-in-the-past for εἶχον). Furthermore, there is clear evidence of ἔχω being used in higher registers, especially towards the end of EMG. In a word, all the necessary signs are there to suggest the further grammaticalization of this future-referring AVC in this period: the rise in frequency of use, the generalization in various contexts including subordinate ones, and the wider sociolinguistic acceptability.

4.3 Θέλω + Infinitive: remaining under shadow

The construction θέλω + Infinitive continued to have a twofold interpretation: on the one hand, it could convey the lexical (volitional) meaning and, on the other, various TAM meanings, including futurity. The development manifested in H–R times, according to which the infinitival complement of the volitional θέλω is gradually replaced by either an ἵνα–clause or a bare Subjunctive form, is further attested in all the texts of EMG.

The perseverance of the V + V$_S$ pattern, which continued in use in EMG, not only for θέλω but also for other similar verbs (cf. *Spiritual Meadow*, CXCIII, for a relevant example involving κελεύω) is noteworthy, as it had remained hitherto unknown. The tripartite complementation of volitional θέλω is shown in Table 4.7:

TABLE 4.7 Complementation of volitional θέλω in EMG

COMPLEMENT*	5th c.	6th c.	7th c.	8th–9th c.	10th c.	Total
+ INF	78 (96.3)	162 (92.6)	123 (90.4)	34 (89.5)	41 (93.2)	438 (92.4)
+ ἵνα (disj.)	2 (2.5)	10 (5.7)	7 (5.1)	3 (7.9)	–	22 (4.6)
+ ἵνα (co-ref.)	–	1 (0.6)	2 (1.5)	–	–	3 (0.6)
+ V$_S$ (disj.)	1 (1.2)	2 (1.1)	4 (3.0)	1 (2.6)	3 (6.8)	11 (2.3)
+ V$_S$ (co-ref)	–	–	–	–	–	–
TOTAL	81	175	136	38	44	474

* The attestations of the formulaic construction "γι(γ)νώσκειν σε θέλω = I want you to know" are excluded from the table

Early medieval Greek 105

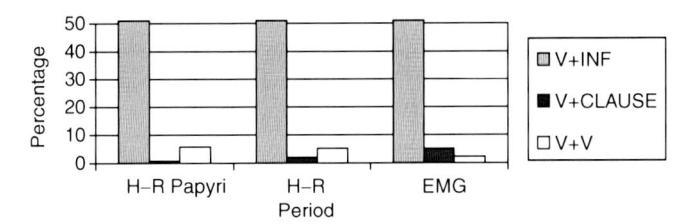

FIGURE 4.2 Θέλω complementation

Table 4.7 is illuminating in two respects: on the one hand, it depicts convincingly the domination of the Infinitive as the main means of complementation of θέλω. On the other hand, it shows that clausal complementation is gaining ground, not really relative to the Infinitive but to the third alternative, the Verbal complement in the Subjunctive, which is still undoubtedly extant, but less frequent now than the ἵνα–clause[8] (cf. Fig. 4.2).

As in the H–R period, the replacement of the Infinitive has not reached the future-referring meaning of the θέλω AVC, or any other modal function for that matter. Concerning the future-referring θέλω, the situation in EMG is seemingly almost identical to the one in the previous period: this meaning *is* attested, but rather sporadically, and almost exclusively in the papyri, as in (14):

(14) ει [leg. ἡ] μητερα σου ασθενι αποθανιν θελι
 the   mother yours is-sick die-INF.AOR. want-3rd PRES.
 "Your mother is sick, she is going to die"

(*PMichael*, 39.10 / 5th–7th c.)

This example is quite representative of the use of future-referring θέλω + Infinitive in the lower registers. It comes from a Byzantine private letter which, according to the editor of the text, is "very obscure and full of mistakes". The latter is evident in the above excerpt, since hardly any word is written without a spelling mistake (e.g. ει for the article ἡ; note also the innovative form μητέρα instead of the AG μήτηρ). All this evidence

---

[8] According to the traditional view, based almost exclusively on Trypanis (1960), there is evidence in the religious hymns of Romanus (6th c.) of a re-positioning of the stress of ἵνα to ἰνά, a development that constitutes the prelude to the emergence of the phonologically shortened form νά. The lack of low-register texts, especially from the 8th till the 10th c., means that we cannot determine whether Trypanis is right or whether this development should be dated later than assumed. But since the papyri contain no instance of νά, despite their occasional low register, even if such a form existed by the early 8th c., it clearly still belonged exclusively to the oral registers of that time, and it must have been generalized to an extent in the subsequent centuries.

proves that the specific text comes from a very low register, where θέλω + Infinitive could obviously be used as an FC. The two other instances of this meaning in the papyri are found again in similar sociolinguistic contexts: the first is found in the very same text, four lines below (and it involves exactly the same phrase), while the second is in a private letter from Alexandria:[9]

(15) σὺν Θ(ε)ῷ γὰρ   θέλω   καταπλεῦσαι εν...........η. ἡ[μέτ]ερον.
     with God prt   want-1st PRES. sail-INF.AOR. prep ???   yours
     μὴ ἀποτύχω   δὲ εἰς   τοῦτο θαρρῶν ὑμᾶς   ἔγραψ[α
     if fail-1st PRES.SUBJ. prt prep this daring to-you wrote
     "God willing, I will arrive at... (yours?). But in case I fail, taking courage, I wrote to you"

(PCair, Mas, 67068r8 / 6th c.)

In absolute figures, the future-referring θέλω AVC is less often attested in EMG than in H–R times, even though the inequality of the number of available texts does not allow for any easy conclusions. More importantly, this meaning of the AVC apparently remains sociolinguistically restricted, as it is still used in low-register texts, and even then not very frequently.

Obviously, contrary to the ἔχω AVC, which gained considerable ground in the domain of future reference, at least in the written registers (cf. 4.2), there is no evidence that a similar development took place for the θέλω AVC. The same holds for the non-papyri texts as well. In these texts, as expected, θέλω + Infinitive is rarely to be seen as an FC. Bănescu (1915: 93) argues that there are actually some instances of such a construction in texts of this period, citing seven examples in total (from Marcus Diaconus, Leontius, and Theophanes). Of all these examples, only the following probably exemplifies a future-referring θέλω AVC:

(16) καὶ γὰρ τοῦ κυρίου εὐδοκοῦντος αὔριον   θέλομεν
     and prt the Lord   willing   tomorrow want-1st PL.PRES.
     ἐνδῦσαι   ὑμᾶς τὸ ἅγιον καὶ ἀγγελικὸν σχῆμα
     clothe-INF.AOR. you the holy and sacred   cloth
     "For tomorrow, God willing, we will clothe you with the holy and sacred cloth"

(Vita Sym. Sali, 65.16 / 7th c.)

---

[9] There is another possible instance of a future-referring θέλω AVC in the papyri (BGU, 2728 / 5th–6th c.), but since the context is rather obscure and allows for multiple meanings, it is not considered as an attestation of future-referring θέλω here.

Despite the fact that a volitional interpretation cannot be excluded here, the future-referring meaning is rather favored. In all other Bănescu's cases, the volitional meaning is equally possible (if not preferable) to the future interpretation. However, there is another instance of the future-referring θέλω AVC in a text of the same author (*V.J.*, 362.2). The existence of two relatively unambiguous examples of future reference does not contradict what we have argued in relation to the papyri attestations and their low register, because both examples are taken from a dialogue and therefore relate to spoken language. It is probable that they actually represent rather closely the oral speech of that time, or at least more closely than Moschos, who even though writing in roughly the same century and incorporating in his work large sections of dialogue does not even once use the θέλω FC. This could perhaps reflect an idiosyncratic choice of the authors, as there can be no explanation for this fact on the basis of the extant evidence.

In any case, the near absence of the θέλω AVC in these texts cannot be disputed, especially in comparison with the attestations of the ἔχω AVC. This phenomenon is somewhat surprising, not only in the light of the facts regarding ἔχω but also because in the H–R period the θέλω construction did start to appear more frequently in some religious texts, as already mentioned (cf. 3.3). It could be accounted for on the basis of the register of these texts, which might not have been appropriate for this construction. Certainly this is very likely to be true for the texts of the 9th–10th c., as *Theophanes*, the works of Constantine VII Porphyrogenitus, the epistle of Arethas, and the *Death poems* cannot really be considered to belong to the low registers, but should be seen rather as texts written in a non-elaborated style. The texts of the first centuries of this period should be seen as being closer to low registers, but yet the θέλω FC is only twice attested.

At face value, these facts might suggest a decline in the frequency of use of θέλω, or at least the complete predominance of the ἔχω AVC in the relevant registers. Bănescu (1915: 93) certainly seems to agree with the latter view, and he argues that θέλω + Infinitive becomes productive as an FC only when the texts in the vernacular emerge (11th–12th c.). This assumption would be difficult to contradict, if no indication of a possible generalization in the use of the construction at an earlier stage could be found. However, there is one significant example, shown in (17):

(17) κελεύομεν τὸν   τὸ δικαίωμα ἔχοντα   προκομίζειν.   εἰ ἀληθῶς δὲ
     order   the   the right   have-PCIPLE bring-INF.   if truly   prt

βλάβην ἐξ αὐτοῦ ὑποστῆναι   θέλει,   μὴ ἀναγκάζεσθαι
damage from this suffer-INF.AOR. want-3rd PRES.,not oblige-INF.PRES.PASS.
προκομίζειν αὐτό· οὐδεὶς γὰρ   ἀναγκάζεται ζημιῶσαι   ἑαυτῷ.
bring-INF. this; no-one prt   obliged   harm-INF. himself
"We order whoever has the right to do so, to bring forth [evidence]. If though truly he is going to bring harm to himself because of this, then [we order him] not to be obliged to bring it forth; for no-one can be made to harm himself."

(*Epanagoge*, 11.18.10 / 9th c.)

In this example, the fact that the complement of θέλω, from a semantic point of view, expresses an undesirable situation for the agent (βλάβην ὑποστῆναι = "to be harmed"), excludes the volitional meaning and argues quite emphatically for the future reference of the θέλω construction. This passage is taken from a legislative text describing what the court or the judge should do in specific and more general cases, in other words it bears a close resemblance to books of civil law. As is well known, this genre of text is always conservative from a linguistic point of view: it is certain to contain archaisms and constructions not attested elsewhere (cf., for example, Tiersma, 1999). In such a text, the existence of an unambiguously future-referring θέλω AVC, as in (17), comes as a surprise, given the scarcity of its attestations in other texts where it would be expected to appear.[10] How are we to reconcile these two facts?

The relative number of attestations of FCs in the *Epanagoge* confirms its register: there are 22 instances of the μέλλω AVC (in both its present and past form), whereas there is absolutely no instance of the ἔχω AVC, and only one of the θέλω AVC, illustrated in (17). With the exception of θέλω, the relative distribution of these constructions complies with the expected linguistically conservative character of the text, even though it is not written in a very elaborated style, an observation based on the type of Infinitive following μέλλω: as has been argued (cf. 3.1, 4.1), the Aorist Infinitive should be regarded as representative of the lower register use, while the Future Infinitive as the learned use, the Present Infinitive being neutral to such a distinction. In the case of the *Epanagoge*, there is no instance of the Future Infinitive, and only

---

[10] One could argue that θέλω + Infinitive in (17) is indeed an archaism, since one example of a future-referring meaning in conditional clauses is already found in Aristophanes (cf. 2.3, ex. 17). However, the numerous legislative papyri do not contain any instance of such a use, despite the abundance of conditionals. Moreover, there is an obvious difference in register between the legislative text in (17) and the comedies of Aristophanes. For these reasons, the example above is taken not to represent an archaizing use.

two instances of the Aorist Infinitive. On that basis, the specific text can be roughly placed in the middle-high registers of use, where the θέλω AVC would normally not be expected to appear.

Since (17) constitutes the only example of the future-referring θέλω in the whole text, it could be attributed to problems in the manuscript tradition of the text. However, the precision required in the copying procedure of legislative texts leaves little room for doubt concerning the authenticity of this attestation. Perhaps, this example represents a momentary slip of concentration on the part of the scribe, because of which he included a form presumably pertaining to the everyday language of his time. But the fact that, for whatever reason, the θέλω AVC found its way into such an official document suggests a rather wider use than the other texts seem to imply, at least for the spoken registers. Despite the lack of evidence, it is plausible to assume that such a development must have occurred between the 7th and the 10th c., that is at the most obscure period in the whole history of post-classical Greek in terms of textual evidence, especially for the low registers. This chronology accounts not only for the scarcity of attestations of the θέλω AVC in the early texts of the period but also for the dramatically altered picture drawn by the texts in the vernacular of the Late Medieval period, as we shall see in the next chapter. The publication of new texts and the more extensive study of the available material of middle registers could certainly help clarify the issue.

It should be noted that it is exactly during these centuries (7th–9th) that the Slavs first migrated and settled into mainland Greece in large numbers, even if smaller waves of immigration might have occurred earlier (cf. Avramea, 2001 for early settlements of the Slavs in the Peloponnese). We cannot discuss at length here the highly controversial issue of the extent to which parts of Greece were inhabited by Slavs, but the ever closer contact between the Greek-speaking populations (and officials) of the Byzantine empire and the Slavs resulted in bilingualism (cf., for example, Dagron, 1994, Nystazopoulou-Pelekidou, 1986). Interestingly enough, the case of the future-referring θέλω AVC has always been regarded as one of the most notable examples of the so-called "Balkan Sprachbund",[11] since Old Church Slavonic, the earliest written form of any Slavic language (*ca.* 9th–11th c.), as well as other early South Slavic texts manifest this construction, which spread throughout the Balkans, with few exceptions (cf. Joseph, 1983). The question remains: is this spread the result of Greek influence,

---

[11] This name has been given to the phenomenon of extensive linguistic convergence involving many Balkan languages (Greek included). It will not be further discussed here (for details, cf. Tomić, 2006, Aikhenvald & Dixon, 2007, among many others).

or had a similar construction developed in the Slavic languages independently? This notorious issue will be examined and, hopefully, clarified to some extent after the discussion of the evidence of Late Medieval Greek in the next chapter.

Apart from the future-referring meaning, the θέλω AVC continued to be used in various contexts that it occurred in H–R times as well. First, the 'particle' use of θέλω in requests ("please") (cf. 3.3) remains quite common in the papyri. The purely grammatical character of θέλω in this context is clearly illustrated in the following example:

(18) θέλησον,   εἴπερ βούλει,   ἐκμισθῶσαι   αὐτὸ
     want-2nd AOR.IMP.   if want-2nd PRES.   rent-INF.AOR.   this
     Καναίῳ τῷ ἁλιεῖ
     Cannaios the fisherman
     "If you want, please rent this to Cannaios the fisherman"

(PPrag, 193r2 / 5th c.)

In this example, the use of the synonymous βούλει indicates rather straightforwardly that θέλησον does not contain any lexical meaning but is used in an adverbial fashion. The fact that this type of use for θέλω + Infinitive does not appear in the non-papyri sources should again be seen as simply an 'accident' due to the character of the body of the papyri, which partly consists of correspondence, where requests are expected to abound.

The modal meanings of the θέλω AVC are similarly attested. In a papyrus of the 6th c., we find the following:

(19) ἐξότε ἀπέστη ἐκ   τοῦ πατρὸς αὐτοῦ, ἄλλας πληγὰς οὐκ ἔλαβεν καὶ
     since left   prep   the father his, other beatings not received and
     θέλει   ὀλίγας λαβεῖν·   ηθεισθη [leg. εἰθίσθη] γὰρ ὀ νῶτος αὐτοῦ
     want-3rd PRES.   some get-INF.AOR.; accustomed   prt the behind his
     καὶ τὴν συνήθειαν ζητεῖ·
     and the idleness   seeks
     "Since he left his father's side, he has not received any beatings and he needs to receive some; for his behind grew soft and wants to stay idle."

(SB, 7655 / 6th c.)

The excerpt comes from a letter where advice is given to "beat some sense" into a boy. Obviously, the register of this kind of correspondence is rather low, and therefore the unmistakably deontic meaning of the θέλω AVC in (19) provides us with the evidence to suggest that this modal use of the AVC was

TABLE 4.8 *Θέλω* AVC in EMG

Meaning	5th c.	6th c.	7th c.	8th–9th c.	10th c.	Total
Future	2 (6.9)	1 (2.7)	2 (14.3)	–	–	5 (6.2)
"Requests"	26 (89.7)	31 (83.8)	12 (85.7)	–	–	69 (86.3)
Obligation	–	4 (10.8)	–	–	–	4 (5.0)
Possibility	1 (3.4)	1 (2.7)	–	–	–	2 (2.5)
TOTAL	29	37	14	–	–	80

not peculiar to a certain register or to a type of texts, namely "grammars", though it certainly continued to be productive in such texts, as the three relevant attestations in *Stephanus* (17.10, 520.22, 576.3 / 6th c.) confirm.

The epistemic possibility meaning is also attested in the texts of EMG, and, to be more precise, in exactly identical contexts in which it was originally attested in H–R times (cf. 3.3), i.e. in questions of the type shown in (20):

(20) Τί   θέλει   εἶναι   τοῦτο;
     What want-3rd PRES. be-INF.PRES. this?
     "What can this be?"

(*Call.*, 43.4 / 5th c.)

This meaning is once more found in the texts of this period, again in a similar question (*Thal.*, 49.8 / 6th c.). This leads us to conclude that it was actually restricted to this specific linguistic / pragmatic context, at least in EMG or, in other words, that it constituted an implicature arising in this specific context. According to what has been argued before, the meaning out of which this 'possibility' implicature arises is most probably obligation, which, as seen in (19), was an extant meaning of the *θέλω* AVC in EMG. Table 4.8 illustrates the token frequency of all uses of the *θέλω* AVC in EMG.

The almost complete absence of any TAM meaning of the *θέλω* AVC in the 8th–10th c. should be attributed more to the character of the textual sources available than to any possible decline in use of the *θέλω* construction. The only exception to this observation, apart from the future-referring example from the legislative text,[12] refers to the use of *θέλω* as a disjunctive marker, attested in the writings of Constantine VII Porphyrogenitus:

---

[12] The occurrence of the *θέλω* AVC in *Epanagoge* as an FC is not included in the table, as this text is not part of the quantitative corpus, due to its rather high register.

(21) «Ἄπελθε μετὰ τοῦ πλούτου σου,   θέλῃς,   εἰς   τὴν χώραν
Leave   with   the   wealth   yours,   want-2nd PRES.SUBJ. prep the country
σου,   θέλῃς,   ἀλλαχοῦ...
yours, want-2nd PRES.SUBJ. elsewhere
"Take your riches and leave, either for your country or elsewhere..."

(*De adm. imp.*, 26.60 / 10th c.)

As has been mentioned (cf. 3.3), the first attestation of this use of θέλεις, previously unnoticed, is found in a papyrus of the 3rd c. AD. In all the texts of these seven intervening centuries included in the corpus, no other attestation occurs. The fact that the second instance of such a meaning comes from a text of an emperor, despite his conscious effort to write in a non-elaborated style, probably implies a continuous—spoken—usage throughout the H–R and Early Medieval periods, which the vast majority of the available texts conceals. One could argue that (21) simply constitutes a fossilized usage, but the numerous attestations of this construction found in the texts of Late Medieval Greek render this hypothesis rather unlikely. The seven-century gap in the textual tradition of the construction corroborates the assumption, put forward above, that the *future-referring* θέλω AVC could have acquired a wider usage in the later stages of this period, a fact that remains hidden to us because of the lack of appropriate textual sources.

Little needs to be said with regard to the past form of the θέλω AVC. The attestations of ἤθελον + Infinitive are very scarce, and therefore our conclusions can only be tentative. All attestations involve the volitional construction, thus consolidating the separation in the development of the present and the past formation of the AVC already evident from the H–R period (cf. 3.3), since the former acquired various TAM meanings, while the latter retained its exclusively lexical character. The only interesting development manifested in EMG is associated with the complement of ἤθελον, as in the *Spiritual Meadow* (Caput LXXVI, CCXII) and in the writings of Leontius (*V.J.*, 384.14 / *Vita Sym. Sali*, 91.26) the first instances of a clausal complementation for ἤθελον are found, all involving disjoint reference. This is to be expected, since the same pattern in the replacement of the Infinitive is manifested for the present counterpart too from the H–R times (cf. 3.3). It is worth pointing out, however, that the diffusion of the new complementation pattern reached ἤθελον many centuries after the same phenomenon occurred for θέλω, confirming the largely separate developments for the two forms.

On the whole, the θέλω construction remained in use in EMG, without showing any overt signs of increasing frequency of use or any morphosyntactic evidence of further grammaticalization (although the data is too meagre to tell with certainty). Obviously, the volitional θέλω remained highly popular, and manifested further traces of the replacement of the infinitival with a different type of complementation, be that a clause introduced by ἵνα or a bare Subjunctive form. On the other hand, the θέλω AVC is undoubtedly attested in its various meanings. With regard to the future-referring θέλω, it remained in use in the low registers, but there is evidence—admittedly scant, but still extant—to believe that its low number of attestations is mostly the result of the problematic textual tradition than a representation of the actual situation of the period, and that it may have been in use in more varied registers as well.

4.4 Conclusions: FCs and registers

In EMG, all three FCs are still in use. Μέλλω + Infinitive is widely attested in all registers, even though there are indications that it is beginning to be mostly associated with the higher registers and with rather elaborated styles. Ἔχω + Infinitive is now enjoying greater popularity, initially in the low-register texts, but eventually in middle registers as well (cf. its attestations in the writings of Constantine VII Porphyrogenitus), without yet acquiring the range of acceptability of μέλλω. Finally, θέλω + Infinitive is seemingly the least frequent of all constructions as far as future reference is concerned; it is possible, though, that the necessarily quite restricted corpus of investigation, especially from the 8th till the 10th c., is largely responsible for this observation. Concerning their grammaticalization status, the μέλλω and ἔχω AVCs became more grammatical on the basis of quantitative and morphosyntactic evidence, while the same cannot be said for θέλω, although this again may be compromised by the unreliability of the available material.

Is there a specific reason for the rise in the frequency of use of the ἔχω AVC? A straightforward answer is impossible to provide, and would probably oversimplify the actual linguistic developments. On the one hand, the μέλλω AVC, in particular after the emergence of competing AVCs with similar meaning, is gradually being restricted to higher and higher registers, since educated authors favor its use because of its AG origin. Ἔχω + Infinitive, on the other hand, already in use for some centuries at the beginning of EMG, and constituting probably an authentic feature of oral speech, must have been a good candidate (among other forms, such as the Present Tense or the Subjunctive) to replace μέλλω in low- and later middle-register texts. Presumably, the equivalent construction of Late Latin could have provided the necessary prestige in order for ἔχω to be more easily used in such contexts. This might also account for the preference by speakers (or writers?) for the ἔχω AVC instead of θέλω + Infinitive, which must have remained in use, but rarely found its way into written texts.

Finally, as has been mentioned, the case of the disjunctive θέλεις is indicative of our near ignorance of the spoken language of the H–R and the Early Medieval period. As for the late centuries of this period, i.e. 8th–10th c., matters are even worse, as no reliable material of the written low-register varieties exists. This is the reason why the importance of a single example (17) from a text of the 9th c. involving the θέλω construction has been stressed as a possible indication of a different situation, if not for the whole period, at least for its late stages. It could be assumed, consequently, that the θέλω FC gained more popularity in these centuries, especially given the decline of Western influence in comparison with the previous period, and the rise of a new linguistic situation in the Balkans probably involving multilingual communities of Greeks and Slavs whose native languages might independently have developed such a future-referring construction.[13] All these observations might help lay the foundations for an account of the totally different situation with regard to the FCs observed in the texts of the subsequent period.

---

[13] Interestingly, Mihăescu (1978) notes that the late Latin attested in Rumania manifests a highly frequent use of a future-referring "volo + Infinitive" construction not attested elsewhere in the Latin-speaking world. It remains to be investigated whether this is connected to the development of cognates in the South Slavic languages.

5

Late Medieval Greek (11th–15th c. AD): the dominance of a single AVC

Introduction: texts and methodology

This was yet another period of great turmoil for the Greek-speaking world. Despite short intervals of growth, both in financial-political and in cultural terms (notably, the 12th and parts of the 14th c.), the Byzantine Empire was losing most of its lands to foreign invaders till its complete downfall with the capture of Constantinople by the Ottoman Turks in 1453. This investigation does not continue after this date (with the exception of the official documents, cf. below), for the reason that this event is conventionally said to mark the end of an era in the Eastern Mediterranean (and not only there); as a consequence, it constitutes a convenient candidate for a cut-off point for linguistic investigation.

That landmarks in economic / political history can also be landmarks in the history of a particular language (or a group of affected languages) is a well-known fact. One of the important landmarks in the history of Greek is the capture of Constantinople by the Franks of the fourth crusade (1204) and the subsequent occupation of large areas of the Greek-speaking world by Franks and Venetians (and in a few areas Genoese). The circumstances for extensive communication or even for bilingualism among Greek-speaking and Romance-speaking populations were immediately created, and the outcome of this cultural and linguistic interchange can still be seen in Modern Greek, most straightforwardly in the lexicon of the language[1] but also on other linguistic levels, as will be argued below (cf. especially 5.4.3).

The major linguistic changes brought about in this period and the characteristic features of Late Medieval Greek (LMG), which are not closely related

---

[1] As already mentioned in chapter 3, another equally important case of language contact and, almost certainly, bilingualism in many parts of Greece of that time (and in the subsequent period of Ottoman rule) involves the Greeks and the Slavs. Some aspects of this instance of language contact, related to this investigation, will be discussed below (cf. 5.4.1).

to the AVCs, will not be discussed here as this would lead us far beyond the scope of the book. Suffice it to say that LMG constitutes the period from which the first substantial textual evidence of a vernacular form of Greek is found, showing quite different properties from the language of the texts of EMG.[2] On the other hand, some brief remarks on the genres and on the kind of textual evidence surviving from these centuries are necessary.

In these years the beginning of a long tradition of folk songs can be traced, in the form of songs about the "akrites", the soldiers at the eastern outposts of the Empire. Furthermore, it seems that in the midst of the imperial court attempts were made to write either in a more day-to-day style, as appropriate to satire (attested in the 12th c. "Ptohoprodromika" written probably by Theodoros Prodromos) or in a genre possibly re-introduced or re-established in the Eastern world by Western influence, namely the novel, albeit in a literary style (the so-called 'literary' novels of the 12th c.). Apparently, the first resurgence of vernacular literature is, at least partly, due to scholars, since all writers of the above works were well-known scholars of their time (with the exception of the unknown writers—if any—of the "akritika", even though the writing down of these songs—especially *Digenis*[3]—might also be due to a scholar interested in preserving a dying tradition). However, this effort was cut short, as the following (13th) century provides us with no texts in the vernacular, a fact that can probably be attributed to the devastating effects of the capture of Constantinople by the Crusaders on the lands of the Byzantine Empire. Although the possibility of historical accident in the textual evidence can be called upon to account for this gap, nevertheless the striking coincidence of textual paucity with political instability renders the explanation in terms of social circumstances more plausible.

Apart from the above-mentioned gap in the textual tradition, the extent of the Frankish and Venetian influence on the Greek-speaking world and, as a consequence, on the Greek language becomes evident from the 14th c. onwards. New novels—or romances—are written in a less literary style than their predecessors of the 12th c. (the works, as noted, of scholars), which were either influenced by the contemporary Western tradition simply in terms of content and structure, or could even be based on, or translated from, a known

---

[2] LMG is the least studied period of Greek. There have been few studies focusing on particular phenomena and problems of LMG (cf., for example, Mackridge, 1993, Pappas, 2004). Recently a major program for the compiling of an LMG grammar has been undertaken (cf. Holton, 2005). For more details on linguistic developments of LMG, cf. Horrocks, 1997: ch. 11, 12.

[3] Some basic information regarding the character of these texts in the vernacular, essential for the better understanding of the following analysis, is given in the bibliography.

novel (cf. Beaton, 1996). Moreover, there now appear texts which are most probably written either by non-native speakers of Greek with a sometimes tenuous, sometimes more complete—as far as we can tell—command of the Greek language or by bilinguals. These texts include, for instance, the famous "Chronicle of Morea" for the conquest of the Peloponnese, as well as poems written in Crete by authors whose lineage is undoubtedly Venetian (e.g. by Dellaportas and Falieros). The Western origin of the authors of these works, among others, has led some scholars (e.g. Jannaris, 1897, Bănescu, 1915) to question the validity of this textual evidence, expressing doubts whether it can be said to represent authentic features and developments of spoken Greek. This issue will be addressed with regard to the specific texts and constructions where it arises.

But any investigation of the texts from this period runs into an important obstacle: the manuscript tradition of most literary works is highly problematic, especially in areas of well-known and widely attested structural and semantic fluctuation, such as future reference, in that there are a great many variant readings found in the manuscripts. And to make matters worse, in the vast majority of cases there exists a chronological gap between the assumed time of production and the oldest manuscript preserving the work. It is essential, then, that a linguistic investigation of any kind, and, in particular, of FCs in LMG, is not exclusively based on the text presented by the critical edition but also on the evidence of the apparatus criticus, especially as many editors have seen fit to make numerous emendations and corrections in the text, sometimes contrary to the evidence of all manuscripts. In some cases, the various manuscripts are so divergent that there can be no single text but only different versions, which ideally should all be consulted. To disregard variant readings and variant textual traditions means to risk distorting the evidence about particular instances of language change (cf. also ch.1).

Accordingly, this investigation aims to encompass almost every literary text written in the vernacular of the period, in order to have as broad a picture as possible of the various FCs found therein. Moreover, the apparatus criticus, when available, and the various versions of a single text, when they have been edited separately, have been consulted, (following Grund's (2006) advice of caution) and this has proved illuminating in many respects, as will be seen below (cf. especially 5.4.3). Regarding the chronology of each text, the editor's opinion is mainly followed, but in some cases, especially in very old editions, specialized works have also been consulted (e.g. Beck, 1988 and Beaton, 1996). Obviously, in the majority of texts, these are only elaborate guesses at best, and this poses a major challenge to the unfettered tracking of linguistic developments in LMG. However, the alternative would be to treat all texts alike in terms of date of production, as the manuscripts containing them date mostly from the 15th century! However, it is suggested here that there are various differences among the texts dating from the early and the later stages of the period, and, therefore, an approximate classification of the texts on the basis of date of production will be attempted. It is acknowledged, though, that this is precarious, hence other textual sources must serve as a controlling factor for the validity of this classification and of the evidence the literary texts present in general.

The same problems have led Manolessou (2003) to doubt the value of the literary texts as source of evidence for the historical linguist, especially in comparison with official and non-literary documents. These texts constitute another important source of material hardly mentioned in any linguistic investigation of the period, apart from some very recent exceptions (e.g. Karantzola, forth., Manolessou, forth., Markopoulos, forth.). The great majority of these documents are drawn from the books of notaries, and include land agreements, dowries, wills, the payment of debts, and any other kind of document that needed the seal of a notary to gain official status. Their main advantage is twofold: (i) their official nature and (ii) the non-literary character of the language. With regard to the former, the official character enables us to trace with near certainty the chronology and the regional origin of these texts, while the literary texts are quite often, as mentioned, of dubious and rather controversial chronology, and their origin, with the exception of specific works whose authors are known, remains a mystery. Moreover, the official documents are often originals, not copies of an unknown original, as is the case with the literary texts, which were usually copied with rather 'loose' standards, resulting in the extensive linguistic variation attested in the manuscripts of the great majority of these works (cf. Beaton, 1996: 164–88). As to their non-literary and prosaic character, this is a valuable corrective in that it is also sensible to assume that at least some of the peculiarities found in the literary texts are due to the fact that a great majority of them are written in verse, and metrical considerations are likely to have intervened in the production of the texts, as is always the case in poetry.

Therefore, an investigation of non-literary documents (contracts, treaties, etc.) has been conducted here, aiming to test and control the validity of the findings of the literary texts (also with regard to their assumed date of production, cf. above). The non-literary documents come from various archives and can be divided into two major classes, according to their geographical origin:

(a) Documents from the archives of the Venetian-ruled parts of Greek-speaking areas: Crete, the Ionian islands (mainly Corfu, Kefalonia, and Kythira) and the Cyclades (mainly Andros and Naxos); and of Venice itself (due to its Greek-speaking community). The oldest text of this category goes back to 1299, but for the most part the material is dated from the 15th–16th centuries.

(b) Documents from the archives of the various monasteries in the Greek-speaking world, mainly from the mountain of Athos, and from various administrative centres of the Byzantine empire (e.g. Mystras). This material is of a much earlier date, in some cases as early as the 10th c.

The language of these official documents has not been properly investigated before. There have been attempts to describe linguistic traits of specific notaries (e.g. Bakker & van Gemert, 1987 for *Varouhas*), but there is no comprehensive account of the overall characteristics of these texts, a fact to be expected considering their quite recent publication (at least for most of the notaries) and the lack hitherto of interest on the part of linguists, based partly on the fact that the legal register of the majority of the texts necessarily implies a language full of formulaic and archaizing elements and constructions (cf. Tiersma, 1999), a distinct drawback for any historical linguistic investigation. On the other hand, there is a sharp distinction between the two categories of documents described above: in the case of the monasteries, the scribes were apparently trained to an extent in the Greek linguistic tradition, a training usually resulting in an archaizing form of the language, although occasional slips prove to be useful in glimpsing an otherwise hidden linguistic reality. In the case of the notaries of the Venetian dukedoms, however, the situation is different, especially in the later stages when an increasing number of native speakers of Greek, minimally familiar with the learned tradition, served as notaries. As a consequence, their language contains elements of the spoken vernacular and is rich in loans from Italian, though still retaining some archaizing constructions of a formulaic character. On the whole, the clear shortcoming of the largely legal character of these texts is outweighed by the fact that they constitute a large body of contemporary prose, often at odds with the poetic character of the literary texts (with the exception of *Mahairas*), and that the linguistic level of the documents is dependent on the very variable level of education of the notaries themselves.

Therefore, the value of the non-literary texts as linguistic material should not be over-estimated. Obviously, such differentiated material presents major problems for a strict quantitative analysis of its linguistic features. That is why no such analysis will be provided for the non-literary texts, as it would arguably be based on unsafe grounds and might prove not only unfruitful but also misleading, for the following reasons:

(a) Many of the AVCs are found in the non-literary documents in formulaic contexts, and, consequently, the high number of their attestations should not be considered as important as it would otherwise be;

(b) The varying degree of linguistic register exhibited in the books of notaries, as well as the different quantity of documents found in each book, effectively renders any quantitative examination extremely difficult.

Given these facts, the treatment of the material will be differentiated as follows: regarding the literary texts, exact numbers of attestations will be provided, when necessary, and comparisons will be made between different genres and works originating from different areas. In other words, a combination of quantitative and qualitative analysis will be followed, as in the previous chapters. On the other hand, in the case of the non-literary documents, the observations will be limited to general tendencies attested in the texts and to particularly interesting examples, without providing any exact numbers of occurrences, unless otherwise stated. Consequently, the validity and importance of observations should be measured according to the relative wealth of the instances of each construction and their geographical distribution, but also be assessed in relation to the comparison between the data in the non-literary and the literary texts of LMG.

Finally, before presenting the investigation of the material, a note on its chronology. Contrary to the literary texts, the non-literary documents dating from the Late Medieval period (11th–15th c.) are rather scarce: most of them are drawn from monastery archives and are written in an archaizing form of the language. Therefore, the corpus of this investigation has been slightly extended to include non-literary texts from the 16th c., which are considerably more numerous and of wider geographical distribution. This decision is supported by the fact that official legal documents constitute a register prone to incorporate linguistic developments at a slower rate than vernacular literary texts, as they are by definition rather normative. Consequently, the texts of the 16th c. may be expected to manifest developments found in the literary texts of previous centuries, providing thus a solid base for comparison between the two types of texts.

The findings concerning each AVC are again presented separately. More emphasis will generally be given to the detailed description and accounting of the data of the literary texts, since they represent relatively well-known territory in terms of their language features; moreover, the data accumulated on the basis of these texts is more easily quantifiable than in the case of the official documents. However, firm conclusions will be drawn only on the basis of evidence from both types of texts. The chapter concludes with the overall picture emerging from the investigation of the data concerning future-reference in LMG.

5.1 High registers and specialization: the case of μέλλω / ἔμελλον

In all studies of future reference in Greek, the story of the μέλλω AVC ends abruptly at the end of the Roman period, or in the Early Medieval years at the latest. Bǎnescu (1915) does not include μέλλω in his table of FCs in LMG, whereas comments about it for this late period are hardly found in wider studies on the history of Greek (Jannaris, 1897, Horrocks, 1997). This attitude is not surprising, as the main interest of scholars was focused on the rise of the θέλω AVC and its various forms, especially since μέλλω, as we have seen in previous sections (cf. 3.1 and 4.1), came steadily to be associated with middle and high registers of use. By the time of LMG it is not the dominant FC, at least not in vernacular texts, while it abounds in the archaizing styles of many scholars and some notaries. Only Aerts (1983) has conducted a study of μέλλω in Medieval Cypriot Greek, for the simple reason that in Cypriot this AVC had a much more influential history than in mainland Greek.

Here it is maintained that this attitude is not wholly justified. Even though μέλλω is now restricted in both its use and meaning in comparison with θέλω (and perhaps ἔχω as well), it still partakes in the system of future-reference in various ways, which will become evident in the analysis that follows. Moreover, it survives in Standard Modern Greek with a particular meaning and in specific constructions, and in some dialects is more productive than in the standard variety. Consequently, the examination below of the μέλλω AVC in LMG will prove to be illuminating.

5.1.1 *The early stages*

The two literary texts of the 11th c. provide a striking contrast, as expected from their quite different styles. Μέλλω is nowhere to be found in *Armouris*, while there are 14 attestations of this construction in *Stratigikon*. At first glance, this observation could be attributable to the different size of the texts, as the former is a song of 197 verses, whereas the latter consists of 104 pages of prose. But although this external factor might have been partially responsible, one additional fact should be noted: *Armouris* contains three instances of the θέλω AVC as a future-referring (and non-volitional) form (cf. 5.4.1). So, it already seems that, in literature written in the vernacular, μέλλω is of secondary importance in comparison with θέλω. This underlines the sharp rise in the frequency of use of the θέλω AVC between EMG and LMG times (cf. below, 5.4.1).

On the other hand, in *Stratigikon,* μέλλω outnumbers both θέλω and ἔχω (the numbers of attestations are 14, 9, and 12, respectively). These facts suggest that the high incidence of μέλλω among the three main FCs constitutes a criterion for specifying the register of the text under examination; so, the situation found in *Stratigikon* would indicate that it is a text of the middle register, as μέλλω is the most common of the AVCs, even though the others exist as well, especially θέλω, which was the last of the three constructions to gain in popularity (cf. 4.3). This criterion is borne out by the data, as will be shown below.

The non-literary texts of these early stages of LMG pattern like the *Stratigikon*. The μέλλω AVC is frequently attested in the archives of the monasteries of Athos and in the documents from South Italy (*Trinchera*: doc. 15, 22, among others) dating from the 11th c. The register of legal documents, to which all these early attestations belong without exception, would presumably be appropriate for a relatively archaizing construction such as μέλλω + Infinitive. This evidence strengthens the assumption of a sociolinguistic specialization to middle and high registers exhibited by the μέλλω AVC from EMG onwards.

A final observation concerning the μέλλω AVC in *Stratigikon* is also relevant here. As revealed in previous chapters (especially 4.1), μέλλω followed a pattern of complementation which was dependent on the register of the text: the Infinitive following μέλλω would be the Aorist one when the text is of the middle register, while its Future and Present forms would occur in works of more archaizing scholars. The data in *Stratigikon* conform to this picture, since in 11 / 14 (78%) of the attestations of the AVC it is the Aorist Infinitive which surfaces, the remaining instances being both the Present (2) and the Perfect Infinitive (!) (but consider that in the last case the verb itself has no other infinitival form, only ἐγρηγορέναι). The pattern is verified, since the complementation of μέλλω in *Stratigikon* is appropriate for its middle register.

Thus, the combined evidence of the two—admittedly very different— literary texts as well as the official documents of the 11th c. seems to illustrate the fact that the μέλλω AVC by the time of LMG must have been rarely used by speakers, being frequent only in relatively high (written) registers. Obviously, this conclusion is disguised by the apparent situation in *Stratigikon* and

Late medieval Greek 123

in the non-literary texts, which is due to their higher register in comparison with the texts written in some form of the vernacular.

The demise of μέλλω from the domain of future reference in the vernacular is more evident in the data of both *Digenis* and the various poems of the 12th c.: the latter contain only one instance of μέλλω, as is also the case with *Digenis*. Compare this with the token frequency of the other AVCs in this work: θέλω FC features 12 times, and ἔχω five. In other words, in this "functional layering" situation, μέλλω represents a tiny minority, with one out of a total of 18 instances (5.6%) of FCs. A very similar picture emerges from the poems of the 12th century (1 / 13: 7.7%). Consequently, it is reasonable to conclude that μέλλω has been restricted to a peripheral position in the domain of future-reference; at this stage speakers could either have stopped using this construction altogether or used it with a more specialized meaning, simultaneously restricting its possible contexts of use. Apparently, the latter occurred, since there is an indication of a possible specialization in the one attestation of *Digenis*:

(1) ... καὶ πάντες μέλλομεν σταθῆν τὴν φοβερὰν ἡμέραν
    and all   will-3rd PL.PRES. stand-INF. the terrible day
    "and we will all stand at that terrible day..."

(*Digenis*, 1755)

This verse refers to the day of the Apocalypse, and is therefore of a specific, religious context. Furthermore, the meaning of the AVC has a strong undertone of certainty about the future, as should be expected in that kind of context, where religious belief does not allow any other semantic nuance. This 'destiny' meaning of the AVC is reminiscent of a similar development for "should" in Old and Middle English (cf. Bybee, Perkins & Pagliuca, 1994: 186), although the semantic pathway leading to it has not been investigated, at least in the μέλλω case. This will be attempted after the evidence from the later stages of the period is examined (cf. 5.1.2).

Before moving to the analysis of the more numerous data of the subsequent centuries, an example found in the documents from South Italy is worth a brief discussion:

(2) Ἰ δ'οὐχί καί οὐ δυνιθή... του   μέλλει   δοῦναι   ὁ ριθείς
    If prt not and not be-able... the-GEN. will-3rd PRES. give-INF. the named
    τοῦ   ριθέντος... τότε καὶ ὁ   ριθείς εἴνα [leg. ἵνα] μέλλει
    the-GEN. named... then and the named that   will-3rd PRES.
    ποιεῖσε...
    do-INF.

> "But if not, and the aforementioned cannot... to give to the previously named... then the previously named should do..."
>
> (*Trinchera*, 323 / d.1270)

In (2), the μέλλω AVC is preceded by a complementizer twice: in the first instance by του, which introduces a complement clause, and in the second case by είνα (=ίνα), which is normally followed by a Subjunctive. In the first case, a more archaizing register would require an Infinitive, and in the second a morphological Subjunctive, instead of this FC. What is common in both cases is the occurrence of the μέλλω AVC in generally speaking future-referring contexts introduced by a complementizer. Recall that the same pattern has been found with relation to έχω in EMG (cf. 4.2) and, as we shall see, is also found with both έχω and θέλω constructions in LMG. It constitutes an instance of overlap between FCs and the morphological Subjunctive in subordinate clauses (cf. especially the discussion in 5.2.3). Therefore, (2) fills in the missing part of the puzzle, since it can now be argued that *all* FCs were used in such contexts, an observation made here for the first time. The early chronology of (2) fits nicely with the fact that μέλλω is the oldest construction of the three, and we should probably assume that it was used in this fashion even earlier, despite the lack of examples. This would comply well with the assumption that old FCs are commonly employed in subordinate contexts (cf., for example, Bybee, Perkins & Pagliuca, 1994: 279). On the other hand, perhaps its sociolinguistic properties might have prevented it from occurring in such contexts, since it was mostly used by learned speakers who were familiar with AG and aware of the normative tradition and could therefore employ the more 'correct' Subjunctive. The fact that (2) comes from South Italy, an area presumably away from the normative pressure of the administrative center of Constantinople, fits well with this scenario regarding the appearance of the μέλλω AVC in subordinate contexts.

5.1.2 *The later stages*

As noted, the 13th century apparently provides us with no literary texts in the vernacular, a fact probably due to extra-linguistic factors. However, the 14th century saw a remarkable rise in the number of such works, at least in comparison with the previous centuries. The abundance of texts produced under quite differentiated political and cultural environments is manifested linguistically in the great variation of syntactic constructions and, in particular, in the FCs.

Although μέλλω remains a peripheral choice, it is still used in most of the literary texts of this century, as can be seen in Table 5.1. The sporadic (and in absolute numerical terms, limited) occurrence of μέλλω is immediately evident, despite its persistence in most of the texts examined. There are, however, some texts that do not include any instance of this verb, namely *Sahlikis, Poulologos, Fysiologos*, and *Iatrosofia*. This could be attributed to the rather low-register character of these texts (especially *Sahlikis*), where μέλλω was simply inappropriate.

The first striking fact in the table is the very high frequency of attestations in *Ermoniakos*, approximately 55% (36 / 65) of the total instances of the construction. This complies with the character of the text and with the circumstances under which it was written, i.e. by order of the Byzantine Duke of Epirus. So, despite the scornful comments of the first editor of *Ermoniakos*, Sathas (1873), who thought that he should probably not have published excerpts of that "barbaric" text, it seems highly plausible that Ermoniakos was well acquainted with the literary tradition, even though he could not avoid some "mistakes"; thus, at first glance, one can find no other characterization for the only instance of μέλλω followed by a Participle (instead of an Infinitive) in his work (N, 99: τὴν μελλοῦσαν γενομένην). Given that the Participle as a verbal form in general must by now have been rarely used in low registers (except for the indeclinable –ο/ώντα(ς) form and the adjectival Passive Participles in –μένος), its use by Ermoniakos could represent an effort at a higher style naturally prone to 'mistakes'. Nevertheless, this construction (μέλλω + Participle) might also have belonged to a pattern followed to a certain extent by other verbs, as we shall see below (cf. 5.2.–5.3). The middle register of *Ermoniakos* can also be verified by the facts regarding the other AVCs (cf. 5.2–5.4), and, just like *Stratigikon*, this text provides a valuable criterion for determining the association of particular linguistic features with registers of use.

Corroborating evidence for the restriction to the middle and higher registers for the μέλλω AVC comes from the non-literary texts. The most characteristic example of this development can be found in two mathematics textbooks, originating probably from Constantinople. In the first book dating from the 14th c. (Vogel, 1968), μέλλω is attested 15 times, all of them involving the old infinitival complementation. In the second (Hunger & Vogel, 1963), dating from the second half of the 15th c., μέλλω is attested only four times (compared with numerous attestations of θέλω), and moreover, the infinitival complementation is only preserved in two cases, the other two involving clausal complementation introduced by νά. Apparently, the different educational level of the authors,

Table 5.1 *Μέλλω* in 14th-c. literary texts

Meaning*	K&H	V&H	L&R	D.P.	Sahl.	CoM	WoT	Ah.	Poul.	Fys.	Iatr.	Erm.	AoT	Pt.	Total
1. Future-reference															
1a. *Μέλλω* + Inf. /	–	1	–	1	–	2	11	–	–	–	–	34	–	3	52 (80.0)
1b. *Μέλλω νά* + Subj. /	–	–	2	–	–	–	–	2	–	–	–	–	1	1	6 (9.2)
1c. *Μέλλει* (imper.) /	–	–	2	–	–	1	1	–	–	–	–	–	–	–	4 (6.2)
1d. *Μέλλει* (intr.) / Will be	–	–	–	–	–	–	1	–	–	–	–	1	–	–	2 (3.1)
1e. *Μέλλω* + Part. /	–	–	–	–	–	–	–	–	–	–	–	1	–	–	1 (1.5)
TOTAL	–	1	4	1	–	3	13	2	–	–	–	36	1	4	65
2. Non-AVC uses															
2a. Nominalized / Fut.	1	1	2	–	–	–	–	–	–	–	–	–	–	–	4
2b. Nominalized / Fate	–	–	–	–	–	–	50	–	–	–	–	2	–	–	52
2c. Adjectival	–	–	–	–	–	–	–	–	–	–	–	2	–	–	2

Key: K&H = *Kallimahos*, V&H = *Velthandros*, L&R = *Livistros-α*, D.P. = *Diigisis*, Sahl. = *Sahlikis*, CoM = *CoM*, WoT = *WoT*, Ah = *Ahilliiá*, Poul. = *Poulologos*, Fys. = *Fysiologos*, Iatr. = *Iatrosofia*, Erm. = *Ermoniakos*, AoT = *AoT*, Pt. = *Ptoholeon*

* The table does not include instances of the past form ἔμελλον, which are very few (24 in total). However, some interesting examples involving the past form will be discussed below.

related to the post-Byzantine character of the second book, can account for this sharp differentiation in the use of μέλλω.

This novel pattern of complementation, namely the replacement of the old Infinitive by a subordinate clause headed by the complementizer νά and with a finite verb form marked for Subjunctive, affected μέλλω beginning the 14th c., as Table 5.1 illustrates.[4] Μέλλω, from a syntactic point of view, behaved like the other auxiliary and modal verbs (such as θέλω, ἔχω, (ἠ)μπορῶ "can" etc.), in the sense that they were the last to comply with this change (cf. Joseph, 1983). As mentioned, this is an argument of the grammaticalization of the μέλλω AVC, which patterned together with other AVCs. However, the μέλλω AVC was the first to be affected in a decisive manner by the new complementation pattern, probably because of its low frequency of use (at least in comparison with the other FCs), which left it vulnerable to the strong analogical pressures of the overall verbal complementation pattern. Note that in most attestations of μέλλω in the non-literary texts of the 14th c. (e.g. in a Cretan document, cf. Manousakas, 1964), it is the old infinitival complementation which occurs (with some notable exceptions, see below), suggesting that the replacement of the Infinitive has not yet reached middle and higher registers.

Related to this issue are the instances of the "impersonal" use of μέλλω, as exemplified in (3):

(3) ὅταν καὶ τὴν νίκην ἤκουσαν ὅτι μέλλει
     when and the victory heard   that will-3rd SING.PRES.
     νὰ ἔχουν
     that have-3rd PL.PRES.
     "when they heard that they will gain the victory…"

(WoT, 2.386)

This use is evident in (3), since μέλλει is a 3rd person singular form, whereas the subject of its complement clause is in the 3rd person plural, as evidenced by the verbal ending in ἔχουν. This development, much in accord with similar developments in the other Greek modals such as πρέπει "must" etc. (cf. Iakovou, 2003), is on the one hand rather surprising, considering that the situation is quite different in the case of the other two future-referring AVCs.[5]

---

[4] The syntactic variation in the complementation between lower and higher registers is now manifested not in the type of the Infinitive but in the type of complementation (infinitival or clausal). This is the reason why, henceforth, the use of the Present and the Aorist Infinitive will not be differentiated. In any case, although the Infinitive remained an authentic feature of LMG (Joseph, 2001b), there is no clear indication of the differences the choice of the Infinitive registered in such contexts.

[5] Concerning the form θέ νά and the debated existence of an impersonal future-referring θέλει νά, see the detailed discussion in 5.4.3.

On the other hand, it is in accord with the progressive specialization of meaning of future-referring μέλλω towards a more deontic nuance, not only as a destiny future (denoting an event that is bound to take place, as in ex. 3) but also as a 'typical' deontic modal, conveying obligation. As we shall see, the same morphosyntactic development occurs in the case of the θέλω AVC but, crucially, only when it conveys a deontic meaning (cf. 5.4.2).

This is hardly surprising, since it is well known that deontic modality tends to correlate cross-linguistically with uninflected forms and impersonal syntactic constructions. More importantly, the impersonal μέλλει constitutes the first clear development along the lines of morphological impoverishment for μέλλω, as it loses now its verbal paradigm, retaining only the 3rd singular form. It is not clear why this morphological reduction in the "decategorialization" parameter (cf. 1.1) occurs in LMG. In this period, the μέλλω AVC is presumably restricted to very specific contexts, and its frequency of use in comparison to the other FCs is substantially lower. Consequently, this morphological reduction can hardly be accounted for on the basis of high frequency of use (with the possible exception of Cyprus, where the μέλλω AVC seems to have been much more frequent, cf. below). But exactly this rarity of use may explain this development: as the μέλλω AVC became increasingly associated with deontic modality, it conformed with the syntactic patterns of the constructions belonging to this semantic domain, and impersonal syntax was clearly the most prominent of the patterns (cf. comment above on πρέπει). Therefore, the ever-growing frequency of the μέλλω AVC occurring in an impersonal syntax can perhaps be regarded as a different kind of decategorialization, as μέλλω was moving away from the domain of futurity into the one of deontic modality. This development never reached a final stage whereby μέλλω would be restricted to an obligation meaning, at least not in most Greek-speaking areas, with the possible exception of Cyprus (cf. below), hence the variation between inflected and uninflected forms of the verb in most texts of LMG.

There are yet more examples of the impersonal syntax of the construction in the domain of the future-in-the past, expressed by the past form ἔμελλε (e. g. *CoM* 885, *WoT* 14041). But a most interesting example of ἔμελλε, illustrating the correlation between syntax and semantics, i.e. impersonal form and deontic meaning, is found in *CoM*:

(4) τὴν πρᾶξιν γὰρ καὶ τὴν στρατείαν ὅπου   ἔμελλεν
 the act   prt and the campaign that-rel will-3rd SING.PRET.
 ποιήσουν
 make-3rd PL.SUBJ.
 "the operation and the campaign that they would / should make..."

(*CoM*, 3702)

Late medieval Greek 129

Three observations are to be made about this example, two from a syntactic point of view. First, it constitutes another instance of the impersonal μέλλει form, since the subjects of the verb and its complement differ (3rd p. sing.–3rd p. pl., respectively). Second and more interesting is the absence of the complementizer νά, producing a "serial" construction (V+V$_S$) that has remained unnoticed hitherto. And even though this "serialization" does not manifest itself again in the corpus in the case of μέλλω, when it is combined with the LMG data concerning the other AVCs, as well as with the evidence already presented from previous periods (cf. mainly 3.2–3.3, 4.3), it could lead us to alter our assumptions with regard to this type of construction in LMG. This issue will be discussed below (cf. 5.4.1).

From a semantic point of view, however, the most interesting fact about (4) is not evident in the example but hidden in the apparatus criticus. For that particular line, the other main manuscript of the text gives the variant reading ἔπρεπε νὰ ποίσουν ("they should / had to make"). Even though there is no way to tell if the meaning of the verse in (4) is simply future-in-the-past or obligation, the variant reading could well offer us an insight into the meaning that μέλλω was felt to have at that time. The deontic undertone of the verb is thus both morphosyntactically (with the impersonal syntax) and semantically (with the variant—presumably synonymous—reading) apparent.

The last observation is also consistent with the tendency of this AVC to be used as a 'destiny future', i.e. in contexts where the action described is bound to happen, such as religious contexts, prophecies, etc. There are numerous examples of that use in the texts of the 14th c., in the romance of *Velthandros* (1214), in *Ahilliid* (N 277), in *Livistros-a* (542), and in many others (cf. also example (3) above). The meaning of 'destiny future' is in accordance with the meaning of obligation alluded to. There is more evidence suggestive of that specialization of the semantics of μέλλω, apart from the fact that it seems to be already in progress in the time of *Digenis*, as noted (cf. 5.1.1): under (2b.) in Table 5.1 is an instance of nominalization unattested before this century, namely the use of a substantive derived from μέλλω, with various forms (τό μέλλον, τά μέλλοντα, τό μελλάμενον, τά μελλάμενα), in the meaning of "fate, destiny". Crucially, this meaning is not exclusively attested in the *WoT*, a text which could be misleading because it constitutes an abridged version / translation of a French original, but also in *Ermoniakos*, whose author, despite any doubts one might have with respect to his language, is after all the only author with the knowledge to use μέλλω in its ancient and certainly obsolete adjectival function (e.g. T49–50), as noted in the same table (under 2c.).

There appears to be an areal differentiation with respect to the productivity of the deontic meaning of μέλλω: the impersonal form μέλλει was very popular in Cyprus, a fact that has been already noted by Aerts (1983), who discusses in detail the extant evidence. In terms of meaning, Aerts only makes a brief comment that μέλλει seems to be moving towards the meaning of πρέπει ("must"). Actually, in accordance with what has been observed above, μέλλει has a clear deontic meaning in the *Assises*, where it is very frequently attested as a deontic verb and can be interchanged with another impersonal verb, ἐντέχεται (=πρέπει). An example of this deontic meaning is given in (5):

(5) Περὶ τοῦ ὅρκου τὸν   μέλλει   νὰ   ποίσῃ   ὁκάποιος
    about the oath   which must-3rd PRES. that make-3rd SUBJ. someone
    ἔμπροσθεν τοῦ   βισκούντη
    in-front-of the   viscount
    "about the oath that one must swear in front of the viscount"

(*Assises*, 259 (ms.A))

This example is taken from the title of a paragraph, where the necessary actions on various occasions are described. Since this text is usually considered to belong to the 14th c., the development of the deontic meaning must have occurred earlier in Cyprus than in other Greek-speaking areas, since it appears already established in the *Assises* at a time when it has a low-token frequency outside Cyprus, as argued above. Recall that such examples of deontic meaning may have been found already in the H–R period (cf. ex. 1 in 3.1) and, consequently, the situation obtaining in Cypriot can be regarded either as a geographically-restricted retention of an old meaning or a recent development. The lack of similar examples from the EMG period, as well as the more clear deontic undertone in all examples from Late Medieval Cyprus in comparison with the H–R data seemingly argues in favor of the latter, although the fact that no text of EMG clearly originates from Cyprus, together with the numerous problems associated with the textual evidence in general from this period (cf. ch. 4) seriously undermine any firm conclusions.

Apart from the μέλλω AVC, we find instances of intransitive use both with μέλλω and ἔμελλον, such as the following:

(6) λοίμη   γὰρ   μεγάλη   μέλλει
    disease prt   big   will-3rd PRES.
    "and a great disease will (occur)"

(*Ermoniakos*, H 224)

Here there is no Infinitive (or subordinate clause) following μέλλω, which by itself conveys a meaning probably along the lines "will occur, will come".[6] This construction is reminiscent of the situation in AG, whereby the Participle could appear without any infinitival complement (when the Infinitive required by the meaning would be a form of the verb "to be"), a fact that led to its nominalization with the meaning of "the future" (τό μέλλον). In the case of AG ellipsis (cf. 2.1), the 'missing' complement of μέλλω was determined—to a great extent—by the linguistic context, whereas the meaning in examples such as (6) is not dependent on the context. The example in (6), which is taken from a middle-register text, is even more interesting if we consider that similar examples are unattested in the case of the other two FCs. This fact highlights the difference between μέλλω and the other two verbs, as the former, despite all developments manifested in LMG, was apparently never so entrenched in the AVC that the speakers lose the ability to extract it from this construction and use it independently with the same meanings. This is also manifested in the new nominalizations of μέλλω with the meaning "fate, destiny".

On the whole, therefore, the data from the 14th century seem to point towards the direction of a semantic specialization for μέλλω in the domain of deontic modality, in the sense of either 'destiny future' or even obligation. This is also reflected on the syntactic level, as μέλλω starts to deviate from the pattern of the other two AVCs: it can now be complemented by a νά–clause and can occur in an impersonal form. These syntactic-semantic developments of μέλλω went in parallel with its decline in frequency of use in the texts of lower registers and the corresponding restriction to higher registers of use, with the possible exception of Cyprus, as will become more evident below.

The picture is unchanged as we move on to the literary texts of the 14th–15th c.,[7] which admittedly contain few instances of μέλλω. However, these attestations comply with the semantic development presented, namely that μέλλω is now used in contexts where the inherent uncertainty engulfing the future gives ground to a fatalistic perspective. This is the case in all examples of μέλλω in these texts (four in *Alfavitos*, two in *Thisiid* (e.g. 92) and one in *Livistros-b* (2814), where μέλλω occurs without a complement, similarly to example (6)).

---

[6] Thus, this intransitive μέλλω is quite different from the Ancient Greek μέλλω$_2$, which, as we saw (cf. 2.1), had the meaning "be late at, delay…". No attestation of μέλλω$_2$ is found in the texts of LMG.

[7] To this category belong texts which cannot be dated with certainty, but were probably written in the late 14th–early 15th c. (cf. bibliography).

TABLE 5.2 *Μέλλω* in 15th-c. literary texts

SYNTACTIC / SEMANTIC PATTERN	P.Xen.	D.V.	CoT	Varni	Fal.	Del.	Kat.	Mah.	Total
1. Future reference									
1a. *Μέλλω* + Inf. /	–	–	2	1	1	10	–	–	14 (20.0)
1b. *Μέλλω νά* + Subj. /	–	2	1	–	4	1	–	8	16 (22.9)
1c. *Μέλλει* (imp.) *νά* + Subj. /	1	–	2	–	2	22	1	8	36 (51.4)
1d. *Μέλλει* (intr.) / Will be	–	–	–	–	3	–	1	–	4 (5.7)
TOTAL	1	2	5	1	10	33	2	16	70
2. Obligation									
2a. *Μέλλω* + Inf. / "should" (Q)	–	1	–	1	–	–	–	–	2
2b. *Μέλλει* (imp.) *νά* + Subj. / "should" (Q)	–	–	–	–	–	–	–	6	6
2c. *Μέλλει* (imp.) *νά* + Subj. / Obl. (Affirm. clauses)	–	–	–	1	–	–	–	–	1
3. Non–AVC uses									
3a. *Μέλλων* / Adj.	1	–	–	–	–	4	–	–	5
3b. Nom./ Future	–	–	–	–	1	2	–	–	3
3c. Nom. / Fate	–	–	–	–	2	–	–	–	2

Key: P.Xen = *Xeniteia*, D.V. = *Velissarios*, CoT = *CoT*, Varni = *O polemos tis Varnis*, Fal. = *Falieros*, Del. = *Dellaportas*, Kat. = *Katalogia*, Mah. = *Mahairas*

Late medieval Greek 133

One interesting example is found in *Spanos*, involving a development that has scarcely been documented: the word μελλοπεθερές ("the mothers-in-law-to-be", rec. A, 481) is a case of compounding exhibited in AG texts and in the papyri (cf. 2.1, 3.1), but hardly anywhere else. Bearing in mind the very low register of the text, we can assume that this example is representative of a rare use of the spoken language which survives even in Modern Greek, though definitely as a relic (mainly in the two words μελλόνυμφος "the spouse-to-be" and μελλοθάνατος "the one who is about to die"). A similar compound (μελλοσύζυγος=the husband-to-be) found in a Byzantine contract of the 13th–14th c. (Gedeon, 1896) probably reflects the continuing existence of such forms in the more legalistic registers. Both examples, however, provide the link from the attestations of that form of compounding in Modern Greek to the period of the papyri. Even though we cannot know whether these compounds had a 'destiny future' meaning in LMG, the fact that they unmistakably do in Modern Greek supports our hypothesis on the development of the deontic meaning of μέλλω in LMG.

The texts of the 15th century are much more representative of the actual reality concerning the μέλλω AVC than those of the 14th–15th c., with regard both to token frequency and the variety of constructions and meanings, as illustrated in Table 5.2.

The developments attested in the previous century are now established. *Μέλλω* is continuously used in specific contexts with the undertone of a 'destiny future': one of the most typical examples of this semantic development is provided by the poems of *Dellaportas*, whereby 90% (30 / 33) of the total instances of the μέλλω AVC follow this norm, as in (7):

(7) καὶ μέλλει   ἐμένα τὸ πουρνὸν στὴν φούρκα νὰ
    and will-3rd SING.PRES. me   the morning at-the gallows that
    κρεμάσουν
    hang-3rd PL.SUBJ.
    "and they are going to hang me at the gallows tomorrow morning"

(*Dellaportas*, A 1.740)

Moreover, the deontic μέλλω AVC was generalized to another context of use (marked as "should" (Q) in the table above) in the wider domain of obligation. This context, exemplified in (8), is a common question about what one should do given the circumstances (the other AVCs also occur in this context, cf. 4.3, 5.2., and 5.3):

(8) καὶ νὰ καθίσουν   εἰς βουλὴν τί μέλλωσι   ποιῆσαι
    and that sit-3rd PL.SUBJ. to counsel what will-3rd PL.SUBJ. do-INF.
    "and to sit for a council about what to do"

(*Velissarios (N)*, 185)

It is worth mentioning that this meaning is usually expressed in Modern Greek with the νά-subj. (and with the morphological Subjunctive in all previous periods of Greek, as already mentioned), but in the texts of LMG it does not constitute the sole case of overlap between 'subjunctive' and 'future' contexts. We will return to this point in the sections on the other AVCs (cf. especially 5.2.3).

In the example above the old pattern of complementation involving an Infinitive is retained. Even though it is still extant, the figures in Table 5.2 leave no doubt that it is on the retreat, as the cases of a complementary νά–clause clearly outnumber those with the Infinitive (cf. Fig. 5.1). Most of the instances of the Infinitive are found in the poetic works of Dellaportas, who in any case is the author who uses μέλλω more than anyone else (39 attestations in total, including substantivized cases). It seems that there is a correlation between the level of literacy exhibited in a particular text, the appearance of μέλλω, and the use of the ancient pattern μέλλω + Infinitive: the higher the register of the text, the more numerous the attestations of μέλλω, and, in particular, its attestations with the old complementation. In this respect, the figures in *Dellaportas* fit neatly into the picture described above for μέλλω, and are suggestive of a quite extended exposure to the learned Greek tradition for the Cretan poet. This is verified by the evidence we have for him, as he apparently had received a rather extensive literary education (cf. Manousakas, 1995).

The absence of *any* infinitival complement in *Mahairas* tempts us to conclude that in the Cypriot dialect this syntactic development took place earlier than in the other Greek dialects, or was at least 'accepted' earlier in written registers. This correlates nicely with the conclusion reached above on the basis of the evidence of the *Assises,* according to which μέλλω was more productive in Cyprus and manifested developments at a faster rate.

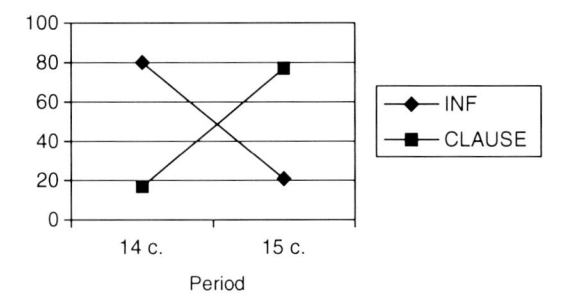

FIGURE 5.1 The complementation of μέλλω AVC

Consequently, the relatively high frequency of use of μέλλω in *Mahairas* should not be seen as an indication of his familiarity with the 'learned' tradition or of a 'higher' register of the text but mainly as a product of the wider popularity entertained by μέλλω in this island.

A further morphosyntactic development concerns the proliferation of the uninflected μέλλει AVC. Table 5.2 illustrates that more than 50% of the total instances of μέλλω involve the impersonal use (43 / 75, 57%), while this pattern was almost non-extant in the 14th century (cf. Table 5.1). The numbers could rise even more if we assume, following Aerts (1983), that all the attestations of the μέλλει form in *Mahairas*, including those where one cannot tell if it is personal or impersonal, should be considered impersonal, because *Mahairas* allegedly contains no single clear example of a personal μέλλω. This observation, even though in agreement with the predominance of uninflected μέλλει in the other Cypriot text of the *Assises*, is not completely accurate, however, since one example of an undoubtedly inflected use of the particular verb has been found[8] (III, §286: ὅτι ἐμέλλαν καὶ τἄλλα κάτεργα νὰ πᾶσιν "for the other ships were bound to go as well"), and, consequently, all the ambiguous cases have been classified as personal, even though one could argue that a firm case cannot be made on the basis of only one clear example. Nevertheless, even this example does not alter the overall pattern, according to which the personal μέλλω is extremely rare in *Mahairas* and under considerable pressure in all the other texts. The fact that, as already mentioned, this development is not common to all three AVCs calls for an explanation (cf. below, 5.1.3).

A final observation concerning the facts presented in Table 5.2 needs to be made: the so-called "intransitive" use of μέλλω, which has been mentioned in connection with the 14th-c. texts, can be found in both *Falieros* and, more importantly, in *Katalogia* (139), the latter arguably representing more straightforwardly the actual low-register language of the time than *Falieros*. Therefore, it can safely be said to constitute an authentic use of μέλλω in LMG.

The contemporary non-literary texts contain relatively few instances of μέλλω. In all the notary books from the Venetian-ruled parts of Greece, μέλλω is found only sporadically. It is attested in Crete (e.g. *Grigoropoulos*, 99 / d.1525) and in Kefalonia (e.g. *De Montesantos*, 3 / d.1535). An example from Kefalonia illustrates its basic context of use:

---

[8] This example involves a past tense form of the verb. As in Table 5.1, Table 5.2 does not contain the attestations of ἔμελλον for this century, for the reasons given above.

(9) τὸν θάνατον ὅπου μέλη   νὰ λάβο
the death   that will-3rd PRES. that take-1st PRES.SUBJ.
καὶ εἰς τὴν κρίσιν   ὅπου θέλο   λάβη...
and to the judgment   that want-1st PRES. take-INF.
"the death that I am destined to receive and the judgment that I will receive..."

(*Amarantos*, 58 / d. 1535)

In this example, μέλλω is found in a religious context, as is usually the case when not attested in some formulaic constructions, for instance in wills. Moreover, (9) contains, as expected, an instance of the impersonal μέλλει syntax. In other words, the non-literary texts of the 15th–16th c. apparently follow the same pattern of use as the literary texts, corroborating the validity of conclusions drawn from them. One qualification needs to be made, though: the impersonal μέλλει pattern is quite rare in the official documents. The syntactic difference should probably be attributed to the register variation exhibited in the non-literary texts, depending on the level of literacy of the notaries themselves: if a notary was educated enough to use this verb, then he would prefer the normative personal construction instead of the everyday impersonal use for his official text.

Finally, it should be noted that the μέλλω AVC was not the only appropriate AVC for 'destiny future' contexts, since other AVCs (and especially θέλω) could also occur in these contexts, as (9) readily shows. Consequently, speakers could select more than one FC, even in the preferred contexts of use of μέλλω, before eventually abandoning altogether the μέλλω AVC by the time of Modern Greek.

5.1.3 Conclusions: the status of μέλλω

The evidence presented indicates that the previously disregarded μέλλω AVC has a rightful place in the expression of future reference in LMG, not only for archaizing texts but also for texts in the vernacular, a fact hitherto unknown. Even though its sociolinguistic distribution is quite restricted in this period, since it was indeed mainly used in texts of middle and high registers, it remains extant in the lower-register texts largely by virtue of a semantic development, which brought its meaning closer to deontic modality, either obligation or 'destiny future'. The latter meaning is observed throughout the Greek-speaking world, while the former was really productive mainly, but not exclusively, in Cyprus. By the token frequency of the μέλλω AVC in each—literary—text, it is possible to establish—roughly speaking—the register of this text, a criterion which might prove useful even for texts written in an archaizing language. As for the syntactic developments, it has been shown that the replacement of the Infinitive by a complement clause headed by νά is almost complete by the 15th c., while μέλλω itself is increasingly used in an uninflected, 3rd singular form, in correlation with the development of its modal meaning, and seems also to be able to be used intransitively, conveying a future-referring, existential meaning.

The cases where the development of μέλλω diverges in comparison with the other AVCs argue for a different grammaticalization stage of this AVC in LMG, as has also been argued for the previous periods (cf. 3.1 and 4.1). First of all, there is semantic evidence which indicates that μέλλω retains its association with a lexical meaning outside the AVC and, therefore, is not as grammatical as the other two verbs forming AVCs. Besides the already mentioned argument from nominalization, it is crucial that μέλλω can also be used without a complement referring to the future, a very idiosyncratic feature that it does not share with either θέλω or έχω. Moreover, the new meaning of its nominalization, "fate, destiny", arises at a time when the μέλλω AVC has already moved into that nuance of meaning; consequently, it could be argued that it is μέλλω itself which expressed this particular meaning, irrespective of its context of use, i.e. whether it formed an AVC or not. Though not conclusive, this evidence is strongly suggestive of a new lexical meaning for μέλλω, which appears less grammatical than θέλω and έχω, with its lexical core in the domain of deontic modality, giving rise to an 'obligation' or a 'destiny future' meaning. This semantic association argues also against a 'split' between lexical μέλλω occurring in nominalizations, compounds, etc. and grammatical μέλλω forming an AVC. The emergence of this new deontic meaning of the AVC goes against typological predictions (Bybee, Perkins & Pagliuca, 1994: 257, 279), which hypothesized that in FCs emerging out of intention as their source, deontic modality should not in principle be attested and, furthermore, that it should not be attested as a development in such a late stage of development, i.e. after prediction had become the main meaning of the AVC.

On the syntactic front, this AVC exhibits two noticeable developments: the gradual and ever-increasing substitution of the finite complement clause for the old Infinitive, as well as the establishment of the impersonal syntax. In the case of θέλω AVC by contrast, leaving aside for the moment details and complications which will be the focus of our attention in the following sections, there is a clear distinction between future reference, manifested by θέλω + Infinitive, and volitional meaning, expressed by θέλω νά + Subjunctive during the whole LMG period; any impersonal use is extremely rare and restricted to the deontic meaning of the construction (cf. 5.4). As for ἔχω, in this period it is mainly used in a variety of modal meanings. Though the FC can occasionally be found with a complement clause, there is a preference for retaining the Infinitive in this use; furthermore, there is almost no example of an impersonal use (cf. 5.2).

Consequently, it seems that the μέλλω AVC is now significantly differentiated from the other two AVCs in syntactic terms. On the other hand, it should be noted that μέλλω originally belonged to the class of modal and aspectual verbs (along with θέλω, ἔχω and others) that retained their infinitival complementation till the LMG period, whereas the vast majority of verbs by that time already had a subordinate clause as complementation (cf., for example, Horrocks, 1997: 227–8). Apparently, this syntactic divergence of μέλλω occurred in LMG, and should evidently be associated with the semantic developments affecting this verb.

It has been argued (cf. 2.1, 3.1, and 4.1) that μέλλω basically constituted a modal verb with a core meaning of intention but that this was easily transformed contextually into prediction, whenever the agent of the clause could have no claim to intentions (e.g. in the case of inanimate subjects), hence the future reference of the μέλλω AVC. This remained the case till EMG and, as a consequence, μέλλω came to be included in that group of, presumably, high-frequency verbs that retained the apparently old-style infinitival complementation in LMG. It never completely lost its lexical meaning, however, and, in that respect, it has similar properties with modal verbs cross-linguistically, such as English modals, which have undoubtedly retained part(s) of their lexical meaning, too (cf., for example, Coates, 1983). In LMG, the μέλλω AVC developed a new modal meaning: its semantics 'shifted' from the domain of intention / prediction to the domain of deontic modality.

It is proposed here that this 'shift' came about through the contextual specialization of the μέλλω FC. In LMG, μέλλω was mostly used in religious and similar contexts where there is little room for doubt regarding the future, leading to the 'destiny future' meaning. It is not clear why this association should have come about; one possibility is based on the observation that μέλλω was restricted in LMG to the higher registers of use. The very low frequency of use of μέλλω in literary texts in the vernacular and in notary books and the specialization of its meaning might be correlated: most of the writers of such works would be familiar with this verb, if at all, through religious texts used for educational purposes (such as the Gospels), which, as mentioned (cf. 3.1), abounded with the μέλλω AVC. Given that, in the LMG period, the expression of future reference was completely different with the θέλω + Infinitive as the dominant FC, speakers might have associated the use of μέλλω with the largely deontic character of usage in these works, resulting in the observed specialization. The likely chain of events is as follows: firstly, μέλλω lost ground as an FC, and was increasingly sociolinguistically restricted to high registers; subsequently, most speakers of LMG used it rarely as shown by the sharp drop in the frequency of use of μέλλω in the texts of the corpus; finally, since speakers familiar with this construction knew it through religious texts and education, specialization of meaning ensued. This scenario fits well with the evidence from *Dellaportas*: it has been argued that his education correlates with his rather extensive use of μέλλω, and, more strikingly, we know that he was heavily influenced by various religious texts, which he knew very well (Manousakas, 1995). At the same time, he uses μέλλω in the deontic meaning almost without exception. In the light of these data, the hypothesis described seems plausible.

The final step, from 'destiny future' to obligation, is easy to imagine, as FCs are often used to convey deontic modality, even without the very strong deontic nuance of the μέλλω AVC. This development might then be considered as a generalization of meaning, since μέλλω could be used in the wide domain of deontic modality and was not restricted to future reference. The 'shift' to deontic modality is also syntactically manifested by the emergence of the uninflected μέλλει form, according to the pattern followed by other modal verbs, such as πρέπει (=must), which appears only in its impersonal form. It is important to note the inter-relation of these developments with the 'frequency of use' factor: as long as the μέλλω AVC retained a high 'frequency of use' (e.g. in EMG), it retained its old syntactic properties. As this started to alter, and the μέλλω AVC was no longer frequently used (in LMG), it was restricted to specific contexts (e.g. religious texts), hence its specialization in meaning; furthermore, its complementation pattern was altered, since it was not the most entrenched FC and was more vulnerable to change than the other FCs. Apparently, the importance given to frequency in recent studies (e.g. Fischer, 2007) is indeed justified, to judge from the Greek data.

Two more observations can be of theoretical interest here. Firstly, the morphological impoverishment of μέλλω occurred at a period when this AVC was rather rarely used and in specific contexts. Therefore, in that case, it is not frequency that led to this reduction but rather its inclusion in the domain of deontic modality, which in Greek is mostly conveyed with impersonal syntax. And secondly, the development "futurity → deontic modality" and especially the fact that its occurrence is mainly due to sociolinguistic factors (e. g. the association of μέλλω AVC with specific written registers), illustrates quite emphatically that the hitherto neglected (for most practitioners of grammaticalization) sociolinguistic properties of AVCs can interfere in a most decisive manner in a grammaticalization process. This is the main reason why the predictions by Bybee, Perkins & Pagliuca (1994) have failed in this particular case, as they are bound to fail in other cases when sociolinguistic developments are not taken into account.

5.2 Ἔχω + Infinitive / subordinate clause: future-reference and modality

The ἔχω AVC is still in use in LMG, even though the future-referring meaning of the AVC is of low frequency. And if we do not include one particular construction found in the 14th c., which will be discussed further below (cf. 5.2.3), ἔχω may even be outnumbered by μέλλω. Nevertheless, it gave rise to various developments surviving in Modern Greek (especially in the domain of the perfect), and therefore it has enjoyed a rather privileged status in the literature in comparison with μέλλω, mostly with regard to its perfect meaning (cf., for example, Aerts, 1965 and Moser, 1988). In his treatment of the diachrony of Future as a category in Greek, Bănescu (1915) offers various examples of the ἔχω FC, but he does not differentiate between its various modal uses and he does not relate the story of ἔχω with that of the other FCs. Otherwise, no systematic account of this construction exists, apart from various comments on specific issues (cf., for example, Joseph, 1983). The examination of the present (ἔχω) and the past form (εἶχα) will be presented here separately, as, contrary to μέλλω, their developments are divergent. This phenomenon is an indication of an advanced grammaticalization stage of the ἔχω AVC (already argued for, cf. 3.2), as the present and the past forms followed different (but not completely unrelated) paths of development, being grammaticalized in different contexts. By contrast, the development of the μέλλω AVC was always related to its past equivalent, as the AVC was less grammaticalized (cf. previous section).

5.2.1 The early stages

Already in the early stages of this period, it seems that the ἔχω AVC rests in the shadow of θέλω, at least as far as future reference is concerned. This is immediately evident in *Armouris*, where ἔχω, like μέλλω, is completely absent. However, one short poem does not provide safe ground for firm conclusions.

The *Stratigikon* offers some interesting insights on the status and function of this AVC in the 11th c. It contains 18 instances of ἔχω + Infinitive. Of these instances, only nine have a purely future-referring meaning, in contrast with the 14 attestations of μέλλω. This suggests that it might have been acceptable to employ this AVC alongside μέλλω for future reference, but perhaps less readily. The ancient ability meaning is also present, attested six times, while the remaining three attestations involve deontic modal uses: two of them in the context of questions (described in the case of μέλλω as a meaning conveyed by "should", e.g. What should we do?), and the last as a prohibition, exemplified in (10):

(10) εἰ δὲ εἴπῃ εἴσελθε εἰς τὴν θάλασσαν, οὐδὲ τοῦτο ἔχεις ποιῆσαι
    if prt says enter   into the sea,   nor this have-2nd PRES. do-INF.
    "If then he says, 'go into the sea', do not do this either!"

(*Stratigikon*, 235, 5)

The observation that the example in (10) constitutes a prohibition is strengthened by the fact that this sentence is preceded in the same paragraph and in the very same context by another prohibition, phrased in the common AG way, i.e. in the Aorist Subjunctive (οὐ μή ποιήσῃς τοῦτο=do not do this). Contrary to the other modal uses, which were available for the ἔχω AVC already from the EMG period (cf. Table 4.5 in 4.2), the context of prohibition appears for the first time in this example; examples such as (10) come as no surprise, since ability and, more particularly, possibility can easily, in the appropriate context, give rise to a prohibition reading (Bybee, Perkins & Pagliuca, 1994: 192–3).

The evidence from the two literary texts of the 11th c. suggests that the ἔχω FC was still in use, especially in the middle register of *Stratigikon*. This is partly verified by the contemporary official documents, which contain sporadic instances of the construction, as the one in (11) taken from a will from the monastery of Esfigmenou in Mount Athos:[9]

(11) Μετὰ δὲ τὴν [ἐ]μὴν ἀπεβίωσην θέλω [καὶ] βούλομαι ἵνα
    After prt the mine death   want   [and] desire   that
    ἀναλαμβάνεσαι   τὸν   ἀγρὸν τῶν   Σελίνων καθὼς
    take-over-2nd PRES. the   field the-GEN. Selinon as
    ἔχει   εὑρεθῆναι   ἐν τῷ τότε καιρῷ...
    have-3rd PRES. find-INF.PASS. in the then time
    "After my death, I want that you take over the field of Selinon in the state that it will be at that time..."

(*Esfigmenou*, 2 / d.1037)

---

[9] Similar examples can be found in the archives of the monasteries of Asia Minor (*MM*: vol.IV, CIV, a.o.), but all of them involve the apparently formulaic expression ἔχεις καταβαλέσθαι ἐξόδους ("you will pay the costs").

It is worth noticing the rather archaizing register of this example, illustrated by the ancient morphology of the Infinitive (εὑρεθῆναι) instead of the common Medieval form εὑρεθῆ (cf. Joseph, 1983: 56). The latter can be found in a contemporary document from South Italy (12), and, consequently, the form found in (11) should not be solely attributed to the early date of production but to a relatively high register:

(12) καὶ ὡς τις [leg. ὅστις] ἂν ἔχει   εὑρεθῆ
     and whoever   prt have-3rd PRES.find-INF.PASS.
     μετατρέπων καὶ διασείων...
       changing and shaking...
     "and whoever is found trying to challenge [this will]..."

(*Trinchera*: 37 / d.1050)

Apart from the morphological aspect, this example is also worth stressing because of its syntax: it contains a relative-conditional clause involving the ἔχω AVC, a pattern not attested elsewhere, with the sole exception of a document from the Cretan notary Patsidiotis written at a much later date (*Patsidiotis* 10, d.1546). Instead, in the texts of subsequent centuries, θέλω and mainly ἤθελα are found in this context, even though εἶχα appears as well (cf. 5.3 and 5.4, 5.5). It could be assumed that the example in (12) reflects an archaism or, perhaps more plausibly, a more generalized use of the ἔχω construction in South Italy as an areal feature. The lack of evidence allows for no elaborate guess.

Given that in the same non-literary texts μέλλω is much more prolific than ἔχω, it can be concluded that the ἔχω FC was not very productive in the higher registers of the official documents. On the other hand, although *Armouris* contains no instance of either μέλλω or ἔχω, the latter seems to have been slightly more frequent in the literary texts than the former. This can be seen in *Digenis*, where the one and only attestation of μέλλω is contrasted with four instances of the ἔχω AVC conveying future reference and another three conveying ability. It is interesting to note in this respect that even *Grottaferrata*, the more learned version of *Digenis*, does not differentiate much between the two FCs in terms of quantity, as it contains five attestations of μέλλω and three of ἔχω. Furthermore, *Digenis* offers two noteworthy examples of ἔχω complemented by another finite verb form, a fact hitherto unnoticed for this AVC in this period. This kind of construction, which has also been noted for the first time in this investigation for μέλλω (cf. 5.1) and for ἔχω in previous periods (cf. 3.2), is illustrated in (13):

(13) ἀπέλθω   ἔχω   καὶ ἐγὼ καὶ νὰ   σᾶς   θεραπεύσω
     leave-1st SUBJ. have-1st PRES. and I   and that   you   serve-1st SUBJ.
     "I will leave as well and I will serve you"

(*Digenis*, 1420)

Again, it is the context which determines the probable future reference of this example. The co-ordination with the independent, future-referring subjunctive[10] (νὰ σᾶς θεραπεύσω) provides evidence in support of this interpretation, which is further corroborated by the fact that this verse is preceded by another, very similar one, whose future reference is unquestionable (*Digenis* 1391: ἔλθει θέλω καὶ ἐγὼ καὶ νὰ τὸν δοκιμάσω "I will come as well and I will test him").[11] The other example of the V + V_S construction, this time with the ability meaning, illustrates the syntactic fluctuation in the form of the AVC, especially at this stage, since the infinitival complementation is found co-ordinated with the finite one:

(14) Οἶδα,   φαγεῖν καὶ πιεῖν   ἔχεις   καὶ λουσθῆς   καὶ
      know,   eat-INF. and drink-INF. have-2nd PRES. and wash-2nd SUBJ. and
      ἀλλάξῃς[12]
      change-2nd SUBJ.
      "I know, you can (have enough to) eat and drink and wash yourself and change clothes"

(*Digenis*, 1779)

This phenomenon of 'serialization', which has often been considered restricted to the case of θέλω, seems in reality to have been more widespread, involving all three FCs. It follows that an account for this development solely on the basis of changes affecting θέλω, as found in the existing literature (cf., for example, Joseph & Pappas, 2002), cannot capture all the relevant facts, either in terms of the chronology or in terms of the spread of these developments. This issue will be addressed when discussing the facts concerning θέλω (cf. 5.4).

The texts of the 12th c. do not contain many instances of ἔχω (ten in total). The majority of these convey an ability meaning (6 / 10), a fact that probably indicates the relatively high level of literacy of the authors of these poems.

---

[10] One could argue that the Subjunctive might be dependent on ἔχω and not have independent future reference in this example. However, there are two reasons why this is probably not the case: (a) the νά-Subjunctive is very commonly used as a future-referring form by itself in many contexts in this period (cf., for example, Horrocks, 1997: 230), and (b) the construction ἔχω νά + Subj. as a future-referring form is hardly ever found (cf. discussion for example (15)).

[11] Actually, the text of Alexiou's critical edition (1985) reads ἀπέλθω θέλω, which constitutes a correction founded on the basis exactly of verse 1420 (ex. 13), and is not a reading found in the manuscript. However, I have reinstated the reading of the manuscript, as Alexiou gives no reason why the perfectly acceptable and widely used construction θέλω + Infinitive should be corrected.

[12] Again Alexiou inserts the subjunctive marker νά in order to avoid the V + V_S construction, and therefore his text reads ἔχεις καὶ νὰ λουσθῆς καὶ ἀλλάξῃς. As Alexiou himself has suggested a correction which creates such a construction (cf. fn. 11), I cannot see why we should accept the insertion of νά. In any case, even accepting this correction would not alter the overall picture of syntactic fluctuation.

However, in *Glykas* the first attestation of ἔχω followed by a νά–clause is found:

(15) ἂν ἔχη   εἰς τὰ ἐπιθάνατα νὰ τὸ εὔρη,
     If have-3rd SUBJ. in the after-life that this find-3rd SUBJ.,
     μὴ σὲ μέλη
     not you worry
     "If he is going to find his doom after death, do not worry"

(*Glykas*, 364)

This example, though, does not signal the onset of a development that would spread in the following centuries, at least not in the domain of future reference. On the contrary, the syntactic construction ἔχω νά + Subjunctive remains in use in subsequent periods (and is still alive in Modern Greek), but mainly carrying modal meanings, such as ability and obligation. Thus, the context in (15) also favors a 'destiny future' interpretation, as it refers to the fate of a person. The strong deontic nuance of this context might be the reason for the replacement of the Infinitive by a clause in (15), since the same thing occurred in the case of μέλλω (cf. 5.1.2). The example from *Glykas* could suggest that the replacement of the Infinitive affected the ἔχω even before the μέλλω AVC, even though there can be no firm conclusion on the basis of a single example. However, it underlines the assumed low frequency of use for the ἔχω FC, since it has been suggested that it was the factor of (low) frequency that led μέλλω to exhibit the new complementation pattern first among the FCs.

The non-literary texts of the 12th–13th c. contain very few occurrences of the ἔχω AVC and only one with a future-referring meaning, in a letter from the Lusignan king of Cyprus to a Turkish ruler (d. 1214) (Lampros, 1908b). Ἔχω is also found in the famous treaty (1299) between the Venetians and Kallergis (Mertzios, 1949), mostly in the sense of obligation:

(16) ἀλλὰ νὰ ἔχειτε   ἀποστέλειν μανδατοφόρους σας…
     but that have-2nd PL.SUBJ. send-INF. heralds   yours
     / set debeatis   mittere nuntios   vestros…
     but owe-2nd PL.SUBJ. send-INF. heralds yours
     "but you have to send heralds of your own…"

(*Kallergis*, 170–1)

Apparently, ἔχω + Infinitive in this context expresses an obligation meaning, probably as a semantic equivalent of the Latin construction "debeo+Infinitive". The ἔχω AVC is repeated three more times in the text of the treaty (229–30 / 253–5 / 290), and in every one of the attestations the equivalent Latin verb is "debeo". Although ἔχω occasionally conveyed this modal meaning, as we have seen above, it was otherwise very rarely attested in this meaning in the non-literary texts: the only attestation except for (16) is found in the 14th c. *Assises* (119, ms. B). Therefore, both literary and non-literary texts suggest that ἔχω + Infinitive was indeed used as a deontic construction, but only rarely. Notice that in (16) the ἔχω AVC is preceded by νά, the result being a construction identical to the one illustrated in (2) involving μέλλω (cf. 5.1.1), whereby νά is followed by a future-referring / modal AVC. This verbal construction will be discussed in detail below (cf. 5.2.3).

On the whole, the evidence from the early stages of LMG shows that, contrary to what has been observed for EMG, ἔχω + Infinitive was not popular as an FC, being used only sporadically in both literary and non-literary texts. Compared to μέλλω, ἔχω is more productive in literary texts in the vernacular and less so in official documents. This probably implies that it was felt to belong to middle registers of use, not quite appropriate either for high, official registers or for lower, vernacular texts. Moreover, the modal (most notably, deontic) meanings that this construction could convey in previous periods are still attested.

5.2.2 *The later stages*

The wholesale retreat of the ἔχω AVC from the semantic field of futurity is clearly evident in the literary texts of the 14th c. The ability meaning of the ἔχω AVC constitutes the most common of its uses. On the other hand, the future-referring meaning has a very meagre token frequency, found in only four of the 14 texts of the corpus. It is rare both in textual distribution and in absolute numbers, suggesting that it was by now almost extinct and probably less used than even μέλλω was (cf. 5.1.2). Apart from those two meanings, the AVC is also used with the sense of obligation, but only twice, both attestations coming from a single text (*WoT*). These facts are summarized in Table 5.3.

The table illustrates beyond doubt the decline in use of the future meaning of this AVC. The total number of attestations is significant: 15 for the ability meaning (62.5%), only seven for the future-referring one (29.2%). Indeed, if we take into account the relevant numbers for μέλλω (52 instances, 18 without *Ermoniakos*), we may draw the conclusion that the ἔχω AVC could hardly be considered an FC any more.

Another observation on the texts of the 14th c. is due here: buried in the critical apparatus are a number of attestations of the V + V$_S$ construction first observed for ἔχω in LMG in *Digenis* (cf. 5.2.1): e.g. in *WoT*, 7.763 the text reads "πῶς νὰ τὸ ἔχω εἰπεί = how to say it", with an infinitival complement of

TABLE 5.3 The ἔχω AVC in 14th-c. literary texts

MEANING	K&H	V&H	L&R	D.P.	Sahl.	CoM	WoT	Ah.	Poul.	Fys.	Iatr.	Erm.	AoT	Pt.	Total
1a. ῎Εχω + Inf. / Ability	–	–	–	–	–	3	1	–	–	–	–	4	–	–	8 (33.3)
1b. ῎Εχω τοῦ νά + Subj. / Ability	–	1	–	–	–	–	–	–	–	–	–	–	–	–	1 (4.2)
1c. ῎Εχω νά + Subj. / Ability	–	–	–	–	3	1	1	–	1	–	–	–	–	–	6 (25.0)
2a. ῎Εχω + Inf. / Future	–	1	–	–	–	2	2	–	–	–	–	–	–	–	5 (20.9)
2b. ῎Εχω νά + Subj. / Future	–	–	–	1	–	–	1	–	–	–	–	–	–	–	2 (8.3)
3. ῎Εχω νά + Subj. / Obligation	–	–	–	–	–	–	2	–	–	–	–	–	–	–	2 (8.3)
TOTAL	–	2	–	1	3	6	7	–	1	–	–	4	–	–	24

ἔχω (εἰπεῖ), while manuscript B reads "πῶς νὰ τὸ ἔχω εἰπῶ = how to say it", with a Subjunctive complement (εἰπῶ) (cf. also WoT, 9.452 and *Ermoniakos*, Ω 155). This further supports the claim made earlier (cf. 5.1.2) that the popularity of this construction was greater and not restricted to the θέλω AVC, contrary to traditional assumptions (further discussion in 5.4).

The literary texts of the 14th–15th c. contain few attestations of the ἔχω AVC, and therefore cannot help us in any significant way in determining its development. There are only 17 instances, nine of which are found in a single text (namely *Florios*), a fact suggestive of a rather sharp decline, even though there are indications of this as early as the 11th c., as noted. As far as future reference is concerned, there are only four examples (three in *Florios*, 1 in *Livistros-b*), the others conveying an ability or an obligation meaning (the latter only once).

The pattern does not alter in the texts of the later stages of this period (15th c.). Again, the ἔχω AVC has a very limited number of attestations (18), most of which are found in one author, this time *Falieros* (11). Regarding its semantic properties, there is no change from the previous texts: the dominant meaning is that of ability, there is one instance of the obligation meaning, and another three of the future-referring meaning, the last found solely in *Falieros*.[13] Concerning the syntax of the construction, it should be noted that the great majority of attestations (12 / 18, 66.6%) contain a complement clause, exactly like the corresponding numbers of the 14th c. (16 / 24, 66.6%); apparently, by the 14th–15th c. the replacement of the Infinitive by a νά–clause has definitely reached its final stages, similar to what has been observed for μέλλω (cf. 5.1.2).

In the official documents of the 14th–16th c., the ἔχω AVC is very rarely attested.[14] There is one clear example of the future-referring meaning in a document from Corfu ("ἔχει λαβεῖν = he will receive", *Hondromatis* 18/ d. 1473), but the archaizing form of the Infinitive (λαβεῖν) argues for a rather obsolete construction, a relic from a previous stage of the language. Apart from this, there is no other clear attestation of the future-referring meaning. Instead, the first instances of the perfect formation dominant now in Modern Greek are found, as in the example (17) from Crete (also attested in *Maras*, IV, 59 / d. 1549 and in a document from Santorini, cf. Delendas, 1949, d. 1554):

---

[13] In a poem of *Falieros*, Ἱστορία καί Ὄνειρο there is another example of the AVC (v. 544), but, since its meaning is obscure, it has not been included in the numbers given above.

[14] With the exception of the construction ἔχω να κάνω με κάποιον ("I have got matters to settle with somebody"), which is widely attested, but is not directly related to the future-referring meaning of the AVC, but rather to the possessive meaning of the verb itself.

(17) *Ἔτι ἀφίνω τῆς Ἄννας Μονοβασιώτησας... ὑπέρπυρα ἑκατόν ἑξῆντα*
More leave the Anna Monovasiotisa... yperpyra hundred sixty
ἀπάνω εἰς ἐκεῖνα τὰ στάμενα ἀποῦ τῆς ἔχω γράψει
apart from those the money that her have-1st PRES. write-
εἰς τοὺς κριτάδες...
INF. at the notaries
"Moreover, I bestow to Anna Monovasiotisa...160 yperpyra apart from the money that I have bestowed to her in the notaries' books..."

(*Grigoropoulos*, 50 / d. 1518)

Apparently, the official documents verify the well-known fact (argued on the basis of the literary texts, cf., for example, Moser 1988, Horrocks 1997) that the perfect formation developed analogically to the corresponding pluperfect formation (εἶχα + Infinitive), as the first attestation of the latter is dated much earlier (probably in the 13th c., cf. 5.3). Furthermore, they reveal another pattern of a perfect formation, whereby ἔχω is followed by the non-finite participial form (-οντα(ς)), as illustrated in (18):

(18) *ὀμπρὸς ἕως τὴν σήμερον ἔχω λαμβάνοντα ὑπὸ σοῦ*
ahead up the today have-1st PRES. receive-PCIPLE by you
μοντάρουν ὅλα καὶ εἶναι 75...
count all and are 75
"till now, I have received from you a total of 75..."

(*Patsidiotis* 148 / d. 1552)

The productivity of this pattern is strengthened by further similar examples, involving not only ἔχω (Panagiotakis, 1986 / d. 1566) but also εἶχα and ἤθελα (cf. 5.3 and the following sections). Therefore, a pattern is established, not an altogether novel one: recall another instance of a similar construction in *Ermoniakos*, this time with μέλλω + Participle (-μένος) (cf. 5.1.2). Consequently, the evidence from the official documents allows us to argue that all these constructions (with the exception of μέλλω, which exhibited a very similar construction nevertheless) constitute attestations of a wider pattern of the type "Auxiliary+Non-finite Participle", which apparently was productive not only in the Medieval period (cf. Karla, 2002) but also in some Modern Greek dialects (e.g. the Cretan dialect, cf. Pagkalos, 1955). This pattern can be seen as a possible parallel of the extensive interplay between Infinitive and Participle found in the papyri (Mandilaras, 1973: 370–3), or as possibly due to (or perhaps strengthened by) Romance influence, even though its exact origins are beyond the scope of this book.

According to the investigation of the extant evidence from LMG, the future-referring ἔχω AVC is certainly obsolete and almost extinct by the 15th c., surviving possibly only as an archaism. The construction continues to be used in modal contexts, especially of ability and obligation. A new perfect meaning emerges, probably in the late 15th–early 16th c., hence its absence from the literary texts of the corpus. The discussion concerning the ἔχω AVC would not be complete, though, without the investigation of the rather peculiar pattern "νά ἔχω + Infinitive", which has been already mentioned in the previous sections and has attracted scholarly interest.

5.2.3 "Νά ἔχω + Infinitive": new evidence and a new interpretation

Thus, Table 5.3 does not tell the whole story about ἔχω, as a further use of this AVC, attested in three texts, namely the *CoM*, the *WoT*, and *Ermoniakos*, has not been included. This use can be exemplified below:

(19) κι   οὐδὲν ἠμπόρεσεν ποσῶς τοῦ   νά   ἔχῃ   ἀπεράσει
     and not could   at-all the-GEN. that have-3rd SUBJ. cross-INF.
     "and he did not manage to cross"

(*CoM*, 2170)

The construction νά ἔχῃ ἀπεράσει has no discernible difference functionally from a simple Subjunctive and, indeed, these two variables are readily placed next to each other many times in the *CoM*. In all the existing literature, this construction has been described as "weird, clumsy", and, possibly, not authentic. Bǎnescu (1915: 90) refers to it as an effort to construct a "Future Subjunctive" probably by someone who has no solid knowledge of Greek, Aerts (1965, 2005) talks about an "unnecessary periphrastic Subjunctive", Joseph (1983) pays little attention to it, while Horrocks (1997: 277) speaks of a "rather clumsy, transitional form". But where does the peculiarity of this construction come from?

The main reason for the attitude of scholars is twofold: on the one hand, the alleged rarity of the form, especially with respect to the number of texts in which it is attested, is considered highly suspicious, leading scholars to assume that it might not be an authentic form at all. On the other hand, underlying these assumptions are the empirical facts of Modern Greek, where να is in complementary distribution with θα, the futurity / modality marker, hence the feeling of peculiarity surrounding this construction, which involves νά + a future-referring AVC. Nevertheless, in what follows it will be demonstrated that the regular assumptions concerning the form are not valid, and a different account will be proposed accordingly. Three claims will be made: (a) this construction is an authentic feature of LMG, originating in EMG, and affecting all FCs; (b) it constitutes an attempt to mark in a more expressive manner the Subjunctive as a subordinating mood, since the morphological Subjunctive had lost much of its distinctiveness; and (c) it is related to the occasional inability of νά to function as a Subjunctive marker.

First of all, with the exception of Horrocks (1997), all other scholars have mistakenly thought this construction an idiosyncratic feature of the *CoM*, whose author, being probably a non-native speaker of Greek, is not to be trusted. However, as already mentioned, the form under investigation is also found in the *WoT*, and more crucially, is even attested once in *Ermoniakos* (Θ 53–4), a text whose middle register has been amply demonstrated. Nonetheless, it is true that the other attestations come from a text written by a non-Greek (*CoM*), or from a translation of an Old French novel (*WoT*). But even if we adhere to the notion of Western influence in the sense of language interference in Greek as L2 by speakers of Romance origin (cf. Thomason, 2001: 146–7 for the notion of "interference"), it is hard to justify it since neither Old French (cf., for example, Foulet, 1916) nor other Romance languages seem to exhibit any similar pattern. The appearance of this construction with θέλω, too (cf. 5.4), a fact noted by Bǎnescu (1915: 90) but again not given any attention except by Horrocks (1997), points to a more widespread use than previously thought. Recall also that in a non-literary text from South Italy, μέλλω is also found in this context, thus completing the picture for all FCs (cf. 5.1.1, ex. 2). In the light of this evidence, it seems reasonable to conclude that the particular construction constitutes an authentic construction of LMG.

TABLE 5.4 "Νά ἔχω + Infinitive" construction in 14th c. literary texts

Clause[15]	CoM*	WoT	Erm.	Total
Final	63 (20)	14	–	77 (32.9)
Complement	79 (29)	28	1	108 (46.2)
Ind. Question	14 (10)	8	–	22 (9.4)
Independent	4 (2)	5	–	9 (3.9)
Command	5 (0)	7	–	12 (5.1)
Temporal	2 (0)	3	–	5 (2.1)
Conditional	1 (1)	–	–	1 (0.4)
TOTAL	168	65	1	234

*The figures in parentheses indicate the attestations occurring in both main manuscripts of *CoM*

[15] One example from the *CoM* (2590), where ἔχω is followed by another νά–clause instead of an Infinitive, which is irrelevant for our purposes here, as well as five more instances ambiguous between a Subjunctive (future-like) and a perfect interpretation have been excluded from the table.

In order to understand the facts better, all instances of the construction νά ἔχω + Infinitive in the literary texts have been examined, and the results are presented in Table 5.4. The left column indicates the type of subordinate clause that νά introduces each time.

In the *CoM* the construction is mainly attested in one manuscript, and is usually replaced (by various means) or omitted in the other. Nevertheless, this is not always the case, as in almost every context there exists a percentage of instances where both manuscripts retain this construction, a percentage which is not negligible: 37% (29 / 79) for complement clauses, 32% (20 / 63) for final clauses, and 71% (10 / 14) in indirect questions, in the three clause-types that share between them the most attestations. Therefore, even though this construction was "regularly replaced" (Horrocks, 1997, Aerts, 2005) in the P(arisinus) manuscript, the tendency was by no means exceptionless, another argument in favor of the authenticity of the pattern.

One could propose an analysis of this construction along two lines: either it constitutes a modally strengthened form of the well-known ἔχω AVC, appearing in specific contexts (as Horrocks, 1997 argues), or it is a way of marking / emphasizing (or clarifying) the future reference or the modal properties of the Subjunctives normally found in these contexts after νά. The figures shown in Table 5.4 are in accordance with the latter hypothesis, for the reason that in most of the cases (e.g. in complement and final clauses) νά is motivated, in the sense that it is expected to appear as a complementizer and, consequently, it is the ἔχω AVC which is encroaching upon the usual context of the morphological Subjunctive. If νά were used to strengthen the future reference of the AVC, one would expect that the majority of attestations of this construction would involve independent, future-like contexts, whereas this is only found four times. Therefore, it is more likely that the construction νά ἔχω + Infinitive came about in an attempt to mark more clearly the subjunctive as a subordinate mood.

Aerts (1965:182) suggests that the above construction is equivalent to the interchange manifested in AG between the Subjunctive and Future Indicative in many contexts. The investigation of EMG showed that he may be right: recall that a similar construction was found in the papyri in a complement clause where the Subjunctive would normally be expected (cf. ex. 7, ch. 4, repeated below):

(20) καὶ τὴν δὲ ἐπιστολήν... γράφω καὶ ἀποδίδωμι μετὰ καὶ προσκυνήσεως
 and the prt letter...   write   and deliver   with and reverence
 μήπως καὶ μετὰ ταῦτα ζητῆσαι   ἔχει   σου   ἡ δεσποτεία
 in-case and after these ask-INF.AOR. have-3rd PRES. you-GEN. the ladyship

καὶ αὐτὰ τὰ χειροψέλλια
and these the armbands
"and this letter... I send and deliver faithfully in case / in the event that, after these, your ladyship asks [i.e. will ask] for these armbands as well"

(*PKöln*, 166 / 6th–7th c.)

Apparently, the 'νά + FC' pattern of LMG has its origins in the EMG period, when the future-referring ἔχω AVC was probably used at times as the ancient Future Tense in "naturally" Subjunctive contexts, possibly in an attempt to overtly mark the futurity of the clause. The difference between EMG and LMG is that, in the latter period, this pattern was generalized to contexts where the normally expected Subjunctive does not complement prototypical future-referring predicates, but for instance verbs like (ἠ)μπορῶ "can" (cf. ex. 19). Consequently, in synchronic terms, this LMG pattern should be regarded as a 'νά + Subjunctive' equivalent: the ἔχω AVC simply functions as a subordination marker, most probably seen by the speakers as conveying the semantics of the morphological Subjunctive.

It should be noted that a similar construction is found in Old and Middle English, when various modal verbs (including the future-referring "should") were used in the place of the Subjunctive and in very similar contexts as the ones mentioned in Table 5.4 (Warner, 1993: 171–2, 178–9). Greek speakers were not the only ones to employ a pattern of marking the Subjunctive through the means of a semantically similar verbal construction. If English, which saw the near complete demise of the category of Subjunctive by early modern times, can be taken as a cross-linguistic parallel, then the equivalent Greek construction should be seen in the light of the steady weakening of the Subjunctive as a distinct morphological category due to phonological overlap with the Indicative, originating in the early Hellenistic period (cf. also 4.2). This is not only an English / Greek peculiarity, as the employment of modal constructions in subordinate contexts has been proved to be a strong cross-linguistic tendency (Bybee, Perkins & Pagliuca, 1994: 214–9). This can be probably regarded as an instance of "modal harmony", a term originally used by Lyons (1977: 807) for situations when a modal and an adverb convey the same type of modality and later expanded by Coates (1983) to include all instances whereby a modal construction co-occurs with another element of the same modality. In modally harmonic contexts, the two elements simply "agree" in modality and do not create a double-marking effect. As Bybee, Perkins & Pagliuca observe (1994: 219), there is a strong cross-linguistic tendency for modal constructions, initially employed in modally harmonic contexts, to generalize in non-harmonic ones, marking simply subordination (like "should" in many cases in Modern English). The Greek pattern must have also followed the same route, in other words the FC involved must have been originally used in future-referring contexts, but it was subsequently re-analyzed as subordinate marker, hence the situation in LMG where FCs are found in non-harmonic contexts also.

There is another factor to be taken into account, namely the properties of *νά* itself. The great overlap between Subjunctive and Indicative is partly resolved in Modern Greek by virtue of *να* functioning as a modal particle, i.e. marking the modality of complement clauses. Apparently, in LMG *νά* retained its role as a complementizer and could only occasionally, and not obligatorily, function as a modal marker (most clearly so when forming a complex complementizer to introduce a clause expressing a real cause, cf. Markopoulos, 2005), hence the occasional need for greater emphasis on the lexical marking of the Subjunctive by means of a future-referring or modal construction (such as *ἔχω* / *θέλω* + Infinitive). A prediction follows that this type of construction would have dropped out of the language in accordance with the obligatory use of *νά* as a particle with modal force and the stabilization of the situation found in Modern Greek. Although further research is needed to determine whether this prediction is fully borne out, the fact that in the Cretan dialect the combination *νά θα* was till recently grammatical, at least in some areas and / or for some speakers (cf. Markopoulos, 2006), suggests that the Standard Modern Greek situation must have been a recent development and that this construction survived for many centuries.

It has been established that the *νά* + FC pattern was authentic, being part of a wider pattern, and that there was a plausible morphosyntactic reason for its appearance (namely the non-distinctiveness of the morphological Subjunctive), even though there is no fully conclusive evidence. But how are we to account for its seeming appearance solely in three texts of the 14th c., and its complete disappearance thereafter? The highly restricted distribution might be interpreted as indicating that the construction involving *ἔχω* is on the brink of extinction. According to our analysis, this should be expected: the construction was in use in such contexts as early as the 6th–7th c., and it is well known (Bybee, Perkins & Pagliuca, 1994: 213–4) that FCs are employed in subordinate contexts only in their latest stage of development, but may survive in embedded clauses as almost relic forms marking subordination. Obviously, *ἔχω* + Infinitive survived in this context up to the 14th c., but it was already very rare in independent clauses. The gap between the 7th and the 14th c. regarding the attestations of this construction is bridged to an extent by evidence found in the official documents: in a document of the late 14th c. from Corfu, the following example is found:

(21) ὅρκον   ἐπιδίδωμι... τοῦ   ἔχο   κραττῆν   καὶ στέργειν
     oath   give...   the-GEN.   have-1st PRES. keep-INF. and obey-INF.
     αὐτό...
     this...
     "I swear... to obey this..."

(*Tselikas*, d. 1391)

In this official document from Corfu, the ἔχω AVC is found in a complement clause introduced by the complementizer τοῦ, very common already from EMG times (cf. Horrocks, 1997: 98–9); in this case, an interpretation of future-reference is favored by the context of an oath, a speech act inherently associated with strong future orientation. It cannot be a coincidence that another example of this construction is attested in an identical context and from the same period (Karydis, 1999: d. 1400). Therefore, it could be argued that these cases reflect a previous stage of development of this construction, in which ἔχω + Infinitive could be used in complement clauses expressing future reference, similar to example (20) dating from the 6th–7th c. The archaizing character of both examples from 14th c. Corfu is evident in their numerous archaizing morphological elements, e.g. the form ἐπιδίδωμι, as this class of AG verbs ending in –μι had been fundamentally altered with regard to their endings as early as the H–R period (Babiniotis, 2002: 143–4). The fact that a scribe with such knowledge of AG would use such a construction signifies that it constituted (a) an authentic and (b) a rather old construction. In accordance with this observation, it could be argued that (21) illustrates the equivalent of the νά + FC for the case of the old infinitival complementation, as the complementizer τοῦ was followed by an Infinitive (at least initially), and in (21) the addition of ἔχω to form the ἔχω FC is not necessary from a semantic point of view, as the same meaning would be expressed by the Infinitives without ἔχω. Therefore, this example does indeed represent a previous stage of development of the νά + FC pattern, namely a stage when not the Subjunctive but the Infinitive was complemented by an Auxiliary to form an FC, originally in modally harmonic contexts (as in 21), and presumably later in non-harmonic ones. Evidently, the νά + FC construction has much deeper roots than previously assumed.

The series of developments argued above can be summarized as follows: the morphological demise of the Subjunctive allowed future-referring / modal AVCs to be used in Subjunctive contexts, originally in future-referring ('modally harmonic') contexts (in EMG), but later in other, not purely future-referring ones (in LMG), where the AVCs were simply used as subordinate markers. This possibility was probably dependent on the optional inability of νά to mark clearly the modality of the clause it introduced directly and in its own right. This pattern involved all FCs, and became rather uncommon in the late LMG period (starting from the 15th c.), probably due to semantic / syntactic developments, especially the ever tighter association felt by speakers between νά and the irrealis modality of such contexts. However, evidence of this pattern involving θέλω not only from the late LMG period but also from Modern Greek dialects suggests that it did not drop out of use till recently.

5.2.4 Conclusions: ἔχω AVC and futurity

In the studies of futurity for LMG, and most prominently in Bănescu (1915), ἔχω + Infinitive figures as a potential FC. However, the results of this investigation suggest that it is over-estimated in this respect, especially when we consider that μέλλω has been rather neglected. The future-referring use of the ἔχω AVC is in fact of a very low frequency, except for the pattern νά ἔχω + Infinitive, which, strictly speaking, is not an FC, but rather a case of modal harmony generalizing in wider syntactic contexts, rendering thus the ἔχω AVC a subordination marker. It is, therefore, undeniable that the ἔχω AVC is mainly present by virtue of its modal (usually ability) interpretation.[16] What has brought about the downfall of the future-referring use?

It is often assumed that the retreat of ἔχω from the domain of future reference is due to the distinct development that originated in the past formation, i.e. the emergence of the pluperfect, which could allegedly cause major ambiguities due to the rather irreconcilable nature of the two meanings (past – future). In any case, the formation of the pluperfect could not have been the sole reason behind the disappearance of future-referring ἔχω, since, according to the findings of this investigation, from the very early stages of LMG ἔχω was in retreat, notably in comparison with θέλω but also more surprisingly with μέλλω. Consequently, the emergence of the 'pluperfect', being most probably precipitated or caused by Western influence (cf. 5.3), could only be responsible for the final 'blow' to the ἔχω FC. Speakers of LMG used mostly the θέλω FC, and the change in the frequency of use of the two AVCs might be partly due to language contact: while communication with late Latin speakers (who would presumably use in

---

[16] The case of the ability meaning can be understood as either an ever-occurring grammaticalization or a retention of a meaning. Both are equally plausible, given that the conditions for the emergence of this meaning through possession are always present.

their majority a variant of the future-referring "habeo + Infinitive") became increasingly rare from the period of EMG onwards, in many parts of the Byzantine empire Greek-speaking populations came in close contact with Slavic populations, who probably already used an FC of volitional lexical origin (cf. 5.4.1 for more details). So, the sociolinguistic situation must have played a role in the rise and fall of the different FCs. In any case, old AVCs are usually replaced in the course of time by another AVC more "expressive"; and the ἔχω FC was certainly old, pretty much entrenched in subordination contexts and, consequently, a prime candidate for replacement in the domain of future reference. The ἔχω AVC remained common only with various modal meanings, as is still the case today in Modern Greek (e.g. έχω να πάω στον γιατρό "I have to go to the doctor").

5.3 Εἶχα + Infinitive: modality and pluperfect

The separate treatment of the past form of the ἔχω AVC is justified by the divergence in its development, which ultimately gave rise to the system of perfect formations found in Modern Greek. As the emergence of this perfect system is now rather well understood (cf., for example, Moser 1988, Horrocks 1997), the investigation here will focus predominantly on the modal uses of the AVC, which remain largely unexplored.

In *Armouris* εἶχα, like ἔχω, is nowhere to be found. This contrasts with *Stratigikon*, which contains five instances of the εἶχα AVC. Even in this severely restricted sample the pattern exhibited in the whole corpus of LMG emerges, namely that the εἶχα AVC has already shifted semantically from the 'ability-in-the-past' meaning to the domain of conditional, or, to be more precise, of counterfactuality. Indeed, this development is attested from Early Medieval times or even before (cf. 3.2 and 4.2) and it proliferates in LMG. In *Stratigikon,* the conditional outnumbers the ability uses, though by a very slight margin (three and two attestations, respectively).

Similar data can be found in *Digenis*, where there are four counterfactual and two ability uses. Notice, however, that the counterfactual εἶχα + Infinitive could surface both in the protasis and the apodosis of the conditional, equally distributed in absolute numerical terms, as exemplified in (22) and (23), respectively:

(22) καὶ ἂν εἶχεν   λείπειν   τὸ δενδρόν, ἐπνίγετον   ὁ Ἀκρίτης
    and if have-3rd PRET. be-absent-INF. the tree, drowned-3rd PRET. the Akritis
    "and if it had not been for the tree, Akritis would have drowned"

(*Digenis*, 1538)

(23) τὸν κόσμον καὶ ἂν ἐγύρευες,   κάλλιον οὐκ   εἶχες   εὗρειν
the world   and if look-2nd PRET., better   not have-2nd PRET. find-INF.
"even if you would look around the world, you would not find a better one"

(*Digenis*, 984)

This should be interpreted as a rather old-fashioned state of affairs, as, in later stages, εἶχα undergoes a syntactic specialization and appears (with few exceptions) in the protasis, with the emerging ἤθελα AVC taking its place in the apodosis, as we will see below (cf. 5.5).[17]

The literary texts of the 12th c. contain only a single example of the εἶχα AVC and, therefore, cannot really tell us anything about its development. But there is an interesting example in the official documents of South Italy:

(24) τα χωράφια τα   ἤχεν   κρατώνταν ο   πάτρας μου
the fields the-rel have-3rd PRET. keep-PCPLE the father   mine
ἤχεν   αυτά αφιερωμένα
have-3rd PRET. them dedicated
"the fields that my father had owned, he had them dedicated..."

(*Trinchera*, 75 / d. 1113)

This example illustrates the second semantic domain for which the εἶχα AVC was regularly used, namely anteriority. It also constitutes another attestation of the construction "Auxiliary + Non-finite participle", already attested for ἔχω (cf. 5.2.1). Consequently, it could be argued that this construction, still extant in the official documents of the 16th c. (e.g. in Crete *Patsidiotis* 1 / d. 1546), is not the result of insufficient knowledge of Greek or of corrupted manuscript tradition but forms a wider pattern, as we shall also see in a following section (cf. 5.5). Furthermore, given the Italian origin of (24), it can no longer be maintained that this construction is a Cretan peculiarity, as Aerts (1965: 174) had suggested.

The independent existence of other εἶχα constructions conveying anteriority meanings (e.g. εἶχα + Object + Passive Participle –μένο(ς), cf. Aerts, 1965 and Moser, 1988) must have facilitated the shift of εἶχα + Infinitive from conditionals (mostly counterfactuals) to pluperfect.[18] This development is

---

[17] Obviously, in the domain of counterfactuals there exists a greater variation than the interplay between the two AVCs, which involves mainly the Past Imperfective (Preterite) form, evident in both examples from *Digenis* above (ἐπνίγετον, ἐγύρευες) (for the correlation between counterfactuality and Imperfective forms, cf. Fleischman, 1995). For more details, cf. Horrocks (1995).

[18] The term "pluperfect" is used without making any precise claims about the semantic content of the construction which might differ significantly from that of the Modern Greek equivalent. This issue needs further research.

fairly well understood (cf. for example, Moser, 1988 and Horrocks, 1995), but the examination of the non-literary texts can shed some light with respect to the dating and the diffusion of this construction. Regarding the former, the following example, found in a document from the archive of the monastery of Patmos but originating from Crete, can be of crucial importance:

(25) ἀπὸ   τὸν εὐγενῆν ἄνθρωπον κύριον Ἰάκωβον Μπαρότζη ... ἦχεν
from the noble   man   sir Iakovon Barozzi ... have-3rd PRET.
δωθῆν   σπιτίου
give-INF.PASS. house-GEN.
γῆς τοῦ   αὐτοῦ Οἰκονόμου ... ἡ ὁποία τὸν καιρὸν ἐκεῖνον
land the-GEN. same Oikonomos ... the which the time that
ἤτονεν διακτίσιμον
were for-building
"The noble Sir Iakovos Barozzi... had given land to the above mentioned Oikonomos... which was then available for house building"

(*MM*, vol. VI, CII / d. 1295)

This example, combined with another attestation in a letter of the Sultan of Egypt to the Byzantine emperor (Schopen, 1828–32 / d.1349) constitutes a strong indication in favor of placing the emergence of the pluperfect construction in the 13th c. at the latest. Corroborating evidence comes from the literary texts, in which the pluperfect εἶχα AVC is attested quite robustly in the 14th c., but only in two texts, i.e. the *CoM* and the *WoT* (cf. Table 5.5). Recall that, with the exception of an obscure verse in the *CoM* (v. 837) and five cases already mentioned (cf. fn. 15) where the 'νά ἔχω + Infinitive' construction might also have a perfect meaning, but obviously not necessarily or even preferably, the pluperfect seems to constitute the only perfect formation involving ἔχω / εἶχα + Infinitive that existed in the 14th c. (*contra* Moser, 1988), since the "present perfect" ἔχω + Infinitive only appears in the non-literary texts of the 16th c. (cf. 5.2.2).[19] The relative chronology of the emergence of the 'perfect' constructions based on ἔχω / εἶχα + Non-finite form is given in (26):

(26)   "εἶχα + Participle" (pluperfect) > "εἶχα + Infinitive" (pluperfect) > "ἔχω + Infinitive / Participle (?)" (present perfect)

---

[19] Ralli, Melissaropoulou, & Tsolakidis (2007) have argued recently that there exist examples of the Perfect ἔχω + Infinitive formation already from the 11th c. in the South Italian documents. But they also agree that this formation was mainly used from the 16th c. onwards. The matter cannot be further discussed here.

TABLE 5.5 The εἶχα AVC in 14th c. literary texts

Contexts of Use / Meanings	K&H	V&H	L&R	D.P.	Sahl.	CoM	WoT	Ah.	Poul.	Fys.	Iatr.	Erm.	AoT	Pt.	Total
1a. Εἶχα + Inf. / Ability	1	–	–	–	–	2	2	–	–	–	–	–	–	–	5 (2.7)
1b. Εἶχα νά + Subj. / Ability	–	–	–	–	–	–	3	1	–	–	–	–	–	–	4 (2.2)
2a. Εἶχα + Inf. / counter-fact. (prot.)	–	–	–	1	–	7	59	1	–	–	–	–	–	–	68 (37.2)
2b. Νά εἶχα + Inf. / Wish (c-fact)	–	6	–	–	3	–	10	–	–	–	–	–	2	–	21 (11.5)
2c. Νά εἶχα + Inf. / C.fact (apod.)	–	–	–	–	–	–	5	–	–	–	–	–	–	–	5 (2.7)
2d. Εἶχα + Inf. / C.fact	–	–	–	–	–	3	8	1	–	–	–	–	–	–	13 (7.1)
3. Εἶχα νά + Subj. / Future-in-the-past	1	–	1	–	–	–	–	–	–	–	–	–	–	–	1 (0.5)
4. Εἶχα νά + Subj. / Habitual (past)	–	1	–	–	–	–	–	–	–	–	–	–	–	–	1 (0.5)
5a. Εἶχα νά + Subj. / Obligation	–	–	–	–	–	5	–	–	–	–	–	–	–	–	5 (2.7)
5b. Τί νά εἶχα + Inf. / "should"?	–	–	–	–	–	–	2	–	–	–	–	–	–	–	2 (1.1)
6. Νά εἶχα + Inf. / Subj.	–	–	–	–	–	1	4	–	–	–	–	–	–	–	5 (2.7)
7. Εἶχα + Inf. / Pluperf.	–	–	–	–	–	23	30	–	–	–	–	–	–	–	53 (29.0)
TOTAL	2	7	1	1	4	41	123	3	–	–	–	–	2	–	183

This schema should not be seen as implying that the oldest construction was replaced by the subsequent but as illustrating the relative order of appearance of different alternatives for the expression of perfect meanings.

Moreover, the case that Horrocks (1995) makes in favor of a Western influence for the actual formation of the pluperfect εἶχα + Infinitive might be plausible, given that this new development is initially attested in an official document from Venetian-ruled Crete and two literary texts of undeniable Western influence, and that there exists a similar pattern in Old French (cf., for example, Brunot, 1966: 346). The wide diffusion of this AVC in the subsequent centuries is illuminated by the official documents, since, by the 16th c., it can be found in many parts of Greece: in the documents from Crete (e.g. *Grigoropoulos*, 11 / d. 1509), Kythira (e.g. *Kasimatis*, 201 / d. 1565) and Corfu (e.g. *Katoimeris*, 220 / d. 1503–07), to name but a few. As most of the literary texts in the vernacular are of unknown geographical origin, it is the evidence of the official documents that clarifies that the pluperfect formation was not restricted to a specific area (or dialect) but was indeed spread throughout the Greek-speaking world by the end of the 16th c., if not earlier.

Apart from the pluperfect meaning, the εἶχα AVC was used in a variety of syntactic contexts and meanings in the 14th c. (cf. Table 5.5). The conditional εἶχα is dominant, though ability uses are also extant. Beside these three uses, various modal nuances of meaning appear, though the number of their attestations is very meagre.

Two constructions involve the pattern νά εἶχα + Infinitive, the first looking like an obligation-related structure (5b. in the table), but the second much more clearly associated with the Subjunctive-like νά ἔχω + Infinitive construction discussed at length in 5.2.3. The related νά εἶχα + Infinitive form (construction 6 in the table) is shown in the following example:

(27) Τὸν θάνατον παρακαλῶ γοργὸν νὰ   μὲ   εἶχε   σφάξει
     The death   implore   quick   that me   have-3rd PRET. kill-INF.
     "I implore Death to kill me quickly"

(*WoT*, 10448)

Apparently, the present and the past form of ἔχω were to some extent interchangeable in this context. Apart from providing corroborating evidence for the productivity and the authenticity of the much more common equivalent ἔχω use, this construction seems to suggest that εἶχα + Infinitive must have been felt by speakers as a modal construction (probably through its use in conditionals) which could then be used appropriately for the modal meaning usually associated with the Subjunctive, even though less readily than present ἔχω + Infinitive. The fact that the εἶχα AVC is used in (27) as an equivalent of the Subjunctive, i.e. as a subordinate marker, is shown by the variant reading in the apparatus criticus (τοῦ νά μέ ἐπάρῃ (ms.A)=that he [Death] takes me) and by the French original "qu'ele m'ocie", which both involve a simple morphological Subjunctive.

Furthermore, the fact that the εἶχα AVC, although morphologically a past construction, does not refer to the past, being employed in a future-referring context, proves its independence from its present counterpart and its separate entry in the 'lexicon' of the speakers. The same development can be observed in the case of the preterite forms of English modals, including the past form of "have", which already in the Old English period started to become independent lexemes (cf. Warner, 1993: 148–50), illustrating once more a common semantic pathway used by speakers of different languages. This is also an indication of the further grammaticalization of the εἶχα AVC in relation to ἔμελλον AVC, since the latter always retained its paradigmatic association with the present form μέλλω.

In the domain of the counterfactuals, it is evident that εἶχα is most commonly used in the protasis of a counterfactual, while in the apodosis it is very rare (five attestations in comparison with 68 in the protasis). Interestingly, the construction pertaining to this semantic domain exhibits no replacement of the Infinitive by a subordinate clause, contrary to the ability-referring structures or the future-referring occurrences of the ἔχω AVC (cf. 5.2.2). This fact plausibly represents the stabilization of an older construction (εἶχα+Infinitive) in a very specific (embedded) syntactic domain, whereas in the case of the domain of ability or futurity, the syntactic flexibility reflects the use of the AVC in a wider array of contexts.

In the domain of future reference, the scarcity of attestations observed for ἔχω is repeated again with εἶχα. There is only one example of a future-in-the-past meaning (*Kallimahos*, 1,331–2), just as there are only seven attestations of future-referring instances of ἔχω. On the other hand, a new development, previously unrecorded for this period, arises, namely the past habitual use, illustrated in (28):

(28) τὰ δάκρυα εἶχε   πάντοτε σὺν   στεναγμῶν νὰ   τρέχῃ
     the tears   have-3rd PRET. always with cries   that run-3rd SUBJ.
     ἅπερ ἡ φύσις τῶν   ἀνδρῶν τὰ ὅπλα νὰ   βαστάζῃ
     as   the nature the-GEN. men   the arms that grasp-3rd SUBJ.
     "and she would cry bitterly all the time / similarly to men who always bear arms"

(*Velthandros*, 415–16)

Even though the example is rather complicated from a syntactic point of view, the habitual interpretation seems the most plausible, especially if seen in the light of the fact that an identical development is found simultaneously for ἤθελα + Infinitive (cf. 5.5). This rather expected semantic change should now be dated much earlier than previously assumed (e.g. Horrocks, 1995, mentions examples only from the 16th–17th c.), i.e. in the 14th c.[20]

The texts of the 14th–15th c. show no further developments concerning the εἶχα AVC, just like the equivalent ἔχω AVC, due to the very small number of instances found. And nothing noteworthy is to be found in the 15th c. either, only that the εἶχα AVC seems to be increasingly restricted to counterfactuals, as 63 / 102 (62%) of the attestations belong to this semantic domain. However, there is an interesting example in *Falieros*:

(29) Κὶ ἄν ἔν' καὶμὲ τὰ κλάματα, μὲ πόνους καὶ μὲ θρήνη
And if is and with the cries, with moans and with laments
ἐδύνετον κι ὁ πόνος σου κι ἡ θλίψη ν' ἀλαφρύνῃ...
could and the pain yours and the sorrow that ease-3rd SUBJ.
ἄλλο νὰ κάμωμε εἴχαμε μὲ τόση πεθυμία;
other that do-1st PL.SUBJ. have-1st PL.PRET. with such willingness?
"If it were that with cries and laments your pain and sorrow could ease, would we do anything else with so much willingness?"

(*Falieros*, Θρῆνος, 83–6)

This example manifests the replacement of the Infinitive by the νά–clause even in the domain of conditionals (in the apodosis). The ancient Infinitive is apparently now restricted to the expression of the pluperfect. This last use is the second most popular in the 15th c. (29 of the remaining 39 non-conditional attestations, 75%), a fact, though, exclusively due to the inclusion in the corpus of two chronicles (*CoT* and *Mahairas*): there is no instance of this pluperfect in any other text. Since both texts are clearly written under Western influence, the language contact account for the pluperfect formation is rendered more plausible, although this development could have come about without any need of external influence, representative as it is of a well-understood semantic change (cf. Horrocks, 1995). Finally, *Falieros* contains two more instances of the pluperfect construction εἶχα + Non-finite participle ('Ιστορία καί Ὄνειρο, 250, 395: καί οὐκ εἶχε λέγοντα σωστόν καί βλέπω... = And he had just finished talking when I saw...), strengthening the assumption of its continuous existence made above.

[20] Bybee, Perkins & Pagliuca (1994: 157) report a similar development for the English form "would", and they argue that the habitual meaning was not related to the modal meaning of the verb. On the other hand, Ziegeler (2006) seems to entertain the opposite view. The Greek evidence is too scarce to clarify the issue, which will not be further discussed.

Apart from the pluperfect formation (involving in the vast majority of cases the infinitival complementation, the alternative being an $-οντα(ς)$ Participle), which has been already discussed, the non-literary texts of the later stages of LMG contain numerous attestations of the use of εἶχα in counterfactuals, similar to what has been noted concerning the 14th c. literary texts (cf. Table 5.5). They also provide indication of a further development in the domain of conditionals, illustrated below:

(30) Μετὰ τουτο να στημαρηστοῦν   με   τὴν στράταν τῆς ἀφέντίας
     After this   that count-3rd SUBJ.PASS. with the order   the lord
     καὶ αν ἦχαν   ξυἄζην   πληότερα   παρα
     and if have-3rd PL.PRET.   worth-INF.   more   than
     το   λεγόμενον...
     the   said
     "After this, they should be counted according to the lord's way, and if they should (prove to) be worth more than what we say..."

(*Olokalos*, 98 / d. 1530)

Contrary to the irrealis interpretation of the counterfactuals, in this example εἶχα + Infinitive is used in a future-referring conditional. This development can be regarded as a case of generalization: εἶχα + Infinitive gained a wider scope of application, from the domain of counterfactuals to the general domain of speculative conditionals. The generalization was made possible as the εἶχα AVC lost its initial temporal restrictions and became productive as a modal construction suitable also for non-past contexts (cf. discussion on ex. 27).

Even though this use of εἶχα is nowhere as frequent as the exactly equivalent use of ἤθελα (cf. 5.5), nonetheless it exhibits a broad distribution geographically speaking, as it is attested, apart from Crete (30), in Kefalonia (e.g. *Sourianos,* 80 / d. 1581) and in Naxos, where the relative-conditional use is found, "if" clauses probably providing the focus for the shift from the simple conditionals to relative-conditionals (cf. also *Polemis*, 25 / d. 1586 for a similar example from Andros):

(31) ὑπόσχεται ὁ λεγούμενος νὰ μαντινιέρου   τὶς λεγούμεναις
     promises   the said   that defend-3rd SUBJ. the said
     ἀγοραστάδες ἀπὸ πᾶσα ἄνθρωπον ὁπού   τ(οὺς)   εἶχ(εν)
     buyers   from any   person   that-rel them   have-3rd PRET.
     ὀχλήσει...
     disturb-INF.
     "the abovementioned promises to defend the abovementioned buyers from whoever would disturb them..."

(*Katsouros*, 4 / d. 1527)

Given that by the 16th c. the predominance of ἤθελα in conditionals is overwhelming (cf. 5.5), the fact that there still exist instances of the use of the εἶχα AVC in this context as a minor pattern provides an important insight with regard to the chronology of the developments of the ἔχω and εἶχα AVCs. The fact that the ἔχω FC is virtually non-extant in those texts (cf. 5.2.2) whereas the εἶχα AVC is still in use in its modal character (i.e. in the conditionals) implies not only that εἶχα was replaced by ἤθελα at a later stage than ἔχω was replaced by θέλω but also, by virtue of this difference in relative chronology, that the ἔχω and εἶχα AVCs did not proceed hand in hand in their developments and might be regarded at that stage as two independent AVCs.

On the whole, the εἶχα AVC specialized in LMG in a very particular semantic–syntactic context, namely the protasis of counterfactual conditionals (and future-referring conditionals in later stages), originating from the ability (or future) in the past meaning, which in its turn gave rise to the grammaticalized pluperfect formation. As mentioned, LMG constitutes the first period when the εἶχα AVC was by and large disassociated from the ἔχω AVC in its various developments. Interestingly, the pluperfect εἶχα AVC constitutes the only construction where the old Infinitive survived as the sole exponent of complementation. The reason for this morphosyntactic 'retention' is not clear, and goes beyond the scope of this investigation: it is perhaps related to the language contact issue between Greek- and Romance-speaking populations, but more evidence is needed before a plausible account can be put forward. On the other hand, the εἶχα AVC manifested in LMG more variation than usually assumed, both on the morphosyntactic and the semantic axis: regarding the former, the –οντα(ς) Participle as a possible complement had not been paid any attention, while concerning semantics, the habitual, conditional, and counterfactual uses had all remained rather unexplored by virtue of the emergence of the pluperfect formation, which has been paid a privileged scholarly attention for the sole reason that it survives in Modern Greek.

5.4 The case of θέλω: untangling the evidence of dominance

The third FC in LMG, the one involving θέλω, has been widely discussed and debated in the literature, especially with regard to its ultimate development to the construction θέ νά and finally to the particle θα (cf., for example, Jannaris, 1897, Horrocks, 1997, Pappas & Joseph, 2001, Joseph & Pappas, 2002). However, all these studies were largely dependent on the data reported by Bănescu (1915). Therefore, as will be demonstrated below, they do not tread on safe ground, since Bănescu's findings are not as decisive as one would hope. This examination challenges some of the widely held assumptions concerning θέλω and sheds some new light on the actual developments attested in LMG, which have been rather controversial. Since the emergence of the particle θα does not take place during this period but undeniably has its roots in LMG with the emergence of its semantic / syntactic source θέ νά, an attempt will be made to clarify what exactly these texts can tell us about this much debated development. As with the ἔχω AVC, the AVC built on the past form ἤθελα will be treated separately, as their developments are again divergent (cf. also Pappas, 2001 for the same conclusion, albeit for a slightly subsequent period).

5.4.1 *The early stages*

The θέλω AVC is undoubtedly the dominant means of expressing future reference in LMG. This fact is already suggested from the very beginning of this period, in *Armouris*. There, this AVC is the only one found, the other two being absent, as noted (cf. 5.1.1, 5.2.1). This observation constitutes by itself a strong indication of the dominant character of the θέλω AVC. Moreover, a pattern is manifested in *Armouris* that is regularly repeated throughout the corpus of LMG, namely the distinction between the morphosyntactically old θέλω AVC, employed for conveying futurity (three times in this text), and the relatively new construction 'θέλω νά + Subjunctive', which implements the lexical, volitional meaning of the verb (another three times). Since this syntactic–semantic correlation has been questioned recently (cf. Joseph & Pappas, 2002), this important issue is one of the main loci of this investigation. It should be noted that, instead of νά, volitional θέλω can also be followed by combinations of complementizers, such as διά νά (once in *Armouris*) and others, as will be illustrated more clearly below.

The other literary text of the 11th c., the *Stratigikon*, exhibits different features, due to its higher register. Consequently, the θέλω + Infinitive pattern is attested overwhelmingly in its ancient, volitional meaning, in comparison with the new, future-referring one (48 and 5, respectively). However, the very existence of the futurity meaning reveals that the FC has started its infiltration into higher registers; recall that a similar assumption has been tentatively made on the basis of the evidence of *Epanagoge* (cf. 4.3), the legal text of the 9th c., and, consequently, the data from *Stratigikon* confirm that the rise in frequency of the θέλω FC must predate the LMG period; on the other hand, the existence of volitional θέλω + Infinitive in any text in this period constitutes a proof of a rather learned character. Despite the character of his work, Kekaumenos, the author of *Stratigikon*, twice utilizes the different syntactic complementation of volitional θέλω involving a subordinate clause, but crucially only in cases of disjoint reference between the subject of θέλω and that of the complement clause. This arguably manifests the path of development which led to the emergence of the νά-clause in the first place, back in the period of the Koine (cf. 3.3).

The ascent up the sociolinguistic scale of the θέλω FC is verified by an example (of a slightly later date) from a monastery in Asia Minor:

(32) ἐθέλει   δῆλον γενέσθαι   τῷ δικαστηρίῳ δι' ἡμεδαποῦ
    will-3rd PRES. evident become-INF. to-the court   prep our
    σημειώματος τὸ ἐλευθέραν πάντη   καὶ αὐτοδέσποτον εἶναι
               note   the free   generally and self-governing is-INF.
    τὴν τοιαύτην μονὴν...
    the this   monastery...
    "it will become evident to the court by virtue of a note of ours that this monastery is free and self-governing..."

(MM, Vol. IV, 7 / d. 1196)

The totally archaizing morphology of (32) confirms that θέλω has by that time started to generalize to higher registers of use, despite the fact that it is not even once attested in the archives of the monasteries of Athos.[21] This example, despite being the only one of its kind before the 14th c., corroborates the assumption that this construction probably enjoyed a wide popularity before the late LMG period, perhaps already in EMG, since it could be employed in the minutes of a court hearing (ex. 32), presumably a rather high register, in the 12th c.

Stratigikon also contains a rather remarkable example, unexpected on the basis of all previous accounts of θέλω:

(33) εἰ δὲ καταγύρωθεν ὅλα [τὰ κάστρα]θέλουν   ἀποστατήσουν[22]
    if prt all-around   all [the castles] want-3rd PL.PRES. rebel-3rd PL.SUBJ.
    "if then all around all [castles] will rebel"

(*Stratigikon*, 168, 31–2)

In this example, both θέλουν and ἀποστατήσουν appear in the 3rd person plural, and this construction could be best regarded as an instance of the V + V$_S$ construction. We have already seen evidence from the other FCs of a rather early attestation of this construction in LMG (cf. 5.1.1 and 5.2.1), and

---

[21] Actually, there is a very early example of θέλω + Infinitive in the archives of the monastery of Vatopedi (doc. 5 / d. 1018). Since the manuscript is corrupted at exactly the point where θέλω is supposedly attested, this example is not considered as a safe attestation of the AVC.

[22] The future reference of the θέλω AVC in this example is verified by the fact that (33) constitutes the last of a long series of future-referring conditionals.

of a wider diffusion than previously (or tacitly) assumed. This instance from *Stratigikon* provides corroborating evidence in favor of the authenticity of the attestations in the other AVCs of this kind. In addition, if proven to be a valid reading, and there is no indication in the apparatus criticus of its being otherwise, then the chronology of its emergence suggested by Bǎnescu (1915) and followed by all scholars subsequently, i.e. the 15th c., should be considered erroneous. Therefore, the whole process suggested for its emergence (cf., for example, Bǎnescu, 1915, Joseph, 1983) becomes doubtful, for two reasons: firstly, this process was based solely on developments involving θέλω, while the pattern involves all three AVCs, as established above, and, secondly, this process was based on developments much later (or so assumed) than the 11th c. Recall that *Stratigikon* is a text of middle register, and consequently not prone to extreme vernacular linguistic features.

Not only is the V + V$_S$ pattern attested in the early LMG period but, as has already been shown (cf. ch. 2, 3, and 4), occurrences of such a pattern are found in the H–R and even in AG. Apparently, this 'serialization' constituted an overall alternative to infinitival complementation, and gained in frequency of use after the latter had lost ground in Greek; in other words, it represents a systematic pattern in its own right. The hitherto unchallenged traditional account (cf., for example, Joseph & Pappas, 2002) attributed the emergence of this construction (which, as noted, was mistakenly placed in the late stages of LMG) to the loss of final "–ν" in the infinitival forms occurring in the θέλω FC, that led to the—partial—reanalysis of the Infinitive as a 3rd person singular, since the two forms coincided phonologically, and subsequently to the generalization of this reanalysis to the other persons, giving a V + V$_S$ pattern. Although this account falls short of explaining the wide textual distribution and the chronology of attestations of this pattern, it certainly isolates a factor which must have safeguarded its continuous presence in LMG. One could argue that this LMG pattern constitutes a novel development, not necessarily related to the ancient attestations of a similar pattern. However, the continuous presence of this construction in all previous periods, including crucially EMG, the link between antiquity and LMG, is itself an argument for the retention of an old pattern instead of the emergence of a new one.[23]

---

[23] The V + V$_S$ pattern might also have been strengthened due to contact with the Arabs: Brincat (2002: 81–2) mentions that the same pattern occurs in Maltese and Pantesco, Arabic dialects in islands of the central Mediterranean, and Stolz (2002: 270) attributes this fact to the lack of Infinitives in all varieties of Arabic. The matter needs further investigation, as the issue of language contact between Greek and Arabic speakers remains largely unexplored.

However, there remains the issue of how this pattern was associated with future reference, as in all previous stages it had been restricted to the volitional meaning of θέλω. This development could perhaps be linked to the simultaneous establishment of the θέλω νά + Subjunctive as the predominant construction conveying volition. As speakers used this construction more and more frequently for the lexical meaning of θέλω, they associated the V + V$_S$ pattern with the other old complementation pattern, namely θέλω + Infinitive, which was increasingly restricted to future reference. In other words, they might have established the following association: "θέλω νά + Subjunctive" = volition, "θέλω + other (ancient) complementation" = TAM meanings. The fact remains that in LMG, already from the early stages, the V + V$_S$ pattern is employed for future reference.

Digenis offers a similar picture to *Armouris*, and, obviously, a completely different one from *Stratigikon*. The construction θέλω + Infinitive has mainly future-referring uses; even though a few volitional uses are still attested, they are heavily outnumbered (4 in comparison with 12 for future reference). The appearance of the volitional meaning in this construction should not mislead us, since it is already most commonly found with a νά–clause (14 instances). So, if we compare the attestations of volitional θέλω in both syntactic constructions, we can conclude that the θέλω νά + Subjunctive pattern is the dominant one in this semantic domain (14 / 18, 77%), and that the existence of the old infinitival pattern with volitional meaning should be seen as an indication of the relative antiquity of the text. This is highlighted in *Grottaferrata*: in this more learned version, the volitional meaning is almost exclusively conveyed by the old infinitival construction (15 / 16 attestations, 93.8%) but, on the other hand, there exist six attestations of the θέλω FC, a fact suggesting that the θέλω FC was already in the early stages of LMG acceptable in middle registers of use.

In *Digenis* one also finds an interesting structure with regard to volitional θέλω, involving two complementizers mutually exclusive in Modern Greek:

(34) Εἰδὲ   ἂν θέλῃς   ὁλόψυχα,   καλή,   ὅτι   νὰ
      See   if want-2nd SUBJ. gladly,   girl,   that   that
      φιλοῦμε
      be-together-1st PL.SUBJ.
      "See if you want with all your heart, my girl, that we be together"

(*Digenis*, 883)

In this example, 'ὅτι νά' presumably form a complex complementizer. This fact, which has been noted before (cf., for example, Horrocks 1997: 211), seems to suggest that in LMG, at least sometimes, νά could function solely as a marker of Subjunctive without any complementizer properties. On the other hand, it has been observed (cf. 5.2.3) that νά also seems to function as a "pure"

Late medieval Greek 169

complementizer when it is followed by an FC. We cannot go into the issue of the origin, the spread and the properties of νά[24] here; suffice it to say that a 'dual' character of νά (complementizer without modal meaning / modal marker) can possibly account for its ambiguous properties in LMG and the lack of ambiguity in Modern Greek (cf. Markopoulos, 2005).

In accordance with the occasional complementizer status of νά, Digenis contains an attestation of θέλω + Infinitive that illustrates the authenticity of the construction νά + FC (cf. 5.2.3) that apparently involved the θέλω FC as well. Consider the following example:

(35) Κύρ Ἥλιε, τί   νὰ ποιήσωμεν   τὸ ἀδέλφιν μας νὰ
      Lord Sun, what that do-1st PL.SUBJ. the sibling ours that
      εὑροῦμεν, | καὶ πῶς νὰ   τὴν γνωρίσωμεν,   νὰ   τὴν
      find-1st PL.SUBJ. and how that her know-1st PL.SUBJ., that her
      θέλωμεν   θάψει;
      will-1st PL.SUBJ. bury-INF?
      "Lord Sun, what should we do to find our sister, and how can we know her, so that we can bury her?"

(Digenis, 91–2)

This instance of the θέλω AVC, attested in an interrogative clause, is exactly parallel to the construction of ἔχω extensively discussed above (cf. 5.2.3), being found in a context where the Subjunctive would be felicitous both syntactically and semantically. Consequently, it is evident that this construction was more popular than often assumed (see also below). Moreover, if the assumption (based on cross-linguistic observations) that the appearance of an FC in subordinate contexts is an indication of its frequent use over an extensive period is correct, then this example constitutes further evidence of extensive use of the θέλω FC prior to the LMG period.

Another example of this construction is found in the non-literary texts, in a document of the 13th c.:

(36) A: ὁσότε νὰ   θέλη   ἐξελθ(εῖν)   νὰ ἠπάγη
         when that will-3rd SUBJ. leave-INF. that go-3rd SUBJ.
         ἠστ(ὸν) αὐθέντην μου...
         to-the lord   mine
      B: ἐπειδὰν ἐξέλθη   καὶ ὑπάγη   εἰς τὸν αὐθέντην μου...
         when   leave-3rd SUBJ. and go-3rd SUBJ. prep the lord   mine
         "when he leaves to go to my lord..."

(Xiropotamou, 9 / d. 1270–74)

---

[24] For syntactic accounts of the developments concerning νά, cf. Roberts & Roussou (2003) and Philippaki & Spyropoulos (2004).

This is yet another instance of the use of the FC in a Subjunctive context. Interestingly, this particular document from the monastery of Xiropotamou survives in two versions, the second being more purist than the first. Consequently, in the second version (B), the AVC is replaced by the morphological Subjunctive, thus implying that the use of θέλω AVC in this context belongs to a lower register, at least at that early date of the document's production (13th c.). This text offers more evidence in favor of the assumption already made (cf. 5.2.3) that the νά + FC pattern had a continuous existence throughout the EMG and the LMG periods, and is not a novelty of the 14th c., as was traditionally postulated.

Finally, in *Digenis* we find the first example where the θέλω νά + Subjunctive construction does not express volition, even though the exact meaning of the example is difficult to determine:

(37) ἀφῶν ἠρξάμην πολεμεῖν εἰς ἕναν   οὐκ ἐβγῆκα...
       since started fight-INF. to   one not went...
       καὶ ἐδὰ ἄρτε εἰς ἕναν μοναχὸν θέλω   νὰ   πολεμήσω;
       and here now to one alone   want-1st PRES. that fight-1st SUBJ.?
       "Since I have started fighting I have not attacked only one opponent, and now against only one should / will I fight?"

(*Digenis*, 1231–5)

The non-affirmative context renders it rather unlikely that this is another instance of purely volitional θέλω, since it is quite difficult to imagine someone asking about his own will (unless he is talking to himself, but this is not the case in the context above, where Digenis is addressing three bandits and refuses their invitation to fight them one by one). On the other hand, a 1st person context is not a prototypical context of "pure" future reference in general, since it more often than not carries modal undertones (such as volition, intention, etc.). Therefore, this example is probably an instance of an obligation meaning, as Digenis expresses disbelief of the situation he finds himself in and wonders if he should indeed fight against only one opponent. The future-referring meaning cannot be excluded, though, and this seems to contradict the split argued above between "θέλω + Infinitive = futurity" and "θέλω νά + Subjunctive = volition". Nevertheless, it is a unique case, while the split is manifested in hundreds of other attestations of the verb and, in addition, it does not convey a clear prediction meaning. We will come back to this issue below; in any case, (37) constitutes the first attestation in LMG of the various modalities involved in a θέλω AVC (for similar meanings in previous periods, cf. 3.3 and 4.3), and also illustrates the difficulties in determining without hesitation the exact meaning of a particular construction.

Interestingly, Coates (1983), in her investigation of the English modals, reports that it is often the case that "will" is found in contexts of "merger", i.e. "contextual neutralization", where it is impossible to tell whether it conveys a particular meaning among its possible meanings.[25] The common semantic basis of both θέλω and "will" seems to favor indeterminacy in some cases.

As with the other two AVCs, the literary texts of the 12th c. provide us with no further insights into the developments of θέλω, because of their relatively high register. Consequently, volitional θέλω + Infinitive not only has a greater token frequency than the expected future-referring meaning (12 in comparison with 8), but also outnumbers the volitional construction θέλω νά + Subjunctive (12 to 6, respectively). The sharp contrast between the situation in *Digenis* (and in *Armouris*) and in the literary texts of the 12th c. shows that the latter provide a rather misleading picture of developments, and should not be taken at face value. On the other hand, the fact that these very texts contain instances of the FC supports the argument made above that this AVC was already so well established as to be used in the poems of well-known scholars of the 12th c. (e.g. Theodoros Prodromos and Mihail Glykas).

In all texts of the early stages of LMG (11th–13th c.), most of the basic properties of the θέλω AVC are already in place:

(a) the great popularity of the future-referring θέλω;
(b) the semantic / syntactic split between future-referring θέλω + Infinitive and volitional θέλω νά + Subjunctive (with occasional exceptions of volitional θέλω + Infinitive due to the higher register of some texts);
(c) the use of θέλω + Infinitive in Subjunctive contexts;
(d) the use of the V + V_S pattern to convey future reference.

The drastic change in the picture of future reference in LMG in comparison with EMG is already apparent: more clearly in the 14th c. (cf. next section), but already from the 11th–12th c., future-referring θέλω + Infinitive is dominant, while it hardly occurred at all in the texts of the previous period. Only indirect evidence from non-literary texts and middle register literary texts (e. g. *Epanagoge* for EMG, *Stratigikon* and the example in 32 for LMG) revealed a possible higher frequency of use for θέλω in EMG. The generalization of use should be seen in combination with the demise of the other two FCs:

---

[25] Coates gives the following example from a dialogue to illustrate the phenomenon (1983: 16–17): 'Newcastle Brown Ale is a jolly good beer. Is it? Well, it ought to be at that price", where "ought" can convey either obligation or epistemic modality. Crucially, in cases of "merger", the actual intended meaning plays no role for the interpretation of the clause, in other words both meanings are found in a "both / and" relationship.

μέλλω was by that time a rather archaizing element, while ἔχω was hardly used any more in future-referring contexts, moving towards the domain of anteriority (cf. 5.1. and 5.2, respectively). But as has been briefly argued (cf. 4.3 and 5.2), language contact might have been the main driving force behind the rise in frequency of use of the θέλω construction; to be more precise, contact with Slavic populations might be partly responsible for this development.

It is well known that the great majority of the modern Balkan languages have an FC based on the verb "want" (cf. e.g. Joseph, 1983). This has been seen as a prototypical case of a language contact phenomenon, even though the details are hotly debated, especially regarding the origin of the construction and the path of diffusion in the various languages. A novel way of looking into the evidence from both Greek and Old Church Slavonic (OCS), the earliest attestation of the South Slavic languages (9th–11th c.), can perhaps illuminate some aspects of this phenomenon. The texts of OCS are mainly translations of the New Testament and other religious works from Greek: crucially, these translations contain FCs built on both "have" and "want" (Birnbaum, 1958). It is only reasonable to argue that the translators would not have used such constructions, especially as there were no exact equivalents in the Greek New Testament (which contains only instances of μέλλω and synthetic future formations), unless they were already in use by the Slavic people. The *xošto* ("want") AVC is predominantly used to translate the μέλλω FC in all its contexts of use (Birnbaum, 1958: 231), while *imam*b ("have") is mainly employed to translate negated future constructions (e.g. οὐ μή + Subjunctive) (Birnbaum, 1958: 196).[26] The systematic use of the Slavic AVCs in relation to completely different Greek constructions renders the assumption of an already established presence of these AVCs in OCS hard to refute (especially for the "have" FC, cf. Andersen, 2006). One could argue that the Slavs might have been already influenced by Greeks before the emergence of OCS, hence the appearance of the "want" future. But this would presuppose the quite early (6th–7th c.) popularity of the future-referring θέλω, which is not verified by the surviving evidence (cf. 4.3), though, as already mentioned, the evidence from EMG is of relatively little value. Nevertheless, one would have to postulate that only the θέλω FC was used more frequently than the texts leave room to suggest, but also that it was used so frequently as to become a pattern for grammatical replication by the Slavic population. This is possible, but rather unlikely.

---

[26] Recall the important role that negation has been argued to have played in the development of the future-referring meaning for the ἔχω AVC (cf. 3.2). Apparently, OCS independently followed a similar path of development for its equivalent construction. Interestingly, Modern Bulgarian still employs the "have" future, mainly in negative contexts (Bubenik, 2000, Heine & Kuteva, 2005: 27).

As already mentioned (cf. 4.3), Slavic populations had settled in Greek-speaking areas from the 6th–7th c., and the inter-relationship between the two populations increased as time progressed, especially in Northern Greece, as Joseph (1983, 2000) has suggested, with extensive language contact and bilingualism. It is, therefore, proposed that it is this close contact with another population *already* speaking a language containing a "want" FC that sparked—at least to an extent—the rise in frequency in the use of θέλω, most probably in the late EMG–early LMG period, without obviously excluding the possibility of other relevant factors, which are far from evident, though. This assumption is in agreement with a recent survey of similar phenomena cross-linguistically, according to which FCs are the most likely to be replicated in situations of language contact (Heine & Kuteva, 2005: 103), and that the increase in the frequency of use of a pattern constitutes "the most common kind of contact-induced grammatical transfer" (Heine & Kuteva, 2005: 48). Even though Greek must have been the "high prestige" language in this language contact situation, this arguably did not inhibit it from being influenced by Slavic, as the findings of the same survey suggest that the process of grammatical borrowing is hardly determined by such sociolinguistic factors (Heine & Kuteva, 2005: 260), i.e. the less prestigious language might equally well provide the source for grammatical borrowing as the more prestigious one. Obviously, in the subsequent centuries, there would be a mutual strengthening of the "want" AVC in both languages due to contact. We will get back to this issue when discussing the development of the θέ νά construction.

5.4.2 *The later stages*

As with the two other AVCs, the literary texts in the vernacular of the 14th c. offer us the first solid basis on which we can construct the actual developments involving θέλω with relative certainty. But this is not to say that the interpretation of the 14th c. facts is a straightforward procedure, as they contain great variation in constructions and meanings. Even so, clear patterns emerge, alongside more controversial ones. The picture of the 14th c. with regard to θέλω is illustrated in Tables 5.6 and 5.7, separating the constructions according to the type of complementation (infinitival or clausal). This separation is motivated by the fact that, in these texts, both θέλω + Infinitive and θέλω νά + Subjunctive were found to express various TAM meanings and, even though this is not novel for θέλω + Infinitive (AVC$_1$), this cannot be said for θέλω νά + Subjunctive (AVC$_2$), which conveys non-lexical meanings for the first time, with a unique exception from the earlier stages of LMG

174 *The future in Greek*

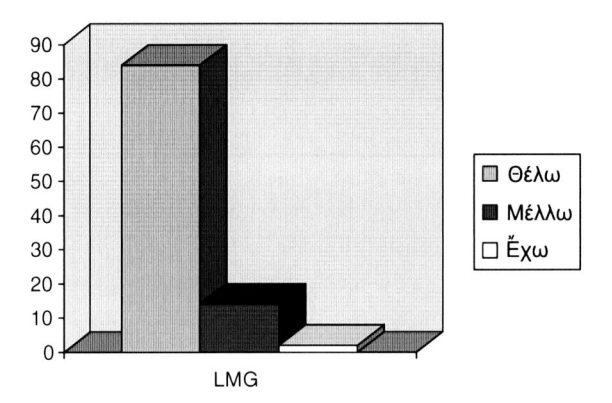

FIGURE 5.2 Token frequency of FCs in LMG (14th c.)

(cf. ex. 37). One question that immediately arises refers to the grammaticalization path of AVC$_2$: is this AVC the result of a novel grammaticalization process, affecting the morphosyntactic construction θέλω νά + Subjunctive, or simply the result of the replacement of the Infinitive in the old AVC? The evidence of the 14th c. texts suggests the former, since, if it were simply a syntactic development, then one would expect that there would be instances of AVC$_2$ conveying future reference, since AVC$_1$ was predominantly employed to express futurity. But this is not what is found: instead, the θέλω AVC$_2$ is employed for other TAM meanings (especially obligation), but not for future reference. It is impossible to tell, however, if the speakers of LMG associated these two AVCs between them and in relation to the volitional construction as well. This seems plausible, on the basis of the developments of the θέ νά construction (cf. 5.4.3).

From the figures in the tables, the overall pattern clearly emerges. The θέλω AVC$_1$ is predominantly used in the domain of future reference, and, furthermore, it constitutes by far the dominant FC in this period;[27] the equivalent numbers for μέλλω and ἔχω are much lower (cf. 5.1.2 and 5.2.2). On the other hand, the volitional meaning is expressed through the construction involving subordinate-clause complementation. There are still instances of the old pattern θέλω + Infinitive conveying volition, but they are significantly fewer than their counterparts involving νά-complementation, which are used in 87.3% (345 / 395) of the total cases of volitional meaning. In addition, 32 / 50 (64%) attestations of lexical θέλω involving infinitival complement are found in two texts, namely *Kallimahos* and *Ermoniakos*,

[27] Hence, the term θέλω FC is taken here to refer to the θέλω AVC$_1$.

Table 5.6 Θέλω + Infinitive in 14th c. literary texts

MEANING	K&H	V&H	L&R	D.P	Sahl	CoM	WoT	Ah.	Poul	Fys	Iatr	Erm	AoT	Pt.	Total
1. Volitional	14	3	3	3	–	–	6	1	–	1	–	18	–	4	50 (10.2)
2. Future-referring	2	2	33	4	19	61	205	24	6	1	9	8	6	11	391 (79.5)
3a. Temporal / Modal compl. (e.g. Ὅταν)θέλω + Inf. / Subj.	–	–	1	–	–	–	5	–	–	–	–	–	–	–	6 (1.2)
3b. Νά θέλω + Inf. / Subj.	–	–	2	–	–	9 (2)	9	2	–	–	–	–	–	–	22 (4.5)
4. Μή θέλω + Inf. / Prohibition	1	–	–	–	–	–	–	1	–	–	–	–	–	–	2 (0.4)
5. "Should" (Q)	–	–	–	–	–	9	5	–	–	–	–	–	–	–	14 (2.8)
6. Epistemic (?)	–	–	–	–	–	–	2	1	–	–	–	–	–	–	3 (0.6)
7. Obligation	–	–	–	–	–	–	1	–	–	–	–	1	–	–	1 (0.2)
8. Generic	–	–	–	–	–	–	–	–	–	2	–	–	–	–	3 (0.6)
TOTAL	17	5	39	4	19	79	233	29	6	4	9	27	6	15	492

Table 5.7 Θέλω + Finite complementation in 14th c. literary texts

MEANING	K&H	V&H	L&R	D.P.	Sahl.	CoM	WoT	Ah.	Poul.	Fys.	Iatr.	Erm.	AoT	Pt.	Total
1a. Θέλω νά + Subj. / Vol.	6	8	14	3	31	69	123	30	8	7	5	3	4	1	312 (87.7)
1b. Θέλω + Compl. (e.g. ὅτι) + νά + Subj. / Vol.	1	–	1	–	–	7	18	1	–	1	–	1	2	–	32 (9.0)
1c. Θέλω μή + Subj. / Vol. (neg.)	–	–	–	–	1	–	–	–	–	–	–	–	–	–	1 (0.3)
1d. Θέ νά + Subj. / Vol.	–	–	–	–	2	–	–	–	–	–	–	–	1	–	3 (0.8)
2. Θέλω νά + Subj. / Hortative	–	–	–	–	–	1	1	–	–	1	–	–	–	–	3 (0.8)
3a. Θέλω νά + Subj. / Obligation (?)	–	–	–	–	–	1(?)	–	–	1	–	–	–	1(?)	–	3 (0.8)
3b. Θέλει (imp.) νά + Subj. / Obligation	–	–	–	–	–	–	–	–	–	–	1	–	1	–	2 (0.6)
TOTAL	7	8	15	3	34	78	142	31	8	9	7	4	9	1	356
4. V + V_S / Future	–	–	–	–	–	1	3	1	–	–	–	–	–	–	6
5. V + V_S / Generic	–	–	–	–	–	–	–	–	–	1	–	–	–	–	1

both (and especially the latter) having been written in an elaborated style and representing a higher register of language. Evidently, apart from some instances of learned usage with a volitional meaning, θέλω + Infinitive is by far the commonest means of expressing future reference in the 14th c. (cf. Fig. 5.2, where the compared frequency of FCs is illustrated: θέλω 84.6%, μέλλω 14.0%, and ἔχω 1.5%).

Apparently, by this period the θέλω FC had also been established in higher registers of use, as is verified by the fact that in the same century, Theodoros Palaiologos, the lord of the Peloponnese, used it in a private letter (*MM*, Vol. III, II, 9 / d. 1390), and in the 15th c., in the oldest surviving text from Naxos (1445), the duke of the Aegean (of Frankish origin) also employs the same AVC (Lampros, 1907). Combining this evidence with that in Table 5.6, according to which the θέλω FC is attested in every single text, we can safely draw the conclusion that, already by the end of the 14th c., θέλω + Infinitive was the predominant AVC in the domain of future-reference, not only in the low registers but also in middle- or high-register contexts, such as administrative documents.[28] It goes without saying then that in the books of the notaries of the 15th–16th c., there are literally thousands of attestations of this specific AVC conveying a future-referring meaning.

As has been mentioned, in the literary texts of the 14th c., the semantic / semantic dichotomy between "θέλω + Infinitive = future reference" and "θέλω νά + Subjunctive = non-future reference" is to a great extent valid, leaving aside some exceptions of the archaic volitional θέλω + Infinitive. This split is largely verified in the official documents: in all the texts included in the corpus, this pattern is unmistakably valid. This observation is important, since it has been repeatedly argued (cf. Joseph & Pappas, 2002, for a recent formulation) that the future-referring θέλω AVC passed through a θέλω νά + Subj. and / or a θέλει (impersonal) νά + Subj. stage in LMG, in order to account for the emergence of the future-referring θέ νά construction. It is argued here that this is not borne out by the data in relation to the θέ νά construction (cf. 5.4.3). Nonetheless, there are a few complications to this assumed split, mainly associated with various modal meanings that the θέλω AVCs could convey. The discussion that follows focuses primarily on the modal uses of the θέλω

---

[28] The sole exception to the wide diffusion of this AVC comes from South Italy, in the documents of which there are no attestations of the θέλω FC, probably because of the early date of the texts (10th–14th c.). This observation further supports our idea of a contact-induced rise in the frequency of use for θέλω + Infinitive (cf. 5.4.1), as the Greek speakers who were not apparently exposed to the same language contact situation did not use this construction.

AVCs (initially alluded to, but not really examined by Bănescu, 1915) that are most relevant to the developments of the FC.

First of all, a specific context of the FC has been isolated, i.e. when it is preceded by temporal / modal complementizers and when it follows νά (3a.–3b. in Table 5.6), since these (and especially the latter) represent cases of intertwining between Future and Subjunctive. As with μέλλω and ἔχω, θέλω participates in a construction headed by νά (i.e. νά θέλω + Infinitive) without a discernible semantic difference from a simple Subjunctive (cf. 5.2.3). Even though the θέλω FC is rarely found in this context, at least in comparison with ἔχω, still the fact remains that this construction should now be regarded as more common than previously thought, since it is also attested in *Ahilliid* and in *Livistros-a*, texts arguably not written under any strong Western influence. Interestingly, as can be seen from row (3b.) in Table 5.6, in the *CoM*, the scribe of the P manuscript regularly replaces θέλω in this structure, sometimes even with ἔχω (in two cases, lines 331, 2638). Apparently, ἔχω was more readily allowed in this construction than θέλω, presumably because it constituted the older of the two FCs (Bybee, Perkins & Pagliuca, 1994: 235).

In the 14th c., the first instance of θέλω + Infinitive conveying epistemic modality is also found, as illustrated below:

(38) κ' ἐκεῖνοι ἐθαυμάζασιν τὴν ὀλιγότητά των
and they wondered the scarcity theirs
< καὶ καθ' αὐτοὺς > ἐλέγασιν, ἔγκρυμμαν θέλουν ἔχει
and among themselves said trap will-3rd PL.PRES. have-INF.
"and they were surprised because of their few numbers, and they said among themselves 'they must have set a trap' "

(*Ahilliid (L)*, 409–10)

In this context, the epistemic reading is quite plausible, as the soldiers are trying to fathom the plans of their enemies. Instances of epistemic meaning are rather rare in LMG: apart from (38) and two possible examples in *WoT* (row 6, Table 5.6), the only other attestation of θέλω + Infinitive with this meaning comes from a letter of the 15th c.:

(39) μὰ κατέχω καὶ στενὸς θὲς εἶσται, ὀγιατὶ ἀλλουνοῦ'
but know and pressed will-2nd SING. be-INF., because else
σαι ὁπλεγάδος . . .
are obliged
"but I know that you must be pressed, as you are obliged to someone else . . ."

(*Legrand*, p. 296 / d. 1499)

This example, found in a letter from G. Carantinos to J. Grigoropoulos, verifies the emergence of the epistemic meaning, which obviously was not as frequent as the other meanings of the AVC, at least in the written registers. Its existence might imply that the future-referring θέλω AVC has reached the final stages of its development, if we believe what Bybee, Perkins & Pagliuca (1994: 279) report, i.e that the epistemic meaning is typologically the last to be expressed by an FC.

More interesting to the overall discussion of the θέλω FC are the examples of the θέλω AVCs conveying deontic modality. These occur rarely with the old, infinitival (row 7, Table 5.6) and mainly with the new, clausal complementation (cf. 40), similarly to developments manifested for the other AVCs (cf. 5.1.2 and 5.2):

(40) Λοιπόν, ὡς ὤμοσα ἐγὼ ἀτὸς μου ποῦ εἶμαι ἀφέντης
Well, as swore I my-self who am noble
καὶ κύριος εἰς τὸν τόπον μου, θέλει κι ὁ βασιλέας
and lord in the place mine, want-3rd PRES. and the king
νὰ ὀμόσῃ γὰρ σωματικῶς, χρυσόβουλλον νὰ ποιήσῃ
that swear-3rd SUBJ. prt by hand, chrysobull that make-3rd SUBJ.
"So, as I myself swore who am noble / and lord of my place, so must also the king / swear by his own hand, make a chrysobull"

(CoM, 8741–3)

The example in (40) is a rather straightforward instance of an obligation meaning, since these words are spoken by a Frankish lord who states that, as he himself has done, the Byzantine emperor (and not the addressee of his words, who is not in a position to swear anything) must also swear in order for this agreement to be valid. In this case the new, clausal complementation is exhibited, but as the subject of ὀμόσῃ is 3rd person singular, similarly to θέλει, there is no way to distinguish between personal and impersonal syntax. The same holds for the first attestation of the deontic meaning with the clausal complementation in the official documents:

(41) διὰ τοῦτο καὶ θέλει νὰ ἔχῃ τὸ στέργον... ἡ τοῦ
for this and want-3rd PRES. that have-3rd SUBJ. the certain... the the-GEN.
καθολικοῦ κριτοῦ κρίσις, ἐὰν ἄρα οὐδὲν εἰσὶν οἱ πρωτεύοντες μοναχοὶ
general judge judgment, if prt not are the primary monks
ὑπογεγραμμένοι εἰς τὸ τῆς καταδοχῆς γράμμα, καθὼς εἴπαμεν.
signed in the the-GEN. agreement letter, as said
"For that reason the judgment of the general judge must be valid, if the primary monks have not signed at the letter of agreement, as we said"

(Koutloumousiou, 32 / d. 1375)

Although the meaning of the construction in (41) is ambiguous between deontic and future-referring, the deontic interpretation is more plausible, as the sentence determines what *needs* to be done if the conditions described in the following conditional clause are met. More examples of such a deontic meaning, suggesting its wide distribution, are found in the contemporary *Assises*, as shown in (42):

(42) ἐκεῖνος ὁποῦ θέλει   νὰ λάβῃ   γυναῖκαν, θέλει
     He   who want-3rd PRES. that get-3rd SUBJ. woman,   want-3rd PRES.
     νὰ   ὀμόσῃ   εἰς τὰ ἅγια...
     that swear-3rd SUBJ. at the sacred...
     "Whoever wants to get married, must swear by the Gospel..."

(*Assises*, 151 (ms. B))

From a syntactic point of view, (41–42) pattern like (40), since it is impossible to tell whether θέλω has a personal or impersonal syntax, as the subject of the verb is in both cases in the 3rd person singular. This is repeated in all the examples found in the *Assises* (e.g. 47, 48 (ms. A), 164 (ms. B)), except for one (272, ms. B), where it is undoubtedly a personal construction.

The issue of the personal or impersonal syntax for these examples is important for the θέλω FC as well. It has been assumed (cf., for example, Joseph & Pappas, 2002, Roberts & Roussou, 2003) that, during the LMG period, an *impersonal future-referring θέλει νά* + Subjunctive AVC emerged, which constitutes presumably the predecessor of the θέ νά construction. However, this impersonal structure is only manifested in considerably later stages of Greek, and Joseph & Pappas (2002: 263) attribute this lack of attestations to the notorious problems of textual tradition, assuming that this AVC passed over quickly before entering the literary language. This assumption is problematic, however, since the corpus of this investigation contains numerous attestations of a great variety of other related constructions, and therefore, their argument is *prima facie* invalid. Nevertheless, the previous examples in (40–42) could be considered as impersonal, although there is no way to tell. But, as shown in Table 5.7 (row 3b.), two instances of this impersonal construction in the literary texts of the 14th c. have indeed been found, but, crucially, both convey a *deontic* meaning, which is exactly the situation obtaining in Modern Greek as well (cf. Roussou, 2005): the example in *Iatrosofia* (142–3) is a straightforward case of medical advice, with a clear obligation meaning (ἀλλὰ ἐκεῖ ὅπου τὴν σικυάνῃς, θέλει νὰ μὴ τὸν κόψῃς ἐκεῖνον τὸν τόπον=but where you apply the remedy (cupping vessel), you must not cut that part), while that in *AoT* is given below:

(43) ἀλήθειαν ὁρίζετε,   γαβρὸν   θέλει   νὰ πάρω
     truth   tell,   son-in-law want-3rd PRES. that take-1st SUBJ.
     "You are right, I have to take a son-in-law"

(AoT, 299)

The interpretation of (43) is far from clear, but thankfully the context is at least indicative of a deontic meaning: the three "candidates" for marrying the king's daughter urge him to make a decision, as it is high time that he did so (AoT, 294–6), and the king responds that they are right, and that he *has* to take a son-in-law. The future interpretation is not excluded, but is arguably disfavored, as it would make little sense for the king to assert that he *will* marry off his daughter, a fact plainly evident; instead, he asserts that it is indeed right that he must marry his daughter (implying, now). The evidence from μέλλω (cf. 5.1.2), whose proliferation of impersonal uses was linked with its strong modal undertones, as well as the unmistakeable case in *Iatrosofia*, render the deontic interpretation preferable. Consequently, although (43) constitutes a case of the impersonal construction sought for (at least by Joseph & Pappas, 2002), it should not be mistakenly taken for a predictive FC.

This pattern is exhibited in other, non-literary texts as well in the subsequent centuries, an observation that strengthens the assumption of its being a systematic development. Apart from a Cretan will of the 15th c. (Sathas, 1873: vol. VI, 1 / d. 1486), where the impersonal θέλει appears again, this pattern is attested numerous times in the mathematics textbook of the 15th c. mentioned above (Hunger & Vogel, 1963). This is unsurprising considering the linguistic context: mathematical problem-solving is bound to involve deontic constructions, of the type "how much should you give in order to...?", and this is exactly what is found, as shown in (44):

(44) καὶ πόσες   ὀργυιὲς θέλει   νὰ εἶναι   ἡ σκάλα
     and how-many "feet"   want-3rd PRES. that is-3rd PRES. the ladder
     νὰ εἶναι σωστή;
     that is correct?
     "and how long should the ladder be in order to be appropriate?"

(H&V, 62)

There are 25 attestations of this construction overall in the textbook. Unfortunately, as in most of them the subject of the clause is in the 3rd person singular, we are again left with no way to tell whether the attested form θέλει signals a personal or an impersonal syntax. There is, however, evidence that it actually could be both: either personal (e.g. no. 67) or impersonal (e.g. no. 99b); on the basis of the relevant attestations in the literary texts of the 14th c., and in the Cretan will mentioned above, one would be more inclined to assume that most of the examples should be considered impersonal, but still there is not enough evidence to support the claim firmly, especially given the fact that the equivalent personal construction is also attested. Finally, it should be noted that this construction could still alternate with the AVC₁ in this deontic meaning (at least in this text), even though rarely: only one example of the old construction bearing a deontic meaning is found (no. 79).

The examples of the non-literary texts of the 15th c. are therefore illuminating in one important respect. They suggest that in the appropriate—deontic—context, the θέλω AVC₂ was quite prolific; as a consequence, they lend more credibility to the deontic interpretation of some ambiguous examples in the literary texts, such as (43).

The deontic construction is also attested in the notary books of the 16th c.: in the documents from Crete, we can find three attestations in *Olokalos* (108, 180, 233), another two in *Grigoropoulos* (38, 90) and one in *Maras* (I, 19), from Corfu there is one example in *Varagkas* (8), and from Kefalonia there is another attestation in *De Montesantos* (140). In all these cases, the deontic nuance is clearly stronger than future reference. Moreover, they all involve a 3rd person singular subject, thus again rendering it impossible to tell whether they constitute impersonal or personal constructions; the exceptions are *Grigoropoulos*, 90 and *Maras*, I, 19, which are undeniably instances of a personal construction. Even though Grigoropoulos was a rather learned notary, this probably cannot be said for Maras, and therefore we can assume that the personal deontic θέλω was still in use, although the frequency of this use, both in absolute numbers and in comparison with the equivalent impersonal construction, remains unknown.

Apart from the expression of deontic modality, two more morphosyntactic facts regarding θέλω in the 14th c. are worth noting. The first concerns the V+V$_S$ pattern. As Table (5.7) illustrates (rows 4–5), this construction is attested in five different texts of this century, another fact corroborating the previously made assumptions about its generalized use. Moreover, one of these instances apparently conveys a generic meaning:

(45) καὶ ὅσοι   θέλουν   ἄψονται   τὰς σάρκας
and those-who want-3rd PL.PRES. touch-3rd PL. the fleshes
τοῦ διαβόλου   εὐθὺς   ἀναπληρόνονται πρὸς φόνους
the-GEN. devil immediately tend   to murders
"And all these who touch the devil, they become straight away murderers"

(*Fysiologos*, 530)

It is worth noting that this instance of generic V+V$_S$ is found in the very same text where more instances of the same meaning, but involving the old AVC$_1$, are attested. Perhaps an indication of the interconnection in the LMG speakers between these two complementation patterns, according to what has been argued for the development of the future-referring meaning of the V+V$_S$ pattern (cf. previous section)? The evidence is suggestive, but not conclusive.

Finally, the literary texts of the 14th c. contain the first instances of the reduced phonological forms of θέλω: in the *WoT* (4826) we find the first attestation of the form θές, which constitutes an abbreviated form of the 2nd person singular θέλεις,[29] while θέ, presumably the reduced form of the 3rd person singular, is attested in *Sahlikis* and in *AoT* (row 1d., Table 5.7). One cannot speak of a reduced paradigm yet, though, since such forms occur only in these two grammatical persons, and the plural and (presumably) the 1st person singular are apparently left unaffected. Moreover, all attestations of this new construction express volition, not future reference. The importance of this phonological development, in connection with the controversial θέ νά construction in particular, will be discussed in detail below (cf. 5.4.3).

The picture concerning the θέλω AVCs does not alter in any significant way in the literary texts of the 14th–15th c. Again, there is a sharp distinction between the future-referring θέλω followed by an Infinitive and the volitional θέλω followed by a complement clause. Some instances of volitional θέλω + Infinitive remain, but they are vastly outnumbered by the clausal complementation construction (13 compared to 67, respectively), and, perhaps even more importantly, ten of those 13 instances are found in the same text, the romance *Florios,* which has already been seen to contain certain archaisms (cf. 5.1.2, 5.2.2). Therefore, the texts of the 14th–15th c. seem to conform to the picture already presented.

Moving on to the 15th century, the texts offer a similar picture yet again as far as the general pattern is concerned: the θέλω AVC$_1$ is utilized mainly for future reference, while θέλω + νά-clause is restricted to the expression of the lexical meaning of the verb and various other modal meanings. A partial exception to this pattern comes from Cyprus. On the face of it, *Mahairas* follows the same pattern found in all texts of LMG, since for future reference the θέλω AVC$_1$ is used (227 attestations), volitional θέλω is always complemented by a νά–clause (129 attestations), and both AVCs are also employed for the expression of various modalities (even epistemic, *Mahairas,* 488).

---

[29] Bănescu (1915: 102) provides another example of θές from *CoM* (2089), but the reading he assumes is not contained in the edition of the text consulted here.

Nevertheless, in this text we also find five instances where θέλω AVC$_2$ has a future-referring meaning, most clearly in the following example (the other being 27, 503, 542 (2)):

(46) *Καὶ θέλετε   νὰ'δῆτε   τὴν κρίσιν   τοῦ Θεοῦ!*
And want-2nd PL. that see-2nd PL.SUBJ. the judgment the God!
Κατεβαίνει   ἕνας κόρπος ἀπὸ τὸ τριπουτζέτειν... καὶ ἐφύγαν
Goes-down   a   missile from the trebuchet...   and left
ἀπὸ τὸν λιμνιόναν μακελλεμένοι καὶ   ἀντροπιασμένοι οἱ Γενουβίσοι.
from the harbor   decimated   and   ashamed   the Genoese
"And now you will see the judgment of God! Down comes a missile from the trebuchet... and the Genoese left the harbor decimated and ashamed"

(*Mahairas*, 498)

Arguably, *Mahairas* constitutes the first text to contain clear examples of such a development, even though there is another attestation in the *Katalogia* (711) which might have a future interpretation, albeit without excluding the possibility of a volitional meaning. Furthermore, a similar instance is attested in *Falieros* (*Ρίμα*, 78), and, if we accept its reading as secure, then we could assume that this development might have occurred prior to its attestation in the texts of the 15th c, although its absence in the texts of the 14th c. renders this assumption risky.

The non-literary texts provide further evidence of this development. Firstly, they contain instances of an intermediate stage, shown in (47):

(47) *ὅ,τι   μέλισες θέλουν   ἀναθραφῆν   καὶ νὰ*
whatever bees   will-3rd PL.PRES. grow up-INF. and that
εὑρίσκουνται   εἰς τὸ λεγώμενον μοναστήρι, νὰ μὴν ἔχι
exist-3rd PL.SUBJ. in the said   monastery, that not have
τινὰς ἐξουσίαν νὰ δόσι οὐδε   να πουλήση
no-one authority that give nor   that sell
"Whatever bees will grow up and exist in this monastery, no-one should have the authority to give away or sell [them] ..."

(*Patsidiotis*, 68 / d. 1550)

In this example, the conjunction *καί* could be seen as connecting the two complements of *θέλουν*, but the second complement is a subordinate clause (*νὰ εὑρίσκουνται*), while the first is an Infinitive (*ἀναθραφῆν*). This is exactly the case in all other attestations of this construction, originating in Naxos (Visvizis, 1951: 21, 27, 42 / d. 1539–40). Joseph & Pappas (2002) cite similar examples from literary texts of LMG, even though almost all examples are taken from texts of the late 15th–16th c., and therefore are not included in the corpus. Furthermore, in the case of the very few examples that do fall within the scope of this investigation, it is impossible to decide whether they convey a future-referring meaning[30] or, in the event that they do express future reference, whether the νά–clause is an independent, future-referring Subjunctive or a complement of θέλω, since the use of the Subjunctive as a future-referring formation is pervasive in all works of LMG, especially in the first centuries (Horrocks, 1997).[31] Although the same indeterminacy could be argued for (47) as well, it seems rather unlikely, as by the 16th c. the future-referring use of the Subjunctive is in decline: according to Bănescu (1915: 88–9), it is attested only three times in "Erotokritos", a 16th–17th-c. Cretan poem of about 10,000 verses! This token frequency is indeed very low, especially compared to the six attestations in the much shorter *Sahlikis*. Therefore, it is more plausible that (47) (as well as the 15th–16th-c. examples mentioned in Joseph & Pappas, 2002) represent a genuine case of two different types of complements for the future-referring θέλω: in this respect, they actuate an intermediate stage where the Infinitive was replaced by a subordinate clause after a conjunction such as καί or, alternatively, in which the Infinitive could appear only adjacent to the verb, a phenomenon already exhibited in the New Testament with regard to the complementation of volitional θέλω (Joseph & Pappas, 2002: 269–70). It is interesting to note that, in her edition of *Livistros-b*, Lentari (2007: 123) remarks that the future-referring νά-Subjunctive is felicitous only when it is dependent upon a previous action, i.e. when future reference is already established in the context. If this is indeed the case for LMG in general, then perhaps examples such as (47) might be one of the prominent syntactic contexts that facilitated the emergence of the future-referring meaning for the θέλω AVC$_2$.

The following example, representing the V + V$_S$ pattern, also relates to (47):

(48) καὶ ὅ, τι   θέλουν   κρίνην   καὶ ἀποφασίσουν...
     and whatever will-3rd PL. judge-INF. and decide-3rd PL.SUBJ.
     "and whatever they will judge and decide..."

(*Amarantos*, 44 / d. 1550)

---

[30] Cf. the following example from *CoM* (3143): ἐν τούτω θέλω ἀπὸ τοῦ νῦν νὰ πάψω ἐδῶ ὀλίγον (= At this point I will / want to stop here for a while). The volitional meaning seems to be perfectly plausible in this context.

[31] Therefore, for the purposes of this investigation, the νά–clauses have been counted as instances of the independent future-referring Subjunctive and have not been included in the tables concerning θέλω.

This type of construction, also attested in another document from Kefalonia (*De Montesantos,* 177 / d. 1546), corroborates our assumption that the νά–clause in (47) is a complement of θέλω, as the form ἀποφασίσουν in (48) cannot express future-reference independently but only as part of a θέλω AVC.³² Consequently, the pattern involving conjunction should be represented as follows:

(49) Θέλω + Infinitive καί (i) subordinate clause
                              (ii) finite form

The example in (48) also illustrates that the θέλω FC includes the V + V_S pattern. This third pattern of complementation, attested in the literary texts of the 14th c. (cf. Table 5.7), is widely attested in the official documents of the 16th c., too, from all areas represented in the archives, e.g. Crete (*Grigoropoulos* 119 / d. 1527), Kefalonia (*De Montesantos* 175 / d. 1546), and Kythira (*Kasimatis* 132 / d. 1564).

The non-literary texts not only exhibit the different complementation alternatives after conjunction for the θέλω FC, they also contain clear-cut instances of the final outcome of this development as well, i.e. of the θέλω AVC₂ with a future-referring meaning, as exemplified in (50):

(50) δηὰ τὸ χ(ωράφ)η   ὅπερ θέλλ(ει)   νὰ γένη   μῆλ(ος)
      for the field   where will-3rd PRES.   that become-3rd SUBJ. mill
      "for the field where a mill will be built"

(*De Montesantos,* 2 / d. 1535)

These instances are quite rare: apart from (50) from Kefalonia, there are three more unambiguous examples from Kythira (*Kasimatis,* 37, 84, 250 / d. 1564–5). If we compare this evidence with the abundance of attestations for the equivalent θέλω + Infinitive construction in the same documents, as well as with the near non-existence of similar examples from the literary texts in the vernacular till the 15th c. (apart from *Mahairas,* cf. ex. 46), then we can draw the conclusion that the development illustrated in (50) must have been quite recent at that time, possibly dating from the mid-15th c. (perhaps earlier for Cyprus), and / or that it was not frequent in written registers, where the older θέλω AVC₁ was clearly dominant. The fact that the θέλω AVC₂ could convey the deontic meaning from as early as the 14th c., in both types of textual evidence, whereas the future-referring meaning for this AVC, exemplified in (50), only appears in the 16th c. in the non-literary texts (and very rarely in the 15th c. literary texts), arguably suggests that the latter development is of a later date.

[32] Alternatively, one can assume that ἀποφασίσουν has nothing to do with the θέλω AVC, being an instance of Subjunctive used in a relative conditional clause, where "bare" Subjunctives such as ἀποφασισουν are quite common. However, despite their numerous attestations in this context, 'Conditional Subjunctives' are never found conjoined to an AVC. Therefore, it seems more likely to assume that these two cases are instances of the V + V_S pattern.

Consequently, the assumed semantic / syntactic split between future-referring θέλω + Infinitive and volitional θέλω νά + Subjunctive was valid till the 15th c., when it started to break down. It is suggested here that a combination of factors contributed to the development of the future-referring meaning for the θέλω AVC$_2$, namely:

(a) The ongoing grammaticalization of the θέλω νά + Subjunctive construction, which could convey deontic modality already from the 14th c. In that instance, one could assume a *second* grammaticalization for θέλω to express future reference, this time in a different syntactic construction (clausal complementation instead of infinitival);

(b) The independent, future-referring νά + Subjunctive which, when used in conjunction with a θέλω AVC$_1$, could be re-analyzed as a complement of θέλω, given the contemporary existence of a θέλω νά + Subjunctive construction. In other words, speakers could make the following reanalysis: [θέλω + Infinitive] καί [νά + Subjunctive] → θέλω + [Infinitive καί νά + Subjunctive]. Such reanalysis must also be the reason for the occurrence of constructions exemplified in (48), involving the V+V$_S$ pattern;

(c) The possible association between the two θέλω AVCs, which could have been related in the way the speakers perceived them.

Obviously, in such situations it is the combination of all these factors that brought about the attested development. Nevertheless, the picture of the θέλω AVCs in LMG is not yet complete, as there remains to investigate the debated θέ νά construction, in order to have the broadest view of all developments affecting θέλω.

5.4.3 *The emergence of "θέ νά": phonological reduction and language contact*

The most controversial θέλω construction in LMG is the θέ νά + Subjunctive, which ultimately gave rise to the particle θα, the futurity / modality particle in Modern Greek. It is quite straightforward that the emergence of this construction should be dated approximately in the 14th c., since the earliest instances are found in the literary texts of this century (cf. Table 5.7).[33] On the other hand, the semantic–syntactic developments associated with this construction have been the subject of a long-standing debate.

---

[33] Horrocks (1997: 232) mentions that this construction might have emerged already in the 13th c., since there is one example in a song called "Porfyris", dating from the early LMG period. However, as Horrocks himself concedes, this is of a very dubious worth, since the song survives in a manuscript dating probably from the 19th c., and therefore cannot be taken at face value.

Two main accounts exist in the literature. According to the first (cf., for example, Jannaris, 1897 and Horrocks, 1997), θέ is a phonologically reduced form of the 3rd person singular θέλει (either personal or impersonal, it is not relevant for this account), which was used to strengthen the future reference of the independent νά-Subjunctive. The fact that a reduced form of θέλω is employed in such a fashion should be attributed to the contemporary dominance of the θέλω FC. The second view, advocated by Joseph & Pappas (2002), assumes that, during the LMG period, θέλω νά + Subjunctive could be used for both volition and future reference, and in the case of the latter meaning, it developed into an impersonal θέλει νά + Subjunctive AVC. This impersonal AVC, which, as Joseph & Pappas admit (2002: 263), never occurs in this period, has to be postulated to account for the emergence of the construction θέ νά + Subjunctive, as θέ was allegedly used as an uninflected form for all grammatical persons. This investigation illustrates that both accounts have important shortcomings and fail to explain the data in a satisfactory manner. Therefore, a novel account will be proposed, accounting for the already known material as well as new material emerging from the non-literary texts. Let us first take a look at the data, which is quite revealing in its own right in many respects.

A. *The data* As mentioned, the θέ νά construction started emerging during the 14th c., since in the works of the Cretan poet Sahlikis and in *AoT* there are three instances of this construction. In all previous accounts of the development of θέλω, this construction has been seen mainly as an FC. Nevertheless, at this early stage, its future-referring meaning is in fact highly doubtful. Starting from *Sahlikis*, the two attestations therein have not been widely discussed and their interpretation remains uncertain, as will become immediately evident. The first example is clearly in favor of the volitional meaning, even though editorial practices have obscured its interpretation to a great extent: (51a) represents Wagner's edition (1874), while (51b) gives the actual reading of the manuscript:

(51a) ἀλλοῦ   ἐρημιὰν   ἐπεθυμᾶ,   ἀλλοῦ   θὲ   νὰ   πτωχάνη
      adv   solitude desires,   adv   wants-?   that   become-poor-3rd
                                                              PRES.SUBJ.

"Sometimes he desires solitude, sometimes he wants to (?) / will (?) lose money"

(*Sahlikis*, 124)

(51b) Ἄλλου   ἐρημίαν   ἐπεθυμᾶ, ἄλλον   θὲ   νὰ
       Other-GEN. destruction wants,   other-ACC. want-3rd SING.PRES. that
       πτωχάνη
       become-poor-3rd PRES. SUBJ.
       "For one he wants destruction, for another he wants him to become poor"

(Ms. P, f. 146 v, ll. 4–5)

Wagner had apparently misread the pronouns "ἄλλου... ἄλλον" for the adverbials "ἀλλοῦ... ἀλλοῦ", obscuring thus the clear meaning of the verse: Sahlikis refers to the gambler, stating that he wants that others be ruined and poor, by beating them at dice. The obviously volitional meaning of the θέ νά construction here is further strengthened by the presence of the synonym ἐπεθυμᾶ in the first semi-verse. Note also that the subject of θέ is 3rd person singular, and therefore θέ could be seen as an abbreviated form of θέλει.

However, *Sahlikis* also offers an example of a further development for this particular construction, as can be seen in (52):

(52) καὶ ἡ   Μανοῦλα ἔφτασε τοῦ   Νίκολο Ἀμπράμω...
     and the mother came   the-GEN. Nicolo Abramo...
     μὲ τὸ φαρίν καὶ φώναζε : λαργᾶτε,   θὲ   νὰ δράμω
     with the horse and shouted   move-2nd PL.IMP. want-? that ride-1st
                                                           SING.SUBJ.
     "And the mother of Nicolo Abramo came... on horse and cried: move away, I want to / will ride"

(*Sahlikis*, 700–2)

The meaning of this example is not as easy to determine as the one in (51), since in (52) both a future-referring and a volitional interpretation seem plausible. The poem describes a tournament of prostitutes, and the verse in (52) is uttered by a prostitute who has just come to participate and, therefore, the context cannot really determine the meaning of the construction. But since the subject of the verb νά δράμω is 1st person singular, one would be inclined to favor the volitional / intentional meaning, since, as already observed (cf. 5.4.1, ex. 37), 1st person contexts can be highly ambiguous and are not readily associated with pure prediction.[34] If this is indeed the case,

---

[34] As further evidence of a volitional (or at least not future-referring meaning) of this example can be seen the fact that there exists a variant of this semi-verse which reads: δέν ἠμπορῶ νά δράμω (="I cannot ride") (Papadimitriou, 1896: v. 749). Arguably, this variant gives a hint of the meaning of the verse, which could be paraphrased as follows: "move away, as I want to ride and / or I cannot ride (if you stay put)".

then θέ itself could be considered either as a reduced form of θέλω (1st person singular), or as a reduced form of θέλει (3rd person singular), but used for other grammatical persons as well, becoming thus akin to a volitional uninflected form (particle). Although volitional particles are rare cross-linguistically (cf. Haspelmath et al., 2005: 502–9), this assumption is probably preferable, as firstly, phonological reduction affecting the 1st person is rarely attested, both cross-linguistically and specifically in Greek, and secondly, contact with Old Venetian might have provided the pattern for the emergence of a volitional particle (cf. further below). In any case, it should be noted that the manuscript tradition of *Sahlikis*, and in particular of the poem which this example belongs to is particularly problematic, and probably reflects an oral tradition (cf. Panagiotakis, 1987). Consequently, the evidence in (51) and especially in (52) should be treated with caution, as they might also represent developments subsequent to the initial writing of the poems in the late 14th c.

Nonetheless, the emergence of the θέ νά construction in the 14th c. is verified by another attestation in *AoT*, a text probably written in Cyprus:

(53) τις   θε   νά   ακούει   άσματα, αινίγματα και λόγους
     who want-? that listen-3rd SUBJ. songs,   riddles   and stories
     και υμνωδίαν τραγωδίων, εις την Ταρσίαν ας πάγει!
     and hymn   tragedies,   to the Tarsian prt go-3rd SUBJ.
     "Whoever wants to hear songs, riddles and stories,
     and tragedy songs, let him go to Tarsos!"

(*AoT*, 614–5)

This attestation of the θέ νά + Subjunctive construction is reminiscent of (51), where the volitional meaning is clearly preferred and there is no indication of person agreement mismatch, if θέ is taken as a reduced form of θέλει. It is important to note that in all three instances of θέ νά in the 14th c., which are the oldest attestations of this construction, the volitional meaning is evident or at least highly preferable. This observation is surprising, given that all recent accounts of the development of this future-referring formation are (tacitly or explicitly) based on its conveying futurity from the very beginning. Joseph & Pappas note that θέ can occasionally convey a volitional meaning (2002: 255–6), but they do not show how this correlates with their account, while Bănescu (1915: 106) and Tonnet (1982) had noted the volitional meaning of the example in (53), but they do not offer a specific account for the phonological reduction and the subsequent developments of the construction. So, it seems that the evidence in the 14th c. already argues for a novel approach.

The literary texts of the 15th c. provide evidence of further developments regarding the form θέ. Two texts, namely *Xeniteia* and *Falieros*, both originating from Crete, contain a construction which has not figured previously in the accounts of the development of the future-referring θέλω AVCs (although the example in *Xeniteia* is mentioned in Bǎnescu (1915: 103)). This construction involves the appearance of the abbreviated form θέ, followed not by a subordinate νά-clause but by an Infinitive,[35] as seen in (54):

(54) Τώρα θωρῶ καὶ θὲ   κοπῇ   πᾶσα σας δυσκολία
     Now think and will-? stop-INF? every your difficulty
     "I think that now all your difficulties will be erased"

(*Falieros*, Ἱστορία καί Ὄνειρο, 733)

This example, as well as all other attestations of this construction with θέ in LMG (*Falieros*, Ἱστορία καί Ὄνειρο 160, 316 / *Xeniteia* 256), convey a future-referring meaning and, moreover, they all have a 3rd person singular subject, in other words θέ is functioning exactly as θέλει would, both in terms of semantics and syntax.[36] Arguably, then, this construction constitutes the future-referring equivalent of the volitional θέ νά + Subjunctive structure exemplified in (51–53). Importantly, the fact that θέ appears in all the contexts where θέλει could appear argues for a phonological process of reduction not triggered by semantic / syntactic considerations, and thus operating across the board.

The same can be said for θές, the form of the 2nd person singular that, as already mentioned (cf. 5.4.2), emerged at the same time as θέ: this form is used in *Falieros* as a 2nd person singular, both in a future-referring context, as an instantiation of the θέλω AVC₁ (cf., for example, ex. 55 and Ἱστορία καί Ὄνειρο 552, among others), as well as in a volitional construction with clausal complementation (e.g. ex. 56 and Ἱστορία καί Ὄνειρο 96, among other examples):

---

[35] The example in (54) could be alternatively regarded as an instance of the V + V_S pattern, since in many cases it is very difficult to decide whether a form constitutes a 3rd person Subjunctive or an Infinitive, as the two forms were homophonous, and their difference in spelling is neutralized by the numerous spelling mistakes of the manuscripts. As long as this example cannot be said to be an attestation of the θέ νά construction, the character of the complement of θέ (be it either Infinitive or Subjunctive) does not alter the essence of the argument here.

[36] This conclusion is further strengthened by evidence from the apparatus criticus in the case of the example above, for which there is a variant reading (man. A) with the full form θέλει instead of θέ.

(55) Κόψει   τὰ   θὲς   τὰ χείλη μου καὶ φὰ   τῆ
    Cut-INF. them-cl. will-2nd PRES. the lips mine and eat-INF. her-cl.
    θὲς   τῆ γλώσσα...
    will-2nd PRES. the tongue...
    "You will cut my lips and you will eat my tongue [if I let you kiss me]"

                        (Falieros, Ἱστορία καί Ὄνειρο, 647)

(56) ...Καὶ ἂν ἔν' καὶ θὲς   νὰ μάθης:
    And if is and want-2nd SING. that know-2nd SUBJ.
    "And if you want to know:"

                        (Falieros, Ἱστορία καί Ὄνειρο, 96)

Therefore, it can be argued that these abbreviated forms (θές, θέ) could function similarly to their fully-articulated equivalents irrespective of the type of construction they are employed in (future-referring or volitional). Only the construction θέ νά + Subjunctive provides a challenge to that conclusion, in the sense of θέ being used as a particle, i.e. with complements containing a subject other than a 3rd person singular.

This construction is attested twice in *Falieros*. The first attestation has arguably a volitional meaning, but θέ is complemented by a 2nd person singular verb:

(57) μὰ   ὅσο   θὲ   νὰ χώνεσαι   κάτεχε κι ἐξανοίκτης
    but as much want-? that hide-2nd SING.SUBJ, know   and were-seen
    "but as much as you want to hide, know that you have been seen"

                        (Falieros, Ἱστορία καί Ὄνειρο, 576)

Superficially, this example is very similar to the one found in *Sahlikis* (cf. ex. 52): the volitional meaning is preferable and the complement of θέ is not in the 3rd person singular. However, the apparatus criticus contains a variant reading for this verse involving θές (mss. NV), instead of θέ, and it is not evident—at least from a linguistic perspective—why the editor of the text (van Gemert, 2006) introduced in the text the *lectio difficilior* θέ, apart from following this particular "rule" of philological practice, since he explicitly (2006: 163) considers (57) as an instance of a volitional construction. The second attestation of θέ, though, is not challenged by different manuscript readings, and is illustrated below:

(58) Καὶ ἂν ἔν' καὶ βλάφτομε κι ἐμᾶς   κι   ἐκείνους δὲ φελοῦμε,
    And if is and hurt   and ourselves and them   not help,

> δὲν ἔν' μεγάλη μας λωλιά νὰ θὲ ν' ἀγανακτοῦμε;
> not is great ours folly that want-? that despair-1st PL.SUBJ.
> "And since we hurt ourselves and we do not help them, isn't it our great folly to be exasperated / to be intent on despairing?"

(Falieros, Ρίμα παρηγορητική, 46)

The interpretation of the θέ νά construction here is far from clear. The overall meaning runs as follows: "Since those who die will gain eternal peace, we should not mourn them so much." Certainly, the volitional meaning cannot be excluded, at least in the sense of "be willing, be intent on"; it is indeed this meaning that the editor of the text subscribes to explicitly in the later edition of a different poem (van Gemert, 2006: 163). From a different perspective, however, this example is suggestive of a parallelism between θέ νά + Subjunctive and simple νά-Subjunctive, and, according to this reading, the θέ νά construction would be used as a variant of the νά-Subjunctive. We have seen (cf. 5.2.3, 5.4.2) that this would not constitute an isolated case, as there have been other instances of an FC being used in contexts where the Subjunctive is normal, bearing very similar semantic nuances. Moreover, a very similar context to the one in (58) obtains in another verse of the very same poem ('Ρίμα', v. 154), where the complement of λωλιά ("folly") is a bare νά-Subjunctive. Yet, in order to postulate a parallelism between (58) and the pattern νά + FC, we have to assume that the θέ νά construction or its phonologically unreduced equivalent θέλω AVC$_2$ was already widely used as an FC, and came to be employed as a subordinate marker as well. No indication of such a development exists, however. Therefore, it seems more likely that the meaning of θέ νά in (58) is similar to "be intent on", i.e. a volition-related meaning.

On the contrary, the first possible instance of a future-referring use of the θέ νά construction is attested in *Mahairas*:

> (59) Ἄν θενὰ μποῦν ἀποὺ τὴν τρύπαν, τ'ἄλογα ἀπόθε
> If will-that? enter-3rd PL.SUBJ. from the hole, the horses from-where
> νὰ τὰ μπάσωμεν;
> that them-cl. put-through-1st PL.SUBJ.
> "If they will go through the hole, from where should / will we put through the horses?"

(Mahairas, 509)

Θέ νά is found here in the scope of a conditional and it could be regarded as conveying a future-referring meaning, since the conditional has a clear future reference. The future-referring interpretation is favored by the context: an assault is being organized, and the captain explains to his underlings that the men will pass the walls of Famagusta through a small hole, and they in turn ask (in ex. 59) if the men will pass through the hole, where they should put through the horses.[37] Recall that in the same century the first attestations of a future-referring θέλω AVC$_2$ occurred (cf. 5.4.2), a facilitating factor for the transition from volition to futurity for the θέ νά construction, if θέ was still associated with the unreduced paradigm, as will be proposed (cf. the analysis further below).

A final remark should be made with regard to these developments. All the instances of θέ in the LMG literary texts, without exception, are attested in texts originating from Crete and Cyprus: this is the case with *Sahlikis*, *Falieros*, and *Xeniteia*, written in Crete, and with *AoT* and *Mahairas*, written in Cyprus. Apparently, the emergence of the θέ νά construction was geographically restricted, and this can be attributed to the distance of these islands, both in geographical and in cultural terms, from the cultural center of the Greek-speaking world, i.e. Constantinople, or, perhaps more likely, to the strong influence of Romance languages (Italian and French) in these regions, even though it cannot be maintained that Crete and Cyprus represent a 'prototypical' linguistic area, given the distance between the two islands (for further discussion, see below).

Since θέ νά occurs in the LMG literary texts already in the 14th c., one could expect it to occur more frequently in the non-literary texts, which were produced in the subsequent centuries. This would not be the case, however, if it was not for the recent publication of some books of Maras, a notary in Kastron (Candia) of Crete in the mid-16th c.: in all other non-literary textual sources, θέ νά is only attested three times, while, surprisingly, *Maras* contains 26 attestations by itself. The later emergence of this construction in the official documents is explained by its apparently oral character, at least in its initial stages, as can be argued on the basis of the literary texts. But the unbalanced distribution of the construction in the non-literary texts arguably constitutes an important fact, which will provide us with new insights into the origin of this form, as will be explained below.

---

[37] It is interesting to note that this reading of (59) is contained only in one manuscript (V) of *Mahairas*, the other two (O, R) containing, instead of the θέ νά construction, variants involving the verb μπορώ = can. Moreover, the wider context in (V) is obscure and its meaning is not readily evident, while the text of the (O, R) manuscripts reads very nicely in this specific part (cf. Pieris & Nikolaou-Konnari, 2003: 358). Perhaps this suggests that the θέ νά construction was still quite rare in written registers, at least as an FC, and was readily replaced by scribes.

The volitional interpretation of the construction, attested in the literary texts (cf. especially ex. 51–53), occurs also in the following example of the late 16th c. from Kefalonia:

(60) φένετε ὤτι θέ   νά   φεύγι   από τό δίκαιων καί νά
     seems that want-3rd PRES. that leave-3rd SUBJ. from the right and that
     φάγι   τό εδικό μου μέ   πονηρίεσ μεγάλεσ
     eat-3rd SUBJ. the my-mine with deceits   great
     "It seems that he wants to abandon justice and to steal my wealth by deceit"

(*Sourianos*, 126 / d. 1582)

Crucially, this example constitutes part of the proceedings of a hearing at a court, a document very rarely found in all the archives of this period. Therefore, it represents a relatively close approximation to the spoken language of that time in what is otherwise a rather official register. In (60), the accuser talks about the accused and describes his actions and purpose; consequently, the volitional interpretation of the example seems quite solid. Therefore, this example provides crucial evidence that θέ νά could still convey a lexical (volitional) meaning, a fact corroborated by more attestations from Crete (e. g. *Maras,* III, 134, 312). Obviously, in some cases, θέ νά is highly ambiguous. In one case (Xanthoudidis, 1912: VI / d. 1590), θέ νά is found in a context ambiguous between a volitional and a future-referring interpretation, while in another the meaning of the construction is again ambiguous, this time between volition and deontic modality, as shown in (61):

(61) Ἀκομῆ   ἔδωκά σου καί ταῖς γραφαῖς   μου διά ἐκίνω ὁποῦ
     Moreover gave   you and the documents mine for that   which
     θέ   νά λάβω   από τόν Κατζαμπανόν
     want-? that receive-1st SUBJ. from the Katzabanos
     "Moreover, I gave you my documents for what I want / have to receive from Kotzabanos"

(*Maras*, I, 272 / d. 1549)

This last example brings us to a possible deontic meaning of the construction, which in some cases is fairly likely, as in (62):

(62) νά   μοῦ τά   δώσῃς τόν Ὀκτώβριον τόν πρῶτον ἐρχόμενον...
     that me them-cl. give   the October   the first   coming...
     ἁμάδη   μέ   τήν ἄλην πᾶγαν   ὁποῦ θέ   νά μοῦ
     together with the other instalment which want-? that me
     δώσῃς   τότε...
     give-2nd SUBJ. then

"You should return it to me next October... together with the other instalment that you have to give me at that time"

(*Maras*, I, 293 / d. 1549)

In (62), the deontic interpretation is favored by the fact that the borrower refers to already agreed instalments that must be paid at a specific time. Similarly, clearly deontic is the meaning of the construction in few other cases (most probably in *Maras* II, 68 / d. 1549 and III, 432 / d. 1538). Nonetheless, in the other possible instances of this meaning (in Andros, *Polemis*, 55 / d. 1593, and in *Maras*: I, 55, 134, 180, 181, 200, 340, 363 / d. 1549, II, 281 / d. 1549, III, 254 / d. 1538, IV, 93, 245a / d. 1549), a future-referring interpretation is not excluded. This difficulty is enhanced by the fact that future-reference is another meaning associated with θέ νά in the official documents, as seen in the following example:

(63) ὁποῦ ἔλαβα σήμερον ἀπὸ σένα μετριτᾶ... διὰ μερτικὸν
which received today from you cash... for part
τοῦ ἐννοικίου τῆς ἀλῆς χρονέας ὁποῦ θὲ νὰ ἔλθη
the-GEN rent the other year which will-? that come-3rd SUBJ.
τοῦ μαγαντζέν(ου)...
the-GEN store room
"which I received in cash from you today... as a guarantee for the rent of the store room for the year to come..."

(*Maras*, I, 130 / d. 1549)

In this example the future reference of the θέ νά construction is evident, since the inanimacy of its subject (χρονέας=the year) effectively rules out volition, while the context is most favoring of future reference. Similarly to deontic meaning, there are few other cases conveying unambiguously future reference (most prominently in *Maras*, IV, 36, 69, 179, 195 / d. 1549), while in three other occurrences of this meaning (*Maras*, I, 51, 202 (2) / d. 1549) the futurity is not so obvious, as the subject of the construction is animate, but it is still preferable.

The discussion of all examples of this construction indicates the great difficulty in distinguishing between the various possible meanings. Leaving aside the indeterminacies, it is relatively clear that θέ νά was used in the non-literary texts to convey three basic meanings: volition, futurity, and deontic modality. As has been observed above, the first two are also attested in the literary texts for the same construction, while the proliferation of the third in the official documents could well be a function of the legal character of these texts, which contains numerous deontic contexts. In any event, this context of occurrence (deontic) is not surprising for θέ νά, since the full form of the verb (either personal or impersonal AVC$_2$) was already quite productive in that meaning from the 14th c. (cf. 5.4.2).

The examination of the data revealed quite interesting facts regarding the θέ νά construction:

(a) It was not only an FC but it could convey volition, obligation, and future reference, in accordance with what has been observed regarding θέλω AVCs. Moreover, the form θέ was not exclusively complemented by a νά–clause but by an Infinitive, too, a fact not paid any attention so far;

(b) It could have an impersonal syntax, in other words θέ could be used as an uninflected form complemented by a verbal form of a different grammatical person;

(c) It is attested in both literary and non-literary texts: concerning the former, it occurs exclusively in texts of specific geographical origin, while in the non-literary texts it is predominantly found in texts written in Crete, with only two exceptions involving Kefalonia and Andros;

(d) It is attested already in 14th c. literary texts, while in the non-literary texts it is only found from the mid-16th c. onwards. There is a further complication regarding the chronology of the θέ νά emergence: all the literary texts containing this construction survive in manuscripts from the 16th c. and, consequently, the possibility of scribal interference in these attestations cannot be ruled out. On the other hand, there is evidence suggesting that θέ νά did not actually emerge in the 16th c. First, the manuscript of *AoT*, according to its editor (Kehagioglou, 2004), dates from the late 15th c.–early 16th c., and, more importantly, is apparently a copy of a much older manuscript. This brings us to the second argument: as far as we can tell, there is no discrepancy between the overall LMG picture and the situation in these texts, in relation to their assumed date of production, at least regarding future reference. In other words, the constructions attested in these texts were expected, given all previous developments in LMG and, therefore, the form of these texts seems to comply well with their assumed date of production. And, finally, the fact that in the mid-16th c. the θέ νά construction found its way into the books of some notaries is indicative that it was considered by them appropriate for written registers by that time. All this evidence arguably suggests that the emergence of θέ νά should probably be placed around the late 14th–early 15th c., while its diffusion in written registers should be placed mostly in the 15th c.

A final note on the facts: there is a remarkable tendency for the θέ νά construction to be used in relative clauses, especially after 'ὁποῦ'. In *Maras*, 21 / 26 attestations are in relative clauses (20 of them after ὁποῦ). More evidence and further research is needed to determine whether this tendency is significant in any respect.

B. *The analysis* The attestations of θέ νά presented here pose a straightforward challenge to the extant accounts for the emergence and further developments of this construction. Specifically, a number of assumptions made by Joseph & Pappas (2002) are difficult to maintain:

(a) They assume that θέλω νά + Subjunctive could convey future reference in LMG; as seen in 5.4.2 and above, this construction started to express such a meaning only in the 15th c., at a time when apparently 'θέ νά' had already emerged;

(b) Their postulation of an impersonal future-referring θέλει νά + Subjunctive as a source for the θέ νά construction is not verified by the data; there are instances of such an impersonal construction, but only with a deontic meaning, as expected given similar developments with other modals in Greek (cf. 5.1.2);

(c) They acknowledge the existence of instances of volitional θέ νά as late as the 17th c. (Joseph & Pappas, 2002: 256), but they do not explain how a construction, allegedly originating from an impersonal FC (θέλει νά + Subjunctive), could subsequently acquire a volitional meaning;

(d) They do not discuss how the form itself ('θέ') came about, even though they consider it "the natural outcome of the widespread use of θέλει" (Joseph & Pappas, 2002: 262), an assumption probably correct, generally speaking, as will be argued below.

The last two points are relevant for the account proposed by Horrocks (1997) as well: this does not explain how and why the form emerged and apparently cannot cope with the volitional uses of the construction; if the origin of θέ νά is to be sought in the independent, future-referring νά + Subjunctive, then, in order to account for the volitional instances of the construction, we would have to postulate that the reduced form 'θέ' was *subsequently* analogically associated with the full forms of the verb. But such a postulation is clearly not intuitive and cannot account for the various contexts of use and developments of θέ. Finally, this account has no explanation for the instances of θέ + Infinitive, where θέ is not used to strengthen the independent future reference of a form, since the Infinitive was not a self-standing element.

Apparently, the extant accounts of this development are rather inadequate. In what follows, a different, novel account is proposed, based on the assumption that the change we should first investigate does not concern a θέ νά construction but the form θέ itself, in other words that it is primarily an instance of phonological change. What remains to be determined is the nature of this change, its spatio-temporal correlates, and its consequences on the expression of future reference.

Three major issues need to be addressed: how and why θέ came about, why this apparently happened in a rather restricted geographical (and not linguistic) area (probably Crete and Cyprus), and how we can explain the development of its meanings. The first two issues are interrelated, since an important factor of the emergence of θέ and its further developments is arguably contact between Greek and Romance speakers, especially Old Venetian and Old French. In order to develop such an account, we need to establish the connection of Crete and Cyprus with Romance speakers.

In the case of Crete, this is evident, as Crete belonged to Venice from the early 13th c., and obviously a language contact situation started to develop. The Venetians established their presence in the island, particularly in cities such as Candia (Kastron), and already from the early 14th c. mixed marriages between the Greek and the Italian population occurred. Very telling is the case of Stefano Bon, a notary of Candia around the years 1303–4, who was Italian, could speak Greek, was married to a Greek woman, and had given a Greek name to his daughter (cf. Maltezou, 1997). Moreover, it is well known that, by the 16th c. at the very latest, Greek was the language mostly spoken on the island, according to reports written for the Venetian administration (cf. Maltezou, 1997: 41). It is argued here that the language contact situation on Crete, where a small—but prestigious—Italian minority was surrounded by the majority of Greek speakers, gave rise to a "shift-induced interference" (cf. Thomason, 2001: 74–6) in Greek; in other words, Italians learned Greek (and eventually shifted completely to Greek), influencing Greek through interference by their own language. It is important to note that, according to Thomason (2001: 75), the results of such contact-induced change are first found in phonology and syntax and later in the lexicon. We will get back to this point below.

As far as Cyprus is concerned, the language contact situation there was more complicated as it involved extensive multilingualism: since the island was ruled by the Frankish family of Lusignan, contact between Greek and (Old) French ensued. Moreover, the Cypriot culture was greatly influenced by the Italians (Venetians and Genoese), who amounted to a considerable proportion of the island's population: in his edition of *AoT*, Kehagioglou (2004: 344–5) mentions various facts that underline this strong influence, not only on the Greek-speaking population but also on the Frankish ruling class, while Richard (1962) and Tomasoni (1994: 223) make reference to documents of the 13th–15th c. coming from Cyprus which manifest a mixing of the languages spoken in the island, namely (Old) French, Venetian (and Genoese), and Greek, with the Italian dialects largely dominant. This is reminiscent of the comment by Mahairas, who writes in his chronicle that "no-one can understand the Cypriots (Greeks), since their language is very mixed and barbarous!" (*Mahairas*, 158), although this comment refers to mixing between Greek and French only, not Italian (for more information on the situation in Cyprus, see Terkourafi, 2005). Therefore, the strong presence and influence of Romance in both Crete and Cyprus is evident.

How then is Romance influence related to the issue of θέ? Arguably, in two main linguistic features that characterized foremost Venetian: the neutralization of number in the 3rd person and the widespread loss of non-tonic vowels. The former, noted already by Rohlfs (1949–54: 299), is considered as an important feature of Old Venetian, and probably resulted in the emergence of subject clitics for the differentiation of number (Caroll, 1981: 33–4). In the case of the verb "want", the Old Venetian dialect exhibited the form "vol" for both the 3rd person singular and plural by the end of the 12th c., while the modern dialects of Veneto have generalized this pattern of identity to the 2nd person as well (Marcato & Ursini, 1998: 366). As to the loss of non-tonic vowels, it is regarded as one of the main isoglosses of the dialects of Veneto (Caroll, 1981: 33–4), affecting both word-initial and word-final positions and exhibiting a wide distribution. The link between Venetian and French lies in the fact that the former was very heavily influenced by the latter in that period (especially during 12th–13th c.), the result being that it is almost impossible now to determine whether some features of Old Venetian were in fact the result of French influence (cf. Caroll, 1981: 16). It is then, perhaps, relevant the fact that the old Provençal paradigm for the verb "voler" (=want, wish) has the same form for the 1st and the 3rd singular person ("volç") in the past tense (Bybee & Brewer, 1980), especially so since the first Frankish settlers of Cyprus spoke a variety heavily influenced by Provençal (cf. Varella, 2006: 87). Therefore, in the discussion that follows, the term "Romance influence" will be taken to mean both Venetian and French influence, although, in the case of Crete, the effect of French can only be indirect, through its influence on Venetian.

It is not difficult to see how these factors might have affected θέλω in the language contact situation described above. On the one hand, speakers of Venetian trying to speak Greek would presumably be very much inclined to leave unpronounced the final unstressed vowels of θέλω, since Old Venetian exhibited extensive vowel loss and, in addition, it is always the most frequently used lexemes that are most prone to such phonological processes (cf., for example, Bybee, 2001: 615–6), and θέλω is certainly one of them. It is also plausible to assume that this change was facilitated by inter-vocalic loss of /l/, which was very weakly pronounced in the Old Venetian dialect and hardly ever retained (Caroll, 1981: 65–7). Such a change must have been optional or geographically dependent, however, as the forms θέλα / θάλα originating from Crete (although from subsequent centuries) seem to suggest a 'θέλ νά' stage (Joseph & Pappas, 2002: 254), even though a final /l/ or a /ln/ cluster are not readily allowed in Greek.

On the basis of these observations, it is proposed that θέ is the product of the loss of the unstressed word-final /i/ of θέλει (possibly following the loss of inter-vocalic /l/), brought about by the high frequency of the verb and the pressure of independent phonological processes attested in Old Venetian. The 2nd person singular also exhibited a similar reduction, from θέλεις to θές, in the same period, as already noted above, a fact suggesting that it belonged to the same pattern. In accordance with what would be expected of a phonological process (although one conditioned by high frequency), this pattern is not particular to θέλω but it affected a series of frequently used verbs ending in –γω /γo/, which in texts both literary and non-literary originating from Crete and Cyprus manifest a reduction in the 2nd and 3rd person singular. These verbs in the corpus are (ὑ)πά(γ)ω ("go"), τρώ(γ)ω and its Subjunctive φά(γ)ω ("eat"), κλαί(γ)ω ("cry"), κρού(γ)ω ("hit"), and λέ(γ)ω ("say, speak"). Only in the case of πά, the reduced form of ὑπάγει, does a parallel generalization in its use for other grammatical persons occur (e.g. 3rd person plural: Maras, I, 13, 14, 25 / d. 1549, Assises, 146 (ms. A), 1st person singular: Falieros, Ἱστορία καὶ Ὄνειρο, 367, 534).[38] In all other cases, we find the reduced forms with the "expected" person value, i.e. λές (2nd singular, Maras I, 89 / d. 1549), πάς (2nd singular, Maras I, 340 / d. 1549), τρώ (3rd singular, Falieros, Ἱστορία καί Ὄνειρο, 497, Sahlikis 779 (Papadimitriou), Assises 255 (ms. B)) κρού (3rd singular, Assises 88 (ms. B)), and so forth (cf. Horrocks, 1997: 239–41). Two observations need to be made at this point: firstly, the reduction of the forms must have taken place after the loss of inter-vocalic /γ/, a process common in Greek (cf., for example, Dieterich, 1898: 86–8, and Hatzidakis, 1905: 241) and in Old French (Brunot, 1966: 167); this is further corroborated by the existence of forms such as πάις (Maras, I, 51 / d. 1549), where the unstressed /i/ survives. And, secondly, this process of phonological reduction was not morphosyntactically conditioned, as it is also

---

[38] Tsakali (2003) mentions that the first attestation of the form πά is found in Armouris, where it constitutes a 3rd person singular form, as expected according to what has been argued above. The details of the development of πά remain largely unknown, but it seems that the example in Armouris can be misleading in terms of chronology, as this form only establishes in the 14th c. or later. Its exact inter-relation with θέ, if any, needs further research.

attested in the case of Infinitives of the very same verbs, for instance φά instead of φάγει (Falieros, 'Ιστορία καί "Ονειρο, 647).³⁹

We have established so far that the forms θές, θέ are part of a wider pattern of a reduction of the unstressed /i/ after a vowel, a phonological environment which was created by the loss of inter-vocalic /γ/ or /l/, the second only in the case of θέλω, which had—strictly speaking—only similar but not identical phonological environment. However, it followed the pattern of the other verbs, probably due to two reasons: (a) its great frequency, which made it a prime candidate for phonological reduction, and (b) Romance influence to create a volitional particle such as θέ, according to what had been argued above. This process could have come about without any external pressure, as Hatzidakis (1905: 211) argues that /i/ was the "weakest" vowel in the Greek system and prone to loss, and Horrocks (1997) discusses a whole restructuring of the LMG verbal paradigms affecting these verbs as well, but the language contact situation must have greatly facilitated it, since it was very prolific in Romance-ruled or -influenced areas.⁴⁰ It affected a series of very commonly used verbs, presumably not only because of their phonological structure but also exactly because of their frequency. Illuminating in this respect is the case of μέλλω: Recall that the μέλλω AVC occurs in its impersonal syntax already from the 14th c. in various literary and non-literary texts (cf. 5.1.2). If the phonological reduction affecting θέλω was of a semantic / syntactic origin, it would presumably have affected μέλλει as well, and even more so, since it was predominantly used in an impersonal form. However, such a reduction is not attested, with the exception of a love poem from Cyprus (16th c.), which contains a form μελά (Aerts, 1983: 157); this is exactly what our account would predict, since it has been argued on independent grounds that μέλλει was apparently much more productive as a vernacular item in Cyprus than in the rest of the Greek-speaking world (cf. 5.1.2).⁴¹

Admittedly, the discussion above seems to indicate the phonological reduction and the emergence of these reduced forms of the verbal paradigm mentioned could very well have occurred without any Venetian or French influence. However, there is no obvious reason why an "internal-only" account

---

³⁹ The same cannot be said for θέ, which does not ever stand for the Infinitive of the verb; however, when the verb appears in the Infinitive, it is in the form θελήσει with another stem.

⁴⁰ It is not a coincidence that the reduced forms of these verbs are attested in various dialects of the Aegean islands, which were for centuries under Italian rule, and particularly so in Hios, ruled by the Genoese (Hatzidakis, 1907: 562–4).

⁴¹ The retention of inter-vocalic /l/ in the case of μελά, contrary to θέ νά, could be attributed to the geminate /l/ of μέλλω, which is retained in the Cypriot dialect, as is well known (cf., for example, Trudgill, 2003). The matter needs further investigation.

is theoretically superior to an account incorporating possible language contact factors influencing a particular language change (cf. Milroy, 1999: 21). Accordingly, various phonological properties of Venetian (that may have been the result of French influence in the first place) have been mentioned, that appear facilitating for such a reduction to occur. Nevertheless, the Romance influence is more evident in the subsequent developments of θέ.

Since θέ was a reduced form of θέλει and since this reduction was not semantically driven, contrary to traditional expectations, θέ could appear in every context in which θέλει occurred: this explains the volitional and deontic uses of θέ, alongside the future-referring ones, as well as its being complemented by an Infinitive. There was nothing extraordinary—at least originally—about this form, as the same thing could be said about θές. But the fact that θέ did not bear any overt agreement features probably allowed it to be used as a volitional particle, i.e. with a volitional meaning but in other grammatical persons. The influence of the similar syncretism in Old Venetian with the form "vol" and in Provençal with the form "volç" must have facilitated this development, and this is the point in the whole diachronic path that θέ followed where Romance influence mainly lies. It is very rare for verbal forms in Greek not to overtly mark the grammatical person, and, since such a situation existed for the very same verb in Venetian at that period (and Provençal as well), the grammatical replication of that pattern appears highly plausible. Moreover, the grammatical patterns are not usually replicated in strictly the same manner (cf. Heine & Kuteva, 2005), and that was verified in this case as well, as Greek speakers generalized the use of θέ for all grammatical persons, and not only for one or two, as was the case in the Romance languages. In other words, contrary to what has been suggested, it is not the syntactic and semantic properties of a presumed θέλει νά + Subjunctive AVC that caused the reduction but an independent phonological reduction which, presumably through interference from Romance, led θέ to become a form marking all grammatical persons.

Furthermore, the very same form was associated with the fuller verbal paradigm of θέλω, (c.f. also 5.5 for the form ἤθε, related to the past paradigm of the verb) hence its use in the very same meanings in which the θέλω AVC$_2$ was employed, such as obligation and future reference. According to this account, the emergence of future reference as a possible meaning for θέ νά is directly related to the emergence of this meaning in the fuller θέλω AVC$_2$, as, apparently, θέ did not become opaque (at least for most speakers) before the end of the 16th c. (if not later), to judge from the volitional uses; therefore, θέ was associated with the verb θέλω, and was used in the same contexts as the full verb, including obviously future-referring contexts. It is telling that the first clear attestation of a future-referring meaning for θέ νά comes from 15th c. Cyprus, from *Mahairas*, where the first instances of the future-referring θέλω AVC$_2$ also occur (cf. 5.4.2). It is reasonable to assume that θέ νά went hand in hand in its development with the full verb, even though we would predict that, as θέ became increasingly (but not totally) opaque on the basis of its lack of agreement features, it would still probably be used in its volitional meaning, but the TAM meanings (and mainly future reference) would certainly be more frequent. This is exactly what is found in the Cretan poetic texts of the 16th–17th c. (cf. Holton, 1993 and especially Markopoulos, 2007). This probably led to another split in the diachrony of θέλω, this time between volitional θέλω νά + Subjunctive and the AVC θέ νά / θα + Subjunctive, which must have occurred in the late 17th c.

According to this analysis, phonological change has facilitated semantic and syntactic developments and not vice versa. This is at odds with most claims in the grammaticalization literature, which emphasize semantics in the domain of causation (cf., for example, Haspelmath, 1999b: 1062). But in the case of θέ νά, the crucial role played by phonology is motivated by language-internal as well as cross-linguistic observations. Thus, the existence of a phonological process that did not apply only to θέλει but also to other verbs, renders a phonological account of this development quite likely; and the subsequent developments of θέ are not only dependent on its phonological form but on the inter-relations with the other extant AVCs involving the full verb. Cross-linguistically, many cases have been reported where phonological change causes syntactic / semantic change (cf. Harris & Campbell, 1995: 75–7), allowing us to include the developments related to θέ in a wider array of cross-linguistic phenomena.

The account sketched here can explain facts concerning θέ that have been largely unsolved:

(a) the volitional uses of the form, attested from the very beginning and as late as the 16th c. (and later, cf. Markopoulos, 2007), as θέ was simply a reduced form of the full lexical verb θέλει and could convey all the meanings associated with the verb;

(b) the absence of a future-referring θέλει / θέλω νά AVC as a morphosyntactic source of θέ νά, since the latter, according to this account, did not have an FC as its origin;

(c) the emergence and development of this form in Crete and Cyprus, probably due to Romance influence: it could be assumed either that θέ emerged independently in these islands, or that it spread from one island to another due to communication between the inhabitants (mainly traders) of these islands. The former seems more plausible due to the sheer distance between Crete and Cyprus and the sociolinguistic situation in both islands; in both Crete and Cyprus, the presence and the influence of Italian speakers was felt everywhere (probably even more so in Crete) and, in addition, the initial conditions that may have led to the properties of Venetian that influenced the Cretan part of the developments were also present in Cyprus: the island was ruled by French, which has been the main influence in the development of the Venetian dialect and, moreover, there existed multilingualism among French, Greeks, *and* Italians. On the other hand, the modern dialects of the islands share various traits, such as velar palatalization (cf., for example, Trudgill, 2003), suggesting that there might be borrowing between these dialects (as with the dialects of other islands in the area, such as the Dodecanese), thus favoring the account of the θέ νά construction spreading from one island to the other through commercial contacts and population movements. More evidence is needed in order to resolve the matter;

(d) the relation between θέ and θές, as well as between similar forms of other verbs, such as πά, since all such forms have been seen as belonging to an overall phonological pattern that affected a series of verbs.

A final comment should be made concerning the distribution of θέ νά (and θέ in general): it has already been remarked that, in the non-literary texts, θέ νά is found almost exclusively in *Maras*: 26 / 29 attestations of this construction occur in the books of this notary, while it is completely absent in contemporary notaries from Crete (e.g. *Patsidiotis*) and elsewhere (e.g. *Kasimatis* from Kythira, *Varagkas* from Corfu, to name but a few). Crucially, Maras was a notary in Kastron (Candia), the capital of Crete; it has been independently argued (Milroy, 1993: 228–9) that linguistic innovations tend to appear in urban areas and spread to other urban centers without immediately affecting the countryside (cf. also Trudgill, 1983, 1986).[42] This observation fits quite nicely with the development of θέ νά as an instance of contact-induced change, since it is only in the cities that Venetians originally settled (cf. Papadia-Lala, 2004 and references therein) and, consequently, it would be mainly in Kastron and other cities that θέ must have emerged. According to

---

[42] This is not to say that the 'gravity model' of diffusion, suggested by Trudgill (cf., for example, 1986), is followed here. Rather, the description of the sociolinguistic situation that follows underlines the independently undisputable major role that urban centers play in the diffusion of language change in general (cf., for example, Taeldeman, 2005), and the importance that should be given to detailed sociolinguistic description in the case of a language change diffusion, much in the spirit of Horvath & Horvath (2001), who criticize the gravity model as not urging scholars to pay attention to crucial details in a sociolinguistic setting.

this assumption, the high frequency of use of θέ in *Maras* comes as no surprise, especially if we also take into account three more facts. Firstly, the Cretan poets of the 14th–15th c. who used this construction (Sahlikis, Falieros) lived in Kastron: Sahlikis certainly knew Italian and was a member of the urban class, while Falieros was a Venetian nobleman (cf. van Gemert, 1997); secondly, the other notary books that have been published so far refer to the agricultural societies of the villages, where the notaries themselves dwelt for the most part, hence the lack of this form; the only exception is Grigoropoulos, a notary of Kastron, who we know to be rather learned (Kaklamanis, 2004) and in whose writing θέ, still a form predominantly of the spoken language, was not readily utilized; and thirdly, the attestation of θέ from Kefalonia comes from a notary in the capital of the island, a fact that again fits with the overall scenario of emergence and spread of θέ in urban centers. As far as Cyprus is concerned, multilingualism must have been a common aspect of its cities, where people of various origins (e.g. French, Greek, Italian, Armenian, and Arabian) were usually in contact (cf. Balletto, 1995, for the situation in Famagusta). Obviously, more material needs to be published in order for this account to be confirmed.[43]

The language contact account sketched above is surprising in a different respect as well, as it does not involve contact between Greek and Slavic languages, although the occurrence in many Balkan languages of an FC based on a (sometimes inflected, sometimes uninflected) shortened form of a verb meaning "want" is considered one of the prototypical instances of the "Balkan Sprachbund" (cf., for example, Aikhenvald & Dixon, 2007: 209–11). Unfortunately, there is simply not enough evidence from the crucial 13th–16th c. not only from LMG but also from many Balkan languages to discover whether the convergence in future reference has its roots in a specific language and how deep in time these roots are. As far as LMG is concerned, there is no literary work in the vernacular that can be traced with certainty in northern Greece (where the language contact situation among the Balkan populations was presumably more intense) up to the mid-15th c., which is the end-point of this investigation. However, on the basis of the extant material, it will be argued that the θέ νά construction is not a grammatical replication of an equivalent Slavic / Bulgarian / Albanian construction, and that the morphosyntactic convergence in the domain of future reference between the Balkan languages probably occurred later, starting from the 16th–17th c. The point of comparison will be the data from Bulgarian, which seems to be fairly well documented even in its Medieval stages.

---

[43] For a similar account for the spread of the loss of the Infinitive in the Balkan languages, see Joseph (2000).

Kuteva (2001: 126) provides an overview of the relevant development in Bulgarian. According to her account, as early as the 13th c. Bulgarian manifested the FC "šta + Infinitive", whereby *šta* constitutes a shortened form of the verb "xotěti" (=want), conjugated in the present. In the following centuries (14th–15th), this FC gave rise to a variety of FCs: "šta + Infinitive", "šta + finite verb", "šta + da (=equivalent to Greek *vá*) + finite verb" and, crucially, "šte + da + finite verb", where "šte" was an invariable particle. In the following centuries, various FCs co-existed, with the FC "šte + finite verb" steadily gaining ground and becoming the standard means of future reference in Modern Bulgarian.

Immediately, numerous similarities between the Bulgarian and the Greek FC strike the eye: the common semantic pathway (originating in volition), the reduced paradigm, which starts to appear at some point in the Medieval period, and the emergence of an uninflected form used with a variety of complementation patterns, including a clause headed by a phonologically similar complementizer ("da" and *vá*, respectively). These morphosyntactic similarities, the close chronological approximation of the relevant developments as well as the sociolinguistic situation linking these two languages seemingly make a good case for arguing that language contact must have played a role in the development of these two FCs. However, it is argued here that this can be the case only for a subsequent stage in the development of θέ vá (i.e. after the 16th–17th c.), not for its emergence, for the following reasons:

(a) The chronology of the data creates several problems. Apparently, the shortened forms appeared in Bulgarian in the 13th c., while θέ (and θές) seems to be a development of the late 14th c., as it is not common in the texts even of the 15th c.;

(b) We can assume that this difference in chronology is the result of the problematic textual tradition of Greek, and that θέ had already emerged from the 13th c. onwards. However, there is a crucial difference in the reduction as manifested in the two languages: while in Bulgarian the whole paradigm of the verb is reduced, in Greek it is only the 2nd and 3rd singular form, similarly to a verbal pattern described above;

(c) The difference between the two patterns of phonological reduction correlates with the difference in meaning: according to Kuteva (2001), the construction "xotěti + Infinitive" expressed *only* future reference already from the late Old Bulgarian period, and the paradigm of the verb was subsequently reduced in this very meaning. On the other hand, as illustrated above, the θέ vá construction was not simply an FC but could also convey volitional and deontic meaning, even in subsequent centuries. In other words,

Kuteva seems to argue that, in the Bulgarian case, the reduction is triggered by the semantic development of the verb, while, in the Greek case, it has been amply demonstrated that this is highly unlikely;

(d) But even if all the above differences can somehow be circumvented, there remains the issue of the geographical distribution of θέ νά. To argue convincingly for a Greek–Bulgarian contact account, one would have to postulate that either there was contact between the two populations in the islands of Crete and Cyprus which could have resulted in such a grammatical replication (rather unlikely), or else that the Greek data is misleading with regard to this development, and that θέ νά had emerged in mainland Greece as well, but this is not attested in the texts or we lack the texts that could have manifested this construction. Although the latter scenario is admittedly possible, we need at least *some* data that might indicate that it is also *likely*, which is missing for the moment, considering especially all the other differences between the two constructions mentioned above.

For these reasons, it is suggested here that the two developments contrasted are at least initially independent, and that the convergence observed in the modern languages must have originated in subsequent periods, when Balkan populations were really intermixed under the Ottoman rule, and language contact situations among them must have been the norm.

Finally, a note on the form θα, arguably the outcome of another reduction of θέ νά: it is attested in the non-literary texts of the 16th c., albeit rarely. The relative scarcity of occurrences of θα has a straightforward explanation; it must have been a quite recent development, probably restricted to the lower registers of use, since it is not found in the literary texts of LMG, while in the official documents it is attested only twice:[44] both examples date from the last decade of the 16th c., and although the first (originating from Crete: Xanthoudidis, 1912: VI / d. 1590) is ambiguous between a volitional and a future-referring interpretation, the second conveys certainly the latter interpretation, as can be seen in (64):

(64) ... κύρ Νικολὸς Κοτύλης καὶ θὰ   ὑπογράψῃ   καὶ ἀτός του
      ... sir Nikolos Kotilis   and will-prt sign-3rd SUBJ. and his-own
      "... Sir Nikolos Kotilis will sign with his own hand"

(*Polemis*, 82 / d. 1598)

---

[44] Seven more attestations of θα can be found in *Varouhas* (Bakker & van Gemert, 1987), which also includes three more instances of the θέ νά construction. However, since all of them are dated from the 17th c., they are not included here.

208　*The future in Greek*

The very late chronology of both examples as well as the absence of this construction in the literary texts of the 15th c. suggest that the emergence of this form should be dated in the late 15th–16th c., and therefore will not be discussed here. The example in (64) is contained in a document from Andros, a fact that gives a possible indication for the early spread of *θα* beyond the island of Crete, if indeed Crete was the place of origin of this form, as is traditionally assumed (cf., for example, Horrocks, 1997: 310).

5.4.4 *Summary: the story of θέλω*

Θέλω exhibited a semantic / syntactic split in LMG: the future-referring AVC was associated with an infinitival complementation, while the volitional construction with a subordinate clause. This split is robustly manifested till the 15th c., when the new clausal complementation was also attested for the first time in a future-referring context. At the same time, various modal meanings (e.g. obligation) could be expressed in both AVCs. Besides these two complementation patterns, there existed a third, the V + V$_S$ construction, that probably represents an older development that was only strengthened, and not brought about, by the late loss of the infinitival endings (especially the final *–ν*), contrary to the standard view hitherto.

In the 14th c., a phonological reduction process affected, among other verbs, the 2nd and 3rd person singular of *θέλω*, resulting in the abbreviated forms *θές*, *θέ* respectively, which shared all contexts of use with the full verb. *Θέ* in particular was generalized to other grammatical persons in the expression of volition, most likely due to a similar pattern in Venetian and the lack of agreement features, which also led to its proliferation in the TAM meanings of the *θέλω* AVC$_2$. The developments concerning *θέ* have been shown to relate to the sociolinguistic situation in the eastern Mediterranean and the language contact between Greek-speaking and Romance (mainly Venetian and French)-speaking populations. The new analysis of these developments explains why *θέ* continued to be used with a volitional meaning, a fact that is verified both by the official documents of the 16th c. (cf. 5.4.3) and the literary texts of the Cretan renaissance (Markopoulos, 2007). Since the exact history of the future-referring *θέλω* AVC has been the subject of extensive debate, Figure 5.3 represents the developments regarding this FC from the AG to the LMG period, according to the findings of this investigation. In the figure, the frequent use of a specific meaning–construction combination is highlighted in bold, while the modal uses have been excluded:

Late medieval Greek 209

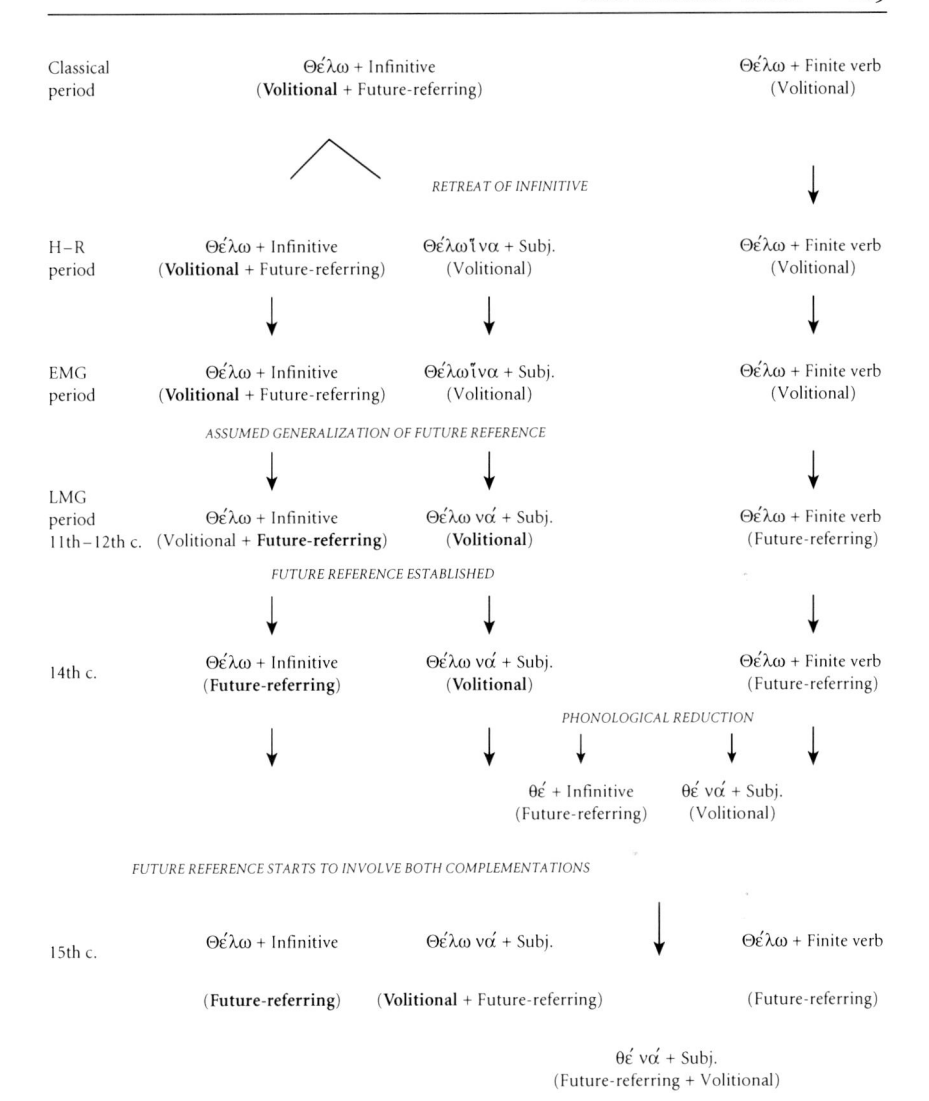

Classical period	Θέλω + Infinitive (**Volitional** + Future-referring)		Θέλω + Finite verb (Volitional)
	↙ ↘ RETREAT OF INFINITIVE		↓
H–R period	Θέλω + Infinitive (**Volitional** + Future-referring)	Θέλω ἵνα + Subj. (Volitional)	Θέλω + Finite verb (Volitional)
	↓	↓	↓
EMG period	Θέλω + Infinitive (**Volitional** + Future-referring)	Θέλω ἵνα + Subj. (Volitional)	Θέλω + Finite verb (Volitional)
	ASSUMED GENERALIZATION OF FUTURE REFERENCE ↓	↓	↓
LMG period 11th–12th c.	Θέλω + Infinitive (Volitional + **Future-referring**)	Θέλω νά + Subj. (**Volitional**)	Θέλω + Finite verb (Future-referring)
	FUTURE REFERENCE ESTABLISHED ↓	↓	↓
14th c.	Θέλω + Infinitive (**Future-referring**)	Θέλω νά + Subj. (**Volitional**)	Θέλω + Finite verb (Future-referring)
	↓	PHONOLOGICAL REDUCTION ↓ ↓	↓
		θέ + Infinitive (Future-referring) θέ νά + Subj. (Volitional)	
	FUTURE REFERENCE STARTS TO INVOLVE BOTH COMPLEMENTATIONS		
15th c.	Θέλω + Infinitive (Future-referring)	Θέλω νά + Subj. (**Volitional** + Future-referring)	Θέλω + Finite verb (Future-referring)
		θέ νά + Subj. (Future-referring + Volitional)	

FIGURE 5.3 The sequence of developments of the θέλω FC

5.5 Ἤθελα + Infinitive / clause: conditionals and volition

Ἤθελα, the past form of *θέλω*, followed a development of its own, associated with, but at the same time differentiated from, the changes involving *θέλω*. This should come as no surprise, if we recall the identical situation of *ἔχω* / *εἶχα* (cf. discussion in 5.3).

The evidence from the earlier texts suggests that *ἤθελα* might have undergone changes similar to *θέλω*, but at a slower rate. In *Armouris*, *ἤθελα* is completely absent, in contrast with the six attestations of *θέλω* both in the volitional and in the future-referring sense. Yet, this observation offers inconclusive evidence, since it might be due to the rather limited length of the text. At the same time and at a different register, i.e. in the *Stratigikon*, ἤθελα is attested 20 times, and conveys a volitional meaning 19 times. This parallels to a large degree the overwhelming dominance there of volitional θέλω over the future-referring AVC, even though the situation in the past is even more striking. The only instance of non-volitional ἤθελα in *Stratigikon* (256, 4) belongs semantically to the domain of the past conditionals, a domain where the frequency of use of ἤθελα will rise dramatically in the following centuries. All the attestations in *Stratigikon* involve the construction ἤθελα + Infinitive, a fact to be expected given the register of the text.

Nevertheless, the facts of *Digenis* are again suggestive of a different rate (and manner) of development for ἤθελα. Firstly, only three instances of ἤθελα can be found in this text, whereas it contains 33 instances of θέλω, while the relative number of attestations for εἶχα / ἔχω is six and nine, respectively. These facts lead us to conclude that, while θέλω is evidently the most common verb in its present form, it is nowhere near as common in the past. Furthermore, each one of the three attestations of ἤθελα represents a different meaning, the first signifying a counterfactual, the second volition, and the last future-in-the-past (65):

(65) Καὶ ὅταν   ἤθελες   δοξασθῆν   καὶ
     And when wanted-2nd PRET. glorify-INF.PASS. and
     ἐπαινεθῆν   μεγάλως, ἐρνήθης   καὶ τὸ γένος σου
     praise-INF.PASS greatly   refused   and the race yours
     καὶ ὅλην   σου   τὴν Συρίαν
     and whole yours the Syria
     "And when you were about to be highly praised and glorified,
     you refused both your race and the whole Syria"

(*Digenis*, 252–3)

This is the first instance of the future-in-the-past meaning of ἤθελα, i.e. the first indication (together with the conditional uses) of ἤθελα + Infinitive becoming an AVC. It further illustrates the association between ἤθελα and θέλω, since the former must have developed this future meaning only in relation to the θέλω FC. Moreover, it is worth mentioning that only the volitional use involves a subordinate clause as a complement,[45] as expected given the previous discussion on θέλω:

[45] On the face of it, the case of the counterfactual meaning also involves a νά-complement, as Alexiou (1985) reads πῶς ἤθελα νὰ κουρασθῶ (v. 1193) (i.e. ἤθελα νά + Subjunctive), following a correction by Trapp, since the manuscript itself reads πῶς ἤθελα κουρασθεῖ (i.e. ἤθελα + Infinitive). The latter reading is arguably preferable (despite the metrical problems it causes), as this construction is robustly attested in many texts of LMG, while the analysis of the Infinitive in this meaning is quite rare and attested at a much later stage.

(66) Καὶ ὁ Θεός οὐκ ἤθελεν ἵνα τὸν ἀπολέσῃ
And the God not wanted that him-cl. destroy-3rd SUBJ.
"And God did not want to destroy him..."

(*Digenis*, 1091)

Interestingly, exactly the same developments are attested in *Grottaferrata*, which contains one example (v. 284) of a volitional ἤθελα νά + Subjunctive construction (among numerous instances of volitional ἤθελα + Infinitive), as well as an example of the future-in-the-past meaning (v. 81). This verifies the authenticity of the picture presented in *Digenis*. The occurrence of one example of the 'future-in-the-past' meaning, at a period when the equivalent θέλω FC is already established (cf. 5.4.1), argues for an association of the type "θέλω → ἤθελα"; it is worth noting that in Bulgarian, the verb "xotěti" was used to convey future reference in the past before the same development was attested for its present form (Kuteva, 2001: 109). This manifests another difference in the development of these FCs in Greek and Bulgarian (cf. also 5.4.3).

On the whole, the evidence from the texts of the early centuries is too meagre to construct any definite picture of developments for ἤθελα. The picture is not clarified either by the poems of the 12th c., which in any case have been proven (cf. 5.1.1, 5.2.1) to be rather misleading with regard to the actual linguistic environment of their time. To be precise, in these poems ἤθελα is attested five times and solely in its lexical meaning. Interestingly, the same poems contain instances of the θέλω FC, as already mentioned, a fact that strengthens the assumption of diverging developments for the two forms of θέλω (present and past). On the other hand, in the poem written by *Glykas* we find an instance of ἤθελα νά + Subjunctive (v. 150), a construction which must have been very common in day-to-day communicative contexts, as the only difference with the archaizing (66) is the replacement of ἵνα by νά.

Moving on to the 14th c., all the major developments are well established, despite the syntactic variation evident in all AVCs. The volitional meaning is the most popular one, attested 192 times, the vast majority of which (172 / 192, 90%) involve a νά–clause. Only in *Ermoniakos* are the subordinate clauses in this context outnumbered by the Infinitive (three to seven respectively), a fact to be expected considering the relatively elaborate character of the text. The variation observed in the way νά–clauses are headed (διά νά, τοῦ νά, τό νά, ἵνα or simply νά) is analogous to the situation found with θέλω; the option of having only νά is the commonest by far.

Apart from the lexical, volitional use, ἤθελα formed an AVC as well (cf. Table 5.8). It is evident that the ἤθελα AVC is mostly found in the scope of counterfactual conditionals, and, more precisely, in their apodoses. Thus, a frequent morphosyntactic pattern was created, according to which εἶχα + Infinitive was used in the protasis (cf. 5.3) and ἤθελα + Infinitive in the apodosis of the counterfactuals, as exemplified in (67):

(67) ...ἂν εἶχε   λείψει /   ἡ   πρέσσα ὁποὺ ἐπέρασε.../
     if have-3rd PRET. miss-INF. / the press   which came/
     ὑπάγει   ἤθελεν   ἐκεῖ ὁποὺ καὶ οἱ ἄλλοι ὑπάγουν
     go-INF. would-3rd PRET. there where and the others go
     "If it hadn't been for the press of the battle... he would have gone where the others go too [he would have died]"

(WoT, 9724–26)

The syntactic specialization described above illustrates a pattern, according to which the more ancient form is retained in the most embedded context, whereas the novel formation (in this case, ἤθελα + Infinitive) is found in independent clauses. The use of the new AVC is then likely to expand into the embedded contexts as well. According to the evidence of the literary texts, this generalization of use is not yet established in the 14th c.; nevertheless, three occurrences of ἤθελα where εἶχα is still normally found, i.e. in the protasis of the conditional (*Poulologos,* 153 / *Livistros-a,* 2408, cf. also ex. 70 below), provide an indication of the ongoing generalization of use of ἤθελα in the protasis of the conditionals as well.

In the non-literary texts, ἤθελα + Infinitive is the most frequently attested AVC. This is mainly due to the character of the texts: being predominantly contracts, agreements and so forth, they are bound to contain numerous conditions, and the ἤθελα AVC was the basic means of expressing conditionals. The generalized use of ἤθελα not only in counterfactuals but also in future-referring conditionals or relative-conditional clauses is already attested in the 14th c., as shown in this document from Crete:

TABLE 5.8 The ἤθελα AVC in 14th-c. literary texts

Grammatical ἬΘελα	K&H	V&H	L&R	D.P.	Sahl.	CoM	WoT	Ah.	Poul.	Fys.	Iatr.	Erm.	AoT	Pt.	Total
1a. "Ἤθελα + Inf. / Counterfact (apod.)	–	–	1	1	2	27	20	2	1	–	–	2	–	–	56 (62.9)
1b. "Ἤθελα νά + Subj. / Counterfact.(apod.)	–	–	–	–	–	4	2	–	–	–	–	–	–	–	6 (6.6)
1c. "Ἤθελα + Inf. / Counterfact. (prot.)	–	–	1	–	–	–	–	–	1	–	–	–	–	–	2 (2.3)
1d. "Ἤθελα νά + Subj. / Counterfact. (prot.)	–	–	–	–	–	1	–	–	–	–	–	–	–	–	1 (1.1)
2. "Ἤθελα + Inf. / Conditional	–	–	–	–	1	–	1	–	–	–	–	–	–	–	2 (2.3)
3. "Ἤθελα + Inf. / Habitual (past)	–	–	–	–	–	1	3	–	–	–	–	–	–	–	4 (4.5)
4a. "Ἤθελα + Inf. / Future in the past	1	–	–	–	–	4	7	–	–	–	–	–	–	–	12 (13.5)
4b. "Ἤθελα νά + Subj./ Future in the past	–	–	–	–	–	–	2	–	–	–	–	–	–	–	2 (2.3)
5. "Ἤθελα + Inf. / "should" (Q)	–	–	–	–	–	4	–	–	–	–	–	2	–	–	4 (4.5)
TOTAL	1	–	2	1	3	41	35	2	2	–	–	2	–	–	89

(68) θέλω ἀπὸ   τοῦ νῦν   καὶ ἔμπροσθεν ἵνα ὑπάρχ(ῃς)   σὺ
     want from the now and onwards   that are   you
     καὶ ἐὰ μέρη σου . . .   διαχωρισμένα . . .   καὶ ἀπὸ   παντοίων φαύλων
     and the parts yours   separated . . .   and from whatever bad
     ὦνμπερ ἤθελον   ἐλθεῖν   πρὸς μὲ
     which would-3rd PL.PRET. come-INF. prep me-cl.
     ὀφλημάτων τε καὶ   ἐμπειριῶν
     debts   and and deeds
     "From now on, I want that you and your relatives are not responsible
     for whatever debts or bad deeds are associated with me . . ."

                                                      (*Manousakas*, 2 / d. 1382)

There are more attestations of approximately the same period, not only from Crete but also from Corfu (Maltezou, 1991: 1 / d. 1414) and Naxos (Lampros, 1907: d. 1445). As in the case of εἶχα, the official documents complement the picture of the literary texts, since they suggest that ἤθελα was not used exclusively in counterfactuals but in other future-referring conditional clauses as well. Note also that in most cases ἤθελα + Infinitive is found in the protasis of the conditional, another context of use that is rarely attested in the literary texts (cf. Table 5.8). Interestingly, an identical construction is found in an Italian document from Andros (Polemis, 1990 / d. 1487): "contra chadauna personna ch(e) volesse contradir" ("against any person who would contradict"); given what has been argued with regard to θέ (cf. 5.4.3), this could be another instance of convergence between Venetian and Greek, especially since such a construction is manifested in the Venetian writer Goldoni (17th c.) and in modern mainland Venetian as well (Rohlfs, 1949–54: III, 39). Clearly more research is needed into this still largely unexplored issue.

Two more complementation patterns of ἤθελα AVC are attested in its use in the protasis of a conditional. The first is found in a non-literary text from Corfu:

(69) διά χάριν τῆς ἄνωθεν ἐκκλησίας . . . καί τόν μοναχῶν ὁποῦ
     for sake the above church . . .   and the monks who
     εἴθελαν   ἠβρήσκοντας εἰς   τὸν ἐώνα   μέλωντας
     would-3rd PL.PRET.   be-PCIPLE   prep the century future-?
     ἅπαντας
     all
     "for the sake of the abovementioned church . . . and all the monks that
     will be in the future"

                                                      (*MM*, vol. V, b. / d. 1371)

This example not only argues in favor of the authenticity of the construction "Auxiliary + Non-finite Participle", attested for ἔχω and εἶχα as well (cf. 5.2.1, 5.3), but also verifies that this pattern encompassed almost all AVCs, with the possible exception of θέλω (and μέλλω, although it exhibits a similar construction, cf. 5.1.2). The second example, attested in a literary text, is shown in (70):

(70) ἐπεὶ   ἂν   ἤθέλαν   νὰ   στραφοῦν   στὴν
     because if   would-3rd PL.PRET.   that   turn-3rd SUBJ. to-the
     Βενετίαν ὀπίσω   ὡς ἐντροπή, κατηγορία, ἦτον τῆς Βενετίας
     Venice back   as shame,   accusation, were the Venice
     "for, if they would turn back to Venice, it would bring shame and accusations to Venice"

(CoM, 521–2)

Apart from the fact that this provides another piece of evidence that speakers started to use ἤθελα instead of εἶχα even in the protasis, the example is interesting in another respect, namely that of the clausal complementation of ἤθελα in this context. Table 5.8 shows that (70) does not constitute an isolated case in terms of complementation, as there are five more instances of the same construction (even though they are all found in the apodosis); however, it does represent the least controversial one, in terms of the meaning of the construction, as it is followed in the next verse by a Preterite (ἦτον), another typical means of conveying counterfactual meaning, apart from AVCs (cf. Horrocks, 1995, 1997: 174–5).

Therefore, this example is probably representative of an existing tendency to replace the Infinitive by a νά–clause, even in this use of ἤθελα. This tendency is also manifested in the official documents, even though sporadically: there are two attestations from the 14th c. *Assises* in Cyprus (251, 269 (ms. A)), while all other attestations come from subsequent centuries: two from Kythira (*Kasimatis*, 70, 127 / d. 1564–5), two from Naxos (*Katsouros*, 5 / d. 1538, 19 / d. 1592), one from Andros (*Polemis*, 43 / d. 1590) and one from Kefalonia, as follows:

(71) καὶ εἴθελεν   ποτὲ τῶ κερῶ   νὰ   τὸ   προστιχήσῃ
     and would-3rd SING.   ever the time   that this-cl. offer-3rd SUBJ.
     ἀλουνόν...   εἰ μέν καί δεν ἤθελεν   τω   προστιχήσῃ...
     somebody   if prt and not would-3rd SING.   this-cl   offer-INF.
     "and if at some point he should offer it to somebody else... if, on the other hand, he would not offer it..."

(*Sourianos*, 317 / d. 1582)

This document offers evidence that this construction was exactly equivalent to the old infinitival one, as the two patterns of complementation are found next to each other in the very same context. Consequently, the official documents provide us with strong evidence in favor of a gradual replacement of the Infinitive by a subordinate clause with regard to the ἤθελα AVC as well.

Apart from its use in conditionals of various kinds, the ἤθελα AVC is also attested in the literary texts of the 14th c. conveying the meaning 'future-in-the-past'. There are even two cases of clausal complementation for ἤθελα in this meaning (cf. Table 5.8), even though the interpretation cannot be certain (*WoT*, 5785, 11787). Even if these two cases are considered as future-referring, this would not imply that the equivalent future-referring θέλω νά+Subjunctive must have developed; it is most probably the case that the replacement of the Infinitive must have reached the past construction earlier than the θέλω FC, as the former was presumably of a much lower frequency. Anyway, the examples are too few to provide any solid basis for conclusions. Unfortunately, the non-literary texts cannot clarify the situation, since they hardly contain any attestation of this meaning, the only possible instance being the following from the monastery of Vazelon in Asia Minor, involving the older infinitival complementation, similarly to the example in *Digenis* (65):

(72) ἤθελεν   δὲ γενέσθαι   ὅρκος, καὶ οὐκ ἀφῆκαν οἱ
      would-3rd SING. prt make-INF.PASS. oath, and not let   the
      γέροντες
      elders
      "an oath was about to be taken, but the elders did not permit it"

(*Vazelon*, 130 / 14th c.)

The scarcity of relevant examples should be partly due to the character of these texts, which do not generally contain narratives in the past that would favor such a meaning. Still, the occurrence of the future-in-the-past meaning very likely signifies the relevant association between θέλω and ἤθελα, apparently not as strong as in the case of μέλλω, which in any case retained a future-referring meaning even when forming an AVC, but apparently stronger than the association between ἔχω and its past equivalent, which was almost never used for this meaning in the 14th c., possibly because of its ongoing grammaticalization in the domain of perfect. However, as already emphasized, this association does not mean that the two forms underwent the same developments at the same rate, as this is clearly dependent on contexts of use in relation to frequency of use.

Finally, the literary texts of the 14th c. are also enlightening with regard to the habitual use of ἤθελα, which is manifested four times, as in (73):

(73) Καὶ εἴ τις   ἤθελ'   ἐγκρεμνισθῇ,   ἔρριπτε ἐκεῖνος δέκα
     And if someone would-3rd SING. throw-INF.PASS, threw he   ten
     "And every time one would fall, he would throw down ten of them"

(WoT, 2448)

Recall that habitual meaning has also been attested for εἶχα in this century (cf. 5.3.2). Consequently, it can be concluded that the emergence of this meaning is typical for such AVCs, as more evidence from other languages seems to argue (e.g. for Old English, cf. Warner, 1993).

So far, ἤθελα seems to deviate from θέλω in two respects: firstly, in the rarity of instances conveying a future reference meaning and the productivity of the hypothetical meaning, and, secondly, in the earlier replacement of the Infinitive by a finite complement clause in non-volitional contexts (conditionals, future-in-the-past). As with ἔχω and εἶχα, θέλω and ἤθελα seem to represent two related, but not identically developed AVCs. One wonders, though, if there is any case of *convergence* in the development of these AVCs. Actually, there is an instance of morphological convergence. In the *Assises* the first example of the 3rd person singular form ἦθε (instead of ἤθελεν) is attested:

(74) καὶ ἐκεῖνος ὅπου εἶχεν ἀγοράσει τὴν κληρονομίαν ἦθεν
     and he   who had bought   the inheritance would-3rd PRET.
     χάσει ἐκεῖνο...
     lose-INF. that
     "and the person who had bought the inheritance would lose that…"

(*Assises*, 79 (ms. A))

In this example, ἦθεν χάσει is in the apodosis of a conditional, a very productive context of the ἤθελα AVC. Only one more attestation of the reduced form ἦθε is found (*Olokalos*, vi / d. 1536), again in a similar context. Two observations are due here: first, it is quite likely that the form ἦθε was formed by analogy with θέ, though more attestations are needed to draw any firm conclusions. Second, ἦθε in both instances seems to retain the exact semantic and syntactic properties of the full form ἤθελε. This apparently corroborates the analysis proposed concerning θέ (cf. 5.4.3), which was initially used simply as a reduced form of θέλει, in the contexts and meanings where the latter was productive. In addition, the fact that one instance of ἦθε comes from Cyprus and the other from Crete fits very well with the assumption of θέ originating from these islands (cf. 5.4.3).

The literary texts of the 14th–15th c. contain few instances of ἤθελα (40 overall), which comply with the general picture described above and, therefore, do not alter our assumptions in any way. The same can be said for the literary texts of the 15th c., even though the attestations of ἤθελα are much more numerous. The infinitival complementation in the volitional meaning is certainly obsolete by this time, as illustrated by its tiny percentage (3 / 44, 7%). Moreover, there are 14 attestations of the future-in-the-past meaning, exemplified in (75), all in the two chronicles (*CoT* and *Mahairas*):

(75) θωρῶντα πῶς δὲν ἔθελεν νὰ τοῦ πουλήσῃ τὴν τζόγια,
thinking that not would-3rd PRET. that him-cl sell-3rd SUBJ. the jewel,
ἐσάστην καὶ ἐπούλησέν του καὶ τὸ καράβιν
agreed and sold him and the ship
"Thinking that he would not sell him the jewel, he agreed to sell him the ship as well"

(*Mahairas*, 95)

This example describes a wrong estimation by a captain, who, thinking that his client did not have the money to buy the jewel he offered him, he agreed to sell him his ship as well, believing that he did not have the money to buy it either (but he found himself without his ship afterwards). In that context, the future-in-the-past meaning of the ἤθελα AVC is most evident. Interestingly, nine of the instances of this meaning involve a clausal complementation, strengthening the assumption that similar attestations found in previous centuries are in fact authentic, and, consequently, that ἤθελα νά + Subjunctive could convey that meaning earlier than the θέλω AVC₂, as argued above. Recall that the instances of futurity in the θέλω AVC₂ were only seven (cf. 5.4.2), even though (or, as we argued, exactly because) the overall occurrences of future reference for the θέλω AVC₁ vastly outnumber the ones for ἤθελα. The similarity between θέλω and ἤθελα regarding these examples lies in the fact that the vast majority are found in *Mahairas* (5 / 7 for θέλω, 8 / 9 for ἤθελα). It is likely that the use of the νά–clause in FCs might have occurred (or at least been reflected in the written registers) earlier in Cyprus than anywhere else in the Greek-speaking areas, even though the reasons for this remain elusive.

As mentioned, in the case of future reference in the past, the majority of instances (9 / 14, 64%) involve a finite subordinate clause. This is not the case for the counterfactuals and conditionals, which are all, irrespective of their exact semantics and the text they are found in, attested with an infinitival complementation. The high number of attestations (47) does not leave any doubt concerning the systematic character of this pattern. As mentioned above, in the non-literary texts of the 16th c. the replacement of the Infinitive in conditionals exists, although rarely. Apparently, the syntactic embedding of the conditionals was most resistant to this morphosyntactic development.

Traces of an ongoing change can be seen in one interesting, though obscure, example from *Falieros*:

(76) κι ἡ τόση λάβρα ποὺ με   καὶ   ἂν ἦτον νὰ σὲ   βράζη...
     and the such heat which me-cl burns if   were that you boil
     δὲν ἤθελα   καὶ νά᾽ φυγες   ἐκ τὴν ἀραθυμία
     not wanted-1st SING?PRET. and that left-2nd AOR. from the dizziness
     "and the heat that burns me, if it boiled you [also] ... you would (?) not recover from your dizziness"

(*Falieros*, Ἱστορία καί Ὄνειρο, 565–9)

Apparently, the example above is the sole exception to the infinitival pattern of the counterfactuals. However, its most remarkable aspect is the apparent disjoint reference between ἤθελα and its complement: ἤθελα, at least at first glance, is a 1st person singular form, and νά᾽ φυγες is a 2nd person singular. One would have to assume, therefore that (76) represents an impersonal construction, even though a peculiar one, as the 1st person singular is hardly ever likely to give rise to an impersonal construction, due to its strong deictic character. Consequently, van Gemert (2006: 162) considers this form as "fossilized" (presumably from ἤθελε νά > ἤθελα, similarly to θέ νά > θα), citing Pagkalos (1955), who has shown that this construction existed in the modern Cretan dialect.[46] However, this account is seriously undermined by the fact that ἤθελα is not followed by a bare Subjunctive, as would be expected if it constituted an amalgamation of ἤθελε νά, but by a full νά–clause, separated from ἤθελα by the conjunction marker καί! Given that this is the first attestation of such a construction, it would be rather far-fetched to assume that fossilized ἤθελα had already become opaque, even more so since the 'bare' impersonal ἤθελε, presumably the basis for such an amalgamation, had apparently not yet emerged. For all these reasons, the above

---

[46] van Gemert also mentions another similar case in *Mahairas* (84), but in this example ἤθελα is followed by an Infinitive and, therefore, the account of ἤθελα from ἤθελα νά becomes impossible to maintain. Moreover, in *Mahairas* ἤθελα/ἐθέλα is normally used as a 3rd person plural, and since in this example the subject of ἤθελα is in the 3rd person plural the occurrence of such a construction might be due to a simple copying mistake, as the scribe might have written ἤθελα instead of ἤθελα.

example should not be considered an instance of a counterfactual apodosis with a fossilized ἤθελα. Therefore, it either constitutes the product of a corrupted manuscript tradition, or it has a different meaning: the verb θέλω also has a meaning "believe, think" in Modern Greek, and this meaning fits very nicely with the verse in (76), which could be paraphrased "I wouldn't believe you would recover from your dizziness", the counterfactuality being conveyed in this case by the Preterite form of ἤθελα. Obviously, such an account presupposes the existence or the emergence of this meaning in LMG, which is far from certain, and needs further research to be confirmed.

On the contrary, the first undeniable instance of this "fossilized" uninflected ἤθελα occurs in *Maras*:

(77) θέλω, ἀνὲν καὶ ἤθελα   λήπεις   τότε...νά   τυχένη
     want, if-is and wanted-? miss-2nd SUBJ. then...that can-3rd SING.
     νά τό   δίδω   τό λεγόμενον σπαθῆ
     that this-cl give-1st SING. the said   sword
     "I want, in case you are away at that time, to be able to give the above mentioned sword [myself]"

(*Maras*, I, 364 / d. 1549)

This development should probably be seen in relation to forms such as μπορά (attested in 16th–17th c. literary texts, e.g. in "Katzourbos", a Cretan comedy, indicating ability or possibility, perhaps from μπορεί να?) and even θα, and it lies beyond our investigation here. It is worth noting, however, that *Maras* contains no instances of θα, and, if this is verified by the publication of more volumes of the same notary, it strengthens our assumption of largely divergent developments (in terms of rate of change) between θέλω and ἤθελα.

It should be stressed that, in the official documents of the 16th c., the ἤθελα AVC abounds in all notary books, irrespective of their geographical origin. It would not be an exaggeration to say that it is found in almost every single document, probably due to the particular character of these texts which favors the appearance of conditional clauses. Because of the sheer number of occurrences, it is almost inevitable that these documents contain otherwise unattested constructions involving ἤθελα, such as the one in (77). The second interesting case involves the V + V$_S$ pattern, which, apparently, the ἤθελα AVC could also exhibit (e.g. Naxos: *Katsouros*, 23 / d. 1596, Kefalonia: *Sourianos*, 2 / d. 1573, Andros: *Polemis*, 1 / d. 1570, Crete: *Maras* I, 9 / d. 1549). This construction was not entirely 'appropriate' for an official document in its earliest occurrences, as the following example nicely illustrates:

(78) A: ἠδεμὴ καὶ ἐθέλασιν   ἀποθάνουν   καὶ τὰ δύω
        if   and would-3rd PL. die-3rd PL.SUBJ. and the both
     B: ἠδὲ καὶ ἠθέλασιν   ἀποθάνει καὶ τὰ δύω
        if   and would-3rd PL. die-INF. and the both
        "if it so happens that both of them die..."

(*Gialeas*, 6 / d. 1529)

In (78), version A represents the original document, which Gialeas later copied after having edited it, thus producing version B. Fortunately, both versions were included in his book, and, therefore, we can detect what changes he made. Apparently, he considered the construction ἐθέλασιν ἀποθάνουν too "vulgar", and he corrected it into the normative ἠθέλασιν ἀποθάνει. These—unfortunately extremely rare—examples provide us with valuable information with regard to what was considered at that time part of the norm and what was seemingly used in lower registers.

A close parallel to this construction is also attested, involving the impersonal form ἤθελε, as exemplified in (79):

(79) ὅσα   πράγματα   ἤθελε   ἀπομείνουν...
     whatever   things   would-3rd SING. remain-3rd PL.SUBJ.
     "Whatever things will be left..."

(*Vagiakakos*, 1 / d. 1509)

This pattern, attested, apart from Zakynthos (79), in Crete (Detorakis, 1996: 7, 3 / d. 1562), in Kefalonia (*De Montesantos*, 29 / d. 1536), in Andros (Polemis, 1982: 1 / d. 1597), and in Cyprus (*Assises*, 138, ms. A), could be considered to be the following stage of the previous construction, if we assume that it is the outcome of the elimination of double agreement exhibited in the ἤθελα + finite form construction. The mechanism behind this development was pervasive throughout LMG in the case of modal verbs: as far as the verbs investigated here are concerned, it affected not only θέλω (deontic, cf. 5.4.2) and ἤθελα but also μέλλω (cf. 5.1) and ἔμελλεν, as the example from the *CoM* (ἔμελλεν ποιήσουν, cf. 5.1.2) suggests.

The fact that the ἤθελα AVC should be regarded in these late stages of LMG as an element not closely associated with θέλω (similar to what has been observed regarding ἔχω and εἶχα, cf. 5.3) is most evidently highlighted in examples such as the following:

(80) ὅπιος   θέλη   ἤθελεν   τὴν   διασήσει...
     whoever will-3rd SING   would-3rd SING. her-cl doubt-INF
     "whoever will doubt her..."

(*De Montesantos*, 78 / d. 1540)

At first glance, it seems that in this future-referring relative-conditional clause, the notary, probably under time pressure, could not decide which form to use and thus wrote both. Alternatively, the use of θέλη can signify an attempt to explicitly mark the future reference of the conditional, which might not have been so evident if only the ἤθελα AVC were used. This overlap was even extended to the morphological level, as forms like ἤθελει (*De Montesantos*, 243 / d. 1550) suggest, since they combine the initial η of the past form with the -ει ending of the present form. Arguably, the generalization of the use of ἤθελα in all conditional clauses, due to its dissociation from past-referring contexts, inevitably led to this morphosyntactic variation in the expression of conditionals.

Finally, a novel use, hitherto unknown, which was not attested in the literary texts, occurs in the official documents: ἤθελα + Infinitive as a pluperfect formation, exactly parallel to the εἶχα AVC. The oldest instance of this development comes from the documents of the Greek-speaking community in Venice:

(81) πως ἔλαβα ἀπό... διὰ ζημίαν ὅπου μᾶς ἤθελεν κάμην
 that received from... for damage which us wanted-3rd SING. do-INF.
 ὁ μισέρ Σιπιόν Μπόν εἰς δύο γριπαρίαις Φωτινοῦ καὶ Βαρσάμο
 the mister Sipion Bon to two ships Fotinou and Varsamo
 τὰ ἤθελεν κουρσέψειν εἰς τὸ πόρτον τῆς Θιάσου.
 which wanted-3rd SING. loot-INF. at the port the Thasos
 "that I received from... for the damage that Mr Sipion Bon had done to us, to two ships, Fotinou and Varsamo, that he had looted at the port of Thasos..."

(*Lampros*, ii / d. 1480)

The same semantic pattern that was observed in the case of εἶχα, i.e. from counterfactual to pluperfect, seems to have been repeated in the case of ἤθελα. The absence of this development from the literary texts of LMG can be attributed to its possibly late emergence, since the use illustrated in (81) is quite productive in the official documents, but not earlier than the 16th c.: it is attested in Naxos (e.g. *Katsouros*, 20 / d. 1596), in Kefalonia (e.g. *Sourianos*, 6 / d. 1581), in Crete (e.g. *Patsidiotis*, 181 / d. 1553), in Kythira (*Kasimatis*, 8 / d. 1563), and in Andros (*Polemis*, 67 / d. 1597). Consequently, it is reasonable to assume that (81) illustrates a common development that should be dated to the late 15th c.

To sum up, the ἤθελα AVC expressed various TAM meanings in LMG, and it was mainly used in conditionals, primarily from the 14th c. In its main use in counterfactuals and conditionals in general, it was the most frequent form in the non-literary texts, a fact allowing us to track the emergence of morphosyntactic variants, such as the fossilized, uninflected form ἤθελα. Moreover, it followed the same semantic path that εἶχα did in developing a pluperfect formation in the late 15th c. In general, it did not pattern like θέλω at the syntactic level, being slightly 'late' in the wholesale replacement of the infinitival complementation with a clause in its volitional meaning, but, on the other hand, extending this development to the non-volitional domains rather earlier than θέλω, possibly because of a lower frequency of use than its present equivalent. Consequently, it would be justified to assume (as Pappas, 2001 also does) that even though interconnected, these two forms followed paths that differ in various respects (not only semantically–pragmatically but also morphosyntactically), and so could be regarded, at least as far as the final stages of LMG are concerned, as partly independent AVCs, similar to what has been argued regarding ἔχω and εἶχα (cf. 5.3).

5.6 Conclusions: future reference in LMG

In LMG, the picture of future reference is significantly differentiated from that of the previous period, partly because of the relatively ample documentation of both literary and non-literary character. The θέλω AVC is undeniably the dominant means of expressing futurity, and the other two constructions are rapidly losing ground. Μέλλω, following the path initiated in EMG (cf. 4.1), is basically associated with middle and high registers; it is only productive as a destiny future or simply with an obligation meaning, and could now be considered to be on the fringes of the domain of futurity. Similarly, ἔχω was hardly used with a future-referring meaning, while εἶχα was increasingly restricted to the domain of the past as a pluperfect, manifested already in the late 13th c. Given that, by the late stages of LMG, the independent, future-referring νά + Subjunctive was also in decline, this period is the first in post-classical times that features a clearly dominant means of future reference, i.e. the θέλω AVC, despite the variation in its syntactic implementation. Thus, the first steps towards the more standardized and "neat" system of future reference of Modern Greek are made in LMG.

These conclusions are largely verified by both types of textual evidence, i.e. literary and non-literary texts. This is important when seen in the light of Manolessou's (2003) investigation of the forms of the indirect object in both types of text, which reaches the conclusion that the official documents may provide evidence totally incompatible with that offered by the literary texts (cf. also Markopoulos, forth.). The convergence of both literary and non-literary texts in the case of the FCs provides a very solid base for the argumentation presented here.

It cannot escape our attention the fact that the picture of LMG regarding FCs is completely different from the one emerging from EMG. It is more than likely that some of the facts attested for the first time in LMG can only constitute the result of developments dating from EMG, but attested systematically and in an emphatic manner in LMG, due partly to a differentiation of the cultural surroundings that allowed for texts to be written in a vernacular, in a style close to oral registers of the time. On the other hand, all FCs investigated manifest developments *internal* to LMG, and, consequently, some of the morphosyntactic changes attested in LMG, especially from the 14th c. onwards (e.g. the emergence of the θέ νά construction), should be considered LMG developments in their own right.

6

Conclusions

6.1 Methodology of historical linguistic investigations

This investigation illustrates the developments of three future-referring AVCs in the history of Greek. It is based partly on re-interpretation of known evidence, and partly on new material, and this great variety of the textual sources consulted has proved to be particularly helpful in assessing the traditional assumptions concerning these constructions. Consequently, many previously unchallenged assumptions have been found inadequate, for instance in relation to the emergence of the future-referring meaning of the ἔχω AVC (cf. 3.2) or the sequence of developments concerning the θέλω AVCs in LMG (cf. 5.4).

One of the major findings is the fact that the three FCs investigated are only partially equivalent. This does not refer merely to the expectedly varied frequency of use throughout their diachronic path of development. Obviously, in AG ἔχω + Infinitive did not express future reference, while in EMG it is firmly established as an FC. Rather, 'partially equivalent' refers to their semantic / syntactic and sociolinguistic properties throughout their history; in other words, although all three AVCs shared the ability to convey future reference (at least from the H–R period onwards), they were not wholly equivalent as they differed with respect to the register of use, the contexts that favored them, their syntactic manifestation (especially in LMG), and the various other (mostly modal) meanings they could also express. Specifically, the μέλλω construction, which owed its future reference to the lexical semantics of the verb itself, was already popular (presumably, in all registers) in AG, but it became increasingly associated with higher registers and deontic modality, a development manifested clearly in LMG. Ἔχω + Infinitive acquired the future-referring meaning approximately in the 1st c. AD and rather rapidly gained higher registers, becoming almost obsolete in LMG. Finally, θέλω + Infinitive, albeit extant as a future-referring AVC from AG, had to wait many centuries before dominating this domain in LMG, while it also had various other modal meanings.

It was the only AVC to exhibit phonological reduction (cf. 5.4.3), a fact that differentiates it rather strikingly from the other constructions. In a nutshell, this investigation has shown that the variation in the expression of future reference, at least as far as the AVCs are concerned, was mostly systematic rather than random, since these constructions exhibited different properties in various linguistic aspects, i.e. "structured heterogeneity" (Weinreich, Labov, & Herzog, 1968: 99–100). Therefore, their traditional treatment as solely synonymous forms is oversimplifying.

In other words, the investigation verifies the commonly made assumption that AVCs in functional layering situations are not wholly equivalent, as their properties are partly dependent on their original semantics. Nevertheless, it should be stressed here that the sociolinguistic properties of the AVCs are also highly relevant, since a possible sociolinguistic specialization can affect most emphatically the further development of an AVC (consider the case of μέλλω in LMG, cf. 5.1). Thus, the differentiating factors among AVCs belonging to the same semantic domain, e.g. futurity, should be sought not only in their contextual meanings and their morphosyntactic properties but also in their acceptance in the various registers of use.

Note that the independently established sociolinguistic specialization is also an important tool for discovering the register level of texts which are rather ambiguous in that respect. For example, the abundance of the μέλλω AVC in a text of LMG would most clearly place it in the higher registers, according to the findings of this investigation. Moreover, the relative distribution of the three FCs in two or more texts would also prove very helpful for determining their relative placement in the register scale. Thus, the sociolinguistic findings of this investigation can be used as a tool for all diachronic examinations on Greek.

The systematic character of variation was also apparent in the interconnection of the developments of the three FCs. There is an important fact that emerges from the investigation of all periods and illustrates this interdependency: the rise in the frequency of use and the establishment of a construction in a specific register almost without exception follows the demise of another in the same register, so that a situation whereby two or more AVCs are equally frequent in a genre or in all contexts in a period never obtains. For instance, in the H–R period the μέλλω construction is clearly dominant in all registers, in the subsequent period ἔχω + Infinitive must have been the favored form in the lower registers (even though lack of reliable evidence necessarily undermines any conclusions regarding EMG), while the striking rise of frequency of use for θέλω + Infinitive in LMG is accompanied by an equally striking decline for the other two AVCs. So, although the exact path of development is distinct for each AVC, as expected given their different lexical sources, all three paths converge insofar as they became dependent on each other, since the AVCs were most probably felt by the speakers to belong to the same overall semantic domain, i.e. futurity. Inevitably, the rise in the frequency of use of any one in the expression of future reference was at least partly responsible for the others taking a different route of development. Consequently, the specialization argued above for each AVC is partially derived from their interconnected developments: for example, the fact that the μέλλω construction was mainly used to convey 'destiny future' in LMG should be seen in the light of θέλω becoming the dominant means in the overall futurity domain.

These two facts, namely the interconnection of developments and the resulting specialization in contexts or registers, could only be ascertained due to the very extensive nature of the corpus investigated, which contains texts belonging to a wide variety of registers, such as literary texts, private letters (especially in the papyri) and non-literary / official documents. If not for the sometimes approximate, sometimes more certain identification of register for the texts examined, a simple quantitative analysis would only obscure the developments, as a number of important observations regarding the frequency of use of the three constructions were dependent precisely on the register of the texts examined. And apart from register information, the fact that, in the case at least of the majority of literary texts in the vernacular in LMG, the differentiated manuscript tradition requires a correspondingly differentiated treatment of almost every text rendered a qualitative assessment of the results of the quantitative examination essential for the correct interpretation of the data. Therefore, in agreement with recent studies on corpus linguistics (cf. Biber, 1998), this investigation highlights most clearly the need for both types of analysis, i.e. quantitative and qualitative, in any historical investigation, as either one alone is simply inadequate to provide the necessary information for a complete picture of developments in a certain period or for a specific construction.

Apart from seeking the relative distribution and frequency of use of each AVC, the main focus of this investigation has been to determine the reasons for the major developments. While the semantic pathways of change were to a large extent traceable, usually through analysis of specific syntactic and pragmatic contexts, the changes in frequency of use, albeit highly significant for the explanation of many developments, could not be easily attributed to a specific reason. However, in many cases, the factor of language contact has been called upon to account for a rise of frequency (in the case of the ἔχω AVC in the H–R period, in the EMG and LMG θέλω construction) or for the emergence of a new construction (the case of θέ νά in LMG). The importance of language contact had been rather neglected in the studies of grammaticalization, but this investigation, in agreement with more recent studies (cf. Heine & Kuteva, 2005), highlights its possible significance in grammaticalization processes. It shows that grammaticalization is not driven only by language-internal cognitive or grammatical (mostly semantic) developments facilitated in various contexts of use, but can be also considerably affected by "external" factors, such as bilingualism and language contact in general.

This investigation also verifies that the influence of language contact complies with the usual path of developments attested cross-linguistically (cf. Heine & Kuteva, 2005); in other words language contact was only observed to have facilitated changes that could independently have emerged. That is perhaps why the role of language contact had not been previously considered to be important for instance in the case of θέ νά, since such a phonological reduction is expected independently for a grammatical form (if θέ νά had originated from an FC, as had been hitherto rather mistakenly assumed). On the one hand, this fact renders rather difficult any attempt to dissociate language-internal and language-external factors in a grammaticalization process. On the other hand, it illustrates that such dissociation might prove to be not only difficult to obtain but also misleading, since both types of factors apparently co-occur and co-operate, as is most aptly demonstrated in the case of θέ νά, whose emergence and subsequent developments were the result of an interplay of contact with Romance speakers and various intra-linguistic factors (cf. 5.4.3).

To sum up, it has been shown that, in order to account successfully for diachronic developments, it is essential to create an extensive corpus representative of different registers of use, to combine quantitative and qualitative analysis, taking into account specific intra- and extra-linguistic properties of the texts included in the corpus, and to seek various factors facilitating or impeding developments, not only from the grammar of the language but also from the sociolinguistic context. Such an investigation leads to the unveiling of patterns hidden in a seemingly random variation, as in the case of the future-referring AVCs. Last but not least, this examination has hopefully revealed the importance of the attention that needs to be paid to the actual data, which, despite its complexities, is the only solid basis for historical explanations, since theoretical principles of historical linguistics may actually be misleading in some cases, as will be exemplified below.

6.2 Theoretical implications: typological predictions and frameworks

The findings of this investigation comply to an extent with the typological predictions regarding FCs (cf., for example, Bybee, Perkins, & Pagliuca, 1994: 243–79). As far as the lexical source is concerned, μέλλω was presumably a modal verb signalling intention, and therefore a very good candidate for expressing futurity; the ability meaning of the ἔχω AVC is known to be a source of futurity, albeit rarely; and the volitional θέλω is virtually predicted to develop a future-referring meaning, as volition is one of the most basic sources of futurity. Furthermore, the interaction between futurity and modality was abundantly manifested in the emergence of various modal meanings for all three constructions.

There are, however, some complications arising from these findings, with respect to the development of all three AVCs. First, the issue of phonological attrition: although these constructions were in use for the expression of futurity for many centuries, they were not phonologically reduced in any obvious way. The only seeming exception is the form θέ, but since, as has been argued, it does not constitute a shortened form of the future-referring θέλει, but an instance of phonological attrition not initially related to grammaticalization, it is not a true exception. Consequently, there is a dissociation of grammatical meaning and phonological attrition, which underlines the fact that the latter is only an optional, albeit frequent, concomitant of grammaticalization (cf. also Heine, 1993: 106–12).

The emergence of θέ νά and its development into a deontic and future-referring marker illustrate, on the other hand, the occasional importance of phonological change for grammaticalization, as, in this case, it is phonology that drove or at least facilitated the subsequent development of a TAM meaning (possibly by analogy with the full form expressing such a meaning). This observation refutes claims that desemanticization, i.e. the partial loss of lexical meaning, constitutes the initial stage of any grammaticalization process (cf., for example, Heine, 2003) and argues for a more complex interaction between linguistic levels in the modeling of language change. Such a model should allow for any grammatical level (i.e. semantics–pragmatics, syntax, morphology and phonology) to provide the trigger for the initiation of a grammaticalization process, either in isolation or (more plausibly) in collaboration with other levels. Nonetheless, the semantics of the lexical elements would retain their importance, since only a subset of lexical elements undergo such changes, due to semantic properties that place them in cognitive domains prone to lead to grammaticalization.

A second finding concerns the possibility of an FC to develop a deontic meaning *after* it is established as an FC, in its last stages of development, a possibility manifested in the case of μέλλω (cf. 5.1.3). This refutes the claim of Bybee, Perkins, & Pagliuca (1994), according to which FCs typically express deontic meanings in their early stages of development, while epistemic meanings take over in their last stages. Apparently, sociolinguistic factors, such as the contextual specialization in a specific text register, can bring about otherwise rare cross-linguistical developments. Therefore, along with the various semantic and syntactic properties, the sociolinguistic embedding of any AVC should be investigated, as typological predictions are only relevant as guidelines, and cannot determine the way speakers will shape their language at any specific time.

Finally, the development of the ἔχω AVC gives rise to a re-formulation of Heine's cognitive schema of Possession / Purpose (1993, 1997), which, as already mentioned (cf. 2.2), assumed the following stages: possession, possession with an abstract goal, obligation, and futurity. That such a cognitive path is possible is well known and manifested in languages such as English (till the obligation stage) or (possibly) Latin. Nonetheless, the development of ἔχω illustrates that this is not the only path leading to futurity that a verb of possession can follow: at least one alternative route exists, according to which possession is followed by "possession of the means / resources (to do something)" that gives rise to ability, which, mainly through the mediation of possibility in specific contexts, leads to futurity. It has been also shown how this last development can occur, since possibility is semantically related to futurity, most evidently in negative contexts, but in other contexts as well. Thus, although the final stage is common in both paths (i.e. future reference), the intermediate stages are different. These may also involve other future-related meanings that the ἔχω AVC has been found to convey, such as 'scheduled future' or 'predestination'. Despite the different route, the fact that the development of ἔχω shares its starting and final point with the one proposed by Heine arguably suggests that it constitutes a variation of the same cognitive schema "possession → futurity". The existence of two (or more) pathways that lead to the same meaning might be considered to undermine the validity of cognitive schemas, since they allow for varied manifestations and do not "impose" on a lexical element a specific route, as would ideally be sought for. Alternatively, and preferably, one would consider variation in the cognitive pathways as a neat way to capture the extensive cross-linguistic variation, since contexts triggering specific changes vary cross-linguistically in terms of productivity.

Finally, some remarks are due concerning the theoretical framework of the investigation. The reasons for adopting a functional–typological over a generative perspective have already been outlined (cf. ch. 1). The analysis of the data arguably supports this view, mainly because of the complexity of the developments examined. More precisely, for each of the AVCs a variety of factors have been found to affect the sequence of developments, usually in combination: register specialization, relevant for all three AVCs, specific contexts for the emergence of future reference in the case of ἔχω, language contact for the emergence and diffusion of θέ νά (and, possibly, for the rise in the frequency of use for both ἔχω and θέλω), phonological processes for the reduction of θέλει to θέ, semantic equivalence and morpho-phonological weakening for the interchange of the FCs with the morphological or the νά-Subjunctive, and so forth. Of all these issues, presumably only the last would be relevant for a generative study (e.g. for example, Roberts & Roussou, 2003: 58–71, for an account of the θέλω AVC, or Lightfoot, 1999, for the account of the development of the English modals). Certainly, a generative study would also emphasize syntactic aspects of such phenomena, resulting in a formal implementation of syntactic changes. However, this investigation has arguably shown that without reference to the factors mentioned above, no comprehensive account can emerge, simply because the developments of the Greek FCs (and presumably of all FCs in general) constitute the result of a complex interplay of a multitude of factors, most notably speakers' manipulation of their language. The exclusion of these factors necessarily limits any examination to a subset of the relevant phenomena, as is most aptly demonstrated in the case of the AVCs investigated here.

On the other hand, as Fischer (2007) remarks, the functional–typological framework has not paid much attention to "form", that is to grammatical / morphosyntactic details relevant to the development of AVCs. It is hoped that this investigation has reversed the balance on that account, by attempting to provide a holistic account—to the greatest possible extent—of the developments affecting AVCs, with attention paid to syntactic patterns, paradigmatic relationships, morphological properties, etc. Moreover, a conscious effort has been made to integrate the functional perspective with a sociolinguistic approach to grammaticalization, by fully investigating the social embedding of the developments attested. This has resulted in the highlighting of one important correlation: it has been observed that whenever an AVC was more frequently used, it was also used in more registers. For instance, the establishment of the ἔχω AVC in EMG went hand in hand with its inclusion in middle registers, while the great rise in the frequency of use of the θέλω AVC₁ in LMG was accompanied by its acceptance in middle and even relatively higher registers. As the progress along the grammaticalization chain of any given AVC implies rise in its frequency of use, and as higher frequency of use implies acceptance in more registers, the following parameter of grammaticalization is proposed here, as addition to the four parameters / correlates of grammaticalization (which refer to the semantic, syntactic, and morphophonological properties of AVCs, cf. ch. 1):

Acceptability (sociolinguistic parameter of grammaticalization):

The further grammaticalized an AVC becomes, the higher up it rises in terms of sociolinguistic (register) acceptability.

Obviously, more evidence is needed to verify the validity of this claim. In any case, however, the sociolinguistic aspect of each grammaticalization case should be added as a relevant factor for its development, next to "extension", "desemanticization", "decategorialization" and "erosion". This can be found important not only for determining the position of an AVC along the cline but also—and perhaps more crucially—for accounting for specific properties, as shown in the case of the μέλλω AVC.

6.3 Three answers—and some further questions

The main aims of this investigation have been summarized in the Introduction (cf. 1.2) in three basic questions, which will be repeated here, together with the answers provided by the examination of the data:

(a) What was the exact process of development for each of the constructions? Is there any interconnection between them? And if so, what exactly?

The sequence of developments for each construction, analyzed in the previous chapters, illustrates that the seemingly random variation in the use of the FCs was in fact at least partially systematic, based on sociolinguistic and semantic differentiation. This is to an extent the outcome of the interdependence of the development of each separate construction.

(b) Which are the possible causes of the attested developments?

A variety of reasons have been proposed for the attested developments, such as cross-linguistically typical cognitive–semantic paths, semantic association (logical square connecting ability with futurity), contextual implicatures, language contact, and loss of morphological distinctiveness (e.g. with respect to the Subjunctive).

(c) What can this investigation tell us about the theory(ies) of language change? More specifically: (i) the phenomenon of grammaticalization and how this is best captured (formal / functional approaches), and (ii) the predictions of the typological literature concerning future-referring forms.

This investigation illustrates that the predictions of the typological literature are borne out by the Greek data to an extent, but with modifications and interesting complications (cf. 6.2). Finally, it argues in favor of a functional–typological perspective in the study of the phenomenon of grammaticalization.

Obviously, many more issues related to this investigation still remain unresolved, as for instance, the relation between these three future-referring AVCs and other, less popular constructions (such as ὀφείλω' ('owe') + Infinitive), the morphological Future and the νά-Subjunctive. On the other hand, this analysis will hopefully be seen as introducing new issues for further research. For example, in the light of the new account for θέ νά, a closer look at the data from subsequent centuries would prove illuminating both for this form and its 'descendant', θα. And the language contact explanation of the same construction (θέ νά) has barely touched the surface of a still largely unexplored issue, the possible grammatical borrowings from Romance (mainly Italian) into Greek in the Late Medieval and in subsequent periods. As always, future-referring constructions leave room for future research.

Abbreviations of texts

The following is a list of all the texts abbreviated in the book. For the whole list of the works consulted for this investigation, see Bibliography.

All the Greek names, from the Classical to the Early Medieval period, are given in their familiar Latin forms or in the TLG forms. The late medieval and modern Greek names / titles (including titles in the Bibliography) are simply transliterated into Latin characters, following largely the Greek spelling (note: η = i, υ = y x = h).

Classical Greek

Agamemnon = Agamemnon. [Murray, G. (1955) *Aeschyli tragoediae*. Oxford: Clarendon Press]

Anabasis = Anabasis. [Marchant, E. C. (1900–21) *Xenophontis opera omnia*, vol. 1–5. Oxford: Clarendon Press]

Antigone = Antigone. [Dain, A. & P. Mazon (1967) *Sophocle*. Paris: Les Belles Lettres]

Areop. = Areopagiticus. [Albini, U. (1955) *Lisia. I discorsi*. Firenze: Sansoni]

Bacchae = Bacchae. [Murray, G. (1902) *Euripidis fabulae*. Oxford: Clarendon Press]

Choephoroe = Choephoroe. [Murray, G. (1955) *Aeschyli tragoediae*. Oxford: Clarendon Press]

De corona = De corona. [Butcher, S. H. (1903) *Demosthenis orationes*, vol. 1. Oxford: Clarendon Press]

De div. som. = De divinatione per somnum. [Ross, W. D. (1955) *Aristotle. Parva naturalia*. Oxford: Clarendon Press]

De Halonneso = De Halonneso. [Butcher, S. H. (1903) *Demosthenis orationes*, vol. 1. Oxford: Clarendon Press]

Electra = Electra. [Dain, A. & P. Mazon (1967) *Sophocle*. Paris: Les Belles Lettres]

Epigr. Gr. = Epigrammata Graeca. [Kaibel, G. (1878) *Epigrammata Graeca ex lapidibus conlecta*. Berlin: Reimer]

Frag. Eur. = Euripides Fragmenta. [Nauck, A. (1889) *Tragicorum Graecorum fragmenta*. Leipzig: Teubner]

Helena = Helena. [Murray, G. (1902) *Euripidis fabulae*. Oxford: Clarendon Press]

Herodotus = Historiae. [Legrand, Ph.-E. (1932–54) *Hérodote. Histoires*, 9 vols. Paris: Les Belles Lettres]

Hippolytus = Hippolytus. [Murray, G. (1902) *Euripidis fabulae*. Oxford: Clarendon Press]

Hist. Anim. = Historia Animalium. [Louis, P. (1964–69) *Aristote. Histoire des animaux*, vols. 1–3. Paris: Les Belles Lettres]

Il. = Ilias. [Allen, T. W. (1931) *Homeri Ilias*, vols. 2–3. Oxford: Clarendon Press]

In Alcib. I = In Alcibiadem 1. [Albini, U. (1955) *Lisia. I discorsi*. Firenze: Sansoni]

Lysias, Fragm. = Lysias Fragmenta. [Thalheim, T. (1913) *Lysiae orationes [editio maior]*. Leipzig: Teubner]
O.T. = Oedipus Tyrannus. [Dain, A. & P. Mazon (1967) *Sophocle*. Paris: Les Belles Lettres]
Od. = Odyssea. [von der Muehll, P. (1962) *Homeri Odyssea*. Basel: Helbing & Lichtenhahn]
Olynth. III = Olynthiaca 3. [Butcher, S. H. (1903) *Demosthenis orationes, vol. 1*. Oxford: Clarendon Press]
Panegyricus = Panegyricus. [Mathieu, G. & E. Bremond (1929) *Isocrate. Discours*. Paris: Les Belles Lettres]
Parm. = Parmenides. [Burnet, J. (1900–07) *Platonis opera, vols. 1–5*. Oxford: Clarendon Press]
Phaedrus = Phaedrus. [Burnet, J. (1900–07) *Platonis opera, vols. 1–5*. Oxford: Clarendon Press]
Philip. 3 = Philippica 3. [Butcher, S. H. (1903) *Demosthenis orationes, vol. 1*. Oxford: Clarendon Press]
Respublica = Respublica. [Burnet, J. (1900–07) *Platonis opera, vols. 1–5*. Oxford: Clarendon Press]
Thuc. = Thucydidis Historiae. [Jones, H. S. & J. E. Powell (1967–70) *Thucydidis historiae, 2 vols*. Oxford: Clarendon Press]
Vespae = Vespae. [MacDowell, D. M. (1971) *Aristophanes. Wasps*. Oxford: Clarendon Press]

Hellenistic–Roman Greek

Acta = Acta apostolorum. [Aland, K., M. Black, C. M. Martini, B. M. Metzger & A. Wikgren (1968) *The Greek New Testament*. Stuttgart: Württemberg Bible Society]
Acta Joannis = Acta Joannis. [Bonnet, M. (1898) *Acta apostolorum apocrypha, vol. 2.1*. Leipzig: Mendelssohn]
Acta X. et P. = Acta Xanthippae et Polyxenae. [James, M. R. (1893) *Apocrypha anecdota*. Cambridge: Cambridge University Press]
Apoc. Esdrae = Apocalypsis Esdrae. [Tischendorf, C. (1866) *Apocalypses apocryphae*. Leipzig: Mendelssohn]
BGU = *Aegyptische Urkunden aus den Königlichen* (later *Staatlichen*) *Museen zu Berlin, Griechische Urkunden*. Berlin. Vols. 1–18 (1895–2000).
Constit. Apost. = Constitutiones Apostolorum. [Metzger, M. (1985–87) *Les constitutions apostoliques, 3 vols*. Paris: Cerf]
Contra Christianos = Contra Christianos [fragmenta]. [von Harnack, A. (1916) *Porphyrius: Gegen die Christen*. Berlin: Reimer]
De adv. = De adverbiis. [Schneider, R. & G. Uhlig (1878–1910) *Grammatici Graeci*. Leipzig: Teubner]
De pronom. = De pronominibus. [Schneider, R. & G. Uhlig (1878–1910) *Grammatici Graeci*. Leipzig: Teubner]

Diss. = Dissertationes. [Schenkl, H. (1916) *Epicteti dissertationes ab Arriano digestae.* Leipzig: Teubner]

Eclogae = Eclogae. [Fischer, E. (1974) *Die Ekloge des Phrynichos.* Berlin: Mouton de Gruyter]

Luc. = Evangelium secundum Lucam. [Aland, K., M. Black, C. M. Martini, B. M. Metzger & A. Wikgren (1968) *The Greek New Testament.* Stuttgart: Württemberg Bible Society]

Mart. Carpi = Martyrium Carpi, Papyli et Agathonicae. [Musurillo, H. (1972) *The acts of the Christian martyrs.* Oxford: Clarendon Press]

Matth. = Evangelium secundum Matthaeum. [Aland, K., M. Black, C. M. Martini, B. M. Metzger & A. Wikgren (1968) *The Greek New Testament.* Stuttgart: Württemberg Bible Society]

PAmh = *The Amherst Papyri, Being an Account of the Greek Papyri in the Collection of the Right Hon. Lord Amherst of Hackney, F.S.A. at Didlington Hall, Norfolk*, ed. B. P. Grenfell & A. S. Hunt. London. Vols. 1–2 (1900–01)

Pausanias = Graeciae descriptio. [Spiro, F. (1903) *Pausaniae Graeciae descriptio, 3 vols.* Leipzig: Teubner]

PBad = *Veröffentlichungen aus den badischen Papyrus-Sammlungen.* Heidelberg. Vols. 1–6 (1923–38)

PBerl Zill = *Vierzehn Berliner griechische Papyri*, ed. H. Zilliacus. Helsingfors: 1941.

PBingen = *Papyri in Honorem Johannis Bingen Octogenarii*, ed. H. Melaerts. Leuven: 2000.

PCair Zen = *Zenon Papyri, Catalogue général des antiquités égyptiennes du Musée du Caire*, ed. C. C. Edgar. Cairo. Vols. 1–5 (1925–40)

PCollYoutie = *Collectanea Papyrologica: Texts Published in Honor of H. C. Youtie*, ed. A. E. Hanson et al. Bonn: 1976

PEnteux = ΕΝΤΕΥΞΕΙΣ: *Requêtes et plaintes adressées au Roi d'Égypte au IIIe siècle avant J.-C.*, ed. O. Guéraud. Cairo: 1931

PFlor = *Papiri greco-egizii, Papiri Fiorentini* (Supplementi Filologico-Storici ai Monumenti Antichi). Milan. Vols. 1–3 (1906–15)

PGrenf = I: *An Alexandrian Erotic Fragment and other Greek Papyri chiefly Ptolemaic*, ed. B. P. Grenfell. Oxford: 1896. II: *New Classical Fragments and Other Greek and Latin Papyri*, ed. B. P. Grenfell & A. S. Hunt. Oxford: 1897

PHamb = *Griechische Papyrusurkunden der Hamburger Staats- und Universitätsbibliothek.* Hamburg. Vols. 1–4 (1911–98)

PHeid = *Veröffentlichungen aus der Heidelberger Papyrussammlung.* Heidelberg. Vols. 1–8 (1956–2001)

PIand = *Papyri Iandanae*, ed. C. Kalbfleisch et al. Leipzig. Vols. 1–8 (1912–38)

PMeyer = *Griechische Texte aus Aegypten.* I, *Papyri des Neutestamentlichen Seminars der Universität Berlin*; II, *Ostraka der Sammlung Deissmann*, ed. P. M. Meyer. Berlin: 1916

PMichael = *Papyri Michaelidae, being a Catalogue of Greek and Latin Papyri, Tablets and Ostraca in the Library of Mr G. A. Michailidis of Cairo*, ed. D. S. Crawford. Aberdeen: 1955

POslo = *Papyri Osloenses.* Oslo. Vols. 1–3 (1925–36)

POxy = *The Oxyrhynchus Papyri.* London. Vols. 1–68 (1898–2003)

PRyl = *Catalogue of the Greek and Latin Papyri in the John Rylands Library, Manchester*. Manchester. Vols. 1–4 (1911–52)
PSakaon = *The Archive of Aurelius Sakaon: Papers of an Egyptian Farmer in the last Century of Theadelphia*, ed. G. M. Parássoglou. Bonn: 1978
PTebt = *The Tebtunis Papyri*. London. Vols. 1–5 (1902–2005)
PWisc = *The Wisconsin Papyri*, ed. P. J. Sijpesteijn. Wisconsin. Vols. 1–2 (1967–77)
Quaest. Conv. = Quaestiones Convivales. [Babbitt, F. C. & H. N. Fowler (1927–36) *Plutarch's moralia*. Cambridge, Mass.: Harvard University Press]
SB = *Sammelbuch griechischer Urkunden aus Aegypten*. Vols. 1–24 (1913–2003)
Strabo = Geographica. [Meineke, A. (1877) *Strabonis geographica, 3 vols*. Leipzig: Teubner]
Test. Abr. (A) = Testamentum Abrahae (recensio A). [James, M. R. (1892) *The testament of Abraham*. Cambridge: Cambridge University Press]
Vita Ad. et Ev. = Vita Adam et Evae. [Tischendorf, C. (1866) *Apocalypses apocryphae*. Leipzig: Teubner]
Vita Antonii = Vita Antonii. [Bartelink, G. J. M. (1994) *Athanase d'Alexandrie: Vie d'Antoine*. Paris: Cerf]

Early Medieval Greek

Call. = Callinicus Hagiographus. [Bartelink, G. J. M. (1971) *Callinicos. Vie d'Hypatios*. Paris: Cerf]
De adm. imp. = De administrando imperio. [Moravcsik, G. & R. J. H. Jenkins (1967) *Constantine Porphyrogenitus. De administrando imperio, 2nd edition*. Washington, D.C.: Dumbarton Oaks]
De cerimoniis = De cerimoniis. [Reiske, J. J. (1829) *Constantini Porphyrogeniti imperatoris de cerimoniis aulae Byzantinae libri duo*. Bonn: Weber]
De insidiis = De insidiis. [de Boor, C. (1905) *Excerpta historica iussu imp. Constantini Porphyrogeniti confecta, vol. 3: excerpta de insidiis*. Berlin: Weidmann]
Death Poems = Death poems. [Ševčenko, I. (1970) "Poems on the Deaths of Leo VI and Constantine VII in the Madrid Manuscript of Scylitzes". *Dumbarton Oaks Papers* 24: 185–228]
Epanagoge = Ecloga Privata Aucta. [Zepos, P. (1931) *Ecloga Privata Aucta [Jus Graecoromanum 6]*. Athens: Fexis]
Historia monachorum = Historia monachorum in Aegypto. [Festugière, A. J. (1971) *Historia monachorum in Aegypto*. Brussels: Société des Bollandistes]
L.Asc. = Liber asceticus. [Cantarella, R. (1931) *S. Massimo Confessore: La mistagogia ed altri scritti*. Firenze: Testi Cristiani]
Malalas = Malalae chronographia. [Thurn, I. (2000) *Ioannis Malalae chronographia*. Berlin: Mouton de Gruyter]
Miracula = Miracula Sancti Artemii. [Papadopoulos-Kerameus, A. (1909) *Varia graeca sacra*. St. Petersburg: Kirschbaum]

Opus 26 = Epistula ad ameram Damascenum. [Westerink, L. G. (1968) *Arethae archiepiscopi Caesariensis scripta minora, vol. 1.* Leipzig: Teubner]

PCair, Mas = *Papyrus grecs d'époque byzantine, Catalogue général des antiquités égyptiennes du Musée du Caire*, ed. J. Maspero. Cairo. Vols. 1–3 (1911–16)

PFuad = *Fuad I University Papyri*, ed. D. S. Crawford. Alexandria: 1949

PKöln = *Kölner Papyri*. Köln. Vols. 1–10 (1976–2003)

PLond = *Greek Papyri in the British Museum*. London. Vols. 1–7 (1893–1974)

PMichael = *Papyri Michaelidae, being a Catalogue of Greek and Latin Papyri, Tablets and Ostraca in the Library of Mr G. A. Michailidis of Cairo*, ed. D.S. Crawford. Aberdeen: 1955

PPrag = *Papyri Graecae Wessely Pragenses*, ed. R. Pintaudi, R. Dostálová & L. Vidman. Firenze. Vols. 1–2 (1988–95)

PSI = *Papiri greci e latini*. Florence. Vols. 1–15 (1912–79)

SB = *Sammelbuch griechischer Urkunden aus Aegypten*. Vols. 1–24 (1913–2003)

Spiritual Meadow = Moschos' Spiritual Meadow. [Migne, J.-P. (1857–66) *Patrologiae cursus completus (series Graeca)* 87: 2852–3112. Paris: Garnier]

Stephanus = Ethnica. [Meineke, A. (1849) *Stephan von Byzanz. Ethnika*. Berlin: Reimer]

Thal. = Ad Thalassium. [Laga, C. & C. Steel (1980) *Maximi confessoris quaestiones ad Thalassium i: quaestiones i–lv*. Turnhout: Brepols]

Theophanes = Theophanis chronographia. [de Boor, C. (1883) *Theophanis chronographia*. Leipzig: Teubner]

V.J. = Vita Joannis. [Festugière, A.-J. & L. Rydén (1974) *Léontios de Néapolis, Vie de Syméon le Fou et Vie de Jean de Chypre*. Paris: Geuthner]

Vita Sym. Sali = Vita Symeonis Sali. [Festugière, A.-J. & L. Rydén (1974) *Léontios de Néapolis, Vie de Syméon le Fou et Vie de Jean de Chypre*. Paris: Geuthner]

Late Medieval Greek

Ahilliid = Ahilliid.

[1. Smith, O. L. (1999) *The Byzantine Achilleid. The Naples version*. Wien: Österreichische Akademie der Wissenschaften

2. Haag, B. (1919) *Die Londoner version der byzantinischen Achilleis*. München: Universitäts-Buchdruckerei Wolf & Sohn

3. Smith, O. L. (1990) *The Oxford version of the «Achilleid»*. Copenhagen: Museum Tusculanum Press.]

Alfavitos = Alfavitos katanyktiki. [Wagner, W. (1874) *Carmina Graeca Medii Aevi*. Leipzig: Teubner]

Amarantos = Amarantos. [Vagionakis, H., O. Katsivela, D. Mihalaga, V. Belovgeni & M. Bletas (2001) *Andreas Amarantos. Notariakes praxeis. Arakli Kefalonias (1548–1562)*. Athina]

AoT = Apollonios of Tyre. [Kehagioglou, G. (2004) *Apollonios tis Tyrou: Ysteromesaionikes kai neoteres ellinikes morfes.* Thessaloniki: Institouto Neoellinikon Spoudon / Idryma Manoli Triantafyllidi]

Armouris = The song of Armouris. [Alexiou, S. (1985) *Vasileios Digenis Akritis kai to asma tou Armouri.* Athina: Ermis]

Assises = Assises. [Sathas, K. (1877) *Mesaioniki Vivliothiki, tomos VI: Asizai tou Vasileiou ton Ierosolymon kai tis Kyprou.* Paris: Maisonneuve]

Hondromatis = Hondromatis. [Konidaris, I. & G. Rodolakis (1996) "Oi praxeis tou notariou Kerkyras Ioanni Hondromati (1472–73)". *EAIED* 32: 139–206]

CoM = Chronicle of Morea. [Kalonaros, P. P. (1940) *To Hronikon tou Moreos.* Athina]

CoT = Chronicle of Tocco. [Schirò, G. (1975) *Cronaca dei Tocco di Cefalonia di Anonimo.* Roma: Accademia dei Lincei]

De Montesantos = De Montesantos. [Zapanti, S. (2002) *Montesantos (de) iereas Stamatios, notarios Eleiou. Katastiho 1535–1553.* Argostoli: Genika Arheia tou Kratous: Arheia Nomou Kefallinias]

Dellaportas = Leonardos Dellaportas. [Manousakas, M. I. (1995) *Leonardou Ntellaporta Poiimata (1403 / 1411).* Athina: Akadimia Athinon]

Diigisis = Diigisis Paidiofrastos. [Tsiouni, V. (1972) *Paidiofrastos diigisis ton zoon ton tetrapodon.* München: Institut für Byzantinistik und Neugriechische Philologie der Universität]

Digenis = Digenis Akritis. [Alexiou, S. (1985) *Vasileios Digenis Akritis kai to asma tou Armouri.* Athina: Ermis]

Ermoniakos = Ermoniakos' Iliad. [Legrand, É. (1890) Ἰλιάδος Ῥαψωδίαι ΚΔ΄. *La guerre de Troie. Poème du XIVe siècle en vers octosyllabes par Constantin Hermoniacos (Bibliothèque Grecque Vulgaire V).* Paris: Maisonneuve]

Esfigmenou = Esfigmenou. [Lefort, J. (1973) *Archives de l'Athos VI: Actes d'Esphigménou.* Paris: P. Lethielleux]

Falieros = Marinos Falieros.
[1. van Gemert, A. (2006) *Marinou Falierou "Erotika Oneira".* Athina: MIET
2. Bakker, W. F. & A. F. van Gemert (1972) "The Ῥίμα Παρηγορητική of Marinos Phalieros". *Studia Byzantina et Neohellenica Neerlandica* 3: 74–195
3. Bakker, W. F. & A. F. van Gemert (1977) *The Λόγοι Διδακτικοί of Marinos Phalieros.* Leiden: Brill
4. Bakker, W. F. & A. F. van Gemert (2002) *Thrinos eis ta Pathi kai tin Staurosin tou Kyriou kai Theou kai Sotiros imon Iisou.* Iraklio: Panepistimiakes Ekdoseis Kritis]

Gialeas = Gialeas. [Bakker, W. F. & A. F. van Gemert (1978) "Oi diathikes tou Kritikou notariou Antoniou Gialea (1529–1532)". *Kritologia* 6: 5–90]

Glykas = Mihail Glykas. [Tsolakis, E. T. (1959) "Mihail Glyka stihoi". *Epistimoniki Epetiris Filosofikis Sholis Aristoteleiou Panepistimiou Thessalonikis,* Appendix 3: 3–22]

Grigoropoulos = Grigoropoulos. [Kaklamanis, S. & S. Lampakis (2003) *Manouil Grigoropoulos, notarios Handaka (1506–1532). Diathikes, Apografes-Ektimiseis.* Iraklio: Vikelaia Dimotiki Vivliothiki]

Grottaferrata = Grottaferrata. [Jeffreys, E. (1998) *Digenis Akritis: The Grottaferrata and Escorial versions*. Cambridge: Cambridge University Press]

H&V = Hunger & Vogel. [Hunger, H. & K. Vogel (1963) *Ein byzantinisches Rechenbuch des 15. Jahrhunderts*. Wien: Österreichische Akademie der Wissenschaften]

Iatrosofia = Iatrosofia-Stafidas. [Legrand, É. (1881) *Bibliothèque Grecque Vulgaire* II. Paris: Maisonneuve]

Kallergis = Synthiki Kallergi. [Mertzios, K. D. (1949) "I synthiki Eneton-Kallergi kai oi sunodeuontes autin katalogoi". *Kritika Hronika* 3: 262–92]

Kallimahos = Kallimahos & Hrysorroi. [Kriaras, E. (1955) *Vyzantina Ippotika Mythistorimata*. Athinai: Aetos]

Kasimatis = Kasimatis. [Drakakis, E. (1999) *Emmanouil Kasimatis, notarios Kythiron (1560–1582)*. Athina]

Katalogia = Katalogia. [Hesseling, D. C. & H. Pernot (1913) $Ερωτοπαίγνια$ *(Chansons d'amour) (Bibliothèque Grecque Vulgaire X)*. Paris-Athènes]

Katoimeris = Katoimeris. [Papariga-Artemiadi, L., G. Rodolakis & D. Karampoula (1997) "Oi praxeis tou notariou Karousadon Kerkyras protopapa Filippou Katoimeri (1503–1507)". *EAIED* 33: 9–436]

Katsouros = Naxos. [Katsouros, A. (1955) "Naxiaka dikaiopraktika eggrafa tou $16^{ου}$ aionos". *Epetiris Mesaionikou Arheiou* 5: 47–91]

Lampros = Venice documents. [Lampros, S. (1908) "Dyo ellinika eggrafa ek ton arheion tis Venetias". *Neos Ellinomnimon* 5: 479–81]

Legrand = Letters. [Legrand, É. (1885) *Bibliographie Hellénique (XVe – XVIe siècles). Tome second*. Paris: Ernest Leroux]

Livistros-a = Livistros & Rodamni (a). [Agapitos, P. A. (2006) *Afigisis Livistrou kai Rodamnis*. Athina: MIET]

Livistros-b = Livistros & Rodamni (b). [Lentari, T. (2007) *Afigisis Livistrou kai Rodamnis (Livistros and Rodamne). The Vatican version*. Athina: MIET]

Mahairas = Chronicle of Mahairas.

[1. Dawkins, R. M. (1932) *Leontios Makhairas: recital concerning the sweet land of Cyprus entitled Chronicle*. Oxford: Clarendon Press

2. Pieris, M. & A. Nikolaou-Konnari (2003) *Leontiou Mahaira "Hroniko tis Kyprou": Paralliili diplomatiki ekdosi ton heirografon*. Leukosia: Kentro Epistimonikon Ereunon]

Manousakas = Cretan documents. [Manousakas, M. I. (1964) "Ellinika notariaka eggrafa apo ta 'Atti antichi' tou arheiou tou Douka tis Kritis". *Thisaurismata* 3: 73–102]

Maras = Mihail Maras.

[I. Drakakis, M. G. (2004) *Mihail Maras, notarios Handaka. Katastiho 149, Tomos A' [16 / 1–30 / 3 1549]*. Iraklio: Vikelaia Dimotiki Vivliothiki

II. Marmareli, T. & M. G. Drakakis (2005) *Mihail Maras, notarios Handaka. Katastiho 149, Tomos B' [1 / 4–28 / 6 1549]*. Iraklio: Vikelaia Dimotiki Vivliothiki

III. Mavromatis, G. (2006) *Mihail Maras, notarios Handaka. Katastiho 148, Tomos B' [2 / 3–31 / 8 1548]*. Iraklio: Vikelaia Dimotiki Vivliothiki

IV. Marmareli, T. & M. G. Drakakis (2005) *Mihail Maras, notarios Handaka. Katastiho 149, Tomos Γ′ [1 / 7–28 / 9 1549]*. Iraklio: Vikelaia Dimotiki Vivliothiki]
MM = Miklosich-Müller. [Miklosich, F. & J. Müller (eds.) (1860–90) *Acta et diplomata graeca medii aevi sacra et profana* (6 vols.). Wien: Gerold]
Olokalos = Olokalos. [Mavromatis, G. (1994) *Ioannis Olokalos, Notarios Ierapetras. Katastiho (1496–1543)*. Venetia: Elliniko Institouto Vyzantinon kai Metavyzantinon Spoudon tis Venetias & Vikelaia Dimotiki Vivliothiki Irakliou]
Patsidiotis = Patsidiotis. [Iliakis, K. & D. Hronaki (2002) *Petros Patsidiotis: Notarios Kainourgiou Horiou ton Karon. Katastiho (1546–1554)*. Dimos Neapoleos]
Florios = Florios & Platziaflora. [Kriaras, E. (1955) *Vyzantina Ippotika Mythistorimata*. Athinai: Aetos]
Fysiologos = Fysiologos. [Legrand, É. (1873) *Le Physiologus. Poème sur la nature des animaux en grec vulgaire et en vers politiques*. Paris]
Polemis = Andros. [Polemis, D. (1999) *Anekdota Andriaka eggrafa tou 16^{ου} aionos. Andriaka Hronika 30*]
Poulologos = Poulologos. [Tsavari, I. (1987) *O Poulologos*. Athina: MIET]
Sahlikis = Sahlikis.
[1. Wagner, W. (1874) *Carmina Graeca Medii Aevi*. Leipzig: Teubner
2. Vitti, M. (1960) "Il poema parenetico di Sachlikis". *Kritika Hronika* 14: 173–200.
3. Papadimitriou, S. D. (1896) *Stefan Sakhlikis i ego stikhotvorenie "Ἀφήγησις Παράξενος"*. Odessa]
Sourianos = Sourianos. [Zapanti, S. (2001) *Giakoumos Sourianos, Notarios Kastrou. Katastiho 1570–1598*. Argostoli]
Spanos = Spanos. [Eideneier, H. (1977) *Spanos: eine byzantinische Satire in der Form einer Parodie*. Berlin: Mouton de Gruyter]
Stratigikon = Stratigikon. [Wassiliewsky, B. & V. Jernestedt (1965) *Cecaumeni Strategikon*. Amsterdam: Hakkert]
Thisiid = Thisiid. [Follieri, E. (1959) *Il Teseida Neogreco. Libro I*. Roma–Atene: Istituto di Studi Bizantini e Neoellenici]
Trinchera = S. Italian documents. [Trinchera, F. (1865) *Syllabus graecarum membranarum*. Napoli: Cataneo]
Tselikas = Early official documents. [Tselikas, A. (1986) "Nikolaou Sparmioti, nomikou Koryfon, «eggrafo eleutherias» (1391)". *Deltion tis Ioniou Akadimias* 2: 168–87]
Vagiakakos = Zakynthos. [Vagiakakos, D. (1950) "Melissinoi kai Kontostavloi. Ek Manis eis Zakynthon 1509". *Epetiris Mesaionikou Arheiou* 3: 141–66]
Varagkas = Varagkas. [Rodolakis, G. & L. Papariga-Artemiadi (1996) "Oi praxeis tou notariou Agiou Matthaiou Kerkyras Petrou Varagka (1541–1545)". *EAIED* 32: 207–340]
Varouhas = Varouhas. [Bakker, W. F. & A. F. van Gemert (1987) *Manolis Varouhas: Notariakes Praxeis. Monastiraki Arakliou (1597–1613)*. Rethymno]
Vazelon = Actes de Vazelon. [Ouspensky, Th. & V. Bénéchévitch (1927) *Actes de Vazélon*. Leningrad]

Velissarios = Diigisis Velissariou. [Bakker, W. F. & A. F. van Gemert (1988) *Istoria tou Velissariou*. Athina: MIET]

Velthandros = Velthandros & Hrysantza. [Kriaras, E. (1955) *Vyzantina Ippotika Mythistorimata*. Athinai: Aetos]

WoT = War of Troy. [Papathomopoulos, M. & E. Jeffreys (1996) *O polemos tis Troados – The War of Troy*. Athina: MIET]

Xeniteia = Peri tis Xeniteias. [Mavromatis, G. (1995) *Ta "Peri tis Xeniteias" poiimata*. Iraklio: Dimos Irakliou – Vikelaia Vivliothiki]

Xiropotamou = Actes de Xiropotamou. [Bompaire, J. (1964) *Archives de l'Athos III: Actes de Xéropotamou*. Paris: P. Lethielleux]

Bibliography

Primary sources

Classical period (5th–3rd c. BC)

Orators
Antiphon. Gernet, L. (1923) *Antiphon. Discours.* Paris: Les Belles Lettres.
Isocrates. Mathieu, G. & E. Bremond (1929) *Isocrate. Discours.* Paris: Les Belles Lettres.
Isaeus. Roussel, P. (1960) *Isée. Discours.* Paris: Les Belles Lettres.
Andocides. Dalmeyda, G. (1930) *Andocide. Discours.* Paris: Les Belles Lettres.
Lysias. Albini, U. (1955) *Lisia. I discorsi.* Firenze: Sansoni.
Demosthenes.
1–26. Butcher, S. H. (1903) *Demosthenis orationes, vol. 1.* Oxford: Clarendon Press.
27–63. Rennie, W. (1921) *Demosthenis orationes, vol. 2.* Oxford: Clarendon Press.
Aeschines. Martin, V. & G. de Budé (1927–8) *Eschine. Discours, vol. 1–2.* Paris: Les Belles Lettres.
Lycurgus. Conomis, N. C. (1970) *Lycurgi oratio in Leocratem.* Leipzig: Teubner.
Dinarchus. Conomis, N. C. (1975) *Dinarchi orationes cum fragmentis.* Leipzig: Teubner.

Poets
Aeschylus. Murray, G. (1955) *Aeschyli tragoediae.* Oxford: Clarendon Press.
Sophocles. Dain, A. & P. Mazon (1967) *Sophocle.* Paris: Les Belles Lettres.
Euripides. Murray, G. (1902) *Euripidis fabulae.* Oxford: Clarendon Press.

Aristophanes.
1. "Acharnenses, Equites, Pax, Aves, Lysistrata, Thesmophoriazusae, Ranae, Plutus": Coulon, V. & M. van Daele (1967) *Aristophane.* Paris: Les Belles Lettres.
2. "Nubes": Dover, K. J. (1968) *Aristophanes. Clouds.* Oxford: Clarendon Press.
3. "Vespae": MacDowell, D. M. (1971) *Aristophanes. Wasps.* Oxford: Clarendon Press.
4. "Ecclesiazusae": Ussher, R. G. (1973) *Aristophanes. Ecclesiazusae.* Oxford: Clarendon Press.
Menander. Sandbach, F. G. (1972) *Menandri reliquiae selectae.* Oxford: Clarendon Press.

Historians
Thucydides. Jones, H. S. & J. E. Powell (1967–70) *Thucydidis historiae, 2 vols.* Oxford: Clarendon Press.
Herodotus. Legrand, Ph.-E. (1932–54) *Hérodote. Histoires, 9 vols.* Paris: Les Belles Lettres.
Xenophon. Marchant, E. C. (1900–21) *Xenophontis opera omnia, vol. 1–5.* Oxford: Clarendon Press.

Philosophers

Plato. Burnet, J. (1900–07) *Platonis opera, vols. 1–5.* Oxford: Clarendon Press.
Aristotle.
1. Ross, W. D. (1964) *Aristotelis analytica priora et posteriora.* Oxford: Clarendon Press.
2. Ross, W. D. (1961) *Aristotle. De anima.* Oxford: Clarendon Press.
3. Oppermann, H. (1928) *Aristotelis 'Αθηναίων πολιτεία.* Leipzig: Teubner.
4. "De audibilibus, De coloribus, De lineis insecabilibus, Mechanica, Mirabilium auscultationes, Physiognomonica, Problemata, De ventorum situ et nominibus, De virtutibus et vitiis, De Xenophane, De Zenone, De Gorgia": Bekker, I. (1960) *Aristotelis opera.* Berlin: Mouton de Gruyter.
5. Moraux, P. (1965) *Aristote. Du ciel.* Paris: Les Belles Lettres.
6. "Categoriae, De interpretatione": Minio-Paluello, L. (1949) *Aristotelis categoriae et liber de interpretatione.* Oxford: Clarendon Press.
7. "De divinatione per somnum, De insomniis, De juventute et senectute + De vita et morte, De longitudine et brevitate vitae, De memoria et reminiscentia, De respiratione, De sensu et sensibilibus, De somno et vigilia": Ross, W. D. (1955) *Aristotle. Parva naturalia.* Oxford: Clarendon Press.
8. Hercher, R. (1873) *Epistolographi Graeci.* Paris: Didot.
9. Susemihl, F. (1884) *Aristotelis ethica Eudemia.* Leipzig: Teubner.
10. Bywater, I. (1894) *Aristotelis ethica Nicomachea.* Oxford: Clarendon Press.
11. Drossaart Lulofs, H. J. (1965) *Aristotelis de generatione animalium.* Oxford: Clarendon Press.
12. Mugler, C. (1966) *Aristote. De la génération et de la corruption.* Paris: Les Belles Lettres.
13. Louis, P. (1964–69) *Aristote. Histoire des animaux, vols. 1–3.* Paris: Les Belles Lettres.
14. "De incessu animalium, De motu animalium, De spiritu": Jaeger, W. (1913) *Aristotelis de animalium motione et de animalium incessu. Ps. – Aristotelis de spiritu libellus.* Leipzig: Teubner.
15. Armstrong, G. C. (1935) *Magna moralia.* In: F. Susemihl (ed.), *Aristotle, vol. 18.* Cambridge, Mass.: Harvard University Press.
16. Ross, W. D. (1953) *Aristotle's metaphysics.* Oxford: Clarendon Press.
17. Fobes, F. H. (1919) *Aristotelis meteorologicorum libri quattuor.* Cambridge, Mass.: Harvard University Press.
18. Lorimer, W. L. (1933) *Aristotelis qui fertur libellus de mundo.* Paris: Les Belles Lettres.
19. van Groningen, B. A. & A. Wartelle (1968) *Aristote. Economique.* Paris: Les Belles Lettres.
20. Louis, P. (1956) *Aristote. Les parties des animaux.* Paris: Les Belles Lettres.
21. "Physica, Physicorum libri octavi textus alter": Ross, W. D. (1966) *Aristotelis physica.* Oxford: Clarendon Press.

22. Kassel, R. (1966) *Aristotelis de arte poetica liber.* Oxford: Clarendon Press.
23. Ross, W. D. (1957) *Aristotelis politica.* Oxford: Clarendon Press.
24. Düring, I. (1961) *Aristotle's protrepticus.* Stockholm: Almqvist & Wiksell.
25. Ross, W. D. (1959) *Aristotelis ars rhetorica.* Oxford: Clarendon Press.
26. "Sophistici elenchi, Topica": Ross, W. D. (1970) *Aristotelis topica et sophistic elenchi.* Oxford: Clarendon Press.
27. Mutschmann, H. (1906) *Divisiones quae vulgo dicuntur Aristotelae.* Leipzig: Teubner.

Theophrastus.
1. Hort, A. (1916) *Theophrastus. Enquiry into plants.* Cambridge, Mass.: Harvard University Press.
2. Dengler, R. E. (1927) *Theophrastus. De causis plantarum, book one.* Philadelphia: University of Pennsylvania Press.
3. "De sensu et sensibilibus, Physicorum opiniones": Diels, H. (1879) *Doxographi Graeci.* Berlin: Reimer.
4. Eichholz, D. E. (1965) *Theophrastus. De lapidibus.* Oxford: Clarendon Press.
5. Coutant, V. (1971) *Theophrastus. De igne.* Assen: Royal Vangorcum.
6. Ross, W. D. & F. H. Fobes (1929) *Theophrastus. Metaphysics.* Oxford: Clarendon Press.
7. Pötscher, W. (1964) *Theophrastos.* Περὶ εὐσεβείας. Leiden: Brill.
8. Steinmetz, P. (1960) *Theophrast. Charaktere.* Munich: Hueber.

Works consulted, but not included in the corpus of the quantitative study

Homer.
1. Allen, T. W. (1931) *Homeri Ilias,* vols. 2–3. Oxford: Clarendon Press.
2. von der Muehll, P. (1962) *Homeri Odyssea.* Basel: Helbing & Lichtenhahn.

Epigr. Gr. Kaibel, G. (1878) *Epigrammata Graeca ex lapidibus conlecta.* Berlin: Reimer.
Lysias (Frag.). Thalheim, T. (1913) *Lysiae orationes [editio maior].* Leipzig: Teubner.
Euripides (Frag.). Nauck, A. (1889) *Tragicorum Graecorum fragmenta.* Leipzig: Teubner.

Hellenistic–Roman period (3rd c. BC–4th c. AD)[1]

3rd century BC
Septuaginta. Rahlfs, A. (1935) *Septuaginta.* Stuttgart: Württembergische Bibelanstalt.

1st century BC–1st century AD
Apocalypsis Esdrae. Tischendorf, C. (1866) *Apocalypses apocryphae.* Leipzig: Mendelssohn.
Vita Adam et Evae. Tischendorf, C. (1866) *Apocalypses apocryphae.* Leipzig: Mendelssohn.

---

[1] The papyri, spanning from the 3rd c. BC to the 8th c. AD, will be listed separately at the end of the corpus of this period.

1st century AD

Novum Testamentum. Aland, K., M. Black, C. M. Martini, B. M. Metzger & A. Wikgren (1968) *The Greek New Testament.* Stuttgart: Württemberg Bible Society.

Apocalypsis Syriaca Baruchi. Denis, A.-M. (1970) *Fragmenta pseudepigraphorum quae supersunt Graeca.* Leiden: Brill.

Assumptio Mosis. Denis, A.-M. (1970) *Fragmenta pseudepigraphorum quae supersunt Graeca.* Leiden: Brill.

Testamentum Abrahae (recensio A). James, M. R. (1892) *The testament of Abraham.* Cambridge: Cambridge University Press.

Apocalypsis Adam. Robinson, J. A. (1893) *Texts and Studies 2.3.* Cambridge: Cambridge University Press.

Isis Prophetissa. Berthelot, M. & C. É. Ruelle (1888) *Collection des anciens alchimistes grecs, vol. 2.* Paris: Steinheil.

Evangelicum Secundum Hebraeos. Klostermann, E. (1910) *Apocrypha II. Evangelien.* Bonn: Marcus & Weber.

2nd century AD

Acta Joannis. Bonnet, M. (1898) *Acta apostolorum apocrypha, vol. 2.1.* Leipzig: Mendelssohn.

Acta Pauli.
1. Schubart, W. & C. Schmidt (1936) *Acta Pauli.* Glückstadt: Augustin.
2. Martyrium Pauli, Acta Pauli et Theclae: Lipsius, R. A. (1891) *Acta apostolorum apocrypha, vol. 1.* Leipzig: Mendelssohn.
3. Testuz, M. (1959) *Papyrus Bodmer X–XIII.* Geneva: Bibliotheca Bodmeriana.

Acta Petri. Vouaux, L. (1922) *Les actes de Pierre.* Paris: Letouzey & Ané.

Martyrium Carpi, Papyli et Agathonicae. Musurillo, H. (1972) *The acts of the Christian Martyrs.* Oxford: Clarendon Press.

Justinus Martyr. Goodspeed, E. J. (1915) *Die ältesten Apologeten.* Göttingen: Vandenhoeck & Ruprecht.

Didache XII Apostolorum. Audet, J. P. (1958) *La Didachè. Instructions des Apôtres.* Paris: Lecoffre.

Evangelium Aegyptium. Klostermann, E. (1910) *Apocrypha II. Evangelien.* Bonn: Marcus & Weber.

Evangelium Petri. Mara, M. G. (1973) *Évangile de Pierre.* Paris: Cerf.

Josephus et Aseneth. Philonenko, M. (1968) *Joseph et Aséneth.* Leiden: Brill.

Martyrium et Ascensio Isaiae. Denis, A.-M. (1970) *Fragmenta pseudepigraphorum quae supersunt Graeca.* Leiden: Brill.

Martyrium Ptolemaei et Lucii. Musurillo, H. (1972) *The acts of the Christian Martyrs.* Oxford: Clarendon Press.

Protevangelium Jacobi. Strycker, E. (1961) *La forme la plus ancienne du protévangile de Jacques.* Brussels: Société des Bollandistes.

Acta Andreae. Prieur, J.-M. (1989) *Acta Andreae.* Turnhout: Brepols.

Apocalypsis Joannis. Tischendorf, C. (1866) *Apocalypses apocryphae.* Leipzig: Mendelssohn.
Evangelium Thomae. Klostermann, E. (1910) *Apocrypha II. Evangelien.* Bonn: Marcus & Weber.
Acta Scillitanorum Martyrum. Robinson, J. A. (1891) *The passion of S. Perpetua.* Cambridge: Cambridge University Press.
Acta Alexandrinorum. Musurillo, H. (1961) *Acta Alexandrinorum.* Leipzig: Teubner.
Acta Justini et Septem Sodalium. Musurillo, H. (1972) *The acts of the Christian Martyrs.* Oxford: Clarendon Press.
Evangelium Ebionitum. Klostermann, E. (1910) *Apocrypha II. Evangelien.* Bonn: Marcus & Weber.
Testamentum Jobi. Brock, S. P. (1967) *Testamentum Jobi.* Leiden: Brill.
Evangelium Philippi. Klostermann, E. (1910) *Apocrypha II. Evangelien.* Bonn: Marcus & Weber.
Acta et Martyrium Apollonii. Musurillo, H. (1972) *The acts of the Christian Martyrs.* Oxford: Clarendon Press.

3rd century AD

Evangelium Bartholomaei. Bonwetsch, N. (1897) "Die apokryphen Fragen des Bartholomäus". *Nachrichten von der Gesellschaft der Wissenschaften zu Göttingen:* Philol.-hist. Kl.
Acta Thomae.
1. Bonnet, M. (1903) *Acta apostolorum apocrypha, vol. 2.2.* Leipzig: Mendelssohn.
2. James, M. R. (1897) *Apocrypha anecdota II.* Cambridge: Cambridge University Press.
3. Poirier, P.-H. (1981) *L'hymne de la perle des actes de Thomas.* Louvain-La-Neuve: Université Catholique de Louvain.

Acta Xanthippae et Polyxenae. James, M. R. (1893) *Apocrypha anecdota.* Cambridge: Cambridge University Press.

4th century AD

Athanasius, "*Vita St.Antonii*". Bartelink, G. J. M. (1994) *Athanase d'Alexandrie: Vie d'Antoine.* Paris: Cerf.
Constitutiones Apostolorum. Metzger, M. (1985–87) *Les constitutions apostoliques, 3 vols.* Paris: Cerf.
Martyrium Pionii. Musurillo, H. (1972) *The acts of the Christian Martyrs.* Oxford: Clarendon Press.
Palladius.
1. Bartelink, G. J. M. (1974) *Palladio. La storia Lausiaca.* Verona: Fondazione Lorenzo Valla.
2. "Proemium ad historiam Lausiacam, Epistula ad Lausum": Butler, C. (1904) *The Lausiac history of Palladius.* Cambridge: Cambridge University Press.
3. Coleman-Norton, P. R. (1928) *Palladii dialogus de vita S. Joanni Chrysostomi.* Cambridge: Cambridge University Press.

4. Berghoff, W. (1967) *Palladius. De gentibus Indiae et Bragmanibus.* Meisenheim am Glan: Hain.

Works consulted, but not included in the corpus of the quantitative study
Strabo (1st c. BC–1st c. AD). Meineke, A. (1877) *Strabonis geographica, 3 vols.* Leipzig: Teubner.
Epictetus, "Dissertationes" (1st c. AD). Schenkl, H. (1916) *Epicteti dissertationes ab Arriano digestae.* Leipzig: Teubner.
Plutarchus (1st–2nd c. AD).
1. Ziegler, K. (1969) *Plutarchi vitae parallelae.* Leipzig: Teubner.
2. Perrin, B. (1914) *Plutarch's lives.* Cambridge, Mass.: Harvard University Press.
3. Nachstädt, W., J. B. Titchener, W. Sieveking, M. Pohlenz C. Hubert, J. Mau, R. Westman, K. Ziegler, W. Pohlenz & F. H. Sandbach (1971) *Plutarchi moralia.* Leipzig: Teubner.
4. Babbitt, F. C. & H. N. Fowler (1927–36) *Plutarch's moralia.* Cambridge, Mass.: Harvard University Press.

Apollonius Dyscolus (2nd c. AD). Schneider, R. & G. Uhlig (1878–1910) *Grammatici Graeci.* Leipzig: Teubner.
Pausanias (2nd c. AD). Spiro, F. (1903) *Pausaniae Graeciae descriptio, 3 vols.* Leipzig: Teubner.
Phrynichus, "Eclogae" (2nd c. AD). Fischer, E. (1974) *Die Ekloge des Phrynichos.* Berlin: Mouton de Gruyter.
Porphyrius, "Contra Christianos (fragm.)" (3rd c. AD). von Harnack, A. (1916) *Porphyrius: Gegen die Christen.* Berlin: Reimer.

Papyri
BGU = *Aegyptische Urkunden aus den Königlichen* (later *Staatlichen*) *Museen zu Berlin, Griechische Urkunden.* Berlin. Vols. 1–18 (1895–2000).
CPR = *Corpus Papyrorum Raineri.* Vienna. Vols. 1–24 (1895–2002).
P.Aberd. = *Catalogue of Greek and Latin Papyri and Ostraca in the Possession of the University of Aberdeen,* ed. E. G. Turner. Aberdeen: 1939.
P.Abinn. = *The Abinnaeus Archive: Papers of a Roman Officer in the Reign of Constantius II,* ed. H. I. Bell, V. Martin, E. G. Turner & D. van Berchem. Oxford: 1962.
P.Achm. = *Les Papyrus grecs d'Achmîm à la Bibliothèque Nationale de Paris,* ed. P. Collart. Cairo: 1930.
P.Adl. = *The Adler Papyri,* ed. E. N. Adler, J. G. Tait & F. M. Heichelheim. Oxford: 1939.
P.Alex. = *Papyrus grecs du Musée Gréco-Romain d'Alexandrie,* ed. A. Swiderek & M. Vandoni. Warsaw: 1964.
P.Alex.Giss. = *Papyri variae Alexandrinae et Gissenses,* ed. J. Schwartz. Brussels: 1969.

P.Amh. = *The Amherst Papyri, Being an Account of the Greek Papyri in the Collection of the Right Hon. Lord Amherst of Hackney, F.S.A. at Didlington Hall, Norfolk*, ed. B. P. Grenfell & A. S. Hunt. London. Vols. 1–2 (1900–01).

P.Ammon = *The Archive of Ammon Scholasticus of Panopolis.* I: *The Legacy of Harpocration*, ed. W. H. Willis & K. Maresch. Opladen: 1997.

P.Amst. I = *Die Amsterdamer Papyri* I, ed. R. P. Salomons, P. J. Sijpesteijn & K. A. Worp. Zutphen: 1980.

P.Anag. = *Corpus Papyrorum Anagennesis*, ed. F. Farid. Athens: 1986.

P.Ant. = *The Antinoopolis Papyri*. London. Vols. 1–3 (1950–67).

P.Aphrod.Lit. = *Hellénisme dans l'Égypte du VIe siècle. La bibliothèque et l'œuvre de Dioscore d'Aphrodité*, ed. J.-L. Fournet. Cairo: 1999.

P.Apoll. = *Papyrus grecs d'Apollônos Anô*, ed. R. Rémondon. Cairo: 1953.

P.Ashm. = *Catalogue of the Demotic Papyri in the Ashmolean Museum.* I: *Embalmers' Archives from Hawara*, ed. E. A. E. Reymond & J. W. B. Barns. Oxford: 1973.

P.Athen. = *Papyri Societatis Archaeologicae Atheniensis*, ed. G.A. Petropoulos. Athens: 1939.

P.Athen.Xyla = *P.Sta.Xyla: The Byzantine Papyri of the Greek Papyrological Society* I, ed. B. G. Mandilaras. Athens: 1993.

P.Aust.Herr. = *P.Trophitis: New Ptolemaic Texts Relating to Egyptian Alimentary and Sale Contracts. Greek Abstracts from a Kibotos Archive*, ed. R. G. Herring. University of Texas: 1989.

P.Bacch. = "The Archives of the Temple of Soknobraisis at Bacchias," ed. E. H. Gilliam. *Yale Classical Studies* 10 (1947): 179–281.

P.Bad. = *Veröffentlichungen aus den badischen Papyrus-Sammlungen*. Heidelberg. Vols. 1–6 (1923–38).

P.Bal. = *Bala'izah: Coptic Texts from Deir el-Bala'izah in Upper Egypt*, ed. P. E. Kahle. London: 1954.

P.Bas. = *Papyrusurkunden der Öffentlichen Bibliothek der Universität zu Basel: Pt. I, Urkunden in griechischer Sprache*, ed. E. Rabel. Berlin: 1917.

P.Batav. = *Textes grecs, démotiques et bilingues*, ed. E. Boswinkel & P. W. Pestman. Leiden: 1978.

P.Benaki = *Greek Papyri in the Benaki Museum, from the Collections of the Historical Archive*, ed. E. Papapolychroniou. Athens: 2000.

P.Berl.Bibl. = *Frammenti di papiri greci asservati nella Reale Biblioteca di Berlino*, ed. G. Parthey. Rome: 1865.

P.Berl.Bork. = *Une description topographique des immeubles à Panopolis*, ed. Z. Borkowski. Warsaw: 1975.

P.Berl.Brash. = *Select Papyri from West-Berlin*, ed. W. M. Brashear. University of Michigan, Ann Arbor: 1973.

P.Berl.Frisk = *Bankakten aus dem Faijûm nebst anderen Berliner Papyri*, ed. H. Frisk. Gothenburg: 1931.

P.Berl.Leihg. = *Berliner Leihgabe griechischer Papyri*. Berlin. Vols. 1–2 (1932–77).

P.Berl.Möller = *Griechische Papyri aus dem Berliner Museum*, ed. S. Möller. Gothenburg: 1929.

P.Berl.Salmen. = *Cartonnage Papyri in Context: New Ptolemaic Documents from Abu Sir al Malaq*, ed. E. Salmenkivi. Helsinki: 2002.

P.Berl.Sarisch. = *Berliner griechische Papyri, Christliche literarische Texte und Urkunden aus dem 3. bis 8. Jh.n.Chr.*, ed. P. Sarischouli. Wiesbaden: 1995.

P.Berl.Schmidt = *Die griechischen Papyrusurkunden der Königlichen Bibliothek zu Berlin*, ed. W. A. Schmidt. Berlin: 1842.

P.Berl.Thun. = *Sitologen-Papyri aus dem Berliner Museum*, ed. K. Thunell. Uppsala: 1924.

P.Berl.Zill. = *Vierzehn Berliner griechische Papyri*, ed. H. Zilliacus. Helsingfors: 1941.

P.Bingen = *Papyri in Honorem Johannis Bingen Octogenarii*, ed. H. Melaerts. Leuven: 2000.

P.Bodl. I = *Papyri Bodleianae I*, ed. R. P. Salomons. Amsterdam: 1996.

P.Bon. = *Papyri Bononienses*, ed. O. Montevecchi. Milan: 1953.

P.Bour. = *Les Papyrus Bouriant*, ed. P. Collart. Paris: 1926.

P.Brem. = *Die Bremer Papyri*, ed. U. Wilcken. Berlin: 1936.

P.Brookl. = *Greek and Latin Papyri, Ostraca, and Wooden Tablets in the Collection of the Brooklyn Museum*, ed. J. C. Shelton. Florence: 1992.

P.Brux. = *Papyri Bruxellenses Graecae*. Brussels. Vols. 1–2 (1974–91).

P.Bub. = *Die verkohlten Papyri aus Bubastos*. Opladen. Vols. 1–2 (1989–98).

P.Cair.Goodsp. = *Greek Papyri from the Cairo Museum*, ed. E. J. Goodspeed. Chicago: 1902.

P.Cair.Isid. = *The Archive of Aurelius Isidorus in the Egyptian Museum, Cairo, and the University of Michigan*, ed. A. E. R. Boak & H. C. Youtie. Ann Arbor: 1960.

P.Cair.Mas. = *Papyrus grecs d'époque byzantine, Catalogue général des antiquités égyptiennes du Musée du Caire*, ed. J. Maspero. Cairo. Vols. 1–3 (1911–16).

P.Cair.Mich. = *A Tax List from Karanis (P.Cair.Mich. 359)*, ed. H. Riad & J. C. Shelton. Bonn: 1976.

P.Cair.Preis. = *Griechische Urkunden des Aegyptischen Museums zu Kairo*, ed. F. Preisigke. Strassburg: 1911.

P.Cair.Zen. = *Zenon Papyri, Catalogue général des antiquités égyptiennes du Musée du Caire*, ed. C. C. Edgar. Cairo. Vols. 1–5 (1925–40).

P.Charite = *Das Aurelia Charite Archiv*, ed. K. A. Worp. Zutphen: 1981.

P.Chic.Haw. = *Oriental Institute Hawara Papyri: Demotic and Greek Texts from an Egyptian Family Archive in the Fayum (Fourth to Third Century BC)*, ed. G. R. Hughes & R. Jasnow. Chicago: 1997.

P.Col. = *Columbia Papyri*. Vols. 1–11 (1929–98).

P.Coll.Youtie = *Collectanea Papyrologica: Texts Published in Honor of H. C. Youtie*, ed. A. E. Hanson et al. Bonn: 1976.

P.Congr.XV = *Actes du XVe Congrès International de Papyrologie II, Papyrus inédits*, ed. J. Bingen & G. Nachtergael. Brussels: 1979.

P.Corn. = *Greek Papyri in the Library of Cornell University*, ed. W. L. Westermann & C. J. Kraemer, Jr. New York: 1926.

P.Customs = *Customs Duties in Graeco-Roman Egypt*, ed. P. J. Sijpesteijn. Zutphen: 1987.

P.David = *Antidoron Martino David oblatum, Miscellanea Papyrologica*, ed. E. Boswinkel, B. A. van Groningen & P. W. Pestman. Leiden: 1968.

P.Diog. = *Les archives de Marcus Lucretius Diogenes et textes apparentés*, ed. P. Schubert. Bonn: 1990.

P.Dion. = *Les archives privés de Dionysios, fils de Kephalas*, ed. E. Boswinkel & P. W. Pestman. Leiden: 1982.

P.Dion.Herm. = *Greek Papyrus Documents from Dionysias and from the Cairo Museum*, ed. M. A. I. Aly. Cairo: 2001.

P.Diosk. = *Das Archiv des Phrurarchen Dioskurides*, ed. J. M. S. Cowey, K. Maresch & C. Barnes. Paderborn: 2003.

P.Dryton = *The Bilingual Family Archive of Dryton, his Wife Apollonia and their Daughter Senmouthis*, ed. K. Vandorpe. Brussels: 2002.

P.Dubl. = *Greek Papyri from Dublin*, ed. B. C. McGing. Bonn: 1995.

P.Dura = *The Excavations at Dura-Europos conducted by Yale University and the French Academy of Inscriptions and Letters, Final Report V, Part I, The Parchments and Papyri*, ed. C. B. Welles, R. O. Fink & J. F. Gilliam. New Haven: 1959.

P.Edfou = Papyri published in *Fouilles Franco-Polonaises* I–III (1937–39).

P.Eleph. = *Aegyptische Urkunden aus den Königlichen Museen in Berlin: Griechische Urkunden*, Sonderheft. *Elephantine-Papyri*, ed. O. Rubensohn. Berlin: 1907.

P.Eleph.Wagner = *Elephantine XIII: Les papyrus et les ostraca grecs d'Elephantine*, ed. G. Wagner. Mainz: 1998.

P.Enteux. = ΕΝΤΕΥΞΕΙΣ: *Requêtes et plaintes adressées au Roi d'Égypte au IIIe siècle avant J.-C.*, ed. O. Guéraud. Cairo: 1931.

P.Erasm. = *Papyri in the Collection of the Erasmus University (Rotterdam)*. Vols. 1–2 (1986–91).

P.Erl. = *Die Papyri der Universitätsbibliothek Erlangen*, ed. W. Schubart. Leipzig: 1942.

P.Fam.Tebt. = *A Family Archive from Tebtunis*, ed. B. A. van Groningen. Leiden: 1950.

P.Fay. = *Fayum Towns and their Papyri*, ed. B. P. Grenfell, A. S. Hunt & D. G. Hogarth. London: 1900.

P.Flor. = *Papiri greco-egizii, Papiri Fiorentini* (Supplementi Filologico-Storici ai Monumenti Antichi). Milan. Vols. 1–3 (1906–15).

P.Fouad = *Les Papyrus Fouad I*, ed. A. Bataille, O. Guéraud, P. Jouguet, N. Lewis, H. Marrou, J. Scherer & W. G. Waddell. Cairo: 1939.

P.Frankf. = *Griechische Papyri aus dem Besitz des Rechtswissenschaftlichen Seminars der Universität Frankfurt*, ed. H. Lewald. Heidelberg: 1920.

P.Freer = *Greek and Coptic Papyri in the Freer Gallery of Art*, ed. L. S. B. MacCoull. University of Washington D.C.: 1973.

P.Freib. = *Mitteilungen aus der Freiburger Papyrussammlung*. Freiburg. Vols. 1–4 (1914–86).

P.FuadUniv. (or P.FuadCrawford) = *Fuad I University Papyri*, ed. D.S. Crawford. Alexandria: 1949.

P.Gen. = *Les Papyrus de Genève*. Geneva. Vols. 1–3 (1896–1996).

P.Genova = *Papiri dell'Università di Genova*. Genova. Vols. 1–3 (1974–91).

P.Giss. = *Griechische Papyri im Museum des oberhessischen Geschichtsvereins zu Giessen*, ed. O. Eger, E. Kornemann & P. M. Meyer. Leipzig-Berlin: 1910–12.

P.Giss.Apoll. = *Briefe des Apollonios-Archives aus der Sammlung Papyri Gissenses*, ed. M. Kortus. Giessen: 1999.

P.Giss.Univ. = *Mitteilungen aus der Papyrussammlung der Giessener Universitätsbibliothek*. Giessen. Vols. 1–6 (1924–39).

P.Got. = *Papyrus grecs de la Bibliothèque municipale de Gothembourg*, ed. H. Frisk. Gothenburg: 1929.

P.Grad. = *Griechische Papyri der Sammlung Gradenwitz*, ed. G. Plaumann. Heidelberg: 1914.

P.Graux = *Papyrus Graux*. Geneva. Vols. 1–4 (1923–2004).

P.Grenf. =

I. *An Alexandrian Erotic Fragment and other Greek Papyri chiefly Ptolemaic*, ed. B. P. Grenfell. Oxford: 1896.

II: *New Classical Fragments and Other Greek and Latin Papyri*, ed. B. P.Grenfell & A. S. Hunt. Oxford: 1897.

P.Gron. = *Papyri Groninganae; Griechische Papyri der Universitätsbibliothek zu Groningen nebst zwei Papyri der Universitätsbibliothek zu Amsterdam*, ed. A. G. Roos. Amsterdam: 1933.

P.Gur. = *Greek Papyri from Gurob*, ed. J. G. Smyly. Dublin: 1921.

P.Hal. = *Dikaiomata: Auszüge aus alexandrinischen Gesetzen und Verordnungen in einem Papyrus des Philologischen Seminars der Universität Halle (Pap.Hal. 1) mit einem Anhang weiterer Papyri derselben Sammlung*, ed. Graeca Halensis. Berlin: 1913.

P.Hamb. = *Griechische Papyrusurkunden der Hamburger Staats- und Universitätsbibliothek*. Hamburg. Vols. 1–4 (1911–98).

P.Harr. = *The Rendel Harris Papyri of Woodbrooke College, Birmingham*. Birmingham. Vols. 1–2 (1936–85).

P.Harrauer = *Wiener Papyri als Festgabe zum 60. Geburtstag von Hermann Harrauer*, ed. B. Palme. Vienna: 2001.

P.Haun. = *Papyri Graecae Haunienses*. Copenhagen. Vols. 1–3 (1942–85).

P.Heid. = *Veröffentlichungen aus der Heidelberger Papyrussammlung*. Heidelberg. Vols. 1–8 (1956–2001).

P.Hels. = *Papyri Helsingienses I, Ptolemäische Urkunden*, ed. J. Frösén, P. Hohti, J. and M. Kaimio & H. Zilliacus. Helsinki: 1986.

P.Herm. = *Papyri from Hermopolis and Other Documents of the Byzantine Period*, ed. B. R. Rees. London: 1964.

P.Herm.Landl. = *Zwei Landlisten aus dem Hermupolites (P.Giss. 117 und P.Flor. 71)*, ed. P. J. Sijpesteijn & K. A. Worp. Zutphen: 1978.

P.Hever = *Aramaic, Hebrew and Greek Documentary Texts from Nahal Hever and Other Sites, with an Appendix containing Alleged Qumran Texts (The Seiyâl Collection II)*, ed. H. M. Cotton & A. Yardeni. Oxford: 1997.

P.Hib. = *The Hibeh Papyri*. London. Vols. 1–2 (1906–55).

P.Hombert = *La Collection Marcel Hombert*, ed. G. Nachtergael. Brussels. Vols. 1–2 (1978–2003).

P.Iand. = *Papyri Iandanae*, ed. C. Kalbfleisch et al. Leipzig. Vols. 1–8 (1912–38).

P.IFAO = *Papyrus grecs de l'Institut Français d'Archéologie Orientale*. Cairo. Vols. 1–3 (1971–75).

P.Jena = *Jenäer Papyrus-Urkunden*, ed. F. Zucker & F. Schneider. Jena: 1926.

P.Jud.Des.Misc. = *Miscellaneous Texts from the Judaean Desert*, multiple editors. Oxford: 2000.

P.Kar.Goodsp. = *Papyri from Karanis*, ed. E. J. Goodspeed. Chicago: 1902.

P.Kellis = *Papyri from Kellis*. Oxford. Vols. 1–5 (1995–99).

P.Köln = *Kölner Papyri*. Köln. Vols. 1–10 (1976–2003).

P.Kroll = *Eine ptolemäische Königsurkunde*, ed. L. Koenen. Wiesbaden: 1957.

P.Kron. = *L'Archivio di Kronion*, ed. D. Foraboschi. Milan: 1971.

P.Laur. = *Dai Papiri della Biblioteca Medicea Laurenziana*. Florence. Vols. 1–5 (1976–84).

P.LeedsMus. = *A Selective Publication and Description of the Greek Papyri in the Leeds City Museum*, ed. S. Strassi. Leeds: 1983.

P.Leid.Inst. = *Papyri, Ostraca, Parchments and Waxed Tablets in the Leiden Papyrological Institute*, ed. F. A. J. Hoogendijk & P. van Minnen. Leiden: 1991.

P.Leipz. = *Die griechischen Papyri der Leipziger Universitätsbibliothek*, ed. C. Wessely. Leipzig: 1885.

P.Leit. = *Leitourgia Papyri*, ed. N. Lewis. Philadelphia: 1963.

P.Lille = *Papyrus grecs (Institut Papyrologique de l'Université de Lille)*. Lille. Vols. 1–2 (1907–12).

P.Lips. (see also *P.Leipz.*) = *Griechische Urkunden der Papyrussammlung zu Leipzig*. Vols. 1–2 (1906–2002).

P.Lond. = *Greek Papyri in the British Museum*. London. Vols 1–7 (1893–1974).

P.Louvre I = *Griechische Papyri aus Soknopaiu Nesos*, ed. A. Jördens mit Beiträgen von K.-Th. Zauzich. Bonn: 1998.

P.Lund = *Aus der Papyrussammlung der Universitätsbibliothek in Lund*. Lund. Vols. 1–6 (1934–52).

P.Marm. = *Il papiro vaticano greco 11*, ed. M. Norsa & G. Vitelli. Vatican City: 1931.

P.Masada = *Masada II, The Yigael Yadin Excavations 1963–65, Final Reports: The Latin and Greek Documents*, ed. H. M. Cotton & J. Geiger. Jerusalem: 1989.

P.Matr. = *Dieci Papyri Matritenses*, ed. S. Daris. Madrid: 1990.

P.Mert. = *A Descriptive Catalogue of the Greek Papyri in the Collection of Wilfred Merton*. London – Dublin. Vols. 1–3 (1948–67).

P.Meyer = *Griechische Texte aus Aegypten. I, Papyri des Neutestamentlichen Seminars der Universität Berlin; II, Ostraka der Sammlung Deissmann*, ed. P. M. Meyer. Berlin: 1916.

P.Mich. = *Michigan Papyri*. Michigan. Vols. 1–19 (1931–99).

P.Michael. = *Papyri Michaelidae, being a Catalogue of Greek and Latin Papyri, Tablets and Ostraca in the Library of Mr G. A. Michailidis of Cairo*, ed. D. S. Crawford. Aberdeen: 1955.

P.Mil. = *Papiri Milanesi*. Milan. Vols. 1–2 (1966–67).

P.Mil.Congr.XIV = *Papiri documentari dell'Università Cattolica di Milano*, multiple editors. Milan: 1974.

P.Mil.Congr.XVII = *Papiri documentari dell'Università Cattolica di Milano*, ed. O. Montevecchi et al. Milan: 1983.

P.Mil.Congr.XVIII = *Papiri documentari dell'Università Cattolica di Milano*, various editors. Milan: 1986.

P.Mil.Congr.XIX = *Papiri documentari dell'Università Cattolica di Milano*, various editors. Milan: 1989.

P.Mil.Vogl. = *Papiri della R. Università di Milano*. Milan. Vols. 1–8 (1937–2001).

P.Mon.Apollo = *Coptic and Greek texts relating to the Hermopolite Monastery of Apa Apollo*, ed. S. J. Clackson. Oxford: 2000.

P.Münch. = *Die Papyri der Bayerischen Staatsbibliothek München*. Munich. Vols. 1–3 (1986).

P.Murabba'ât = *Les grottes de Murabba'ât*, ed. P. Benoit, J. T. Milik & R. de Vaux. Oxford: 1961.

P.NagHamm. = *Nag Hammadi Codices. Greek and Coptic Papyri from the Cartonnage of the Covers*, ed. J. W. B. Barns, G. M. Browne & J. C. Shelton. Leiden: 1981.

P.Naqlun = *Deir El-Naqlun: The Greek Papyri*. I: ed. T. Derda. Warsaw: 1995.

P.Neph. = *Das Archiv des Nepheros und verwandte Texte*, ed. B. Kramer, J. C. Shelton & G. M. Browne. Mainz: 1987.

P.Ness. = *Excavations at Nessana*. London – Princeton. Vols. 1–3 (1950–62).

P.NYU = *Greek Papyri in the Collection of New York University*. New York. Vols. 1–2 (1967–2004).

P.Oslo = *Papyri Osloenses*. Oslo. Vols. 1–3 (1925–36).

P.Oxf. = *Some Oxford Papyri*, ed. E. P. Wegener. Leiden: 1942.

P.Oxy. = *The Oxyrhynchus Papyri*. London. Vols. 1–68 (1898–2003).

P.Oxy.Astr. = *The Astronomical Papyri from Oxyrhynchus*, ed. A. Jones. Philadelphia: 1999.

P.Oxy.Hels. = *Fifty Oxyrhynchus Papyri*, ed. H. Zilliacus, J. Frösén, P. Hohti, J. Kaimio & M. Kaimio. Helsinki: 1979.

P.Panop. = *Urkunden aus Panopolis*, ed. L. C. Youtie, D. Hagedorn & H. C. Youtie. Bonn: 1980.

P.Panop.Beatty = *Papyri from Panopolis in the Chester Beatty Library Dublin*, ed. T. C. Skeat. Dublin: 1964.

P.Paris = *Notices et textes des papyrus du Musée du Louvre et de la Bibliothèque Impériale*, ed. J. A. Letronne, W. Brunet de Presle & E. Egger. Paris: 1865.

P.Petaus = *Das Archiv des Petaus*, ed. U. Hagedorn, D. Hagedorn, L. C. Youtie & H. C. Youtie. Opladen: 1969.

P.Petr. = *The Flinders Petrie Papyri*. Dublin. Vols. 1–3 (1891–1905).
P.Petr.² I = *The Petrie Papyri, Second Edition* 1, *The Wills*, ed. W. Clarysse. Brussels: 1991.
P.Petra = *The Petra Papyri* I, ed. J. Frösén, A. Arjava & M. Lehtinen with contributions by Z. T. Fiema, C. A. Kuehn, T. Purola, T. Rankinen, M. Vesterinen & M. Vierros. Amman: 2002.
P.Phil. = *Papyrus de Philadelphie*, ed. J. Scherer. Cairo: 1947.
P.Polit.Jud. = *Urkunden des Politeuma der Juden von Herakleopolis (144/3, 133/2 v Chr.)*, ed. K. Maresch & J. M. S. Cowey. Wiesbaden: 2001.
P.Pommersf. = *Ein frühbyzantinisches Szenario für die Amtswechslung in der Sitonie: die griechischen Papyri aus Pommersfelden (PPG), mit einem Anhang über die Pommersfeldener Digestenfragmente und die Überlieferungsgeschichte der Digesten*, ed. A. J. B. Sirks, P. J. Sijpesteijn & K. A. Worp. Munich: 1996.
P.Prag. = *Papyri Graecae Wessely Pragenses*, ed. R. Pintaudi, R. Dostálová & L. Vidman. Firenze. Vols. 1–2 (1988–95).
P.Prag.Varcl = *Papyri Wessely Pragenses*, ed. L. Varcl. *Listy Filologické*. Vols. 1–2 (1946–61).
P.Princ. = *Papyri in the Princeton University Collections*. Princeton. Vols. 1–3 (1931–42).
P.Quseir = "Papyri and Ostraka from Quseir al-Qadim", ed. R. S. Bagnall. *Bulletin of the American Society of Papyrologists* 23 (1986): 1–60.
P.Rain.Cent. = *Festschrift zum 100-jährigen Bestehen der Papyrussammlung der Österreichischen Nationalbibliothek, Papyrus Erzherzog Rainer*. Vienna: 1983.
P.Rein. I = *Papyrus grecs et démotiques recueillis en Égypte*, ed. T. Reinach, W. Spiegelberg & S. de Ricci. Paris: 1905.
P.Rev. = *Revenue Laws of Ptolemy Philadelphus*, ed. B. P. Grenfell. Oxford: 1896.
P.Ross.Georg. = *Papyri russischer und georgischer Sammlungen*. Tiflis. Vols. 1–5 (1925–35).
P.Ryl. = *Catalogue of the Greek and Latin Papyri in the John Rylands Library, Manchester*. Manchester. Vols. 1–4 (1911–52).
P.Sakaon = *The Archive of Aurelius Sakaon: Papers of an Egyptian Farmer in the last Century of Theadelphia*, ed. G. M. Parássoglou. Bonn: 1978.
P.Sarap. = *Les archives de Sarapion et de ses fils: une exploitation agricole aux environs d'Hermoupolis Magna (de 90 à 133 p.C.)*, ed. J. Schwartz. Cairo: 1961.
P.Select. = *Papyri Selectae*, ed. E. Boswinkel, P. W. Pestman & P. J. Sijpesteijn. Leiden: 1965.
P.Sel.Warga = *Select Papyri*, ed. R. G. Warga, Jr. University of Illinois at Urbana-Champaign: 1988.
PSI = *Papiri greci e latini*. Florence. Vols. 1–15 (1912–79).
PSI Congr.XI = *Dai papiri della Società Italiana: Omaggio all'XI Congresso Internazionale di Papirologia*. Florence: 1965.
PSI Congr.XVII = *Trenta testi greci da papiri letterari e documentari editi in occasione del XVII Congresso Internazionale di Papirologia*. Florence: 1983.

PSI Congr.XX = *Dai papiri della Società Italiana: Omaggio al XX Congresso Internazionale di Papirologia.* Florence: 1992.

PSI Congr.XXI = *Dai papiri della Società Italiana: Omaggio al XXI Congresso Internazionale di Papirologia.* Florence: 1995.

PSI Corr. I = *Correzioni e riedizioni di papiri della Società Italiana* I, ed. M. Manfredi. Florence: 1977.

P.Sorb. = *Papyrus de la Sorbonne.* Paris-Atlanta. Vols. 1–2 (1966–94).

P.Soter. = *Das Archiv des Soterichos*, ed. S. Omar. Opladen: 1979.

P.Stras. = *Griechische Papyrus der Kaiserlichen Universitäts- und Landes-bibliothek zu Strassburg.* Leipzig. Vols. 1–9 (1912–89).

P.Tebt. = *The Tebtunis Papyri.* London. Vols. 1–5 (1902–2005).

P.Tebt.Tait = *Papyri from Tebtunis in Egyptian and Greek*, ed. W. J. Tait. London: 1977.

P.Tebt.Wall = *New Texts in the Economy of Tebtunis*, ed. E. W. Wall. Duke University, Durham, N.C.: 1983.

P.Theon. = *The Family of the Tiberii Iulii Theones*, ed. P. J. Sijpesteijn. Amsterdam: 1976.

P.Thmouis = *Le Papyrus Thmouis 1, colonnes 68–160*, ed. S. Kambitsis. Paris: 1985.

P.Thomas = *Essays and Texts in Honor of J. David Thomas*, ed. T. Gagos & R. S. Bagnall. Oakville: 2001.

P.Tor.Amen. = *L'Archivio di Amenothes figlio di Horos. Testi demotici e greci relativi ad una famiglia di imbalsamatori del secondo sec. a.C.*, ed. P. W. Pestman. Milan: 1981.

P.Tor.Choach. = *Il Processo di Hermias e altri documenti dell'archivio dei choachiti, papiri greci e demotici conservati a Torino e in altre collezioni d'Italia*, ed. P. W. Pestman. Turin: 1992.

P.Turner = *Papyri Greek and Egyptian Edited by Various Hands in Honour of Eric Gardner Turner on the Occasion of his Seventieth Birthday*, ed. P. J. Parsons, J. R. Rea, et al. London: 1981.

P.Ups.Frid = *Ten Uppsala Papyri*, ed. B. Frid. Bonn: 1981.

P.Vars. = *Papyri Varsovienses*, ed. G. Manteuffel, L. Zawadowski & C. Rozenberg. Warsaw: 1935.

P.Vat.Aphrod. = *I Papiri Vaticani di Aphrodito*, ed. R. Pintaudi. Rome: 1980.

P.Vind.Bosw. = *Einige Wiener Papyri*, ed. E. Boswinkel. Leiden: 1942.

P.Vind.Sal. = *Einige Wiener Papyri*, ed. R. P. Salomons. Amsterdam: 1976.

P.Vind.Sijp. = *Einige Wiener Papyri*, ed. P. J. Sijpesteijn. Leiden: 1963.

P.Vind.Tand. = *Fünfunddreissig Wiener Papyri*, ed. P. J. Sijpesteijn & K.A. Worp. Zutphen: 1976.

P.Vind.Worp = *Einige Wiener Papyri*, ed. K. A. Worp. Amsterdam: 1972.

P.Warr. = *The Warren Papyri*, ed. M. David, B. A. van Groningen, & J. C. van Oven. Leiden: 1941.

P.Wash.Univ. = *Washington University Papyri.* Washington. Vols. 1–2 (1980–90).

P.Wisc. = *The Wisconsin Papyri*, ed. P. J. Sijpesteijn. Wisconsin. Vols. 1–2 (1967–77).

P.Würzb. = *Mitteilungen aus der Würzburger Papyrussammlung*, ed. U. Wilcken. Berlin: 1934.

P.Yale = *Yale Papyri in the Beinecke Rare Book and Manuscript Library.* Yale. Vols. 1–3 (1967–2001).
P.Zen.Pestm. = *Greek and Demotic Texts from the Zenon Archive,* ed. under the general direction of P. W. Pestman. Leiden: 1980.
SB = *Sammelbuch griechischer Urkunden aus Aegypten.* Vols. 1–24 (1913–2003).
UPZ = *Urkunden der Ptolemäerzeit (ältere Funde),* ed. U. Wilcken. Berlin-Leipzig. Vols. 1–2 (1927–57).

Early Medieval period (5th–10th c. AD)

5th century
Callinicus Hagiographus. Bartelink, G. J. M. (1971) *Callinicos. Vie d'Hypatios.* Paris: Cerf.
Marinus Neapolitanus.
1. Masullo, R. (1985) *Marino di Neapoli. Vita di Proclo.* Napoli: d'Auria.
2. "Commentarium in Euclidis data": Menge, H. (1896) *Euclidis opera omnia.* Leipzig: Teubner.

Sozomenus. Bidez, J. & G. C. Hansen (1960) *Sozomenus. Kirchengeschichte.* Berlin: Akademie-Verlag.
Historia monachorum in Aegypto. Festugière, A. J. (1971) *Historia monachorum in Aegypto.* Brussels: Société des Bollandistes.
Antonius Hagiographus. Lietzmann, H. (1908) *Das Leben des heiligen Symeon Stylites.* Leipzig: Hinrichs.
Nilus Ancyranus.
1. Conca, F. (1983) *Nilus Ancyranus. Narratio.* Leipzig: Teubner.
2. Guérard, M.–G. (1994) *Commentaire sur le Cantique des cantiques.* Paris: Cerf.

6th century
Joannes Malalas. Thurn, I. (2000) *Ioannis Malalae chronographia.* Berlin: Mouton de Gruyter.
Stephanus. Meineke, A. (1849) *Stephan von Byzanz. Ethnika.* Berlin: Reimer.
Moschos, "Spiritual Meadow". Migne, J.-P. (1857–66) *Patrologiae cursus completus (series Graeca)* 87: 2852–3112. Paris: Garnier.
Maximus Confessor.
1. Laga, C. & C. Steel (1980) *Maximi confessoris quaestiones ad Thalassium i: quaestiones i–lv.* Turnhout: Brepols.
2. Declerck, J. H. (1982) *Maximi confessoris quaestiones et dubia.* Turnhout: Brepols.
3. "Opusculum de anima, Mystagogia, Liber asceticus, Hymni": Cantarella, R. (1931) *S. Massimo Confessore. La mistagogia ed altri scritti.* Firenze: Testi Cristiani.
4. "Expositio in Psalmum lix, Expositio orationis dominicae": van Deun, P. (1991) *Maximi confessoris opuscula exegetica duo.* Turnhout: Brepols.
5. Ceresa-Gastaldo, A. (1963) *Massimo confessore. Capitoli sulla carità.* Roma: Editrice Studium.
6. Lucà, S. (1983) *Anonymus in Ecclesiasten commentarius qui dicitur catena trium patrum.* Turnhout: Brepols.

7th century
Chronicon Paschale. Dindorf, L. (1832) *Chronicon paschale*. Bonn: Weber.
Miracula Sancti Artemii. Papadopoulos-Kerameus, A. (1909) *Varia graeca sacra*. St. Petersburg: Kirschbaum.
Leontius.
1. Festugière, A.-J. & L. Rydén (1974) *Léontios de Néapolis, Vie de Syméon le Fou et Vie de Jean de Chypre*. Paris: Geuthner.
2. Déroche, V. (1994) "L'Apologie contre les Juifs de Léontios de Néapolis". *Travaux et Mémoires* 12: 61–63, 65–71, 79–84.

8th–9th centuries
Theophanes Confessor. de Boor, C. (1883) *Theophanis chronographia*. Leipzig: Teubner.

10th century
Constantinus VII Porphyrogenitus.
1. Moravcsik, G. – R. J. H. Jenkins (1967) *Constantine Porphyrogenitus. De administrando imperio, 2nd edition*. Washington, D.C.: Dumbarton Oaks.
2. Reiske, J. J. (1829) *Constantini Porphyrogeniti imperatoris de cerimoniis aulae Byzantinae libri duo*. Bonn: Weber.
Arethas, "Epistula ad ameram Damascenum". Westerink, L. G. (1968) *Arethae archiepiscopi Caesariensis scripta minora, vol. 1*, 233–45. Leipzig: Teubner.
"Death poems". Ševčenko, I. (1970) "Poems on the Deaths of Leo VI and Constantine VII in the Madrid Manuscript of Scylitzes". *Dumbarton Oaks Papers* 24: 185–228.

Works consulted, but not included in the corpus of the quantitative study
Epanagoge (9th c.).
1. Zepos, P. (1931) *Leges Imperatorum Isaurorum et Macedonum* [Jus Graecoromanum 2]. Athens: Fexis.
2. Zepos, P. (1931) *Ecloga Privata Aucta* [Jus Graecoromanum 6]. Athens: Fexis.
Constantinus VII Porphyrogenitus, "de insidiis" (10th c.) de Boor, C. (1905) *Excerpta historica iussu imp. Constantini Porphyrogeniti confecta, vol. 3: excerpta de insidiis*. Berlin: Weidmann.

Late Medieval period
I. Literary texts in the vernacular (editions and basic information)
11th century
The song of Armouris (197 verses). Alexiou, S. (1985) *Vasileios Digenis Akritis kai to Asma tou Armouri*. Athina: Ermis.
This is probably the oldest surviving song of the "akritika", and even though the manuscripts which contain it date from the 15th–16th c., nevertheless its linguistic features and its content allow us to place its date of composition at the very early stages of LMG, and to regard it as one of the earliest attestations of the vernacular.

Stratigikon (104 pp.). Wassiliewsky, B. & V. Jernestedt (1965) *Cecaumeni Strategikon*. Amsterdam: Hakkert.

This is a text written in prose by Kekaumenos, a provincial aristocrat without much literary education, and its chronology is basically secure. It is included in the corpus, since it is considered as representative of the middle register of Greek for that time, and, despite the often sharp contrast with more vernacular texts, it provides us with valuable information concerning the diffusion and the sociolinguistic embedding of FCs.

11th–12th century
Digenis Akritis (1867 v.). Alexiou, S. (1985) *Vasileios Digenis Akrites kai to Asma tou Armouri*. Athina: Ermis.
One of the most famous texts of LMG, and one of the most controversial, too. This "epic poem" has survived in five different versions, with the Escorial (E) version used here being the least literary among them. The actual genre of the text, its oral or written character, its chronology, as well as the exact relation between the different versions are highly controversial.

Grottaferrata (3749 v.). Jeffreys, E. (1998) *Digenis Akritis: The Grottaferrata and Escorial versions*. Cambridge: Cambridge University Press.
This is the longer and more learned version of *Digenis*, which has been examined in order to compare the properties of the FCs in the two versions belonging to different registers.

12th century
Ptohoprodromika (1347 v.). Eideneier, H. (1991) *Ptochoprodromos (Neograeca Medii Aevi* V). Köln: Romiosini.
These are four poems, probably written by Theodoros Prodromos, a scholar deeply involved in imperial court life. It constitutes one of the earliest experimentations of scholars in the vernacular language, as Prodromos himself admits in his poems.

Mihail Glykas (581 v.). Tsolakis, E. T. (1959) "Mihail Glyka stihoi". *Epistimoniki Epetiris Filosofikis Sxolis Aristoteleiou Panepistimiou Thessalonikis*, Appendix 3: 3–22.
Glykas, a scholar like Prodromos, was the writer of one poem in the vernacular, by which he entreats the emperor to allow him out of jail.

Spaneas (674 v.). Wagner, W. (1874) *Carmina Graeca Medii Aevi*. Leipzig: Teubner.
The poem known by this name was allegedly written by a member of the imperial family of the Komninoi, and it contains pieces of advice for youth, which are stereotypically found in many works of this kind in LMG.

14th century
Kallimahos & Hrysorroi (2607 v.). Kriaras, E. (1955) *Vyzantina Ippotika Mythistorimata*. Athinai: Aetos.
This text constitutes one of the Byzantine "romances" based on, but not translated from, equivalent Western works. Since it also follows an older tradition of romances written in the 12th c. by scholars, its language could be regarded as less vernacular than other texts of the 14th c.

Velthandros & Hrysantza (1348 v.). Kriaras, E. (1955) *Vyzantina Ippotika Mythistorimata.* Athinai: Aetos.

The second of the romances referred to above, it shares its basic linguistic features with *Kallimahos.*

Livistros & Rodamni (version a) (4407 v.). Agapitos, P. A. (2006) *Afigisis Livistrou kai Rodamnis.* Athina: MIET.

Yet another romance, which survives in two versions, the oldest of which dates from the 14th c.

Diigisis Paidiofrastos (1082 v.). Tsiouni, V. (1972) *Paidiofrastos diigisis ton zoon ton tetrapodon.* München: Institut für Byzantinistik und Neugriechische Philologie der Universität.

This text belongs to a long series of similar works whose content seems to have been inspired by the lives of animals. This trend was apparently very popular in LMG, hence the numerous works following it.

Sahlikis (1527 v.).
1. Wagner, W. (1874) *Carmina Graeca Medii Aevi.* Leipzig: Teubner.
2. Vitti, M. (1960) "Il poema parenetico di Sachlikis". *Kritika Hronika* 14: 173–200.
3. Papadimitriou, S. D. (1896) *Stefan Sakhlikis i ego stikhotvorenie "'Ἀφήγησις Παράξενος".* Odessa.

Sahlikis' poems can be considered the earliest attestation of Cretan literature. The chronology of these poems (*ca.* 1390) has very recently been ascertained, and it was previously thought that they belonged to a much later period (early 16th c.). It should also be noted that they are the first rhymed poems in LMG. Their manuscript tradition is very problematic: they survive in three different manuscripts dating from the 16th c.

Chronicle of Morea (9235 v.). Kalonaros, P. P. (1940) *To Hronikon tou Moreos.* Athina: Dimitrakos.

This long poem tells of the conquest of the Peloponnese by the Franks, and is probably written by a Greek of Frank descent ("gasmulos"), as the rather hostile attitude of the author towards Greeks seems to indicate. Deprived of any—at least strong—influence from the Greek literary tradition, this work might be highly representative of the lower register of Greek at LMG, even though the presumed non-Greek origin of its author has given rise to intense controversy with regard to the authenticity of the linguistic characteristics featuring in the text. The textual tradition of the chronicle includes two main manuscripts (H and P).

War of Troy (14401 v.). Papathomopoulos, M. & E. Jeffreys (1996) *O polemos tis Troados – The War of Troy.* Athina: MIET.

Despite its bulk, this novel actually constitutes an abridged translation of a well-known French original, *La guerre de Troie* by Benoît de Sainte-Maure.

Ahilliid (3901 v.: N-1820 v., L-1320 v., O-761 v.).
1. Smith, O. L. (1999) *The Byzantine Achilleid. The Naples version.* Wien: Österreichische Akademie der Wissenschaften.

2. Haag. B. (1919) *Die Londoner version der byzantinischen Achilleis*. München: Universitäts-Buchdruckerei Wolf & Sohn.
3. Smith, O. L. (1990) *The Oxford version of the «Achilleid»*. Copenhagen: Museum Tusculanum Press.

Another novel, without any known Western original. As there is no critical edition which would provide us with one text from the three different versions in which it is found (and maybe there can be *no* one critical edition for all three of them), all of its versions have been investigated as basically different texts.

Poulologos (668 v.). Tsavari, I. (1987) *O Poulologos*. Athina: MIET.

This is yet another token of the allegorical works dedicated ostensibly to the lives of animals.

Fysiologos (1131 v.). Legrand, É. (1873) *Le Physiologus. Poème sur la nature des animaux en grec vulgaire et en vers politiques*. Paris: Maisonneuve.

This belongs to the same circle of works as *Poulologos*. It enjoyed great popularity, as some versions of it go back to the late Roman period.

Iatrosofia – Stafidas (27 pp.). Legrand, É. (1881) *Bibliothèque Grecque Vulgaire* II. Paris: Maisonneuve.

This is a body of work that contains medical advice about a variety of illnesses. Typically, this advice is a mixture of herbal knowledge and prayers, or incantations.

Ermoniakos' Iliad (8799 v.). Legrand, É. (1890) Ιλιάδος Ραψωδίαι ΚΔ΄. *La guerre de Troie. Poème du XIVe siècle en vers octosyllabes par Constantin Hermoniacos (Bibliothèque Grecque Vulgaire* V). Paris: Maisonneuve.

Ermoniakos, the author of this poetic work, seems to have been a scholar or grammarian in the court of the Duke of Epirus in Arta. Little else is known about him. This *Iliad* constitutes an attempt to render the Homeric epic accessible to people with no educational training. It is written not in the usual political (15-syllable) verse of LMG, but in the more learned iambic 8-syllable verse. Its language arguably belongs to the middle register, as it features some archaizing constructions.

Apollonios of Tyre (870 v.). Kehagioglou, G. (2004) *Apollonios tis Tyrou: Ysteromesaionikes kai neoteres ellinikes morfes*. Thessaloniki: Institouto Neoellinikon Spoudon [Idryma Manoli Triantafyllidi].

This is a novel based on a well-known Western original with versions in French, Italian, Spanish, and other languages. It is quite likely that the Greek version originated in Cyprus. The main manuscript dates from the late 15th–early 16th c., but palaeographic evidence suggests that it is a copy of a much older manuscript, written probably not long after the supposed date of production.

Ptoholeon (1332 v.: a-971 v., P-361 v.). Kehagioglou, G. (1978) *Kritiki ekdosi tis Istorias Ptoholeontos*. Thessaloniki.

This constitutes a very popular narrative in verse, telling the story of the wisdom of an old man. It survives in two versions from this period and two more from the subsequent centuries.

14th–15th century

Spanos (1833 v.). Eideneier, H. (1977) *Spanos: eine byzantinische Satire in der Form einer Parodie.* Berlin: Mouton de Gruyter.

This is a text found in numerous versions of an almost "vulgar" character: it is a low-register satire of the orthodox mass.

Florios & Platziaflora (1843 v.). Kriaras, E. (1955) *Vyzantina Ippotika Mythistorimata.* Athinai: Aetos.

Another romance, most probably a translation from a Western original.

Imperios & Margarona (893 v.). Kriaras, E. (1955) *Vyzantina Ippotika Mythistorimata.* Athinai: Aetos.

This rather short romance is another work translated or heavily influenced by a foreign original.

Thisiid (1118 v.). Follieri, E. (1959) *Il Teseida Neogreco. Libro I.* Roma – Atene: Istituto di Studi Bizantini e Neoellenici.

This romance constitutes a translation from the Italian original by Boccaccio. Most of its books remain unpublished, and here only the first book has been investigated.

Livistros & Rodamni (version b) (4013 v.). Lentari, T. (2007) *Afigisis Livistrou kai Rodamnis (Livistros and Rodamne). The Vatican version.* Athina: MIET.

This rather different and later version of the 14th c. romance survives in only one manuscript (V).

Alfavitos katanyktiki (120 v.). Wagner, W. (1874) *Carmina Graeca Medii Aevi.* Leipzig: Teubner.

This is a poem with a moralizing purpose, based on the alphabet, a technique commonly utilized in LMG.

15th century

Peri tis xeniteias (547 v.). Mavromatis, G. (1995) *Ta "Peri tis Xeniteias" poiimata.* Iraklio: Dimos Irakliou – Vikelaia Vivliothiki.

This anonymous poem arguably originates from Crete, as can be seen by its language. It refers to the misery of those who find themselves far away from home. It survives in two manuscripts of the 16th c.

Diigisis Velissariou (972 v.: x-580 v., N^2-392 v.). Bakker, W. F. & A. F. van Gemert (1988) *Istoria tou Velissariou.* Athina: MIET.

This is the tale of Velissarios, a famous general of the time of Justinian (6th c.). Its content speaks for an original Byzantine novel, without any Western influence. It survives in two different versions.

Chronicle of Tocco (3923 v.). Schirò, G. (1975) *Cronaca dei Tocco di Cefalonia di Anonimo.* Roma: Accademia dei Lincei.

This chronicle, much shorter than the *Chronicle of Morea*, refers to the dominion of the family of Tocco in the Ionian islands in the 14th–15th c. As with the *Chronicle of Morea*, it could have been written by a foreigner (Italian?).

O polemos tis Varnis (466 v.). Moravcsik, G. (1935) *Ellinikon poiima peri tis mahis tis Varnis.* Budapest.

This somewhat obscure text constitutes a versed account of the battle of Varna, in Bulgaria, even though it is written probably by a Greek in the middle of the 15th c.

Falieros (1920 v.).
1. van Gemert, A. (2006) *Marinou Falierou "Erotika Oneira".* Athina: MIET.
2. Bakker, W. F. & A. F. van Gemert (1972) "The Ρίμα Παρηγορητική of Marinos Phalieros". *Studia Byzantina et Neohellenica Neerlandica* 3: 74–195.
3. Bakker, W. F. & A. F. van Gemert (1977) *The Λόγοι Διδακτικοί of Marinos Phalieros.* Leiden: Brill.
4. Bakker, W. F. & A. F. van Gemert (2002) *Thrinos eis ta Pathi kai tin Staurosin tou Kyriou kai Theou kai Sotiros imon Iisou.* Iraklio: Panepistimiakes Ekdoseis Kritis.

Falieros was a noble of Venetian origin whose poems, five in total, provide valuable information with regard to the Cretan dialect of the 15th c., at least as far as the form spoken in the Kastro (today's Iraklio) by the Greek-speaking Venetians is concerned. All the manuscripts containing the poems date from the 16th c.

Dellaportas (4221 v.). Manousakas, M. I. (1995) *Leonardou Ntellaporta Poiimata (1403 / 1411).* Athina: Akadimia Athinon.

Leonardo Dellaporta was yet another Cretan of Italian origin, whose career mainly as a diplomat can be easily traced thanks to the Venetian archives from Crete. He wrote four poems in the early 15th c., which provide corroborating evidence for the Cretan dialect of that time.

Katalogia (714 v.). Hesseling, D. C. & H. Pernot (1913) Ἐρωτοπαίγνια *(Chansons d'amour) (Bibliothèque Grecque Vulgaire X).* Paris-Athènes.

This title refers to a collection of folk love songs. In this corpus only those songs have been included which are mentioned in a manuscript of the 15th c., and not the whole collection.

Chronicle of Mahairas (342 pp.).
1. Dawkins, R. M. (1932) *Leontios Makhairas: recital concerning the sweet land of Cyprus entitled Chronicle.* Oxford: Clarendon Press.
2. Pieris, M. & A. Nikolaou-Konnari (2003) *Leontiou Mahaira "Hroniko tis Kyprou": Parallili diplomatiki ekdosi ton heirografon.* Leukosia: Kentro Epistimonikon Ereunon.

This is a chronicle written in prose by L. Mahairas, which relates the history of the conquest of Cyprus by Western rulers and their reign up to the 15th c. Mahairas himself was in the entourage of the rulers, or at least his family was. This chronicle is one of the earliest and more robust attestations of the Cypriot dialect. For the purposes of this investigation, the text of the edition by Dawkins was checked against the text(s) of the manuscripts, when necessary. All three manuscripts date from the 16th c.

II. Non-literary texts
<u>Venetian- / Frankish-ruled areas</u>
I. Crete

Detorakis, Th. (1980) "Didaskalikes kai vivliografikes symvaseis sti Venetokratoumeni Kriti". *Kritologia* 8: 231–56.

Detorakis, Th. (1996) *Venetokritika meletimata (1971–94)*. Dimos Irakliou: Vikelaia Vivliothiki.

Gerland, E. (1899) *Das Archiv des Herzogs von Kandia*. Strassburg.

Gerland, E. (1907) *Histoire de la noblesse Crétoise au Moyen Age*. Paris: Leroux.

Gialeas. Bakker, W. F. & A. F. van Gemert (1978) "Oi diathikes tou Kritikou notariou Antoniou Gialea (1529–32)". *Kritologia* 6: 5–90.

Grigoropoulos. Kaklamanis, S. & S. Lampakis (2003) *Manouil Grigoropoulos, notarios Handaka (1506–32). Diathikes, Apografes-Ektimiseis*. Iraklio: Vikelaia Dimotiki Vivliothiki.

Kaltsounakis, I. E. (1928) "Anekdota Kritika symvolaia ek tis Enetokratias". *Praktika Akadimias Athinon* 3: 483–519.

Kiskiras, I. P. (1968) *I symvasis mathiteias en ti Venetokratoumeni Kriti*. Athinai.

Koder, J. (1964) "Eine kretische Urkunde des 15. Jh". In: Koder, J. & E. Trapp (eds.), Ἀκροθίνια. Wien: Institut für Byzantinistik.

Manousakas, M. I. (1960–1) "I diathiki tou Aggelou Akotantou (1436), agnostou Kritikou zografou". *Deltion Hristianikis Arhaiologikis Etaireias* 1: 139–51.

Manousakas, M. I. (1961) "Venetika eggrafa anaferomena eis tin ekklisiastikin istorian tis Kritis tou 14^{ou}–16^{ou} ai. (Protopapades kai protopsaltai Handakos)". *Deltion tis Istorikis kai Ethnologikis Etaireias tis Ellados* 15: 149–233.

Manousakas, M. I. (1962) "Ena palio idiotiko gramma (1420;) se Kritiki dialekto". *Kritiki Protohronia* 2: 35–9.

Manousakas, M. I. (1963) "Dyo palies Kritikes diathikes (1506, 1515)". *Kritiki Protohronia* 3: 73–9.

Manousakas, M. I. (1964) "Ellinika notariaka eggrafa apo ta 'Atti antichi' tou arheiou tou Douka tis Kritis". *Thisaurismata* 3: 73–102.

Manousakas, M. I. (1970) "Eggrafa agnoston notarion tou Rethemnou (1535–50)". *Kritika Hronika* 22: 285–97.

Maras.
I. Drakakis, M. G. (2004) *Mihail Maras, notarios Handaka. Katastiho 149, Tomos A' [16 / 1 – 30 / 3 1549]*. Iraklio: Vikelaia Dimotiki Vivliothiki.
II. Marmareli, T. & M. G. Drakakis (2005) *Mihail Maras, notarios Handaka. Katastiho 149, Tomos B' [1 / 4 – 28 / 6 1549]*. Iraklio: Vikelaia Dimotiki Vivliothiki.
III. Mavromatis, G. (2006) *Mihail Maras, notarios Handaka. Katastixo 148, Tomos B' [2 / 3 – 31 / 8 1548]*. Iraklio: Vikelaia Dimotiki Vivliothiki.

IV. Marmareli, T. & M. G. Drakakis (2005) *Mihail Maras, notarios Handaka. Katastiho 149, Tomos Γ' [1 / 7 - 28 / 9 1549]*. Iraklio: Vikelaia Dimotiki Vivliothiki.
Mertzios, K. D. (1949) "I synthiki Eneton-Kallergi kai oi synodeuontes autin katalogoi". *Kritika Hronika* 3: 262–92.
Mertzios, K. D. (1961–2) "Stahyologimata apo ta katastiha tou notariou Kritis Mihail Mara (1538–78)". *Kritika Hronika* 15–16: 228–308.
Mertzios, K. D. (1965) "Kritika symvolaia ton xronon tis Enetokratias". *Kritika Hronika* 19: 111–45.
Olokalos. Mavromatis, G. (1994) *Ioannis Olokalos, Notarios Ierapetras. Katastiho (1496–1543)*. Venetia: Elliniko Instituto Vyzantinon kai Metavyzantinon Spoudon tis Venetias & Vikelaia Dimotiki Vivliothiki Irakliou.
Panagiotakis, N. (1986) "I kritiki periodos tis zois tou Dominikou Theotokopoulou. Palaies kai nees eidiseis". In: V. Kremmydas, Chr. Maltezou & N. Panagiotakis (eds.), *Afieroma ston Niko Svorono*. Rethymno.
Panagiotakis, N. (1990) *Fragkiskos Leontaritis. Kritikos mousikosynthetis tou dekatou ektou aiona. Martyries gia ti zoi kai to ergo tou*. Venetia.
Patsidiotis. Iliakis, K. & D. Hronaki (2002) *Petros Patsidiotis: Notarios Kainourgiou Horiou ton Karon. Katastiho (1546–54)*. Dimos Neapoleos.
Varouhas. Bakker, W. F. & A. F. van Gemert (1987) *Manolis Varouhas: Notariakes Praxeis. Monastiraki Arakliou (1597–1613)*. Rethymno.
Vourdoumpakis, A. (1913) "Kritika eggrafa ek tis Enetokratias kai Tourkokratias". *Hristianiki Kriti* 2: 339–424.
Vourdoumpakis, A. (1939) "Dyo anekdota eggrafa ek Sfakion". *Epetiris Etaireias Kritikon Spoudon* 2: 256–62.
Xanthoudidis, S. (1912) "Kritika symvolaia ek tis Enetokratias". *Hristianiki Kriti* 1: 1–288.
Xanthoudidis, S. (1939) "To diploma (proveleggion) ton Skordilon Kritis". *Epetiris Etaireias Kritikon Spoudon* 2: 299–312.

II. Corfu

Alexakis. Karampoula, D. & L. Papariga-Artemiadi (1998) "Oi praxeis tou notariou Doukadon Kerkyras Arseniou Alexaki (1513–16)". *Epetiris tou Arheiou Istorias Ellinikou Dikaiou (EAIED)* 34: 9–126.
Asonitis, S. (1993) "Tria Kerkyraika notariaka eggrafa ton eton 1398–1458". *Eoa kai Esperia* 1: 9–44.
Hondromatis. Konidaris, I. & G. Rodolakis (1996) "Oi praxeis tou notariou Kerkyras Ioanni Hondromati (1472–73)". *EAIED* 32: 139–206.
Eustratiadis, S. (1925) "Kerkyraikon proikosymfonon tou *IE'* aionos". *Theologia* 3: 47–50.
Karydis, S. & P. Tzivara (1994–6) "O naos tou Agiou Lazarou Poleos Kerkyras kai i koinotita ton «adynaton»". *Eoa kai Esperia* 2: 83–109.
Karydis, S. (1999) "Antigrafa notariakon praxeon tou 15^{ou} ai. sta katastixa tou Kerkyraiou notariou ierea Stamatiou Kontomari". *Parnassos* 41: 157–71.

Katoimeris. Papariga-Artemiadi, L., G. Rodolakis & D. Karampoula (1997) "Oi praxeis tou notariou Karousadon Kerkyras protopapa Filippou Katoimeri (1503–1507)". *EAIED* 33: 9–436.

Kazanaki, M. (1977) "Eidiseis gia to zografo Thoma Mpatha (1554–99) apo to notariako arheio tis Kerkyras". *Deltion tis Ioniou Akadimias* 1: 124–38.

Kontogiannis, S. & S. Karydis (1994) "I moni Palaiokastritsas Kerkyras". *Epistimoniki Epetiris tis Theologikis Sxolis Pan / miou Athinon* 29: 591–704.

Lampros, S. (1910) "Kerkyraika eggrafa anekdota". *Neos Ellinomnimon* 7: 464–8.

Maltezou, Chr. (1986) "«Ospitia kai ospitohalasmata»". *Deltion tis Ioniou Akadimias* 2: 37–53.

Maltezou, Chr. (1991) "Arheiakes martyries gia pente metavyzantinous naous tis Kerkyras". In: *Eufrosynon: Afieroma ston Manoli Hatzidaki*. Athina: Tameio Arhaiologikon poron kai apallotrioseon.

Pentogalos, G. (1976) "Agora kai diathesi Kefalonitikon krasion stin Kerkyra to 1502". *Kerkyraika Hronika* 20: 114–19.

Pentogalos, G. (1980) "Georgios Moshos, notarios Kerkyras sto telos tou *IE'* ai.". *Kerkyraika Hronika* 23: 293–302.

Theotokis, S. (1914) *Anamnistikon teuhos tis Panioniou Anadromikis Ektheseos – Tomos A': Enetokratia*. Kerkyra.

Tselikas, A. (1986) "Nikolaou Sparmioti, nomikou Koryfon, «eggrafo eleutherias» (1391)". *Deltion tis Ioniou Akadimias* 2: 168–87.

Tzivara, G. & S. Karydis (1993) "«Ego Georgios o Moshos dimosios notarios ton Koryfon egrapsa »". *Istor* 6: 19–27.

Varagkas. Rodolakis, G. & L. Papariga-Artemiadi (1996) "Oi praxeis tou notariou Agiou Matthaiou Kerkyras Petrou Varagka (1541–45)". *EAIED* 32: 207–340.

Vranianitis. Karydis, S. (2001) *Theodorou Vrianiti, dimosiou notariou poleos kai nisou Kerkyras. Oi sozomenes praxeis (1479–1516)*. Athina.

Vrokinis, L. (1973) "Palatinis Komiteias pronomiaka dikaiomata en Kerkyra". *Kerkyraika Hronika* 17: 109–39.

Zaridi, K. (1993) "O Kerkyraios stihourgos Iakovos Trivolis (stoiheia apo to istoriko arheio Kerkyras, 1515–46)". *Eoa kai Esperia* 1: 145–89.

Zaridi, K. (1994–6) "Plirofories gia ti stoiheiodi ekpaideusi stin Kerkyra ton 16° aiona". *Eoa kai Esperia* 2: 110–34.

Zaridi, K. (1995) *O Megas Protopapas Kerkyras Alexios Rartouros. Logios tou $16^{ου}$ ai. (1504–74)*. Kerkyra.

III. Kefalonia

Amarantos. Vagionakis, H., O Katsivela, D. Mihalaga, V. Belovgeni & M. Bletas (2001) *Andreas Amarantos. Notariakes praxeis. Arakli Kefalonias (1548–62)*. Athina.

Hrisohoidis, K. (1977) "To metohi tou Panagiou Tafou stin Kefalonia (teli $16^{ου}$ ai.)". *Kefalliniaka Hronika* 2: 195–214.

De Montesantos. Zapanti, S. (2002) *Montesantos (de) iereas Stamatios, notarios Eleiou. Katastiho 1535–53*. Argostoli: Genika Arheia tou Kratous: Arheia Nomou Kefallinias.

Garmpis, D. (1999) "Nees eidiseis gia ti moni ton Agion Faneston stin Kefalonia kai ena anekdoto eggrafo". *Kefalliniaka Hronika* 8: 407–14.
Pentogalos, G. (1975) "Ithi kai anthropines sheseis stin Kefalonia ton $I\varSigma T'$ aiona". *EAIED* 22: 59–145.
Pentogalos, G. (1976) "Hristoforou i Hristodoulou Krassa diathiki (1584) kai akyrosi tis (1584)". *Kefalliniaka Hronika* 1: 144–56.
Pentogalos, G. (1977) "Notariako antigrafo katalogou tou IE' aionos gia dorites kai ktimata tis ekklisias tou Agiou Nikolaou sto Rifi tis Kefalonias". *Kefalliniaka Hronika* 2: 45–59.
Pentogalos, G. (1999) "Eggrafa anaferomena ston Agio Gerasimo tou 16^{ou}, 17^{ou} kai tou 18^{ou} ai.". *Kefalliniaka Hronika* 8: 85–110.
Sourianos. Zapanti, S. (2001) *Giakoumos Sourianos, Notarios Kastrou. Katastiho 1570–98.* Argostoli.

IV. Andros
Pashalis, D. P. (1928–29) "O Spartiatis Stratigopoulos, dimosios upo vasilikin exousian notarios en Andro. Eidiseis peri ton en Andro notarion epi Fragkokratias kai Tourkokratias (meta trion panomoiotypon)". *Byzantinisch-neugriechische Jahrbücher* 7: 87–98.
Polemis, D. & M. Foskolos (1987) "To arheion tis Katholikis Ekklisias Androu". *Epetiris Etaireias Vyzantinon Spoudon* 47: 109–48.
Polemis, D. (1982) "Apeleutherosis aihmalotou en Andro kata ton 16° aiona". *Petalon* 3: 81–90.
Polemis, D. (1995) *Oi afentotopoi tis Androu. Petalon: parartima 2.* Andros.
Polemis, D. (1999) *Anekdota Andriaka eggrafa tou 16^{ou} aionos. Andriaka Hronika 30.*
Vogiatzidis, I. K. (1910) "O Lakedaimonios vivliografos Stratigopoulos". *Byzantinische Zeitschrift* 19: 122–26.

V. Naxos
Katsouros, A. (1955) "Naxiaka dikaiopraktika eggrafa tou 16^{ou} aionos". *Epetiris Mesaionikou Arheiou* 5: 47–91.
Lampros, S. (1907) "Doukikon Gramma Iakovou Krispi B' tou Doukos tou Aigaiou". *Neos Ellinomnimon* 4: 467–75.
Visvizis, I. (1951) "Naxiaka Notariaka eggrafa ton teleutaion hronon tou Doukatou tou Aigaiou (1538–77)". *EAIED* 4: 1–167.
Zerlentis, P. (1924) *Grammata ton teleutaion Fragkon doukon tou Aigaiou Pelagous.* Ermoupolis.
Zerlentis, P. (1925) *Feoudaliki politeia en ti niso Naxo.* Ermoupolis.

Athos
Chilandar I. Živojinović, M., V. Kravari & C. Giros (1998) *Archives de l'Athos XX: Actes de Chilandar I (–1319).* Paris: P. Lethielleux.
Dionysiou. Oikonomidès, N. (1968) *Archives de l'Athos IV: Actes de Dionysiou.* Paris: P. Lethielleux.

Docheiariou. Oikonomidès, N. (1984) *Archives de l'Athos XIII: Actes de Docheiariou.* Paris: P. Lethielleux.
Esphigménou. Lefort, J. (1973) *Archives de l'Athos VI: Actes d'Esphigménou.* Paris: P. Lethielleux.
Iviron I. Lefort, J., N. Oikonomidès & D. Papachryssanthou (collab. H. Métrévéli) (1985) *Archives de l'Athos XIV: Actes d'Iviron I (–1050).* Paris: P. Lethielleux.
Iviron II. Lefort, J., N. Oikonomidès & D. Papachryssanthou (collab. H. Métrévéli) (1990) *Archives de l'Athos XVI: Actes d'Iviron II (XI–1204).* Paris: P. Lethielleux.
Iviron III. Lefort, J., N. Oikonomidès & D. Papachryssanthou (collab. H. Métrévéli) (1994) *Archives de l'Athos XVIII: Actes d'Iviron III (1204–1328).* Paris: P. Lethielleux.
Iviron IV. Lefort, J., N. Oikonomidès & D. Papachryssanthou (collab. H. Métrévéli) (1995) *Archives de l'Athos XIX: Actes d'Iviron IV (1328–XVI).* Paris: P. Lethielleux.
Kastamonitou. Oikonomidès, N. (1978) *Archives de l'Athos IX: Actes de Kastamonitou.* Paris: P. Lethielleux.
Kutlumus. Lemerle, P. (1988^2) *Archives de l'Athos II: Actes de Kutlumus.* Paris: P. Lethielleux.
Lavra I. Lemerle, P., A. Guillou, N. Svoronos & D. Papachryssanthou (1970) *Archives de l'Athos V: Actes de Lavra I (–1204).* Paris: P. Lethielleux.
Lavra II. Lemerle, P., A. Guillou, N. Svoronos & D. Papachryssanthou (1977) *Archives de l'Athos VIII: Actes de Lavra II (1204–1328).* Paris: P. Lethielleux.
Lavra III. Lemerle, P., A. Guillou, N. Svoronos & D. Papachryssanthou (1979) *Archives de l'Athos X: Actes de Lavra III (1329–1500).* Paris: P. Lethielleux.
Pantocrator. Kravari, V. (1991) *Archives de l'Athos XVII: Actes du Pantocrator.* Paris: P. Lethielleux.
Philothée. Regel, W., E. Kurtz & B. Korablev (1975) *Actes de l'Athos VI: Actes de Philothée.* Amsterdam: Hakkert.
Prôtaton. Papachryssanthou, D. (1975) *Archives de l'Athos VII: Actes du Prôtaton.* Paris: P. Lethielleux.
Saint-Pantéléèmôn. Lemerle, P., G. Dagron & S. Ćirković (1982) *Archives de l'Athos XII: Actes de Saint-Pantéléèmôn.* Paris: P. Lethielleux.
Vatopédi. Bompaire, J., J. Lefort, V. Kravari & C. Giros (2001) *Archives de l'Athos XXI: Actes de Vatopédi I (–1329).* Paris: P. Lethielleux.
Xénophon. Papachryssanthou, D. (1986) *Archives de l'Athos XV: Actes de Xénophon.* Paris: P. Lethielleux.
Xéropotamou. Bompaire, J. (1964) *Archives de l'Athos III: Actes de Xéropotamou.* Paris: P. Lethielleux.

Greek documents related to the Turkish rule

Ahrweiler, H. (1969) "Une lettre en grec du Sultan Bayezid II (1481–1512)". *Turcica* 1: 150–60.
Amantos, K. (1936) "Oi pronomiakoi orismoi tou Mousoulmanismou yper ton Hristianon". *Ellinika* 9: 103–66.

Babinger, F. & F. Dölger (1949) "Mehmed's II frühester Staatsvertrag (1446)". *Orientalia Christiana Periodica* 15: 215–58.

Bombaci, A. (1954) "Nuovi firmani Greci di Maometto II". *Byzantinische Zeitschrift* 47: 298–319.

Giannopoulos, I. (1974) "Epistoli eis tin Ellinikin tou Bostanzi Basi Skentir Bei pros ton Andrea Gritti (1503)". *Thisaurismata* 11: 128–35.

Lampros, S. (1892) "Ellinika eggrafa en to arheio tis Venetias en ois kai eggrafa Tourkon arhonton ellinisti". *Deltion tis Istorikis kai Ethnologikis Etaireias tis Ellados* 4: 634–52.

Lampros, S. (1908a) "Ellinika dimosia grammata tou Soultanou Vagiazit B'". *Neos Ellinomnimon* 5: 155–89.

Lampros, S. (1908b) "I elliniki os episimos glossa ton Soultanon". *Neos Ellinomnimon* 5: 40–78.

Lefort, J. (1981) *Documents grecs dans les archives de Topkapi Sarayi*. Ankara: Türk Tarih Kurumu Basimevi.

Wittek, P. (1951) "Ein Brief des Kaisers Johannes VIII. an den Osmanischen Wesir Sariga Pasha vom Jahre 1432". *Byzantion* 21: 323–32.

Zahariadou, E. (1962) "Mia ellinoglossi synthiki tou Hidir Aidinoglou". *Byzantinische Zeitschrift* 55: 254–65.

South Italy / Sicily

Guillou, A. (1967) *Saint-Nicolas de Donnoso (1031–60 / 1). Corpus des actes grecs d'Italie du Sud et de Sicile I*. Città del Vaticano: Biblioteca Apostolica Vaticana.

Guillou, A. (1968) *Saint-Nicodème de Kellarana (1023 / 4–1232). Corpus des actes grecs d'Italie du Sud et de Sicile II*. Città del Vaticano: Biblioteca Apostolica Vaticana.

Guillou, A. (1972) *La Théotokos de Hagia-Agathê (Oppido) (1050–64 / 5). Corpus des actes grecs d'Italie du Sud et de Sicile III*. Città del Vaticano: Biblioteca Apostolica Vaticana.

Guillou, A., S. G. Mercati & G. Giannelli (1980) *Saint-Jean-Théristès (1054–1264). Corpus des actes grecs d'Italie du Sud et de Sicile V*. Città del Vaticano: Biblioteca Apostolica Vaticana.

Trinchera, F. (1865) *Syllabus graecarum membranarum*. Napoli: Cataneo.

Various

Assises. Sathas, K. (1877) *Mesaioniki Vivliothiki, tomos VI: Asizai tou Vasileiou ton Ierosolymon kai tis Kyprou*. Paris: Maisonneuve.

Bénou, L. (1998) *Le codex B du monastère Saint-Jean-Prodrome Serrès XIIIe–XVe siècles*. Paris: Editions de l'Association "Pierre Belon".

Delendas, I. (1949) *Oi katholikoi tis Santorinis*. Athinai.

Drakakis, A. Th. (1967) "I Syros epi Tourkokratias – I Dikaiosyni kai to Dikaion". *Epetiris Etaireias Kykladikon Meleton* 6: 63–492.

Gedeon, M. (1896) "Vyzantina symvolaia". *Byzantinische Zeitschrift* 5: 112–17.

Gerland, E. (1903) *Neue Quellen zur Geschichte des Lateinischen Erzbistums Patras*. Leipzig: Teubner.

Hunger, H. & K. Vogel (1963) *Ein byzantinisches Rechenbuch des 15. Jahrhunderts*. Wien: Österreichische Akademie der Wissenschaften.
Kasimatis. Drakakis, E. (1999) *Emmanouil Kasimatis, notarios Kythiron (1560–82)*. Athina.
Lampros, S. (1908) "Dyo ellinika eggrafa ek ton arheion tis Venetias". *Neos Ellinomnimon* 5: 479–81.
Lampros, S. (1909) "Naupliakon eggrafon tou oikou Poulomati en etei 1509 kai o vivliografos Mihail Souliardos". *Neos Ellinomnimon* 6: 273–83.
Lampros, S. (1910) "Enthymiseon itoi hronikon simeiomaton syllogi proti". *Neos Ellinomnimon* 7: 113–313.
Lampros, S. (1914) "Anekdota eggrafa tis monis Xirohorafiou i Ieras". *Neos Ellinomnimon* 11: 401–13.
Lampros, S. (1914) "Konstantinos Palaiologos Graitzas". *Neos Ellinomnimon* 11: 260–88.
Legrand, É. (1885) *Bibliographie Hellénique (XVe–XVIe siècles). Tome second*. Paris: Ernest Lerouy.
Maltezou, Chr. (1975) "I Kritiki oikogeneia Kaldouri sta Kythira". *Thisaurismata* 12: 257–91.
Maltezou, Chr. (1987) "Tria Kypriaka afierotiria eggrafa. Symvoli sti meleti tis latinokratoumenis Kyprou". *Symmeikta* 7: 1–17.
Manousakas, M. I. (1960) "Stefanos Katrarios: O protos gnostos ellinas notarios tis Hiou". In: *Eis mnimin K. Amantou (1874–1960)*. Athinai: Typografeion Mina Myrtidi.
Manousakas, M. I. (1962–63) "I proti emporiki paroikia ton Veneton sta Palatia (Milito) tis M. Asias". *Deltion Hristianikis Arhaiologikis Etaireias* 3: 231–40.
Manousakas, M. I. (1981) "Un acte de donation à l'église Saint-Kyriaké de Mouchli (1457)". In: *Travaux et Mémoires* 8: *Hommage à M. Paul Lemerle*.
Manousakas, M. I. (1984) "Mia diathiki apo to Nauplio (1534) me plousio glossiko yliko". In: *Antihari: afieroma ston kathigiti Stamati Karatza*. Athina.
Mavroeidi-Ploumidi, F. (1971) "Eggrafa gia tis erides ton Ellinon tis Venetias". *Thisaurismata* 8: 115–87.
Mertzios, K. D. (1949) "Diathiki Annas Palaiologinas Notara [1493]". *Athina* 53: 17–20.
Mertzios, K. D. (1953) "Arheiaka Analekta". In: *Prosfora eis Stilpona P. Kyriakidin. Ellinika: Parartima* 4: 474–85. Thessaloniki.
Mertzios, K. D. (1967) "Un mandat du XIVe siècle en grec vulgaire". *Byzantinische Forschungen* 2: 265–8.
Miklosich, F. & J. Müller (eds.) (1860–90) *Acta et diplomata graeca medii aevi sacra et profana* (6 vols.). Wien: Gerold.
Odorico, P. (1998) *Le codex B du monastère Saint-Jean-Prodrome Serrès XVe–XIXe siècles*. Paris: Editions de l'Association "Pierre Belon".
Papadia-Lala, A. (1993) "Oi Ellines kai i venetiki pragmatikotita: Ideologiki kai koinoniki sygkrotisi". In: Chr. Maltezou (ed.), *Opseis tis istorias tou Venetokratoumenou Ellinismou: Arheiaka tekmiria*. Athina: Idryma Ellinikou Politismou.

Ploumidis, G. (1998) "Naulosi ploiou sti Zakyntho". *Kefalliniaka Hronika* 7: 85–8.
Richard, J. (1962) *Documents chypriotes des Archives du Vatican (XIVe et XVe siècles)*. Paris: Institut Français d'Archéologie de Beyrouth.
Rodolakis, G. (1997) "To «vlisidi» kai i sermagia sto emporio kata tous metavyzantinous hronous". *EAIED* 33: 457–72.
Romanos, I. (1959) "Gratianos Zorzis, authentis Leukados". *Kerkyraika Hronika* 7: 127–330.
Sathas, K. (1872–77) *Mesaioniki Vivliothiki* (6 vols.). Venetia / Parisi.
Schopen, L. (1828–32) *Ioannis Cantacuzeni eximperatoris historiarum libri iv, 3 vols*: vol. 3, 94–9. Bonn: Weber.
Skopeteas, S. (1950) "Eggrafa idiotika ek D. Manis ton eton 1547–1830". *EAIED* 3: 60–117.
Vagiakakos, D. (1950) "Melissinoi kai Kontostavloi. Ek Manis eis Zakynthon 1509". *Epetiris Mesaionikou Arheiou* 3: 141–66.
Vazelon. Ouspensky, Th. & V. Bénéchévitch (1927) *Actes de Vazélon*. Leningrad.
Visvizis, I. (1968) "Tina peri ton proikoon eggrafon kata tin Venetokratian kai tin Tourkokratian". *EAIED* 12: 1–129.
Vogel, K. (1968) *Ein byzantinisches Rechenbuch des frühen 14. Jahrhunderts*. Wien.

Secondary sources

Adams, J. N. (1991) "Some neglected evidence for Latin *habeo* with Infinitive: the order of the constituents". *Transactions of the Philological Society* 89: 131–96.
Adams, J. N. (2003) *Bilingualism and the Latin language*. Cambridge: Cambridge University Press.
Aerts, W. J. (1965) *Periphrastica*. Amsterdam: Hakkert.
Aerts, W. J. (1983) "Periphrastic constructions of the Future Tense especially with Μέλλειν, in Mediaeval Cypriotic". *Epetiris tou Kentrou Epistimonikon Erevnon* 12: 149–69.
Aerts, W. J. (2005) "The Lexicon to the *Chronicle of the Morea* as a tool for linguistic studies". In: E. Jeffreys & M. Jeffreys (eds.), *Anadromika kai Prodromika: Approaches to texts in Early Modern Greek. Neograeca Medii Aevi V*. Oxford.
Aijmer, K. (1985) "The semantic development of will". In: J. Fisiak (ed.), *Historical Semantics. Historical Word Formation*. Berlin: Mouton de Gruyter.
Aikhenvald, A. Y. & R. M. W. Dixon (2007) *Grammars in contact. a cross-linguistic typology*. Oxford: Oxford University Press.
Andersen, H. (2006) "Periphrastic futures in Slavic: divergence and convergence". In: K. Eksell & T. Vinther (eds.), *Change in verbal systems. Issues in explanation*. Bern: Peter Lang.
Anderson, G. D. S. (2006) *Auxiliary verb constructions*. Oxford: Oxford University Press.

Anderson, J. (2000) "Auxiliary". In: G. Booij, C. Lehmann & J. Mugdan (eds., in collab. with W. Kasselheim & S. Skopeteas), *Morphologie: Ein internationales Handbuch zur Flexion und Wortbildung*. Berlin: Mouton de Gruyter.

Avramea, A. (2001) "Les Slaves dans le Péloponnèse". In: E. Kountoura-Galaki (ed.), *Oi skoteinoi aiones tou Vyzantiou (7th–9thc.)*. Athina: Ethniko Idryma Ereunon.

Babiniotis, G. (2002) *Synoptiki istoria tis ellinikis glossas*. Athina.

Balletto, L. (1995) "Ethnic groups, cross-social and cross-cultural contacts in the 15th century Cyprus". In: B. Arbel (ed.), *Intercultural contacts in the Medieval Mediterranean*. Portland: Frank Cass.

Bănescu, N. (1915) *Die Entwicklung des griechischen Futurums*. Bukarest: Söhne.

Basset, L. (1979) *Les emplois périphrastiques du verbe grec "Μέλλειν"*. Lyon: Maison de l'Orient.

Beaton, R. (1996) *The Medieval Greek Romance, 2nd edition*. London: Routledge.

Beck, H.-G. (1988) *Istoria tis Vyzantinis dimodous logotehnias* [transl. from German]. Athina: MIET.

Bennett, C. (1910) *Syntax of early Latin*. Boston: Allyn & Bacon.

Bertinetto, P. M. (1990) "Perifrasi verbali italiane: criteri di identificazione e gerarchia di perifrasticità". In: G. Bernini & A. Giacalone-Ramat (eds.), *La temporalità nell'acquisizione di lingue seconde*. Milano: Angeli.

Biber, D. (1998) *Corpus linguistics*. Cambridge: Cambridge University Press.

Binnick, R. (1991) *Time and the verb: a guide to tense and aspect*. Oxford: Oxford University Press.

Birnbaum, H. (1958) *Untersuchungen zu den Zukunfts-umschreibungen mit dem Infinitiv im Altkirchenslavischen*. Stockholm: Almqvist & Wiksell.

Biville, F. (2002) "Greco-Romans and Greco-Latin: a terminological framework for cases of bilingualism". In: J. N. Adams, M. Janse & S. Swain (eds.), *Bilingualism in ancient society. Language contact and the written text*. Oxford: Oxford University Press.

Blass, F. & A. Debrunner (1961) *A Greek grammar of the New Testament and other early Christian literature [transl. by R. W. Funk]*. Chicago: University of Chicago Press.

Borsley, R. (ed.) (2000) *The nature and function of syntactic categories (syntax and semantics 32)*. London: Academic Press.

Brincat, J. (2002) "Linguistic cross-currents in the central Mediterranean. Malta as a focal point". In: P. Ramat & T. Stolz (eds.), *Mediterranean languages. Papers from the MEDTYP workshop, Tirrenia, June 2000*. Bochum: Universitätsverlag Dr. N. Brockmeyer.

Browning, R. (1983) *Medieval & Modern Greek*. Cambridge: Cambridge University Press.

Brunot, F. (1966) *Histoire de la langue Française. Tome I: De l'époque latine à la Renaissance*. Paris: Librairie Armand Colin.

Bryer, A. & J. Herrin (eds.) (1977) *Iconoclasm*. University of Birmingham: Centre for Byzantine Studies.

Bubenik, V. (2000) "On the nature of innovations in the aspectual systems of Medieval Greek and South Slavic languages". In: H. Tzitzilis & H. Symeonidis (eds.), *Valkaniki Glossologia. Syghronia kai Diahronia [Balkanlinguistik. Synchronie und Diachronie]*. Thessaloniki.

Bybee, J. (1985) *Morphology: A study of the relation between meaning and form*. Amsterdam: Benjamins.

Bybee, J. (1988) "The diachronic dimension in explanation". In: J. A. Hawkins (ed.), *Explaining language universals*. Oxford: Blackwell.

Bybee, J. (2001) *Phonology and language use*. Cambridge: Cambridge University Press.

Bybee, J. (2006a) "From usage to grammar: the mind's response to repetition". *Language* 82: 711–33.

Bybee, J. (2006b) *Frequency of use and the organization of language*. Oxford: Oxford University Press.

Bybee, J., D. Perkins & W. Pagliuca (1994) *The evolution of grammar: tense, aspect and modality in the languages of the world*. Chicago: University of Chicago Press.

Bybee, J. & M. A. Brewer (1980) "Explanation in morphophonemics: changes in Provençal and Spanish preterite forms". *Lingua* 52: 201–42.

Bybee, J. & S. A. Thompson (1997) "Three frequency effects in syntax". *Berkeley Linguistics Society* 23: 378–88.

Bybee, J. & W. Pagliuca (1987) "The evolution of future meaning". In: A. G. Ramat, O. Carruba & G. Bernini (eds.), *Papers from the 7th International Conference on Historical Linguistics*. Amsterdam: Benjamins.

Bybee, J., W. Pagliuca & D. Perkins (1991) "Back to the Future". In: E. C. Traugott & B. Heine (eds.), *Approaches to grammaticalization*. Amsterdam: Benjamins.

Campbell, L. (ed.) (2001) *Grammaticalization: a critical assessment (special issue of Language Sciences, 23 (2–3))*.

Caroll, L. (1981) *Language and dialect in Ruzante and Goldoni*. Ravenna: Longo Editore.

Chila-Markopoulou, D. (2000) "Thelo na... alla den tha...: Fainomena grammatikopoiisis kai tropikis polyekmetalleusis". *Studies in Greek Linguistics* 21: 822–33.

Christidis, A.-F. (ed.) (2007) *A history of Ancient Greek: from the beginnings to late antiquity*. Cambridge: Cambridge University Press.

Coates, J. (1983) *The semantics of the modal auxiliaries*. London: Croom Helm.

Coleman, R. G. G. (1971) "The origin and development of Latin *habeo* + Infinitive". *Classical Quarterly* 21: 215–32.

Comrie, B. (1985) *Tense*. Cambridge: Cambridge University Press.

Comrie, B. (1989) "On identifying future tenses". In: W. Abraham & T. Janssen (eds.), *Tempus – Aspekt – Modus*. Tübingen: Max Niemeyer Verlag.

Cristofaro, S. (2003) *Subordination*. Oxford: Oxford University Press.

Croft, W. (1990) *Typology and universals*. Cambridge: Cambridge University Press.

Croft, W. (2000) *Explaining language change: an evolutionary approach*. Harlow–New York: Longman.

Dagron, G. (1994) "Formes et fonctions du pluralisme linguistique à Byzance (IXe–XIIe siècle)". *Travaux et Mémoires* 12: 219–40.

Dahl, Ö. (1985) *Tense and aspect systems*. Oxford: Blackwell.

De Melo, W. D. C. (2007) "The present tense with future meaning in the accusative and infinitive construction in Plautus and Terence". *Transactions of the Philological Society* 105: 105–25.

Denison, D. (1993) *English historical syntax: verbal constructions*. London: Longman.

Devine, A. M. & S. D. Stephens (2000) *Discontinuous syntax: hyperbaton in Greek*. Oxford: Oxford University Press.

Dieterich, K. (1898) *Untersuchungen zur Geschichte der griechischen Sprache von den hellenistischen Zeit bis zum 10. Jahrh. n. Chr.* Leipzig: Teubner.

Diewald, G. (2002) "A model for relevant types of contexts in grammaticalization". In: I. Wischer & G. Diewald (eds.), *New Reflections on Grammaticalization*. Amsterdam: Benjamins.

Dryer, M. S. (1998) "Why Statistical Universals are Better Than Absolute Universals". *Chicago Linguistic Society 33: The Panels*: 123–45.

Fewster, P. (2002) "Bilingualism in Roman Egypt". In: J. N. Adams, M. Janse & S. Swain (eds.), *Bilingualism in ancient society. Language contact and the written text*. Oxford: Oxford University Press.

Finegan, E. & D. Biber (1994) "Register and social dialect variation: an integrated approach". In: D. Biber & E. Finegan (eds.), *Sociolinguistic Perspectives on Register*. Oxford: Oxford University Press.

Fischer, O. (1997) "On the status of grammaticalisation and the diachronic dimension in explanation". *Transactions of the Philological Society* 95: 149–87.

Fischer, O. (2004) "What counts as evidence in historical linguistics?" *Studies in Language* 28 (3): 710–40.

Fischer, O. (2007) *Morphosyntactic change. Functional and formal perspectives*. Oxford: Oxford University Press.

Fleischman, S. (1982) *The future in thought and language: Diachronic evidence from Romance*. Cambridge: Cambridge University Press.

Fleischman, S. (1995) "Imperfective and irrealis". In: J. Bybee & S. Fleischman (eds.), *Modality in Grammar and Discourse*. Amsterdam: Benjamins.

Foulet, L. (1930) *Petite syntaxe de l'ancien Français*. Paris: H. Champion.

Gignac, F. T. (1976–81) *A grammar of the Greek papyri of the Roman and Byzantine periods*. Milan: Istituto Editoriale Cisalpino – La Goliardica.

Goodwin, W. W. (1875) *Syntax of the moods and tenses of the Greek verb*. New York: St. Martin's Press.

Gregersen, F. & I. L. Pedersen (2001) "A la recherche du word order not quite perdu". In: S. C. Herring, P. van Reenen & L. Schøsler (eds.), *Textual Parameters in Older Languages*. Amsterdam: Benjamins.

Grund, P. (2006) "Manuscripts as sources for linguistic research. A methodological case study based on the *Mirror of Lights*". *Journal of English Linguistics* 34: 105–25.

Haiman, J. (1994) "Ritualization and the development of language". In: W. Pagliuca (ed.), *Perspectives on Grammaticalization*. Amsterdam: Benjamins.
Haiman, J. (1998) *Talk is cheap. Sarcasm, alienation, and the evolution of language.* Oxford: Oxford University Press.
Haiman, J. (1999) "Action, speech, and grammar: the sublimation trajectory". In: M. Nänny & O. Fischer (eds.), *Form miming meaning.* Amsterdam: Benjamins.
Haldon, J. (1997) *Byzantium in the seventh century: the transformation of a culture.* Cambridge: Cambridge University Press.
Harris, A. & L. Campbell (1995) *Historical syntax in cross-linguistic perspective.* Cambridge: Cambridge University Press.
Harris, M. & P. Ramat (eds.) (1987) *Historical development of auxiliaries.* Berlin: Mouton de Gruyter.
Haspelmath, M. (1995) "The converb as a cross-linguistically valid category". In: M. Haspelmath & E. König (eds.), *Converbs in cross-linguistic perspective: structure and meaning of adverbial verb forms – adverbial participles, gerunds.* Berlin: Mouton de Gruyter.
Haspelmath, M. (1999a) "On the cross-linguistic distribution of same-subject and different-subject complement clauses: economic vs. iconic motivation". *Paper presented at the International Conference on Cognitive Linguistics, Stockholm, July 1999.*
Haspelmath, M. (1999b) "Why is grammaticalization irreversible?" *Linguistics* 37: 1043–68.
Haspelmath, M. (2000) "Periphrasis". In: G. Booij, C. Lehmann & J. Mugdan (eds., in collab. with W. Kasselheim & S. Skopeteas), *Morphologie: Ein internationales Handbuch zur Flexion und Wortbildung.* Berlin: Mouton de Gruyter.
Haspelmath, M. (2005) " 'Want' complement clauses". In: M. Haspelmath, M. S. Dryer, D. Gil & B. Comrie (2005) *The world atlas of language structures.* Oxford: Oxford University Press.
Hatzidakis, G. (1905) *Mesaionika kai Nea Ellinika. Tomos A.* En Athinais: Typois P. D. Sakellariou.
Hatzidakis, G. (1907) *Mesaionika kai Nea Ellinika. Tomos B.* En Athinais: Typois P. D. Sakellariou.
Heine, B. (1993) *Auxiliaries: cognitive forces and grammaticalization.* Oxford: Oxford University Press.
Heine, B. (1997) *Possession: Cognitive sources, forces and grammaticalization.* Cambridge: Cambridge University Press.
Heine, B. (2002) "On the role of context in grammaticalization". In: I. Wischer & G. Diewald (eds.), *New reflections on grammaticalization.* Amsterdam: Benjamins.
Heine, B. (2003) "Grammaticalization". In: B. Joseph & R. Janda (eds.), *The Handbook of Historical Linguistics.* Oxford: Blackwell.
Heine, B. & T. Kuteva (2002) *World lexicon of grammaticalization.* Cambridge: Cambridge University Press.
Heine, B. & T. Kuteva (2005) *Language contact and grammatical change.* Cambridge: Cambridge University Press.

Heine, B., U. Claudi & F. Hünnemeyer (1991) *Grammaticalization: A conceptual framework*. Chicago: University of Chicago Press.

Herring, S. C., P. van Reenen & L. Schøsler (2001) "On textual parameters and older languages". In: S. C. Herring, P. van Reenen & L. Schøsler (eds.), *Textual parameters in older languages*. Amsterdam: Benjamins.

Holton, D. (1993) "The formation of the future in Modern Greek literary texts up to the 17th century". In: N. Panagiotakis (ed.), *«Arhes tis Neoellinikis Logotehnias»: Praktika tou Deuterou Diethnous Synedriou "Neograeca Medii Aevi"*. Venetia.

Holton, D. (2005) "The Cambridge grammar of Medieval Greek project: aims scope, research questions". *Paper presented at the Neograeca Medii Aevi VI conference, Ioannina*.

Hopper, P. (1991) "On some principles of grammaticalization". In: E. C. Traugott & B. Heine (eds.), *Approaches to Grammaticalization*. Amsterdam: Benjamins.

Hopper, P. & E. C. Traugott (1993) *Grammaticalization*. Cambridge: Cambridge University Press.

Hopper, P. & E. C. Traugott (2003) *Grammaticalization. 2nd edition*. Cambridge: Cambridge University Press.

Horn, L. (1972) *On the semantic properties of logical operators in English*. Ph.D. dissertation, University of California, Los Angeles.

Horn, L. (1989) *A Natural History of Negation*. Chicago: University of Chicago Press.

Horrocks, G. (1995) "On condition: aspect and modality in the history of Greek". *Proceedings of the Cambridge Philological Society* 41: 153–73.

Horrocks, G. (1997) *Greek: a history of the language and its speakers*. London: Longman.

Horvath, B. M. & R. J. Horvath (2001) "A multilocality study of a sound change in progress: The case of /l/ vocalization in New Zealand and Australian English". *Language Variation and Change* 13: 37–57.

Humbert, J. (1930) *La Disparition du datif en grec*. Paris: Champion.

Iakovou, M. (2003) "«Prepei» kai «mporei»: I grammatikopoiisi tis apostasis". In: D. Theophanopoulou-Kontou, Ch. Laskaratou, M. Sifianou, M. Georgiafentis & V. Spyropoulos (eds.), *Syghrones Taseis stin Elliniki Glossologia*. Athina: Ekdoseis Pataki.

Itkonen, E. (1983) *Causality in linguistic theory: a critical investigation into the philosophical and methodological foundations of "non-autonomous" linguistics*. London: Croom Helm.

Itkonen, E. (2005) *Analogy as structure and process: approaches in linguistics, cognitive psychology and philosophy of science*. Amsterdam: Benjamins.

Janda, R. (2001) "Beyond 'pathways' and 'unidirectionality': on the discontinuity of language transmission and the counterability of grammaticalization". In: L. Campbell (ed.), *Grammaticalization: a critical assessment (special issue of* Language Sciences, 23 (2–3)).

Jannaris, A. (1897) *An historical Greek grammar*. London: MacMillan.

Janse, M. (1993) "La position des pronoms personnels enclitiques en grec néo-testamentaire à la lumière des dialectes néo-helléniques". In: Brixhe, C. (ed.), *La Koinè grecque antique*. Nancy: Presses Universitaires.

Joseph, B. (1983) *The synchrony and diachrony of the Balkan infinitive: a study in areal, general, and historical linguistics*. Cambridge: Cambridge University Press.

Joseph, B. (2000) "Processes of spread for syntactic constructions in the Balkans". In: H. Tzitzilis & H. Symeonidis (eds.), *Valkaniki Glossologia. Syghronia kai Diahronia [Balkanlinguistik. Synchronie und Diachronie]*. Thessaloniki.

Joseph, B. (2001a) "Is there such a thing as 'grammaticalization'?" In: L. Campbell (ed.), *Grammaticalization: a critical assessment (special issue of* Language Sciences, 23 (2–3)).

Joseph, B. (2001b) "Textual authenticity: evidence from Medieval Greek". In: S. C. Herring, P. van Reenen & L. Schøsler (eds.), *Textual parameters in older languages*. Amsterdam: Benjamins.

Joseph, B. (2004) "Rescuing traditional (historical) linguistics from grammaticalization theory". In: O. Fischer, M. Norde & H. Perridon (eds.), *Up and down the cline – the nature of grammaticalization*. Amsterdam: Benjamins.

Joseph, B. & P. Pappas (2002) "On some recent views concerning the development of the Greek future system". *Byzantine and Modern Greek Studies* 26: 247–73.

Karantzola, E. (forth.) "Stoiheia gia tin grammatikopoiisi tou *tha* (16th–17th c.)". *To be published in the proceedings of the 8th International Conference on Greek Linguistics, Ioannina, 2007*.

Karla, G. (2002) "Metafrazontas metohes se dimodi logo to 1600". In: P. Agapitos & M. Pieris (eds.), «T'adonin keinon pou glyka thlivatai». *Ekdotika kai ermineutika zitimata tis dimodous ellinikis logotehnias sto perasma apo ton Mesaiona stin Anagennisi (1400–1600). Praktika tou 4^{ou}diethnous synedriou Neograeca Medii Aevi*. Iraklio: Panepistimiakes Ekdoseis Kritis.

Kazhdan, A. (in collab. with L. F. Sherry & Ch. Angelidi) (1999) *A history of Byzantine literature (650–850)*. Athens: The National Hellenic Research Foundation.

Keller, R. (1994) *On language change: the invisible hand in language* [transl. from German]. London: Routledge.

Kountoura-Galaki, E. (ed.) (2001) *Oi skoteinoi aiones tou Vyzantiou (7th–9th c.)*. Athina: Ethniko Idryma Ereunon.

Kuteva, T. (2001) *Auxiliation: an enquiry into the nature of grammaticalization*. Oxford: Oxford University Press.

Lass, R. (1990) "How to do things with junk: exaptation in language evolution". *Journal of Linguistics* 26: 79–102.

Lass, R. (2004) "Ut Custodiant Litteras: editions, corpora and witnesshood". In: M. Dossena & R. Lass (eds.), *Methods and data in English historical dialectology*. Bern: Peter Lang.

Lehmann, C. (1995) *Thoughts on grammaticalization*. München: Lincom Europa.

Levinson, S. (2000) *Presumptive meanings: the theory of generalized conversational implicature*. Cambridge, Mass.: MIT Press.

Lightfoot, D. (1979) *Principles of diachronic syntax*. Cambridge: Cambridge University Press.

Lightfoot, D. (1999) *The development of language: acquisition, change, and evolution*. Oxford: Blackwell.

Lightfoot, D. (2003) "Grammatical approaches to syntactic change". In: B. Joseph & R. Janda (eds.), *The handbook of historical linguistics*. Oxford: Blackwell.

Loprieno, A. (1995) *Ancient Egyptian. A linguistic introduction*. Cambridge: Cambridge University Press.

LSJ (1996^9) = Liddell, H., R. Scott et al. (eds.), *Greek-English Lexicon*. Oxford: Clarendon Press.

Lyons, J. (1977) *Semantics*. Cambridge: Cambridge University Press.

Mackridge, P. (1993) "An editorial problem in Medieval Greek: the position of the object clitic pronoun in the Escorial *Digenes Akrites*". In: N. Panagiotakis (ed.), «*Arhes tis Neoellinikis Logotehnias*»: *Praktika tou Deuterou Diethnous Synedriou "Neograeca Medii Aevi"*. Venetia.

Magnien, V. (1912) *Emplois et origines du futur grec*. Paris: Champion.

Maltezou, Chr. (1997) "To istoriko kai koinoniko perivallon". In: Holton, D. (ed.), *Logotehnia kai Koinonia stin Kriti tis Anagennisis*. Iraklio: Panepistimiakes Ekdoseis Kritis.

Mandilaras, B. (1973) *The verb in the Greek non-literary papyri*. Athens: Hellenic Ministry of Culture and Sciences.

Manolessou, I. (2000) *Greek noun phrase structure: a study in syntactic evolution*. Ph. D. dissertation, University of Cambridge.

Manolessou, I. (2003) "Oi mi logotehnikes piges os martyries gia ti glossa tis Mesaionikis periodou". *Lexikografikon Deltion* 24: 61–88.

Manolessou, I. (2005) "From participles to gerunds". In: M. Stavrou & A. Terzi (eds.), *Advances in Greek generative syntax*. Amsterdam: Benjamins.

Manolessou, I. (forth.) "Glossiki epafi sti Mesaioniki Ellada: i antonymia 'o opoios'". In: Chila-Markopoulou, D., H. Haralampakis, A. Moser & A. Mpakakou (eds.), "*Glossis Harin*". Volume in honor of Prof. G. Babiniotis. Athina: Ellinika Grammata.

Marcato, G. & F. Ursini (1998) *Dialetti Veneti: grammatica e storia*. Padova: Unipress.

Markopoulos, T. (2005) "Categorial features and grammaticalization: the case of Medieval Greek 'na' ". *Paper presented at the 7th International Conference on Greek Linguistics, York*.

Markopoulos, T. (2006) "The development of futurity / modality markers: evidence from Modern Greek dialects". In: A. Ralli, M. Janse & B. Joseph (eds.), *Proceedings of the 2nd International Conference on Modern Greek Dialects and Linguistic Theory, Mytilene, September 2004*. Patras: University of Patras.

Markopoulos, T. (2007) "Grammatikopoiisi kai glossiki poikilia: o Mellontas sta hronia tis 'Kritikis Anagennisis' (16th–17th c.)". *Studies in Greek Linguistics* 26 (in memory of A. F. Christidis): 251–63.

Markopoulos, T. (forth.) "I ereuna tis glossikis allagis sta keimena tis Mesaionikis Ellinikis: methodologiki diereunisi ton pigon". *To be published in the proceedings of the 8th International Conference on Greek Linguistics, Ioannina, 2007.*

Matthews, P. (1981) *Syntax.* Cambridge: Cambridge University Press.

Mayser, E. (1934) *Grammatik der griechischen Papyri aus der Ptolemäerzeit.* Berlin: Mouton de Gruyter.

McCawley, J. D. (1981) *Everything that linguists have always wanted to know about logic but were ashamed to ask.* Chicago: University of Chicago Press.

Meillet, A. (1912) "L'évolution des formes grammaticales." *Scientia* 12: 26, 6.

Mihăescu, H. (1978) *La langue Latine dans le Sud-Est de l'Europe.* Paris: Les Belles Lettres.

Milroy, J. (1993) "On the social origins of language change". In: C. Jones (ed.), *Historical linguistics: problems and perspectives.* London: Longman.

Milroy, J. (1999) "Toward a speaker-based account of language change". In: E. H. Jahr (ed.), *Language change: advances in historical sociolinguistics.* Berlin: Mouton de Gruyter.

Moravcsik, G. (1938) "Ta syggrammata Konstantinou tou Porfyrogennitou apo glossikis apopseos". *Studi Bizantini e Neoellenici* 5: 514–20.

Moser, A. (1988) *The history of the perfect periphrases in Greek.* Ph.D. dissertation, University of Cambridge.

Nevalainen, T. (2004) "Three perspectives on grammaticalization: lexico-grammar, corpora and historical sociolinguistics". In: Lindquist, H. & C. Mair (eds.), *Corpus approaches to grammaticalization in English.* Amsterdam: Benjamins.

Newmeyer, F. (2001) "Deconstructing grammaticalization". In: L. Campbell (ed.), *Grammaticalization: a critical assessment (special issue of* Language Sciences, 23 (2–3)).

Nystazopoulou-Pelekidou, M. (1986) "Les Slaves dans l'Empire Byzantin". In: *The 17th International Byzantine Congress. Major Papers (Washington, D.C., August 3–8, 1986).* New York: Aristide D. Caratzas.

ODB = Kazhdan, A. et al. (1991) *The Oxford dictionary of Byzantium.* Oxford: Oxford University Press.

Pagkalos, G. (1955) *Peri tou glossikou idiomatos tis Kritis.* Athina.

Palmer, F. R. (2001) *Mood and modality.* 2nd edition. Cambridge: Cambridge University Press.

Panagiotakis, N. (1987) "Meletimata peri Sahliki". *Kritika Hronika* 27: 7–58.

Papadia-Lala, A. (2004) *O thesmos ton astikon koinotiton ston elliniko horo kata tin periodo tis Venetokratias (13th–18th c.). Mia synthetiki proseggisi.* Venetia: Elliniko Instituto Vyzantinon kai Metavyzantinon Spoudon Venetias.

Pappas, P. (2001) "The microcosm of a morphological change: Variation in *thelō* + infinitive futures and *ēthela* + infinitive counterfactuals in Early Modern Greek". *Diachronica* 23: 59–92.

Pappas, P. (2004) *Variation and morphosyntactic change in Greek: from clitics to affixes.* New York: Palgrave.

Pappas, P. & B. Joseph (2001) "The development of the Greek future system: setting the record straight". In: G. Aggouraki et al. (eds.), *Proceedings of the 4th International Conference on Greek Linguistics*. Thessaloniki: University Studio Press.

Philippaki-Warburton, I. & V. Spyropoulos (2004) "A change of mood: the development of the Greek mood system". *Linguistics* 42: 791–817.

Pinkster, H. (1987) "The strategy and chronology of the development of future and perfect tense auxiliaries in Latin". In: M. Harris & P. Ramat (eds.), *Historical development of auxiliaries*. Berlin: Mouton de Gruyter.

Pulvermüller, F. (2002) *The neuroscience of language. On brain circuits of words and serial order*. Cambridge: Cambridge University Press.

Ralli, A., D. Melissaropoulou & S. Tsolakidis (2007) "O Parakeimenos sti Nea Elliniki kai stis dialektous: paratiriseis gia tin morfi kai tin exelixi tou". *Studies in Greek Linguistics* 26 (in memory of A. F. Christidis): 361–72.

Ramat, P. (1987) "Introductory paper". In: M. Harris & P. Ramat (eds.), *Historical development of auxiliaries*. Berlin: Mouton de Gruyter.

Roberts, I. & A. Roussou (2003) *Syntactic change: a minimalist approach to grammaticalization*. Cambridge: Cambridge University Press.

Rohlfs, G. (1949–54) *Historische Grammatik der italienischen Sprache und ihrer Mundarten*. Bern: Francke.

Roussou, A. (2005) "The syntax of non-volitional 'θelo' in Greek". In: M. Stavrou & A. Terzi (eds.), *Advances in Greek generative syntax*. Amsterdam: Benjamins.

Schreiner, P. (1988) "Der byzantinische Bilderstreit. Kritische Analyse der zeitgenössischen Meinungen und das Urteil der Nachwelt bis heute". *Settimane di Studio del Centro Italiano di Studi sull' Alto Medioevo* 34: 319–427.

Schwyzer, E. (1950–71) *Griechische Grammatik*. München: Beck.

Slobin, D. I. (1997) "The origins of grammaticizable notions: beyond the individual mind". In: D. I. Slobin (ed.), *The crosslinguistic study of language acquisition, Vol. 5. Expanding the contexts*. Mahwah: Erlbaum Associates.

Steele, S. (1978) "The category AUX as a language universal". In: J. H. Greenberg (ed.), *Universals of Human Language*. Stanford: Stanford University Press.

Stolz, T. (2002) "No Sprachbund beyond this line!" In: P. Ramat & T. Stolz (eds.), *Mediterranean languages. Papers from the MEDTYP workshop, Tirrenia, June 2000*. Bochum: Universitätsverlag Dr. N. Brockmeyer.

Taeldeman, J. (2005) "The influence of urban centres on the spatial diffusion of dialect phenomena". In: P. Auer, F. Hinskens & P. Kerswill (eds.), *Dialect change: convergence and divergence in European languages*. Cambridge: Cambridge University Press.

Taylor, A. (1994) "The change from SOV to SVO in Ancient Greek". *Language Variation and Change* 6: 1–37.

Terkourafi, M. (2005) "Understanding the present through the past: processes of koineisation in Cyprus". *Diachronica* 22: 309–72.

Thomason, S. G. (2001) *Language contact: an introduction*. Edinburgh: Edinburgh University Press.

Tiersma, P. (1999) *Legal language*. Chicago: University of Chicago Press.
Tomasoni, P. (1994) "Veneto". In: L. Seriani & P. Trifone (eds.), *Storia della lingua italiana. Volume terzo: Le altre lingue*. Torino: Giulio Einandi.
Tomić, O. M. (2006) *Balkan sprachbund morpho-syntactic features*. Dordrecht: Springer.
Tonnet, H. (1982) "Note sur la constitution du futur grec moderne". *Cahiers balkaniques* 3: 105–19.
Traugott, E. C. (1999) "Grammaticalization and lexicalization". In: K. Brown, J. Miller, & R. Asher (eds.), *Concise Encyclopedia of Grammatical Categories*. Amsterdam: Elsevier.
Traugott, E. C. & R. Dasher (2002) *Regularity in Semantic Change*. Cambridge: Cambridge University Press.
Trudgill, P. (1983) *On dialect*. Oxford: Blackwell.
Trudgill, P. (1986) *Dialects in contact*. Oxford: Blackwell.
Trudgill, P. (2003) "Modern Greek dialects: a preliminary classification". *Journal of Greek Linguistics* 4: 45–64.
Trypanis, C. A. (1960) "Early Medieval Greek ἵνα". *Glotta* 38: 312–13.
Tsakali, V. (2003) "On the Greek verbs *erhome* 'come' and *pijeno* 'go' ". Unpublished M.Phil dissertation, University of Cambridge.
Tsangalidis, A. (1999) *Will and Tha: a comparative study of the category future*. Thessaloniki: University Studio Press.
Van der Auwera, J. (2001) "On the typology of negative modals". In: J. Hoeksema, H. Rullmann, V. Sanchez-Valencia & T. van der Wouden (eds.), *Perspectives on negation and polarity items*. Amsterdam: Benjamins.
Van der Auwera, J. & V. A. Plungian (1998) "Modality's semantic map". *Linguistic Typology* 2: 79–124.
Van Gelderen, E. (2004) *Grammaticalization as economy*. Amsterdam: Benjamins.
Van Gemert, A. (1997) "Logotehnikoi prodromoi". In: Holton, D. (ed.), *Logotehnia kai Koinonia stin Kriti tis Anagennisis*. Iraklio: Panepistimiakes Ekdoseis Kritis.
Varella, S. (2006) *Language Contact and the Lexicon in the History of Cypriot Greek*. Bern: Peter Lang.
Vincent, N. (1991) "The role of periphrasis in theory and description". *Paper presented at the 10th International Conference on Historical Linguistics, Amsterdam*.
Warner, A. (1993) *English auxiliaries: structure and history*. Cambridge: Cambridge University Press.
Weinreich, U., W. Labov & M. Herzog (1968) "Empirical foundations for a theory of language change". In: W. P. Lehmann & Y. Malkiel (eds.), *Directions for historical linguistics: a symposium*. Austin: University of Texas Press.
Ziegeler, D. (2006) "Omnitemporal *will*". *Language Sciences*: 28: 76–119.

Name Index

Adams, J. N. 62, 70
Aerts, W. J. 11, 19, 60, 92, 94, 121, 130, 135, 140, 149, 151, 157, 201
Aijmer, K. 48
Aikhenvald, A. Y. 109 (n. 11), 205
Alexiou, S. 143 (n. 11, 12), 210 (n. 45)
Andersen, H. 172
Anderson, G. D. S. 12–13
Anderson, J. 12
Apollonius Dyscolus 78–79, 83
Arethas 96, 107
Aristotle 21
Avramea, A. 109

Babiniotis, G. 154
Bakker, W. F. 119, 207 (n. 44)
Balletto, L. 205
Bănescu, N. 1, 60, 64, 94, 96, 97 (n. 6), 106–107, 117, 121, 140, 149–150, 155, 164, 167, 177, 182 (n. 29), 184, 189, 190
Basset, L. 19, 22
Beaton, R. 16, 117–118
Beck, H.-G. 117
Bennett, C. 39
Bertinetto, P. M. 12
Biber, D. 16, 227
Binnick, R. 40 (n. 18)
Birnbaum, H. 172
Biville, F. 63 (n. 7)
Blass, F. 49, 53
Bon, S. 198
Borsley, R. 12
Brewer, A. 199
Brincat, J. 167 (n. 23)
Browning, R. 1, 89, 94, 97
Brunot, F. 160, 200
Bryer, A. 87
Bubenik, V. 172 (n. 26)
Bybee, J. 2–4, 9–11, 18, 21, 35, 41, 43–44, 48, 56, 64, 66, 68, 70, 73, 78–79, 99, 123–124, 137, 140–141, 152–153, 162 (n. 20), 177–178, 199, 229–230

Campbell, L. 2, 39, 203
Carantinos, G. 178

Caroll, L. 199–200
Chalkokondyles 97 (n. 6)
Chila-Markopoulou, D. 19, 40
Christidis, A.-F. 1, 46
Claudi, U. 4
Coates, J. 10, 138, 152, 171 (n. 25)
Coleman, R. G. G. 70
Comrie, B. 9, 32
Constantine VII Porphyrogenitus 89, 91, 96, 98, 107, 111, 113
Cristofaro, S. 39 (n. 17)
Croft, W. 8, 10

Dagron, G. 109
Dahl, Ö. 9, 43
Dasher, R. 4, 69
De Melo, W. D. C. 32
Debrunner, A. 49, 53
Delendas, I. 147
Dellaportas, 117, 132–134, 139
Demosthenes 55 (n. 4)–56
Denison, D. 71
Detorakis, Th. 221
Devine, A. M. 27
Dieterich, K. 200
Diewald, G. 21
Diggle, J. 32
Dixon, R. M. W. 109 (n. 11), 205
Dryer, M. S. 5

Ermoniakos 125–126, 129–130, 145, 147–150, 174, 212

Falieros 117, 132, 135, 147 (n. 13), 162, 183, 190–193, 200–201, 205, 218–219
Fewster, P. 50
Finegan, E. 16
Fischer, O. 3–4, 6–8, 18, 139, 231
Fleischman, S. 9–10, 41, 62, 157 (n. 17)
Foulet, L. 150

Gedeon, M. 133
Gignac, F. T. 46, 61 (n. 6)
Glykas, Mihail 144, 171, 211
Goldoni, 214

284   *Name Index*

Goodwin, W. W. 19–20, 23, 30–31, 38–39, 41, 43, 61, 71 (n. 10), 98–99
Gregersen, F. 15
Grigoropoulos, J. 178
Grigoropoulos, M. 135, 148, 160, 181, 185, 205
Grund, P. 16, 117

Haiman, J. 8, 18
Haldon, J. 88
Harris, A. 39, 203
Harris, M. 12
Haspelmath, M. 2, 11, 24, 74, 189, 203
Hatzidakis, G. 200, 201 (n. 40)
Heine, B. 2–5, 12, 21–22, 25, 27–28, 34–35, 37, 62, 64, 172 (n. 26), 173, 202, 228–230
Herrin, J. 87
Herring, S. C. 15
Herzog, M. 226
Holton, D. 116 (n. 2), 203
Homer 20, 22–24 (n. 8), 27, 34, 36 (n. 14) 39 (n. 16), 40, 43–44, 61
Hopper, P. 2, 5, 23, 36, 44
Horn, L. 68, 80
Horrocks, G. 1, 15, 46–47, 50 (n. 3), 60–62, 75, 89, 94, 116 (n. 2), 121, 138, 143 (n. 10), 148–151, 154, 156, 157 (n. 17), 158, 160, 162, 164, 168, 184, 186 (n. 33), 187, 197, 200–201, 208, 215
Horvath, B. M. 204 (n. 42)
Horvath, R. J. 204 (n. 42)
Humbert, J. 46
Hunger, H. 125, 180
Hünnemeyer, F. 4

Iakovou, M. 68, 127
Itkonen, E. 2, 4, 8

Janda, R. 4
Jannaris, A. 1, 20, 30, 32, 46, 53, 60–62, 64, 117, 121, 164, 187
Janse, M. 46
Joseph, B. 2–3, 54, 74, 94, 109, 127 (n. 4), 140, 142–143, 149, 164–165, 167, 172–173, 176, 179–180, 183–184, 187, 189, 197, 200, 205 (n. 43)

Kaklamanis, S. 205
Kallergis 144
Karantzola, E. 118
Karla, G. 148
Karydis, S. 154
Kazhdan, A. 87

Kehagioglou, G. 196, 198
Kekaumenos 165
Keller, R. 8
Korrah ben Scharik 91
Kountoura-Galaki, E. 87
Kuteva, T. 3, 5, 12–13, 22, 28, 62, 172 (n. 26)–173, 202, 206–207, 211, 228

Labov, W. 226
Lampros, S. 144, 176, 214, 222
Lass, R. 16, 67
Lehmann, C. 2–3, 26
Lentari, T. 184
Leo VI 89
Leontius 95–96, 106, 112
Levinson, S. 68
Lightfoot, D. 5, 7, 231
Loprieno, A. 72
Lyons, J. 9, 41 (n. 19), 48, 152
Lysias 25, 30 (n. 11), 32

Mackridge, P. 116 (n. 2)
Magnien, V. 1, 21, 29
Maltezou, Chr. 198, 214
Mandilaras, B. 46, 75 (n. 12), 81, 97, 148
Manolessou, I. 46, 50, 118, 223
Manousakas, M. I. 127, 134, 139, 214
Maras 147, 181, 193–196, 200, 204–205, 220
Marcato, G. 199
Marcus Diaconus 106
Markopoulos, T. 118, 153, 169, 203, 208, 223
Matthews, P. 11
Mayser, E. 46
McCawley, J. D. 9
Meillet, A. 2
Melissaropoulou, D. 158 (n. 19)
Mertzios, K. D. 144
Mihăescu, H. 114 (n. 13)
Milroy, J. 202, 204
Moravcsik, G. 91 (n. 4)
Moschos, J. 89 (n. 1), 95–97, 107
Moser, A. 140, 148, 156–158

Newmeyer, F. 5
Nikolaou-Konnari, A. 193 (n. 37)
Nystazopoulou-Pelekidou, M. 109

Pagkalos, G. 148, 219
Pagliuca, W. 2–4, 9–11, 21, 35, 41, 44, 48, 64, 66, 68, 70, 73, 78–79, 99, 123–124, 137, 140–141, 152–153, 162 (n. 20), 177–178, 229–230

Name Index

Palaiologos, Theodoros 176
Palmer, F. R. 11
Panagiotakis, N. 148, 189
Papadia-Lala, A. 204
Papadimitriou, S. D. 188 (n. 34), 200
Pappas, P. 2, 116 (n. 2), 143, 164–165, 167, 176, 179–180, 183–184, 187, 189, 197, 200, 223
Pedersen, I. L. 15
Perkins, D. 2–4, 9–11, 21, 35, 41, 44, 48, 64, 66, 68, 70, 73, 78–79, 99, 123–124, 137, 140–141, 152–153, 162 (n. 20), 177–178, 229–230
Philippaki-Warburton, I. 169 (n. 24)
Phrynichus, 33, 55, 59
Pieris, M. 193 (n. 37)
Pinkster, H. 36, 62
Plato, 38, 42
Plungian, V. A. 11
Polemis, D. 163, 195, 207, 214–215, 220–222
Prodromos, Theodoros 116, 171
Pulvermüller, F. 6

Ralli, A. 158 (n. 19)
Ramat, P. 12
Richard, J. 198
Roberts, I. 7, 169 (n. 24), 179, 231
Rohlfs, G. 97 (n. 6), 199, 214
Romanus 105 (n. 8)
Roussou, A. 7, 169 (n. 24), 179, 231

Sahlikis 125, 126, 182, 184, 187–189, 191, 193, 200, 205
Sathas, K. 125, 180
Schopen, L. 158
Schøsler, L. 15
Schreiner, P. 87
Schwyzer, E. 1, 20, 61
Slobin, D. I. 6
Spyropoulos, V. 169 (n. 24)
Steele, S. 12

Stephens, S. D. 27
Stolz, T. 167 (n. 23)

Taeldeman, J. 204 (n. 42)
Taylor, A. 27
Terkourafi, M. 199
Theophanes 102, 106–107
Thomason, S. G. 63 (n. 7), 150, 198
Thompson, S. A. 56
Thucydides 25 (n. 9), 30 (n. 11), 32, 55 (n. 4), 56
Tiersma, P. 108, 119
Tomasoni, P. 198
Tomić, O. M. 109 (n. 11)
Tonnet, H. 189
Traugott, E. C. 2, 4–5, 23, 36, 69
Trudgill, P. 201 (n. 41), 204 (n. 42),
Trypanis, C. A. 105 (n. 8)
Tsakali, V. 200 (n. 38)
Tsangalidis, A. 9
Tsolakidis, S. 158 (n. 19)

Ursini, F. 199

Van der Auwera, J. 11, 69
Van Gelderen, E. 7
Van Gemert, A. F. 119, 191–192, 205, 207 (n. 44), 219 (n. 46)
Van Reenen, P. 15
Varella, S. 199
Vincent, N. 12
Visvizis, I. 183
Vogel, K. 125, 180

Wagner, W. 187–188
Warner, A. 12, 152, 161, 217
Weinreich, U. 226

Xanthoudidis, S. 194, 207

Ziegeler, D. 43, 162 (n. 20)

Subject Index

Ability (as modal notion) 11, 33–35, 37–38, 45, 60–61, 63, 64 (n. 9), 65–72, 85, 96–97, 100–101, 103–104, 141–147, 149, 155 (n. 16)–156, 159–161, 164, 220, 229–230, 232
  Ability-in-the-past 37–38, 70–71, 101, 156, 159–160, 164
Adjacency 12, 26–27, 44, 52–53, 184
Ancient Greek (AG) *see also* Classical Greek 19–45, 46–49 (n. 2), 51–58, 60–61 (n. 6), 71 (n. 10), 72–74, 76–78, 84, 89, 91, 99, 105, 113, 124, 131, 133, 141, 154, 167, 208, 225
Andros 119, 163, 195–196, 208, 214–215, 220–222
Anteriority 157, 172
Aspect 9, 10, 13, 30 (n. 11)–33, 40 (n. 18), 57–59, 89, 138
  Imperfective 19 (n. 2), 30–31, 57–58, 89, 157 (n. 17)
  Perfective 19 (n. 2), 30, 49 (n. 2), 57–59, 89
Athos 119, 122, 141, 166
Atticism, *see also* diglossia 15–17, 79
Auxiliary 5–6, 11–13, 24, 26, 44, 48, 80, 127, 148, 154, 157, 215

Balkan Sprachbund, *see also* language contact, Slavic languages 109, 205
Bilingualism, *see also* language contact 62, 63 (n. 7), 109, 115 (n. 1), 117, 173, 228
Bulgarian, *see also* language contact 172 (n. 26), 205–207, 211
Byzantium, Byzantine Empire 87–88, 90, 92, 105, 109, 115–116, 119, 125, 127, 133, 156, 158, 178

Classical Greek, *see also* Ancient Greek 1–2, 15, 17–18, 53–54, 58–59, 85, 88–89, 98, 209
Cline, *see also* grammaticalization 5–6, 232
Code alternation 63 (n. 7)
Complementizer 39 (n. 16), 98–99, 124, 127, 129, 151, 153–154, 165, 168–169, 177, 206
  Complex complementizer 153, 168

Compounding 27, 51, 79, 133, 137
Conditionals 37–38, 45, 71, 96, 101–102, 108 (n. 10), 142, 150, 156–157, 160, 162–164, 166 (n. 22), 179, 192, 209–210, 212–214, 216–218, 220–222
  Apodosis 37, 71, 96, 101, 156–157, 161–162, 212, 215, 217, 220
  Counterfactuals 37, 71, 85, 101–102, 156, 157 (n. 17), 161–164, 210 (n. 45), 212–215, 218–219, 222
  Protasis 42, 156–157, 161, 164, 212, 214–215
Constructional meaning 12, 72
Convergence 109 (n. 11), 205, 207, 214, 217, 223
Co-reference 75–76
Corfu 119, 147, 154, 160, 181, 204, 214
Cretan dialect, *see* Crete
Crete 117, 119, 127, 134–135, 142, 147–148, 153, 157–158, 160, 163, 180–181, 184–185, 187, 190, 193–194, 196, 198–200, 203–205, 207, 208, 212, 214, 217, 220–222
Cypriot dialect, *see* Cyprus
Cyprus 92, 121, 128, 130–131, 134–136, 144, 182, 185, 189, 193, 198–201 (n. 41), 203–205, 207, 215, 217–218, 221

Diglossia *see also* Atticism 15–17
Disjoint reference 74–75, 112, 166, 219
Divergence 73, 92, 138, 156
Dodecanese 204

Early Medieval Greek (EMG) 16–18, 87–114, 116, 122, 124, 130, 138–139, 141, 145, 149, 151–152, 154–156, 166–167, 170–173, 209, 223–226, 228, 231
Egyptian (Demotic) 72
Ellipsis 24, 25 (n. 9), 52, 131
Embedding,
  Syntactic 219
  Sociolinguistic 8, 15, 17, 230–231
English, *see also* Old English, Middle English 3, 10–11, 34, 40 (n. 18), 41, 43–44, 48, 138, 152–153, 161, 162 (n. 20), 171, 230–231
Exaptation 67–68

Subject Index

Franks, *see also* French 115–116, 176, 178, 198
French, *see also* Romance languages,
    language contact, Provençal 82, 129,
    150, 160–161, 193, 198–202, 204–205, 208
Frequency of use 6, 18, 23, 26, 42, 55–57,
    63, 74, 89 (n. 1), 94–96, 101, 104,
    107, 112–113, 122, 125, 127–128, 131, 135,
    138–140, 144, 155, 165, 167, 171–173,
    176 (n. 28), 181, 200–201, 205, 210,
    216, 223, 225–228, 231–232
    Token frequency, 18, 23, 26–28, 31–32, 35,
        42, 49, 59, 75, 84, 100–101, 103, 111, 123,
        130, 133, 136, 145, 171, 174, 184
Future
    Destiny Future 123, 128–129, 131, 133,
        136–139, 144, 223, 227
    Future-in-the-past 38, 64 (n. 9), 70–71,
        89, 102–104, 128–129, 159, 161, 210–211,
        216–218
    Future Tense 2, 8–10, 14, 19–21, 23, 40
        (n. 18), 41, 43 (n. 21), 44, 47, 49, 61
        (n. 6), 96–99, 152
    Predestination Future 64, 70, 230
    Scheduled Future 64 (n. 8), 65, 70, 230

Generalization of use / meaning 6, 54, 60,
    72, 75–76, 96, 97, 104, 107, 139, 163, 167,
    171, 200, 209, 212, 222
Generative grammar / framework 5–8, 231
Genericness 40 (n. 18), 41, 43–44, 73, 76–78,
    80, 83–84, 175, 181–182
Genoese 115, 183, 178–199, 201 (n. 40)
Gradualness of change 4–6, 13, 55, 73
Grammatical categories 6, 9–10, 12–13, 39,
    41 (n. 19), 54, 58, 98, 128, 140, 152
    Non-distinctiveness of 13, 153
Grammatical replication 62, 67, 172, 202,
    205, 207
Grammaticalization 2–8, 11, 13–14, 22, 26,
    28, 33, 34, 44–45, 49, 73, 83, 85, 93, 95,
    101, 104, 112–113, 127, 137, 139–140, 155
    (n. 16), 161, 174, 186, 203, 216, 228–233
    Functional–typological perspective 2–4,
        6–8, 231, 233

Habeo + Infinitive construction, *see also*
    Latin, language contact 34, 62, 70, 81, 156
Habitual 40 (n. 18), 77–78, 80, 159, 161,
    162 (n. 20), 164, 213, 217
Hellenistic–Roman Greek (H-R) 1–2, 15,
    17–18, 25, 27–28, 45, 46–86, 89–94,
    98–102, 104–107, 110–112, 114, 130, 154,
    167, 209, 225–226, 228
Hios 201 (n. 40)
Hyperbaton 27

Iconoclasm 87
Impersonal form, *see also* θέλει impersonal,
    uninflected form 39, 127 (n. 5)–131,
    135–139, 176, 178–181, 187, 196–197, 201,
    219, 221
Implicature 33, 69, 111, 232
Impreciseness 9
Indo-European 39, 41, 82
Infinitive
    Aorist 19, 28–30, 32–33, 37–38, 42,
        53–56, 89 (n. 1)–93, 108–109, 122, 127
        (n. 4)
    Future 19, 24, 28–33, 38, 42, 49, 53–59,
        89 (n. 1), 90 (n. 3)-91, 93, 108, 122
    Present 19, 28–33, 37–38, 42,
        53–59, 89 (n. 1)–91, 93, 108, 122,
        127 (n. 4)
    Replacement of 49, 53–54, 56, 58, 73–74,
        92–93, 104–105, 113, 127, 134, 137, 144,
        147, 161–162, 174, 184, 205 (n. 43), 211,
        215–216, 217–218
Intention 21–22, 25, 27–28, 33, 35,
    41–44, 48, 51, 70, 77, 137–138, 170,
    188, 229
Interference (shift-induced), *see also*
    language contact 150, 198, 202
Irrealis, *see also* markers 37, 71 (n. 10), 73,
    101–103, 155, 163
Italian (Old) 97 (n. 6)

Kefalonia 119, 135, 163, 181, 185, 194, 196, 205,
    215, 220–222

Language contact *see also* bilingualism,
    multilingualism 14, 39, 58, 72, 176
    (n. 28), 186, 202, 205, 207, 227–228,
    231–232
    Contact between Latin and Greek 39, 62,
        63 (n. 7), 70, 72, 81, 155
    Contact between Slavic and Greek 109,
        115 (n. 1), 155–156, 172–173
    Contact between Bulgarian and
        Greek 205–207, 211
    Contact between Romance languages
        and Greek 162, 164, 189, 198–199, 201,
        205, 208, 228, 233

288   Subject Index

Language contact (*cont.*)
   Contact between Arabic and
      Greek 167 (n. 23)
   Contact-induced change 173, 198, 204
Late Medieval Greek (LMG) 1, 15–18, 38, 72,
    74, 88, 109–110, 112, 115–224, 225–228,
    232–233
Latin, *see also* "habeo + Infinitive
   construction", language contact 32,
   34, 36, 39, 62, 67, 70, 72, 81–82, 113, 114
   (n. 13), 144, 155, 230
Layering 36
   Functional layering 44, 123, 226
Lingua franca 46
Literary texts 15, 17, 70, 116–122, 124–126,
   131–132, 136, 138, 141, 145–151,
   157–160, 163, 165, 171, 173, 175–176,
   179, 181–183, 185–186, 190, 193–196,
   200–201, 205, 207–208, 212–217, 220,
   222–223, 227
Logical square 68–69, 232
Lusignan, *see also* Cyprus, Franks 144, 198

Manuscripts/Manuscript tradition 16–17,
   33, 109, 117–118, 129, 143 (n. 11), 147,
   150–151, 157, 166 (n. 21), 177, 186 (n. 33),
   187, 189, 190 (n. 35), 191, 193 (n. 37), 196,
   211 (n. 45), 219–220, 227
Markers 30
   Conjunction 219–220
   Disjunction 111
   Future certainty 48
   Irrealis / Potential 71 (n. 10)
   Modality / Futurity 149, 153, 170, 229
   Subjunctive 143 (n. 12), 150, 168
   Subordination 152, 153, 155, 161, 192
Metre 32, 118, 211 (n. 45)
Middle English 43, 71, 123, 152
Modal branching 70, 85
Modal harmony, *see also* "νά + FC"
   construction 152, 155
Modality, *see also* modality marker,
   TAM meanings 8, 9, 10, 11, 68–69, 140,
   152–153, 155–156, 229
   Agent-oriented modality 11
   Deontic modality, *see also* obligation 9,
      11, 48, 53, 59, 78–80, 83–84, 99, 100,
      110, 128–131, 133, 136–139, 141, 144–145,
      178–181, 185–186, 194–195, 197, 202,
      206, 221, 225, 230
   Dynamic modality 11

Epistemic modality 9, 11, 78, 80, 82–83,
   111, 171 (n. 25), 175, 178, 182, 230
Modal verb 20–22, 25, 33, 44, 127, 138,
   139, 152, 221, 229
Speaker-oriented modality 11
Modern Greek 1, 20, 37, 64 (n. 8), 82, 115,
   121, 133–134, 136, 144, 147–149, 153,
   155–156, 157 (n. 18), 164, 168, 169, 179,
   186, 220, 223
Modern Greek dialects, *see* Modern Greek
Morphosyntactic agreement 19, 50, 54, 189,
   202, 203, 208, 221–222
Morphosyntactic properties 5–6, 22, 33,
   226, 231
Multilingualism, *see also* language
   contact 114, 198, 204, 205
Mutual reinforcement, *see also* language
   contact 62, 63 (n. 7), 72, 173

Naxos 119, 163, 176, 183, 214, 215, 220, 222
Nimboran 41
Non-finite forms, *see also* Infinitive,
   Participle 19, 44, 47–50, 58, 84, 85, 148,
   157–158, 162, 215
Non-literary texts, *see also* notaries 16,
   118–120, 122, 123, 125, 127, 135–136, 142,
   144–145, 150, 158, 163, 169, 171, 180–181,
   183, 185, 187, 193, 195–196, 200–201, 204,
   207, 212, 214, 216, 219, 222–223, 227
Norm, normative behaviour 59, 63, 76, 120,
   124, 136, 221
Notaries, *see also* non-literary texts 16, 17,
   118–121, 135–136, 138, 142, 176, 181, 193,
   196, 198, 204–205, 220–221

Obligation, *see also* deontic modality, TAM
   meanings 2–3, 11, 35, 60, 62–64 (n. 9),
   65–70, 79, 85, 99–101, 103, 111, 128–129,
   131–133, 136–137, 139, 144–147, 149,
   159–160, 170, 171 (n. 25), 174–175,
   178–179, 196, 202, 208, 223, 230
Old Bulgarian, *see* Bulgarian
Old Church Slavonic (OCS), *see also*
   Slavic languages, language
   contact 172 (n. 26)
Old English 41, 43, 71, 123, 152, 161, 217
Old French, *see* French
Old Venetian, *see* Venetian

Papyri 17, 46–49, 51–60, 61 (n. 6), 65–67, 70,
   72, 75–77, 80–84, 88, 90–101, 105 (n. 8),

Subject Index

106 (n. 9), 107, 108 (n. 10), 110, 112, 133, 148, 151, 227
Participle 19, 23, 24, 25, 37, 44, 48, 50, 72, 84, 125, 131,
   Adjectival / Nominal 23, 24 (n. 8), 25, 49, 51
   Complement of FCs 97 (n. 6), 125, 148, 157, 158, 162, 163, 164, 214
   Verbal 23, 24 (n. 8), 49, 51
Particle 26, 82, 110, 165, 186, 191, 206
   Futurity / Modality 153, 164, 186
   Volitional 189, 201, 202
Perfect 11, 19, 46, 122, 140, 147–150 (n. 15), 156, 158(n. 19), 160, 216
Periphrasis, periphrastic constructions 1, 2, 9, 11–13, 55 (n. 4), 72, 149
Phonological change 186, 189, 190, 198, 200–201, 203, 226, 228, 229, 230
Pluperfect 19, 148, 155–157 (n. 18), 158, 160, 162–164, 222–223
Possession 33–34, 35, 147 (n. 14), 155 (n. 16), 230
   Abstract possession 37, 230
   Possession / Purpose cognitive schema 34, 35, 64, 230
Possibility 9, 60, 65, 66–70, 80, 81, 83, 84, 85, 97, 98, 111, 141, 220
   As a source for future reference 66–70, 230
   Epistemic possibility see also epistemic modality 9, 78, 80, 82, 83, 85, 111
Prediction (core meaning of futurity) 10, 13, 21, 28, 37, 43, 137, 138, 170, 188
Prohibition 141, 175
Provençal, see also French, language contact 199, 202

Reanalysis 7, 34 (n. 13), 36 (n. 14), 167, 186
Reduction,
   Morphosyntactic 48, 50, 72, 85, 128, 139
   Phonetic / Phonological 6, 186, 189–190, 200–202, 206–209, 226, 228, 231
Register, see also sociolinguistic variation 16, 17, 47, 59, 73, 75 (n. 11), 79, 81, 83, 84, 85, 88, 91, 94, 95, 96, 107, 108 (n. 10), 110, 111, 113, 119, 120, 122, 124, 125, 133, 136, 142, 194, 209–210, 224, 225, 226, 227, 228, 230, 231, 238
   High registers 17, 75, 77, 78, 81, 85, 92 (n. 5), 94, 95, 96, 104, 109, 111 (n. 12), 113, 121, 122, 123, 125, 127 (n. 4), 131, 134, 135, 136, 138, 139, 142, 145, 165, 166, 171, 176, 223, 225, 226, 232
   Low registers 16, 17, 46, 47, 52, 59, 73, 81, 84, 85, 87, 88, 89, 91, 92, 93, 94, 95, 96, 105 (n. 8), 106, 107, 108, 109, 113, 114, 125, 127 (n. 4), 131, 133, 135, 136, 170, 176, 207, 221, 226
   Middle registers 17, 47, 77, 80, 83, 84, 85, 90 (n. 3) 91, 95, 96, 100, 109, 113, 122, 125, 127, 131, 136, 141, 145, 150, 167, 168, 171, 176, 223, 232
   Written registers 78, 106, 114, 122, 134, 139, 178, 185, 193 (n. 37), 196, 218
Requests 81, 83, 84, 85, 110, 111
Restructuring 201
Retention 9, 44, 59, 73, 130, 155 (n. 16), 164, 167, 201 (n. 41)
Romance languages, see also French, Venetian, language contact 115, 148, 150, 164, 193, 198–199, 201–203, 208, 228, 233

Santorini 147
Scribes, see also manuscripts 16, 50, 54, 109, 119, 154, 177, 193 (n. 37), 219 (n. 46)
Serialization, see also V + V$_s$ pattern 129, 143, 167
Slavic languages, see also Old Church Slavonic, language contact 109, 110, 114 (n. 13) 156, 172, 173, 205
South Italy 39, 122–124, 142, 150, 157, 158 (n. 19) 176 (n. 28)
Specialization,
   Sociolinguistic (register) 73, 81, 121, 122, 138, 226, 227, 230, 231
   Morphosyntactic / semantic 23, 44, 73, 123, 128, 129, 131, 138, 139, 157, 212, 227
Split (semantic / syntactic) 73, 137, 170, 171, 176, 186, 203, 208
Spoken language 14–15, 39, 45, 47, 75, 82, 107, 109, 114, 119, 133, 194, 205
Standard Modern Greek,
   see Modern Greek
Structured heterogeneity 226
Subjunctive, see also "νά + Subjunctive"
   As a subordinating mood 19, 38, 39 (n. 16), 73, 81, 84, 92, 98, 99, 104, 113, 124, 126, 127, 132, 137, 144, 146, 151, 159, 165, 168, 176, 179, 218
   Deliberative 75 (n. 12)

Subjunctive, (cont.)
  Future-referring (independent) 47,
    60, 61, 98, 113, 172, 184 (n. 31), 186,
    187, 197, 223
  Interchange with Indicative (Future) 47,
    61 (n. 6), 99, 143, 150 (n. 15), 151,
    152, 153, 177
  Interrogative 37, 39
  In prohibitions 141
  Morphological 60, 200–201
  Overlap with AVCs 98, 99, 104, 124, 134,
    149, 151, 152, 153, 154, 160, 161, 169, 170,
    171, 192, 231
  Subordination marker 39, 147, 149, 151, 152
  Weakening 152, 154, 184, 232
Swahili 41
Syntactic borrowing, *see also* grammatical
  replication 39
Syntactic cohesion, *see also* syntagmatic
  bondedness 26, 44
Syntagmatic bondedness, *see also* syntactic
  cohesion 26, 45, 52, 72, 84

TAM (Tense-Aspect-Modality)
  meanings 9, 12, 19, 39 (n. 17),
    40, 43, 73, 76, 82, 83, 84, 85, 100,
    101, 104, 111, 112, 173, 174, 203,
    208, 222, 229
Telicity 32–33
Tok Pisin 41
Turks 115, 144
Typological findings / predictions 6, 10,
  11, 14, 39 (n. 17), 85, 137, 140, 178, 229,
  230, 233

Unidirectionality 4, 5
Uninflected form, *see also* impersonal
  form 12, 82, 128, 135, 137, 139, 187, 189,
  196, 205, 206, 220, 222

V + V$_s$ pattern, *see also* serialization 38–39,
  72, 74, 75, 76, 104, 129, 143, 145,
  166–167 (n. 23), 168, 171, 175, 181,
  182, 184, 185 (n. 32), 186, 190 (n. 35),
  208, 220
Variation 7, 13, 16, 24, 35, 118, 164, 173, 226,
  228, 230–232
  In the complementation of AVCs 29,
    127 (n. 4)
  Manuscript 17, 117, 129, 161, 188 (n. 34),
    190 (n. 36), 191, 193 (n. 37)
  Morphosyntactic 124, 128, 157 (n. 17),
    211, 212, 222, 223

Sociolinguistic (register) 73, 83, 136
Venetian, Venetian influence, *see also*
  Romance languages, language
  contact 115, 116, 117, 119, 135, 144, 160,
  189, 198–202, 204–205, 208, 214
Vernacular, *see also* literary texts 15–17,
  107, 109, 116 (n. 3), 117, 119–124,
  136, 138, 145, 160, 167, 173, 185, 201,
  205, 224, 227
Volition, Volitional meaning of
  constructions, *see also* volitional
  particle 2, 29, 40, 41, 42, 43, 44,
  73, 77, 78, 79, 82, 83, 85, 104, 107,
  108, 137, 156, 165, 168, 170, 174–176,
  182, 183, 184 (n. 30), 187, 188 (n. 34),
  189–197, 202, 203, 206, 207, 208, 209,
  210, 211, 212, 217, 223, 229
Volitional (ἐ)θέλω, 27–28, 38, 41, 42, 74,
  75, 76, 84, 104, 112, 113, 165, 166, 168, 170,
  171, 174, 176, 182, 184, 186, 190, 197, 203,
  209, 210, 211, 229

Willan, *see also* Old English, Middle
  English 41, 43

Zakynthos 221

῎Ηθε 217
῎Ηθελα (fossilized) 219–220 (n. 46), 222
Θα, *see also* "θέ νά construction" 149,
  153, 164, 186, 203, 207 (n. 44), 208,
  220, 233
Θέ, as a form of the verb θέλω 186–189,
  190 (n. 35, n. 36), 191–199, 200 (n. 38),
  201 (n. 39), 202–208, 214, 217,
  229, 231
Θέ νά construction 14, 98, 127 (n. 5), 164,
  173–174, 175–176, 179, 182, 186–189,
  190 (n. 35), 191–192, 193 (n. 37),
  194–200, 201 (n. 41), 202–206, 207
  (n. 44), 208–209, 219, 224, 228–229,
  231, 233
Θέ + Infinitive 197–198, 209
Θέλει (impersonal) 127 (n. 5), 175–176,
  178–181, 187, 197, 202, 203, 229
Νά + clause, *see also* Νά + Subjunctive,
  replacement of Infinitive 127, 147,
  150 (n. 15), 162, 166, 168, 174, 182,
  184 (n. 31) 185, 190, 196, 212, 215
  In AVCs 92, 131, 134, 137, 144, 210 (n. 45),
    218
Νά + Subjunctive, *see also* Subjunctive,
  νά + clause 134, 192

As complement of θέλω, *see also* "θέ νά construction", θέλει (impersonal) and "θα" 137, 165, 168, 170, 171, 173, 174, 175, 176, 179, 182, 186, 187, 197, 203, 209, 211, 213, 218

Future-referring 184, 186, 187, 197, 223, 231, 233

In AVCs 14, 132, 146, 159, 216, 218, 231, 233

Νά + FC construction, *see also* "νά έχω construction" 98, 145, 149–155, 169, 170, 175, 177

Νά έχω construction 98, 149–155, 158, 160